The Women Of The Mayflower And Women Of Plymouth Colony

Ethel Jane Russell Chesebrough Noyes

The Women of the Mayflower

and

Women of Plymouth Colony

By

Ethel J. R. C. Noyes

Plymouth, Massachusetts
1921

Linotyped and Printed by Memorial Press, Plymouth, Mass.

FOREWORD.

The Pilgrim Women have been written about so little that it is indeed a pleasure to welcome a book bearing the title, "The Women of the Mayflower and Plymouth Colony." History has dwelt long and minutely upon the Pilgrim Fathers and their great adventure, but has passed over the women with a generalization and occasionally a tribute. Even their contemporaries have had but little to say about them. The author of this little book is to be highly commended therefore for this much needed addition to our meagre store of literature about the mothers of this Nation.

There is much need to-day to perpetuate their spirit, to practise their faith, to maintain their ideals. They loved liberty and endured hardship, sacrifice and suffering for its sake. They built the homes of the Nation on the foundation of English ideals of home and family life which we cherish to-day as ours. They served their homes and the community life of the colony with loyal and unswerving devotion. They brought up their families in those rugged virtues and a living faith in God, without which nations perish. They have a message for us to-day, calling us back, not to their austerities but to their righteousness and spirituality. Such books as this help to spread that message throughout the Nation.

(Signed) ANNE ROGERS MINOR,
President General,
National Society, Daughters of the American Revolution.

The Women of the Mayflower

and

Women of Plymouth Colony

Contents

THE GREAT NORTH ROAD.

Part of design of sampler made by Lora Standish.   May be
seen in Pilgrim Hall, Plymouth.

THE GREAT NORTH ROAD.

THREE HUNDRED and a few more years ago the Great North Road leading from London to Edinburgh ran through and by an English village in Nottinghamshire just as it had done three hundred years earlier than that and as it has these three hundred years. The streets of the village ran toward it and into it as brooks flow to a river, it being the main thoroughfare of travel and therefore source of all outside interests for the inhabitants of the village.

At the corner as one could say, of one of these little streets or roads where it joined the Great Road, one spring day of the sixteenth century, we might see a group of some of the villagers, young people principally, and it is plain some event of unusual interest has called them together; they are laughing and waving to a young man who rides away from them down the road, a friend who has been one of them from childhood and popular as evidenced by the number who have been wishing him a safe journey and all the usual farewells of any time and place. This young man with the pleasing face and manner is the son of the postmaster of the village and he goes to college; his erstwhile companions gaze after his retreating figure down the Great Road through the meadows and

farm lands and there is one girl looks the longest —
a girl named Mary.

Other times other manners in some things — yet
even today in another country village we have seen
the postmaster's son leave home for college, not on
horseback but in an automobile, and a gay crowd of
his friends seeing him off, his presence to be missed
in much the same degree as among those we are now
viewing with the mind's eye. Though time and
circumstance be the result of the passing of three
hundred years, human nature remains as unchanged
as the sky and sea; the student of the present whom
we mention may be cousin of a Cabinet official, that
scarcely is remembered at the moment, neither is it
thought of that the boy who rides on the Great
Northern Road is a member of one of the most substantial county families, with powerful friends
ecclesiastical and lay. As the turn of the road will
soon take him from sight, he looks back at the group
watching him for a final wave of his hat, then rides
on towards his destination, Cambridge, thinking,
perhaps, of the gentle Mary, whom we have noted,
whose fine character and winning ways are already
an influence with him and not thinking at all, or
knowing, of another Mary who is to be perhaps an
equal if not more potent influence in his life — a
woman in as great a contrast in rank and circumstance as the difference may be between a queen and
a village maid.

The gay group now lessens as some turn their
steps towards their daily tasks, a few of the boys

perchance to a long walk to the nearest school, few
and far between in those days; others to help in
the farm work, if parents could not spare them;
the girls to look after the flocks on the Commons, or
home work, such as cooking, wool spinning, caring
for the children or the sick. In this time and locality no hospitals, orphanages or homes for the aged
were there to relieve the sick or homeless; friendship and charity must indeed have reached a crest
among these only moderately well to do people,
education was backward from conditions easily
found, yet a thread of knowledge of life in other
countries as well as their own came almost daily to
these quiet, rustic people, not by books or news-
papers, (the first seen rarely, the last not existing),
nor by letters which were not publicly delivered by
the government until some time later, but by the
constant travellers on foot or on horseback by the
Great Road. The post house, both an inn, relay
station and receptible for news, though not a post
office as is today thought of by the words, was the
finest house in this particular town and well known,
from the north country to London. The position
of postmaster was a coveted benefaction of the government, the salary being large and enabling the
official to lease the manor house from a wealthy
ecclesiastic. The office at this time had been retained in one family for several generations. Thus
the men and women and children, of course, had
plenty to talk about beside their local interests at
gatherings at the inn or after church services on

Sundays, for the old Church still was revered and followed, the changes that were coming to some of its then supporters not yet discernable.

As we have selected a spring day for our glimpse into this long ago life we may hear conversation among our young friends of the coming May Day fetes and procession.of mummers and maskers, and plans being formed and opinions given as to who should act the usual characters in the masque of Robin Hood. It was a pity indeed that "Will" would not be with them this year; who might be Alan a Dale in his stead? But Will was graver since learning Latin and Greek, perhaps he would not care for their good times as much as he used to. A mistake surely — Will was just as sociable and genial as ever.

Thus Mary and an Alice and Elizabeth and another Mary and Katherine chatted away of coming pleasures and absent friends as blithe as any similar bevy of girls in a far futured century from theirs can do.

In front of one of the cottages another group has gathered; a peddler has come in and the older women have let the brew and baking wait a few moments to hear the news of the towns he has come from on his chain of travel, where other friends dwell, and to see his merchandise. The girls' eyes gleam as they join the listeners and prospective buyers, departing Will and coming dances forgotten for the moment in this new interest of the day. Joy! Patty, across the river, has sent a message to

Bess; not a written note, oh, no, for neither she could write nor Bess could read it, but a message well delivered by the friendly vender of trifles, so why give a thought to a lack of ability to read or write just then, when one has learned, nevertheless, the latest important event in the life of a dear friend in her very own words. The peddler was a reliable and patient transmitter of words or gifts; a telephone and parcel post in one, and always a welcome visitor. Today he might be telling of the pageant lately given in a city not far away in distance, but far in fact to them, to entertain the Queen on a visit she had made there in the interests of the enterprise and industry that "Good Queen Bess" endeavored to prosper in her land. Fashions were also described, as the old time peddlers were indeed specialists in much beside selling commodities and fancies. It is decided that Molly "shall have a new ribbon to tie in her nut brown hair." A new clasp knife is needed by some one;—listen to the tale of the strange vegetables now being brought for the nobles and gentry from the place called the Queen's kitchen garden in Holland. He had seen them and they were good to taste;—a measure of linen? yes; starch just imported and the use explained; a looking-glass, none too many on hand for comfort; a Bible printed in English by a Dutch printer — he has just sold one to the rector in a neighboring town — and so the peddler passes by.

An arrival at the inn, later in the day, of a high dignitary of the Church with his train of employees

made bustle about the village while horses were
changed. Towards evening, many of the people
gathered about the manor house, old in their day,
and while the sunset gleamed in the fish ponds on
the estate and touched the church's spire, they
talked of that day's and other day's events, discussed the curtailment of the commons, as the land-
lords enclosed more and more, whereof one had said
not that geese were stolen from the common but
the common taken from under the geese; stories
heard from travellers, or doubted what they could
not believe. A noted personage had passed that way
quite recently who had made more than ordinary
impression, a gentleman of the court going on an
important mission to Scotland, then quite as foreign
seeming a country as Holland, where this gentleman
had lived also. He had talked especially with Will,
the postmaster's son and seemed glad to hear about
his studies, and was altogether friendly. But few
travellers changed the course of the lives of any of
the dwellers in this community as this same pleasant
gentleman was to do for some. Could Mary have
dreamed that she should see her Will one day riding
away again, not to studies of Latin and Greek but
in company with this same gallant gentleman, to
the study and knowledge of a new world and
language, as private secretary of Queen Elizabeth's
ambassador to Holland?

Neighborly visits, while the twilight lingers after
babies are in their cradles, for recounting impressions and retelling news; thus the women of that

little village close a day like many another of which
their lives were made.

"Weaving through all the poor details
And homespun warp of circumstance
A golden woof-thread of romance."

Time to measure of several years, is spent almost
unnoted by these quiet dwellers in the village of
Scrooby, the village we have pictured; life for them
does not greatly change, but for William Brewster,
the postmaster's son, change, variety, experience,
have filled each day since Mr. Davidson, the Queen's
ambassador and advisor, called him to become his
secretary and confidential friend. The experiences
of this period both abroad and in his own country
have been narrated by many and. may be read in
various writings. At the close of these interesting
years, when all things pointed to a continuance of
the brilliant life stretching before him as courtier
or politician, suddenly all was changed. One day,
news came to Scrooby, as to the rest of the country,
that Mary the Beautiful, exiled Queen of Scots, was
dead. How this event directly affected William
Brewster and brought him to his home again may
also be read elsewhere. He became once more a
country resident, welcomed and beloved by all his
old friends. The day of days dawned for Mary and
smiled upon her marriage with Will. He received
the appointment to the Scrooby post, in succession
to his father, so the old manor house became home
to Mary for many years, and as the wife of the most

respected and admired man of the community — the
leader in thought and opinion, her days must have
been filled with honest pride and pleasure and love
for her husband and children. That these happy
years should close with anxiety, distress, poverty as
her portion was because of the very importance of
her husband's position.

The causes which made for the startling contrast
were slow in gathering yet when accumulated, the
effects followed with rapidity. Naturally, as William Brewster settled back into his old place at the
home of his boyhood, the differences he had noted
between life on the Continent and in his native
country made an ever recurrent impression. The
word pictures he drew of vastly different scenes and
manners, customs and dress found an ever ready
audience and were recounted in the effort to broaden
and educate his hearers. At the same time, he
resumed acquaintance with college friends in other
places and persuaded some to move into his locality.

During these years, the farmers found living
much more difficult, owing to landlord's selfishness
who were growing richer while their tenants grew
poorer, also these country people found their
religious life growing more difficult. Church and
State were one, and ordered its subjects' lives from
the beginning to the end; persons who did not care
to be so controlled were soon made to see the error
of their ways. Nevertheless, as the Bible was made
accessible to more of the people from being printed
in their own language, and as workers from the Con-

tinent, chiefly Holland, came to live and mix with
the English, other ideas and views were taken by
some, quite different from the long dominant ones
of the State Church.

Enough of these persons who thought alike separated from the old Church to call themselves a new
Church and held religious services among themselves
at their own houses. William Brewster was the
leader in his part of the country, and so many gladly
followed his teachings and example that the Church
tried in every way to restrain them. Brewster's
personal charm and influence, his intellect and generous spirit drew countless numbers of men and
women for miles around to his home for the worship
they conducted according to their ideas of right and
liberty of conscience. After the service in the old
Chapel of the manor house, he entertained all the
company at dinner.

Just here we can see Mary Brewster, the sympathetic and charming hostess, her fair face silhouetted
against the dark, age old wainscot of the refectory
or dining-room, of the manor inn, surrounded by her
and her husband's early friends and those of later
years, loved by them all for herself no less than as
the wife of their revered leader.

These gatherings came to be held in secret, of
necessity, as the members were liable to arrest for
absenting themselves from the regular Church services and teaching other views. Spies were set to
report their actions, and some were called before
the magistrates and sent to prison. It became plain

that they could not continue in that manner — uncertainty and anxiety becoming daily companions.

Queen Elizabeth died; her successor rode down from Scotland on the Great North Road and stopped with all his retinue at Scrooby. This was doubtless the last brilliant assembly that the manor saw, when the home of the Brewster's. The people hoped for better things at his accession, but soon learned that he was to be just as hard upon them and times would be worse. Plans were made among them under the guidance of Brewster for emigration to Holland where, as he knew, there was liberty and welcome for all.

It is not difficult to realize the reluctance with which they came to this decision, to leave all their natural associations, to give up much that was dear with almost no hope of a return. Sad indeed were these days for Mary Brewster and the other women of the community who were preparing like her to part with much of their belongings, their homes and friends who could not think as they did but were cherished, notwithstanding.

"Well worthy to be magnified are they
Who with sad hearts of friends and country took
A last farewell, their loved abodes forsook,
And hallowed ground in which their fathers lay."

The final summer for them in the old home passed; that each sunset brought a certain regret, each rose that bloomed a more than passing attention we may believe. Yet it seemed the best thing they could do for themselves and their children. In the place where they would make their new home others of English birth and similar experiences were already settled, having been, as they, forced to leave their own land; at least they would be welcomed by and could have intercourse and sympathy with those of their own race and country, advice and help also in the matter of the problem of living — a somewhat staring one, as they were ignorant of any solution but their own. Curiosity, too, supposed ever to be an attribute of women, might pierce their melancholy a little, and they had heard enough to wish to behold for themselves since the opportunity had come; the enthusiasm for adventure on the part of the children must have lightened the prospect as well. The pain was in giving up the dear interests, the fond associations of their lives.

Dull indeed the eye of fancy which cannot see Mary Brewster with her two little daughters coming down the stone steps of the manor house in a golden evening, to follow the path through the meadow fields towards Ryton stream and there wander on its banks, visiting favorite nooks and listening to the bird's good night, for them seeming notes of farewell. As Experience wears ever the same dress, her mirror must reflect for each of us some such scene as this.

THE SWORD OF THE SPIRIT.

Design of carving on pew back from old Church at Scrooby,
England.   May be seen in Pilgrim Hall, Plymouth.

THE SWORD OF THE SPIRIT.

A Ship had been engaged to meet them at Boston from where these travellers were to sail. The first stage of their journey was accomplished by their arrival at that town. Since the edict that whoever did not subscribe to and uphold the State Church must leave the country, one would suppose that their proposed departure would not have been difficult, but when it was discovered how many desired to go and had so arranged, malice itself must have been the cause of the refusal of the authorities to permit it. The ship's master then had to be well paid to consent to take them away in secret. Instead of meeting them at the appointed time in daylight, he kept them waiting until night, but they all were finally on board with their baggage. Before the ship had gotten a fair start, however, they were stopped by the port authorities who had been warned by the ship's owner, himself. The voyagers were taken from the ship back to the town in small boats, their belongings examined and those of most value as well as all their money taken from them, the women having to undergo as thorough a search of their persons as the men, which their own chronicler speaks of with indignation. Still further embarrassment awaited these women when they were all marched through the town in the early morning and people hurried into the streets to stare at them as at a spectacle, and followed them into the court room. Here the magistrates were more favorably disposed toward them but were obliged to order their imprisonment until the Lords in Council should decide their case. After a month's confinement, which was made only less trying and uncomfortable by the kind hearted magistrates — to their great credit—the women and children and most of the men were dismissed and sent back whence they came, by order of the Council; the more prominent men were kept till the autumn was far advanced before their freedom was granted.

The wounds to their feelings were healed by determination, and after an unexpected winter among their friends, who in vain urged the abandonment of their plans, some of them were ready to make a second attempt to accomplish their object.

Brewster and several men, especially his friend, John Robinson, made other and as they thought safer arrangements for this venture. So one bleak day at the end of the winter, the women and children, with the necessary baggage, embarked in a small boat at an inconspicuous place on the coast, and sailed out on the sea. The large boat chartered for the voyage was to await them at an appointed place near the shore, between Grimsby and Hull, and the men were to go by land to meet it and the small boat bringing their families and possessions; all were to board it, and hoping for a more trusty master of this ship before news of their plans would get to unfriendly ears, would be away.

Such good time was made by the little boat from shore to rendezvous, that it reached the appointed place before the larger ship arrived and must ride at anchor in a choppy sea. The women being unaccustomed to travel by sea were most uncomfortable, and the weather becoming worse, with the boat pitching and tossing so continuously they were driven to desperation and begged the seamen to run the boat into an inlet where the water was quiet, that they might have some rest. The men evidently compassionate, did so, but it was a most unfortunate move, though seemingly harmless. The night was spent in that strange and lonely place, while their thoughts must have been busy with questionings as to the non-arrival of the ship and the possibility of the men being arrested before they could get to them; the cold was penetrating and in their efforts to keep the children warm and quiet, the keeping up of their own courage was under long odds.

In the dimness of the dawn, they could see the ship making anchor, and on shore, their men could also be seen, so hope arose with the morning, soon to be overcast, however, when it was realized that their little boat was fast on shore, and no chance of release till the tide rose. The resourceful Dutch captain of the larger ship, endeavoring to honestly earn his money, sent his own small boat to shore to gain time by taking on the men. These activities gave the children some entertainment at least, we suppose, and they doubtless waved and called to their fathers and friends as the first boat load left shore and boarded the ship; the second trip was begun when suddenly the watchful captain saw an armed company appearing in the distance; one glance and his efforts were all in the direction of getting himself and his boat to safety, no matter who might be on it or who not on it. His sails were quickly run up, his anchor raised, notwithstanding the entreaties of the men, who also realized the situation, to send them ashore, at least, if he would not stay. The plight of the women and children, helpless onlookers of this tragic end of their plans, drove the men wellnigh frantic, both on the ship and on shore. The ship was soon out of sight, flying before a good wind, but into as great a storm as they left breaking behind.

Quick consultation among the remaining men decided who should try to escape and who would remain with the women. It was wiser that not all should be taken this time if it could be avoided. Some of them, therefore, thus leaving their friends and families in this dire situation, got safely away, though their position was no more enviable than those husbands and brothers who were taken away on the ship. No marvel that the women, even the bravest, were heartsick and in tears, with their husbands apparently lost and the children, frightened, cold and sobbing, clinging to them. But they had two or three of the men, and well could Mary Brewster be a tower of strength to most, seeing her own husband still on the shore and knowing what a rock he would be for them all to lean on.

When the company of men on horseback and on foot came to the water's edge, where the boatload of women and the few men awaited their fate at their hands, they placed them under arrest and hurried them to the nearest town, to the court.

With their former experience in mind, they anticipated a long, dreary imprisonment; but unlooked for circumstances pleaded their cause. Each magistrate before whom they were taken in turn, with ever increasing haste, seemed anxious to shelve the responsibility of a sentence. Their case seemed so innocent and pitiable, the appearance of so many despondent women and chilled and shivering children, so appealing, that no justice could harden his heart sufficiently to imprison them, more especially when their only crime seemed to be the desire to be with their husbands, wherever they went, which was certainly a compliment to men in general. When urged to go to their homes, their reply that they had no longer any homes, capped the climax, and, fearing criticism of any harsh treatment, the magistrates were most eager to be rid of the matter on any excuse to themselves. Without realizing it, as the nerves of the women were strained to the breaking point, they certainly affected the nerves of the men, and when the judges dismissed them, finally, from sheer desperation, even the men of the company being included, it would have been hard to say which parted from the other with most pleasure.

That day's experience, in all its misery, however,

advertised them in an unimagined way, for, though they only desired an inconspicuous and quiet life, the story of their wanderings and hardships was soon talked of and many came to hear of them and consider their cause with interest and sympathy, and, indeed, led to their making new friends and gaining help later on. Nevertheless, their weariness was far from over, and, throughout that spring, Brewster and Robinson, in the face of other disappointments and difficulties, used their final resources to get the women and children and themselves out of their net of trouble.

Yet in the end their dauntless efforts were successful. Their own historian tells us that, notwithstanding, they all got away after a time and "met together again according to their desires, with no small rejoicing."

This happy place of meeting and rejoicing was Amsterdam, the city of their intentions when planning to leave England. The comparing of adventures since they had been swept apart by the tumultuous circumstances of their departure must indeed have been a refreshment to their minds as the safe arrival at their destination gave rest to their bodies.

The anticipated welcome of the English people, who had already settled in the city and had churches for worship according to their several ideals, was cordial and sympathetic. We may be sure that the women of the longer residence were only too happy

to show and tell of this wonderful city, to the newcomers, and that the women in whom we are especially interested would have been glad indeed that
such guides and advisors should have been there to
help them assimilate the countless new impressions
which were next in the path of their experience.
While each old friend or comparatively new
acquaintance who had been of their original party
at home, must have grown doubly dear by similar
situation in the surrounding strangeness of this new
world with all its marvels and perplexities. The
contrast between the quiet existence they had led so
long and the bustling, colorful life into which they
were plunged, might well have dazed them for a
time had not a certain sort of commotion and
change attended them, in the interval, and been an
unforseen preparation for steadiness in any confusion of circumstance.

We may picture Mary Brewster, an example of
their steadfast purpose, meeting the new and trying
conditions of poverty, a new language and different
modes of living in calm cheerfulness. Love and loyalty to the men of their families would actuate every
woman to do her best in making the homes these same
men had now to struggle to provide. Mutual understanding and common interests were great factors
in smoothing the rough places. These men, now or
afterwards, never thought of going first as pioneers
to provide a home for their wives and sisters to
come to; they well knew that the women were the
ones to make the homes for them. It was such a

matter of course that the question seems never to have arisen, likewise never commented on; one of the reasons why we encounter such a scarcity of details that we would gladly read in their records.

At this time even the names of the women seem hidden as by the very secrecy of their journeyings. Later the mist clears for us somewhat. Only the figures of Mary Brewster and her young daughters, Fear and Patience, Mrs. Robinson, the pastor's wife, and her daughters are comparatively clearly outlined in the picture we try to see just here.

Nevertheless, it was because of a woman and her clothes, especially a velvet hood, that was a prime cause of their moving from this scarcely established home; even as the long shadow of a woman had already fallen indirectly upon them in their original home and ultimately made for their departure thence.

Let us seem to be standing on the banks of a canal of Amsterdam. It is a brilliant winter afternoon and the scene is animated and full of color, for skaters are flying over the ice and spectators are watching them or walking about. Here is a group of women, there are one or two whom we recognize, at least, having seen them in England. The wife of the pastor of the Separatist Church which is seeking a home, Mrs. Robinson, and the wife of the leader of his congregation, Mrs. Brewster, with them a lady much more elaborately dressed than either of them, the wife of the pastor of the Separatist Church already established in Amsterdam, Mrs. Johnson. We

feel quite sure it is she, for what is the advantage of
having fine clothes if one may not wear them where
many can see, on a gay afternoon in a big city especially, and has it not been a matter of indifference
to her what comments are made or how nearly her
husband's church is rent asunder? These new
friends are a pleasure to her since they do not criti-
cize but only admire her appearance. Their
attitude, if reflected from the male members of their
party is that the style of woman's costume is a
detail, and may be according to her station, the one
point being that it should be paid for.

Mrs. Johnson is probably giving her point of view
of the matter and an opinion of her brother-in-law,
in the controversy, which is a matter of record.
Meanwhile, the eyes of the mothers see the bright
faces of their children, and their voices come to
them from the ice. John and Jonathan are being
called to by a number of girls as they start to race
to a goal.

The girls have some of their new friends with
them, fair English roses like themselves, all for the
present blooming together in this country of tulips
— Bridget and Mercy Robinson, Fear and Patience
Brewster, Jacquelin and Dorothy May, the latter,
daughters of the elder of Mr. Johnson's church.
Dorothy and Patience, lighthearted children, never
giving thought to the web Fate is weaving for them.
Soon to part, after a brief acquaintance, but to
renew it in a few years, because Dorothy is a mag-
net to draw back to Amsterdam the grave young

man so frequently seen with her father and Mr. Brewster, at this time, and will herself leave her home there to join these friends again. And Patience is to become the wife of a man of prominence and influence just as her mother had done. These are future visions indeed, yet these two girls, as they stand side by side, are the presentment of the women (though ship and Colony were then undreamed of) causing the special designation in the title of this story.

Therefore because of the turmoil regarding Mrs. Johnson's apparel and other matters affecting the congregation, John Robinson and William Brewster thought it wiser to remove their people from such ensuing contentions, notwithstanding it would entail the search for new employments and cause some more expense.

It was ever the Sword of the Spirit — the spirit of self-sacrifice, "whatsoever it should cost them," to attain their cherished object, democratic religious and civil government, that led them onward, step by step, to the victory which was to be theirs.

This change of surroundings was accomplished with much less stress and strain than their former one. Their new companions in Amsterdam were sorry to have them go; while a welcome from strangers awaited them in the city of their choice.

UNDER THE LINDENS OF LEYDEN.

UNDER THE LINDENS OF LEYDEN.

THE CHIMES from the spire of the State House rang out an evening hour. There seemed no unusual portent in this daily custom to the ear of workers in the busy city turning homewards at close of day. Yet in that hour on that calm evening of early summer, history was being made for that city, and to its honored name was added an interest for thousands of a future day by the seemingly unimportant event then taking place.

A large canal boat, one of the many that plied between Amsterdam and Leyden, was nearing its mooring at the close of the day's trip and a number of persons were on the quay apparently awaiting its arrival. The boat was heavily ladened with freight and passengers, the household belongings and persons of a number of families. If some of the members looked a trifle anxious, all seemed happy and still interested in all to be viewed at the end of a pleasant journey that had been full of new sights for the majority. A pleasanter voyage than many had experienced within the year, and with much uncertainty and strangeness eliminated from this landing at Leyden which had harassed their arrival at Amsterdam; for these are the pilgrims from England, to whom the authorities of this city had recently given permission for residence, in reply to a petition sent in their behalf from Amsterdam, by their pastor, John Robinson.

The English were already well known in Leyden and some of this party had been there to rent houses and survey the prospect. More than casual glances were given these new arrivals, for, though evidently poor people and certainly, as yet, unknown, their appearance was distinguished even in their plain clothes of English fashion, different to the gay apparel of the natives.

The accounts of this beginning of their sojourn in a new locality are somewhat meagre, nevertheless they furnish ground for speculation and conclusions not unjustified. Our interest follows the women we already know and others whom we are soon to know, as they once more endeavor to solve the problems of home-keeping with slender resources, their characteristics of patience and courage again to the test. An admonition surely given by their beloved pastor must have dwelt in their thoughts to "stand fast in one spirit, with one mind striving together . . . and in nothing terrified."

The advantages of living in a prosperous, progressive and highly civilized city were not long in being realized by these women. Though, at first, their homes were in the poorer part of the city, their industry and energy supplementing that of the men, who soon found plenty of employment in the trades of the city, particularly the cloth and silk weaving, enabled them to live fairly comfortably. The markets of fish and vegetables saw them as daily

customers, and even the flower market found them
as occasional visitors to delight the children as well
as themselves. The public schools gave to many of
the children more of an education than their mothers
had had; this opportunity for free knowledge, as
well as the hospitals, homes for the aged, orphan
asylums, were some of the marvels of this new life.
Books and pictures were so moderate in price as to
be available for all.

The contrasts between the conditions which tended towards the benefit and advancement of the plain
people in their present home and those which were
only for the benefit of the wealthy and aristocratic
class in their old home were as easily seen by his
companions now as they had been by William
Brewster years before.

The objects above all the planning for the routine
of practical life were that they might have food and
comfort, peace and quiet to worship God.

They were not without news of England, for their
community was constantly increased by new arrivals, who, hearing of the success of their venture,
came to try the experiment themselves; some
remaining as true friends and burden sharers, others returning.

Scarcely three years passed before the women
had the joy of moving into attractive newly built
cottages on a piece of ground in a very desirable
location for their needs, bought by several of the
men for all in common. All were now in good circumstances retained by continual labor, however.

The nearness of the famous University was a satisfaction to the many intellectual men of the party, both to enter as students or to read in its library.

That the content of the men was reflected by the women is without doubt, for if the men in a family are fairly happy it is easy for the women to be so, and, on their own account they had reason to be lighthearted. Their cosy little houses were built at the sides of the piece of property, the center becoming a small park or community garden with sanded walks, flower bordered. The pastor's house, at one end, was the largest and finest, for in it the Sunday services and three teaching services or lectures were held, as they had been held in the old manor house in Scrooby.

Besides their two indefatigable and honored leaders, the pastor and William Brewster, now an elder in their Church, the community was fortunate in having among them the young doctor, a widower, whose home was kept by his sister, Anna. Her self-reliant, decisive character must have been highly sympathetic and congenial to her brother. The life of Anna Fuller is one of those most discernable to us in that coterie of women, after the lapse of the long years. Tactful and clever she was, and a favorite with all. Between her and Mary Brewster there grew a warm attachment.

A friend to them both and to many others, was Katherine Carver (the wife of John Carver, a prominent and valued man of their company) whose lovely character endeared her to them, but whose

chief interest in life was her husband and what concerned him.

Ann Tilly and the wife of James Chilton added to
the group of these young matrons who enjoyed their
quiet but not altogether uneventful lives in mutual
sympathy and esteem. We must admire the smooth-
ness with which they managed their affairs, taking
into consideration the varying temperaments among
them; tact and unselfishness, wisdom and charitable-
ness must indeed have been taught them by "the
grave Mistress Experience," and not only among
themselves was it observable, but also with their
new, interested and friendly neighbors, the women
of that Dutch city, through whom they became ac-
quainted with its manners and customs and to feel
quite familiar with them. Their children and the
Dutch children soon became friends and through
them the mothers of each began their knowledge of
one another, to their mutual advantage. We know
the pride of the native women in their city and how
ready and willing they were to show its sights and
relate its history to these interested strangers.

Thus we can easily fancy a party coming along
Belfry Lane and through other streets on their way
to visit the Burg, a promised treat to the children
and desired by their elders. Ann Tilly is taking the
children of her household — two little cousins and a
niece — having none of her own, whom she has mothered. Mistress Chilton has with her, her daughter;
Mary Brewster and her two daughters walk with
Katherine Carver; Anna Fuller and the Carpenter

girls — one soon to be her sister-in-law — and one or two boys, a lively party, all accompanied by some Dutch friends as guides.

Leyden was at that time full of reminders of the war with Spain, its part of it having been the great siege. Up on the Burg the country for miles around lies before them, and as they look, the story is told and they try to picture just where and how the battle was fought. Doubtless some old soldier was on the Burg, that bright afternoon, living for himself again that time of suffering and valor, and glad to recount many of the details and describe where had been a particular Spanish redoubt, or just where such a regiment had been stationed, or the location of a General's headquarters.

We of days far from theirs are yet joined to their experiences of that afternoon of our fancy if we have chanced on a similar recital from one who had participated in another war with Spain in a very different country and setting, a war in which the descendants of some of these women had a part. From the wall of an old Spanish castle near Manila, a party of women, one of them the present writer, looked over the surrounding plain on an afternoon not many years ago, while the then American owner, their host, related just such details and anecdotes of the Philippine incident in the war.with Spain, already some years in the past; there was a battery of the United States regulars; the insurgents came in here; a far glimpse of the sunlit harbor showed where Dewey's ships lay; and so on. By such a touch does a string on the harp of life sing on through the centuries.

Coming home, they would visit the City Hall, where were then kept many mementos and relics of victory upon which they could look with wondering earnestness, feeling as we when today viewing objects closely connected with the World War, so recently in our thoughts.

The blossoms of the lindens fell over the grey wall enclosing the old cloister wherein the veiled nuns had walked, fell over into another garden and around other women of whom the cloistered nuns had never heard, and to whom they were but a name; lives in deepest contrast, lived in neighboring environment yet divided by a grey stone wall and many years.

At a well by the old wall several young women have gathered, some to get water for their household use, others to meet them there for a gossip — for even in the little colony of English Separatists living so quietly on their own ground, itself almost a cloister, in the gay city of Leyden there was, of course, gossip in its friendly and sociable meaning. But chat between the women only is interrupted, and apparently to their amusement, by small boys and girls all eagerness at a tale one of their number is telling of an exciting event in their school life that day; no less than the story of how the Prince's ball fell into the canal and he took the boat hook belonging to an old woman who lived near, never thinking she would object, and fished the ball safely out. A tale with an apparently happy ending, but not so, the old woman mistaking Prince Frederick for just an everyday boy scolded him well, and when some one called out that it was the Prince who had borrowed her boat hook, she was so overcome and frightened that she ran in her house and they could not coax her out, for she said they would take her to prison.

Smiles fade as a shadow of remembrance crosses the minds of some of the listeners at prison experiences they have known, and perhaps a thought of contrast that here, in this democratic land, their children have as playmate a prince of the blood, while in their own country they might scarcely ever have seen one. A few of the young men have wandered towards the well, since evening is advancing and their day's employments are over; here are Edward Southworth, William Bradford, Robert Cushman, William White,— and, severally, Alice Carpenter, Mary Singleton and Anna Fuller may no longer be monopolized by the children, while Patience Brewster is glad to hear of her friend in Amsterdam, Dorothy May, from William Bradford, who visits Elder May rather frequently.

In fact, news from Amsterdam was quite regularly brought by visitors as well as by those of their own company returning, since seeds of romance sown in the early days of their sojourn were bearing fruit, and engagements were so frequent that one was scarcely talked of before another came up for consideration.

Thus it was not surprising to see Samuel Fuller leaning across the half door of the Carpenter's cottage, while Agnes, presumably waiting for Alice to return from the well, on the other side of the door, smiled at him. Not unlikely that Edward Southworth and the doctor will both be asked to supper, for the Carpenter household, with five gay, pretty girls in it was not a dull one. One of the households soonest to break away, however, from the present surroundings; after three of his daughters married, Alexander Carpenter moved the rest of his family to his old home in England. Anna Fuller noticing her brother's absorption and knowing from rather frequent experience that he may forget about the supper she will provide for him, decides on spending the evening away from home, herself. To her neighbor and special friend, Mary Allerton, she will be a gladly welcomed guest — she who, a year ago was Mary Norris, and for whom Anna had been a witness at her marriage to Isaac Allerton. Sarah, Isaac's sister, who lived with them, was good company also, and if Degory Priest should happen by, as was more than likely, to walk with Sarah to the weekly lecture at Pastor Robinson's and if William White should come too, still less unlikely, she would tell him that — "yes she would marry him, when Samuel married Agnes Carpenter and was off her hands and mind."

In this group of pilgrims there were many young

men and girls, therefore many were the love tales
told under the lindens and marriages frequent
during their sojourn.

The Botanical Gardens at Leyden, one of the
city's proud possessions, must have held the usual
charm for walks of sweethearts and wives and the
men of their choice on a Sunday afternoon that
seems to be evident everywhere there are Gardens,
in any era and place, from Edinburgh to Hong
Kong.

The annual Kermiss also witnessed many visitors
from among these strangers, and the other holidays
and sports came in time to be almost as familiar and
enjoyable as though known in their own country.

Good health and fairly comfortable living made
comparatively light hearts, among the younger set
especially.

We are glad to picture these years of their life
in Leyden when their industry and thrift brought
them to pleasant days of living, and the cheerfulness
and peace of their little community attracted visitors and favorable comments. These days were
lighted by hope, a hope that they might through
some fortunate possibility be able to return to their
beloved England and live in the unmolested peace
and independence there which they had found here.

Prosperity again found Mary Brewster, for her
husband becoming a much respected teacher of
languages in the University, was soon able to win
a comfortable and adequate living for his family,
and, as always, the Brewsters were ever ready with

sympathy and help to those less well off than they; indeed one of the chief supports in this thoroughly religious body of people was their convention of mutual help and friendliness.

Mary, as well as her husband, was always available as the confidant of their neighbors, therefore a frequent witness for the young couples who went to the State House, according to the custom of the country, to declare their intentions of marriage, and we feel sure the interest did not stop there, and that she and her daughters helped with the simple festivities connected with these marriages. A member of the University was exempt from tax on home-made wines and brew, and as both were common beverages at that time, and made in all households, her wine and cooking receipts must have been frequently used.

While the history of these Pilgrims may be told, and has been, with casual if any reference to the women, the story of the women must hinge on reference to the whole Pilgrim story. Looking at them from our position, down the long vista, seeing the background of which they were hardly conscious, the foreground invisible to them, their reality and aliveness should be vividly lighted by all the colors of romance which only distance may give and we should be able to get the feeling that things had for them, at least. A few plain, loyal, trustful women living their daily lives with no dream of a place in history, yet on whom else may we look entitled to a softer, more caressing glow from the flame of fame?

Julianna Carpenter, the eldest sister, married
George Morton, before the lindens bloomed again,
followed soon by the marriages of Agnes to the wise
and popular young doctor, the doctor's sister to
William White, as she had said, and the lively young
widow, Sarah, sister of Isaac Allerton, to Degory
Priest.   Their mutual satisfaction and happiness
was punctured by the shock of the sudden death
of one of their number, Agnes Fuller; the whole
community was stirred by the fact that so unexpectedly, the doctor was again a widower.   Thus their
recurring measure of joy and sorrow, pleasure and
trouble, success and endeavor.

We may well hope that, in the fullness of time,
our days may be looked upon with the same search-
light of sympathy and understanding which we turn
upon theirs.

Another year more wedded couples were added
to the list—it was a sign of their hopefulness that
marriage among them was encouraged and the remarriage of the widowed favored.   Alice Carpenter
married Edward Southworth and William Bradford
brought his bride from Amsterdam, Dorothy May.
It was in the late autumn that she came to
Leyden to renew some childhood's friendships.   The
marriage of another friend of Alice Southworth occurred at a slightly later date when
Robert Cushman married Mary Singleton.   So
these younger and important men of the settlement
took on new responsibilities, and after a while Dr.
Fuller tried a third time and found with Bridget

Lee a more permanent happiness in matrimony. The very little girls, as the years passed, were replaced by others, while they grew into the places of maidenhood left vacant by the younger matrons. Thus Mary Chilton, Bridget Robinson, Priscilla Mullins, Patience and Fear Brewster, Desire Minter, Humility Cooper, formed a lively group in which Elizabeth Tilly and Mercy Robinson claimed membership though somewhat younger.

The famous storks of Holland were good enough to bring many rosy babies to the little homes of this English colony, so the joy and amusement of babyhood was never lacking.

Into this little world a passing traveller entered, a young man of some wealth and position in England, who having heard of the community, thought to look upon it as of transient interest, and desiring to meet William Brewster, John Robinson and others whose writings printed by their own established press were attracting attention. In truth he was more interested in the printing press than the writings, being reputed himself a printer, and as a worker in one art or trade or profession desires to see the results or products of another in that same class, Edward Winslow entered the life of the Brewsters, the Robinsons, the Allertons, the Bradfords, but most particularly into the life of Elizabeth Barker, and since it was her world it became his, too, henceforth. Almost the last romance of these peaceful years witnessed by the lindens and the old grey wall.

Soon thereafter a rift became apparent in the harmony of existence in the garden colony and it was Mary Brewster who heard it first. Again she experienced the haunting anxiety on her husband's account, which she well knew of old, and from the same source — persecution by the royal authorities in England and their representatives in Holland. The cause was the printing press and the sentiments it set forth. The hunt for the unknown though suspected printer at that time is an entertaining story told by various chroniclers of the history of these people and reminds one of the somewhat similar search for the hidden printer of our modern times who issued the prescribed little Belgian newspaper during the occupation of that country by the Germans.

Suddenly in addition to this personal touch of unrest came a focus in the national affairs of their adopted country, which centered in Leyden, and while of great interest to them, as such matters have been, and are, to us, are always bound to increase uncertainty and instability of daily concerns.

The scope of the present work is not to dwell on the general events of history, but only as their effects touched the lives of the women of our story. Gradually it had come to be recognized, also, that the younger generation among them was fast becoming more Dutch than English, as was natural from environment. And since their object had never been other than to remain English people and to send the enlightening word of their religious freedom and church's independence back to their own people, now that the advantage of their printing press was about to be denied them this advancement was at an end.

These subjects for reflection and others equally compelling brought them to a point in their destiny for which Providence in the preceding years had been preparing them by the variation of their experience, the widening of their horizons, the increasing knowledge of humanity and capacity for labor and economy which came as assets of their exile from home in a land of comparative freedom.

The women had as much opportunity for facing these questions and facts and discussing them among themselves as the men, and the possibility of giving up all that they had won for the sake of their faith and ideals loomed as evident before them as to those upon whom they not only depended but supported by their love and loyalty.

Thus prior to the all-important conference called at Pastor Robinson's house, many of them had set to withdraw their thoughts from the comparative ease and prosperity of the past ten years, and drill their minds to becoming again way-farers and makers of new homes elsewhere. Where else, indeed! Many suggestions were made before the answer was determined. When it became definitely known to the city authorities that these peaceful, industrious and altogether desirable inhabitants were thinking of severing their connection with them, they announced their regret publicly in complimentary terms. Also an offer was made that these would-be pioneers continue under the flag of the Netherlands as colonists. But it was their own flag, their own nationality for which they were about to sacrifice much and for which they stood ready to endure more in the future.

At the assembly at John Robinson's house where the congregation met for final decision, it was resolved that if the vote showed a majority in favor of remaining a while longer, the Pastor should remain with them, and for those who wished to emigrate immediately, William Brewster, their Elder, should be their spiritual leader, while awaiting the coming of the rest.

In regard to this vote, one writer has said, "It cannot be known whether or not the women of the church had a vote in the matter. Presumably they did not, for the primitive church gave good heed to the words of Paul, 'Let your women keep silence in the churches.' Neither can it be known — if they had a voice — whether the wives and daughters of some of the embarking Pilgrims, who did not go themselves at this time, voted with their husbands and fathers for removal." If this exactness is lacking, we may feel a certain knowledge that each woman was aware of how the vote which affected her and hers would be cast. One is somehow reminded of the old story, though of modern times, of a certain pastor receiving a call to a larger field of usefulness who retired to seek Divine guidance. During this time a member of the congregation called for information on the subject. The pastor's little daughter received the visitor, and in reply to the important question said, "I can't say exactly — Father is praying but Mother is packing."

During the time between the actual decision and final satisfactory arrangements for departure — we can fancy the women's days being particularly trying. Breaking up homes — deciding what would be needed most in the unknown land and in the restricted space alloted to each one's belongings on a small ship. Cooking and table utensils were commonly of pewter and wood — so anxiety of modern movings regarding breakage was lessened — books, clothing and furniture required the same attention as we experience in packing. And looking-glasses! Mrs. Robinson's sister, Jane White, had married soon after their arrival in Leyden, Randolph Tickens, a manufacturer of looking-glasses, so although the Tickens family were not to go among the first, a looking-glass or two were certainly to be found space for. If they were such as the mirror of Mary, Queen of Scots, though of earlier make, and shown to visitors in Holyrood Castle, they were not very desirable or useful, giving but a hazy reflection of any one's good looks — but they may have been satisfactory when new.

The day before the breaking up of the community came at last, as all days do, though seemingly far off when first recognized as approaching. That evening was spent by all, at the Pastor's house, at supper and with music. If verging on tragedy to us, as on-lookers, what must it have been for them?

The barges are moored at the quay — near the Nuns Bridge — were any of their thoughts flung back, as ours are, to the day of their arrival at Leyden eleven years before? This party is large, as many who would return, for a time, are going with the others to see them depart. Some have already gone and are in England making final arrangements — so Mary Brewster, Katherine Carver, and Mary Cushman are without their husbands at present — though the sons of the Brewster and Cushman families are at their mother's side — while Katherine Carver has the unfailing attention of the tall, strong, young man, devoted to her husband's interests, John Howland.

Anna Fuller White (since her marriage called more often by her full name, Susanna), has her husband and little son, Resolved, a fitting name for the first born of this woman. Her brother, the doctor, is of the emigrating party, (with a young assistant), but his wife and baby will stay behind. The children of some are to go with them, while those of others will remain with relatives — thus the little son of Dorothy and William Bradford has gone to his grand-parents at his mother's old home in Amsterdam. The sadness in the eyes of some of the women as they look back at the fair and beautiful city, which has sheltered them so kindly, is formed of regret that all may not remain together in this departure, as well as a sigh for the happy years now gone.

THE FIRE OF FAITH.

The cradle that was brought across the
sea for the first New England baby.
May be seen in Pilgrim Hall, Plymouth.

THE FIRE OF FAITH.

As ONE GOES along the road of remembrance, some readers as well as the writer may see before them the outlines of a ship at the wharf of, perhaps, an unfamiliar city, towards which they have travelled after careful planning and arrangements for a voyage which is, after all, to carry them towards the unknown —. Just so, and with the same feelings the eyes of the women passengers on the canal boats from Leyden, looked upon the form of the "Speedwell", the little ship on which their thoughts and plans had for some time focused, now appearing before them with all the suddenness of reality and accomplished effort. Those whose former knowledge of ships had been far from pleasant, saw it with bravely stiffened reluctance or repugnance, while the younger were in contrast as eager to experience this new thing.

Some of the girls, whose memories, real or imagined, could stretch back to their coming from England, almost as babies, were in great favor and admiration with those whose life and experience had been only in Holland. So Bartholomew Allerton and his little sisters, Resolved White, John Cooke, Samuel Fuller (nephew and namesake of the doctor), relied on the good nature that would reply to their numerous questionings of Humility Cooper, Desire

Minter, Mary Chilton, Elizabeth Tilly and Priscilla Mullins, for the older boys were too interested and too busy in the matters of moving the baggage and the preparations on the ship to give attention to those who had no higher travelling lineage than a canal boat.

It was evening when they arrived at Delfshaven and their ship could not sail until morning. That July night was too full of excitement and emotion for ordinary rest, even for many of the inhabitants of the town, who were drawn to the wharves by curiosity and interest to see this decidedly unusual party who were to sail from their port.

Though their old tower had seen the sailing of many a ship and the farewells of countless friends in its centuries of guardianship of the little city, no scene had ever been quite like this, and curiosity turned quickly to sympathy.

Friends came also from Amsterdam to see them sail, so that an animated picture filled the evening and morning hours. The fatigue of the women was forgotten or disguised in the sad enjoyment of these last hours with the members of their families who were not to go with them.

Fear and Patience Brewster see naught else but their mother's face, filled with its well-known love, sympathy and energy, as she made one more effort at self-sacrifice and endurance for her husband's sake, choosing to go with him and two of her boys who would need her more in the new life than the two daughters, left to the protection of their oldest

brother and the care of the Robinsons and other
loyal friends in the safety and comfort of their
Leyden home, cheering them and others with the
prospects of a speedy reunion. Hope and courage
gilded these prospects at the time. Sarah Priest,
who is to have the care of little Sarah Allerton, her
namesake niece, has her husband to part from, as
well as her brother and his gentle wife. The doctor's
wife has a similar farewell to make to her husband,
though her sister-in-law goes with her family —
husband and son — and the wife of Edward Fuller
goes with him and their son. Susanna White having
all with her whom she holds most dear (her brothers,
her husband and little boy) may be looked upon as
one of the most fortunate of the company; it is the
friends of Anna Fuller (as she still seems to them)
who remain behind, who shall have heavier thoughts
at parting than Susanna White, though her cheerfulness and kindness are not wanting.

Other women who are happy in having their
families with them are Mrs. Chilton and her sweet
daughter, Mary, who has ever a special attendant
in the person of one of Edward Winslow's brothers
(two of whom had joined him in his life at Leyden
and preparations for this adventure), so her valuable bundles of baggage are well looked after in their
transportation into the ship.

All is well too, in the heart of Elizabeth Tilly,
whose father is more than half her world, and next
in it, the object of her girlish admiration, Desire
Minter — the ward of lovely Mrs. Carver. Her step-

mother and uncle's family are all part of the out-
going company also, so her spirits may be light
enough to amuse the children — herself but little
past the boundaries of their land — Elizabeth Tilly
with sparkling eyes and wind-blown hair, as we see
her then, child of mystery and of argument after
centuries have gone. Doubtless any or all of the
older members of that company could have answered
a question that still burns for some of us — who was
her mother? Why the airy tradition floating down
the years that she was grand-daughter of John
Carver? As much, that, at one time, seemed un-
fathomable, has come to light regarding these people,
this question may one day be definitely answered.

Katherine Carver and Elizabeth Winslow, feeling
that since their husbands believed in this venture,
and since they could make new and comfortable
homes for them anywhere, all was well, are anxious
to be off, especially as the former had for some
time been separated from her husband, and looked
forward to seeing him soon, at Southampton, where
he was to meet their ship. Also the wife of Captain
Standish, who had joined this expedition, thought
that any undertaking with which her martial husband connected himself was right, and so long as she
could be with him in any part of the world, happiness would be hers. These three women, having only
their husbands to think of, are naturally drawn
together, and each can appreciate the beauty and
charm of the others, being equally lovely herself.

Like Mary Chilton and her mother, Priscilla

Mullins and her's are happy in the thought that they are not to be separated from one another nor from the men of their family.

Among the friends of all these women accompanying them from Leyden, for the sweet sorrow of parting, is Juliana Morton, sole representative of the Carpenter family, whose daughters had been gay companions with them all, in past days. Juliana and her husband and family alone remained in Leyden, to this date, and for a time thereafter. The parents and the two younger sisters, Mary and Priscilla, returned to their old home in England; Agnes Fuller slept under the shadow of St. Peter's church and Alice Southworth with her husband and two boys were at this time living in London — business affairs of Edward Southworth having shortened their stay in Leyden. They, however, were thoroughly in touch with the plans of their old friends, and knew of the difficulties with which they had contended. They also knew of the preparations being made for another ship with passengers, some of them strangers, some friends, to sail from London to meet the ship from Delfshaven, at Southampton, and together cross the ocean. Like others of the original company their affairs did not admit of themselves being voyagers at this time.

Sarah Fletcher and Hester Cooke are two others whose hearts we feel are heavy, as their husbands are to precede them to a new country, and they must remain with all the others who will await the first opportunity to follow.

The tide has come in, the wind is fair. Now gaily clad sailors are getting up anchor on the little ship, filled with those whose trust is in her. All ashore for those not going — the last, the very last farewells must be said. Their beloved pastor once more leads them all in prayer, his entire flock about him for the last time. And so they "took their leave one of another; which proved to be the last leave to many of them."

The ship moves out from the wharf, the wind shakes the flag — their English flag — above them, token of their regained nationality. A volly of shot from shore and three guns fired from the ship echo over the watchers waving to each other as long as individuals may be distinguished, and longer. How eagerly the imagination pictures the scene. The *Speedwell* on that fair summer morning, sails into the unseen fog of disappointment and failure that shall prove her name a sad mistake. But for all on board of her "the fire of their faith lights the sea and the shore."

So they leave forever, Holland, that refuge which for twelve years had sheltered them, that school wherein they have been shaped and prepared for the great enterprise before them. Their own country's flag above them, their own little vessel to carry them once more to England, if only for a farewell. Thus the spirits of sadness and expectation attend them and of gratitude and hope.

The summer breezes blowing from England's

shores came out to meet the little ship and caressed the hair and cheeks of that group of England's daughters who stood, drawing their long cloaks about them, on the deck of the *Speedwell* as it entered Southampton water. Once more, as so often in their dreams these past years, they behold their native land. An interlude of vision. Only two of them will ever return; for the rest it will remain a dream, a memory — for "Memory draws from delight ere it dies an essence that breathes of it many a year."

An animated day this proves to be, with greetings from old friends and new acquaintances who have come in the ship from London to join them. The ship! They view it riding at anchor. Of its name or history few of them care. Yet what other ship has held more truly the form of fate for its passengers and of epoch for the world! But they could not know and it seemed then only their guide to cross the sea, their means of accomplishing the only way out of their difficulties.

A company of shrewd business men, as profiteering a syndicate as ever crushed the individual, had happened on this ship at the time they needed one of its size and accommodations for the enterprise they were planning to undertake in sending a homeless, well-nigh friendless, but dauntless company of men and women to colonize in America, chiefly on the money of these same people but supplemented by some of their own, and many directions, conditions and restrictions for their endeavors to which they had reluctantly to agree. King nor country cared, the merchants, their nominal backers, cared less than nothing for the personal success or good fortune of these voyagers, except only where advancement of their own selfish interests or claims for territorial advantage accrued and might be returned.

These two boat loads of pioneers regarded thus with indifference, may be viewed for a moment in contrast to that subsequent fleet of English ships carrying English passengers on whom all England from Crown to Commons looked with interest and in whom hope and pride were centered — the ships bearing colonists under the leadership of John Winthrop, to the same shores, ten years later, saluted by royal guns as they sailed away as voyagers whose adventure would reflect honor and renown to the kingdom, whose loss would be a disaster to the nation, while if either or both of these two unimportant ships with all on board had sunk at sea, as so nearly happened, the incident would not have seemed worth recording for a paragraph of history by the country, who treated these loving children with contempt and disdain. Nevertheless these brave pilgrims prepared the way for all others who later sought homes on the far shores of their intent and gave them aid and comfort by personal contact as well as by their example of unfaltering purpose. For their recompense to the merchants commercially interested in their adventure, the account shows them more than over-paid, at length.

For their advantage to the country they left forever, since it did not understand them and did not want them, in long, long years from that day, perhaps the arrival of the first contingent of American destroyers in British waters, in the spring of 1917, to give a certain aid and comfort to England, may be accounted a return.

But thoughts like these were not in their minds as they are in ours. The ship from London, by name, *Mayflower*, was before them — an actuality, while for us it is a vision.

This vessel was twice the size of the little *Speedwell* and bore a popular and one of the oldest names for British ships. A predecessor of the name had in 1415 borne the flower of knighthood to France, to fight at Agincourt. Another had been flagship of the Duke of Gloucester. *This Mayflower* had already a noteworthy career, the equal, of any, as a warship. She had been a member of Queen Elizabeth's fleet, contributed to it by a city guild, and took a brilliant and prominent part in the fights of the Spanish Armada to the final, desperate and victorious one. Nevertheless in spite of this, her name would not have gilded a page in history, but on the day she sailed from London for Southampton, equipped for a long voyage across the sea, destiny began to weave for her the wreath of fame. Not a large ship — 120 or more tons — and about 82 feet long, but what other is greater? Which more inspiring to poets and artists? The true and accepted model of the *Mayflower* is on exhibition at the National Museum in Washington, this was made by Capt. J. W. Collins, an expert in naval architecture, by order of the United States Government.

At Southampton the companies of each ship mingled on shore and on shipboard while the vessels were being made ready for departure. The allotments to the respective ships, the designation of quarters in the ships, were necessarily made chiefly with regard to the needs and comfort of the women and children. The number of each was increased by the wife and family of Stephen Hopkins and of John Billington, also by four children named More. These children, three boys and a girl, were protegees of Mr. Weston, one of the merchants interested, and, having no apparent connection with any one of the company; just what reason he had for sending them on this voyage seems likely to remain an unanswered question. The loving natures of Mary Brewster, Katherine Carver and Elizabeth Winslow accepted them as their special charges, and Jasper was thereafter considered with the numerous and varied family of the Carvers, Ellen, with the Winslows, while Richard and his other brother, increased the Brewster's number of boys. For only a short time were these children to know these new and kind friends. Another unexpected addition to their numbers was in the person of the young man of Southampton, John Alden by name, who joined their company, as cooper, for the sake of the voyage and adventure — but who remained as one of them for the sake of the love and admiration he gained for some in particular. Their business affairs being concluded, the *Speedwell* and *Mayflower* sailed from the harbor, but soon the *Speedwell* was found in a dangerous condition from leaks,—though she had been thoroughly overhauled after her trip from Holland. It was decided to put into the nearby port of Dartmouth, where a stay was made of ten days, at much cost to the pilgrims both in time and money. However, after this set-back, the ships sailed again and all had hopes of comfortable progress. Land's End was behind them about a hundred leagues on the 23rd of August, when the Captain of the *Speedwell* again proclaimed that disaster to his ship was imminent. There was nothing else to do but turn both ships back to the nearest port. Plymouth welcomed them and kind-hearted people there tried to comfort and cheer the disappointed passengers. For some, these several returns to England began to affect their spirits as a portent or warning, but to others they but served to make stronger the desire to carry out their plans, in spite of discouragement, in spite of the charm of England's summer days beside the sea, in spite of the bright and friendly town through whose massive gateways they had to pass to visit the busy streets and get their last glimpses of gay shops — sights which they realized they would never again see when they had emigrated to the new and lonely land. This acid test lasted fourteen days.

About this time, in their house in Dukes's place, Edward and Alice Southworth received a letter

written by Robert Cushman, while at Dartmouth,
relating the unpleasant events that had transpired.
Their sympathies were doubtless awakened, but even
more their surprise, when, not long after, Robert
and Mary Cushman and their son, returned to London; they and a number of others both from choice
and necessity had left the company at Plymouth
when it was finally decided to abandon the thought
of the *Speedwell* making the voyage and that the
Mayflower would go on alone.

Such of the passengers who had come from Leyden
and who were to continue their voyage, were transferred with their effects to the other ship, and in this
unexpected turn of their affairs, all had to make
themselves as comfortable as possible. Disappointment and the discouraging delay could not have lent
much enthusiasm to the re-arranging of themselves
and their family belongings, especially in such
crowded quarters as now became necessary. Finally,
all being adjusted, the *Speedwell* sailed for London
and the *Mayflower* for her long voyage.

Compactness could never have had a more effective demonstration, when one considers what actually was required by these colonists in the way of
equipment, the number of people and the size of
the ship. Though the Leyden contingent had brought
little more than personal belongings, and as few as
possible, the *Speedwell* had little spare space, while
on board the *Mayflower* when she sailed from London
were not only the passengers and their accessories,
but supplies for the enterprise as a whole — other

necessaries being added at Southampton — also the regular ship's supplies for the vessel and crew for a long voyage and return.

Let us glance at a list of articles which we know were part of the load: building materials for houses and boats, clothing materials, beds and bedding, rugs, spinning-wheels, chairs, chests, cradles, cooking utensils, carpentering tools, books, weapons, gunpowder and shot, cannon, garden and farm implements, seeds and plants, medicines, trinkets for trading with the Indians, goats, chickens, pigs, pigeons, dogs, beer and butter, food for the animals, dried and salted foods for the people. And some of these things we may see this day, as they have been seen on any day of these three hundred years since they were shipped on the *Mayflower*.

We have heard careless or would-be witty remarks as to the countless china tea pots, which came in the *Mayflower* and are in every state in the Union, or household furnishings which would supply largely populated cities by the number claimed as authentic. Such amusing remarks cause a smile indeed, not however, from the cause the sarcastic authors assume, but from the ignorance or exaggeration willingly or unconsciously evinced. The known freight the *Mayflower* carried was a ship load and no more — and some of it remains to the present hour. China tea pots, or even one, never was part of her invoice; tea and coffee were not then known as beverages to these people, nor in their world; what a solace and comfort therefore was missing for the

women of the voyage — for at sea, how seemingly
indispensable are these important factors of present
day life.

The women of the *Mayflower* — let us look at
them now, since all who ever may be called by that
name are together on the ship, and fair days and
moonlight nights give possible encouragement to
them as the voyage opens. We see the forms of those
we have known in England and Leyden, heretofore,
some more familiar to us than others, but we are
interested in all, however slight our acquaintance:
and their new companions, lately from London,
claim our attention likewise. Among these latter
we note Mrs. Stephen Hopkins as an addition of
great advantage; her vigor of mind and body, her
decidedly wholesome and attractive personality
wins regard from all. Her own little daughter,
Damaris, and her step-daughter, Constantia, added
one each to the quota of childhood and girlhood on
board. Against the name of Elizabeth Hopkins, as
against the names of two others of the matrons of
this passenger list, (Mary Brewster and Susanna
White) destiny set a shining mark.

Mrs. John Carver has her maid and her young
ward, Desire Minter, also the frequent company of
her dear friends, Mrs. Myles Standish and Mrs. Edward Winslow. It needed not for John Carver to
be one of the leading men of this company, nor for
him and his wife to have more of worldly goods than
many, for Katherine Carver to have the love and admiration of all who knew her.

Quite a stranger to all is Mrs. Christopher Martin, and scarcely known during her brief stay among them; she and her husband were among the passengers from London.

Two pairs of mothers and daughters, — Mrs. Chilton and Mary, Mrs. Mullins and Priscilla — engage our attention, as Cupid's entanglements are even in this serious adventure, since Mary has lost an admirer and Priscilla gained one. There was not room for both of Edward Winslow's brothers on the larger ship, when the *Speedwell* failed their hopes, so John had to seek the new world and his winsome Mary, at a later day. John Alden, the young cooper, engaged for the voyage at Southampton, has already met his fate in acquaintance with the buoyant Priscilla. The names of these two sweet maids of the *Mayflower*, (soon to become sorrow-touched women of the new colony) ripple as music through poetry and romance, or staid fact and history to our imagination.

Here is a group whom we know far less well; Mrs. Thomas Tinker, Mrs. John Rigdale, Mrs. Francis Eaton, yet we feel sure their qualities of mind and heart must be the equal of many of their companions.

Here are the sisters-in-law, wives of John and Edward Tilly, each with a young girl to mother — not her own — for Humility Cooper is cousin to Ann Tilly, and Elizabeth is a step-child to John Tilly's wife.

Mrs. Edward Fuller, sister-in-law of the doctor

and Anna White, is one of those sailing for another
haven than some of the others, though knowing it
not.

From London has come Mrs. John Billington, so
different in style and manner from her women companions as to be quite noticeable, yet not lacking
in desirable qualities to say the least; and little
Ellen More, now in Mrs. Winslow's care.

Mrs. William Bradford — standing in the shadow
of tragedy — and Mrs. Isaac Allerton with her two
little girls, Remember and Mary, complete the
count. Mary Allerton's namesake daughter stands
nearest to us, of all that company, between that day
and this.

"How slow yon tiny vessel plows the main!
Amid the heavy billows now she seems
A toiling atom — then from wave to wave
Leaps madly, by the tempest lashed, — or reels,
Half wrecked, through gulfs profound.
Moons wax and wane,
But still that lonely traveller treads the deep."

What words can better picture the *Mayflower* at
sea than these of Mrs. Sigourney? The monotony,
the discomfort, the terrors day after day. Since the
waning of the September moon, under which the
voyage began, the weather had become cold and
stormy; the sea dangerous — whose roughness affected many and made the labors and duties of those
able to withstand it, increase.

The ship's cook was of slight service to the passengers, since his work was for the benefit of the

officers and crew only, therefore the preparing of
their meals fell to the different individuals whose
health and abilities so enabled them. With slight
cooking facilities, it was necessary to rely chiefly
upon such fare as did not require to be prepared by
fire; gin and brandy were relied upon for warmth,
and beer a tonic.

To this tossing ship, on one of these stormy days,
there comes a stranger, promptly and appropriately
called Oceanus, and the Hopkins family becomes one
of especial interest, with its new baby for all the
women and children to delight in.

Another day's excitement is provided by one of
the young men, who chafing under the restraint of
staying below decks, imposed by the storm, ventures
above and is no sooner out than over the side of the
ship, in the grip of a wave. His presence of mind
to grasp a rope, which trailed from the rigging in
the water and his grit in holding on, making his
rescue possible by the sailors, make a topic of conversation with sufficient thrill. One wonders if John
Howland became invested with a new interest for
Elizabeth Tilly from that day, or the few subsequent ones, when the great, hearty fellow was somewhat the worse for his adventure.

The shock of death enters when a particularly
rough sailor, who had terrorized the women and
children and annoyed the men by his language and
manners, is stricken suddenly, buried at sea, and
so one of their trials is removed.

The storm increases and all doubt not that their

end is approaching, since the ship is giving way, but
this crisis passes, by the energies of the captain and
crew and the aid of an iron screw, or jack, which
was brought by a passenger from Leyden. That
screw was the instrument which saved the *Mayflower*, and we know not the owner — whose name
seems of more interest to us than it did to them to
whom the screw was the thing.

Another day brings a blow to Doctor Fuller and
to all, since one of their own company is summoned
by death, the young assistant to the doctor, William
Button. Many begin to show the effects of the
dreary weeks on the ship and look worn, weary and
ill.

At last, at last, in a November dawn, land is in
sight! A day spent in running southward looking
for a favorable harbor, but none appearing, they
turn about and return to the point of land first
seen, and by nightfall are safely riding at anchor.

With the episode immediately following, the
women had no actual connection, yet to some we
know it was of interest, as their husbands signed
the document drawn up in the cabin, and because
of it Katherine Carver was made the "first lady"
of the little group of friends, since her husband was
then duly elected governor of this colonial company.
More love, more respect, they could not give her as
their governor's wife than they had always given
her as just one of themselves — tested and trained
as all had been together in the years of friendship
amid all the shades of mutual experience.

The next day new life and animation was evident among all on board the *Mayflower*. Hope flung aside the grey veils that had almost enveloped her for many weeks and stood in the radiant garments of expectancy — they would not recognize the vagueness, the emptiness of her background. They had been brought across the sea in safety — they were about to disembark on the solid ground of their new country. Ambition stirred the weakest to prove the wisdom of their choice.

In the cabin of the *Mayflower*, next day, their Elder led them in prayer and hymns of thankfulness. Around were those who had listened to him in the old hall at Scrooby Manor, and others who, since then, had made his way their way through life. We may easily picture, again, Mary, his devoted wife, seated in the old chair (which, at least, we may see actually), her gentle, anxious face silhouetted against the grim old cabin walls of the *Mayflower*, as lovely to her friends who looked at her that day, as when its fairness had as a background her old home in the stately manor in England. All who were able were at this service, on what, for them, was Expectation Sunday, (though some were too weak and ill to leave their berths), and afterwards, walked on the decks looking at the new, mysterious land before them — recognizing various familiar trees, growing almost to the water's edge, and accepting the attention of the surprised but welcoming sea-gulls. The little pool, across a stretch of nearby beach, partly surrounded by juniper trees, attracted

the eyes of the women with delight at prospect, if
tomorrow was fair, for a grand and general wash
day, with plenty of water, instead of the restricted
supply that had had to suffice them for more than
a hundred days' effort at cleanliness.

The cold, foggy morning of the 23rd of November
witnessed much energy among the company on the
ship, riding at anchor in its lonely harbor. Small
boats brought many of the women ashore with kettles and big bundles, — the first time that they set
foot on the soil of their new country—and Monday
wash day was established. The men who were not
employed repairing the small boat, or shallop, which
had been stored in the hold of the *Mayflower*, and
which they wished to use for exploration as soon as
possible, cut the fragrant cedars or junipers about
the pool, made cheerful, pungent fires, and swung
the kettles for the boiling water. Some, no doubt,
looked on it as quite a picnic, with lunch served by
the fire, and the whole thing a change from the life
of the past weeks.

The dusk saw the footprints of many English
women marking for the first time that sea-washed
shore, and the ashes of the first fires of civilized life,
(with women as an important half of that life),
mingling with the sands. The women went "home"
to the ship, with contentment in their minds, but
wet, cold and tired. Small wonder that colds became evident next day — with little vitality left to
resist them. Misery had plenty of company.

Another day and the anxious wives whose hus-

bands made up the first exploring party watched
them row away in the ship's long boat, land and
march along the shore, out of sight, under the
watchful lead of Captain Myles Standish.

Through the two days and nights of their absence,
knowing not what dangers or disasters might befall
them, we can never doubt that the secret prayers of
Rose Standish unceasingly appealed for the safe
return of her husband and the husbands of the other
women, her dear friends, for whom he was responsible. And not her's only we know were answered,
when, on the third morning, the welcome sound of
guns from shore, signaling the long boat, relieved
the tension on the ship. What rejoicing, interest
and even amusement was the result of their safe
arrival, with curious trophies of their first land journey and descriptions of what they had seen and
done.

After a few days, their own shallop being repaired,
another and larger party went away for discovery.
Another safe return and tales of interest followed
this. And news of importance awaited them, also
— for they found the White family rejoicing in the
arrival of a son and brother; Dr. Fuller and Mr.
and Mrs. Edward Fuller in a new nephew, and Samuel in a cousin, in the little Pilgrim. Probably
Oceanus Hopkins looked at his future playmate with
interest, not unmixed with surprise that he was no
longer the new baby of the *Mayflower*.

Before the next attempt to find the place most
desirable for their permanent location, another

event, far less cheerful, drew attention to the Whites. A young man in their employ, Edward Thompson, died, and thus became the first of the *Mayflower* passengers to be buried in American soil.

The following day, one of the Billington boys in search of diversion, finding a loaded gun in the cabin and a barrel of gunpowder, promptly shot it off then and there; his pleasure was short-lived, but those who were ill or much startled by the noise, probably did not care what happened to him. The jeopardy in which he placed the ship and every soul on board was doubtless beyond his comprehension. The restlessness of the small boys in those cramped quarters was one of the trials the mothers had to bear. Our sympathy is for both.

On the 16th of December, reckoning by the calendar as we know it, the third and, as it proved to be, the final and successful attempt at finding the place for their settlement was made. But while much happened to the exploring party, in the seven days of its absence, and while the thoughts of those left on the ship followed them, at all times, hearts were heaviest there, and gloom as great as that surrounding the storm-tossed shallop settled on the *Mayflower*. The moments were tense to the family of James Chilton, whose illness daily became more acute, and hope of his recovery faded in the hearts of his loving wife and daughter. Into the loving sympathy of their friends and their own deep sorrow, there entered a shock and excitement of stunning effect, when it was discovered that Dorothy

Bradford was missing. Someone had seen her on deck — we see her, too — standing, in the sunset, wrapped in her long cape, looking over the water, alone.

We recall her as, years past, we saw her on another winter afternoon, in Amsterdam, standing with Patience Brewster on the banks of the canal. gay with skaters — the elder's daughter, then, now the wife of one of the principal men of this company.

One who kept a record of those days wrote: "At anchor in Cape Cod harbor. This day Mistress Dorothy Bradford, wife of Master Bradford, who is away with the exploring party, to the westward, fell overboard and was drowned." A woman of the *Mayflower* whose experience of the New World was destined to be brief — and never of Plymouth Colony — the one appointed to lead the way into a New Country for many of the women who sorrowed that night for her sudden going. That no further comment or record was made of this tragedy seems remarkable. Out of the silence conjectures arise, as will in such conditions, without form or foundation in truth as far as can ever be known.

Mr. Chilton died the next day — the first head of a family to be taken. The illness which was gradually affecting many of the company, grew out of the colds and run down condition they had reached. It seems like grip or influenza of our modern knowledge, with other complications; its fatality was appalling. Mary Chilton and her mother had need

of the uplifting sympathy and companionship of
such friends as Mary Brewster and Susanna White
in the dark hours of their sorrow. Theirs was the
first test of faith. The little family of three had
expected to face the new life together, with whatsoever pleasure or privation it might bring, and to
have the one taken for whom and with whom the
other two had willingly ventured, strong in their
love and determination to bear their part in the
work which needed women's hands to secure even
a semblance of home, was crushing indeed. Yet
these women, already proven brave, would now be
braver still and rejoice in the safe return in the
shallop of the other husbands and fathers who
brought the good news of a satisfactory place to
establish their settlement.

The enthusiasm of these men at the happy ending
of their uncomfortable and dangerous journey was
soon lessened by knowledge of the grievous and
unexpected events which had happened while they
were away.

We think it was Elder Brewster who gave the sad
explanation to William Bradford as to why Dorothy
was not with the cluster of women and girls who
crowded so eagerly at the ship's rail to catch first
glimpse of their men as the discoverers returned.
These men had lately seen and touched a rock, for
them a stepping-stone, that day of exploration, to
solid ground — they saw it not as the gateway of a
mighty nation; a rock which had wandered to that
place from far away; a traveller, a pilgrim who had

waited long to welcome these pilgrims. They returned now to the rock of their community, William Brewster, keystone of the arch of their high aspirations, molder and guardian of the firm principles that other rock so fitly typified.

One more storm and struggle for the *Mayflower* on weighing anchor again, one more disappointing return to a harbor which she desired to leave, but after all a calm day's sail across the bay and rest in that quiet harbor guarded by the lonely rock. Her work nobly performed, her name immortal, she had reached the goal.

THE FIRST STREET.

THE FIRST STREET.

THE FIRST STREET of Plymouth, the first street of New England, was in the making. From the decks of the *Mayflower* the women looked longingly toward the land, whither the men went daily, hearing the sounds of hammering and sawing which came across the harbor, for as yet none of them had been permitted to go ashore in these new surroundings. The hill which arose at the water's edge, behind the rock, was snow-crowned; around and beside it a path had been cut and worn by the men as they went to the work of making houses for their families.

By the maps and charts of the company, it was found that this situation, which they had all approved for their permanent residence, was the place visited and named by an earlier explorer of whom they had heard, and some had seen, Captain John Smith. The appellation he gave to it suited them well — Plymouth; if they had had the selection of a name as well as the site for their New World home, it could not have been better chosen, in view of the fact that Plymouth was the last place their feet had trod and their eyes seen in their Old World home, and the inhabitants of that town had been kind to them.

Nevertheless it was of Leyden that they thought when building. The larger hill at the end of the street, which they at first saw in the mind's eye, even as we do now, reminded them of the eminence crowned by the fort at Leyden, and upon it they would build their fort and it would be a constant reminder of the Burg.

But first must be built the store-house to hold all their belongings moved from the ship, and then the few houses necessary to shelter themselves. Of these plans they talked at night when the men returned to the ship or on the days when the weather was so inclement that no trip could be made ashore; these delays were a constant strain upon the nerves of all, as the need for haste was so evident, with winter's storms increasing and the impatience of the crew growing therewith, to say nothing of the failing health and strength of so many of themselves.

The fortitude and patience of the women who had braved all the dangers, shared all the trials, and now, in spite of courage and cheerfulness seemed fading before their eyes was enough to urge every man to use his own last reserves of energy and strength to provide better conditions for them. They well realized the important asset to their venture, of the women. Without them not even the magnetism and charm of Brewster, the indomitableness and courage of Myles Standish, the business ability of Allerton, the experience of Hopkins, the worldly wisdom of Winslow, the youth and strength of John Howland and John Alden or the zeal and fervor of Bradford and Carver could have assured the stability and success of this colony. Previous settlements

in this region and others further south bore witness
to a lack of something making for continued interest
and permanence on the part of the men, who were
not wanting in necessary personal qualities. The
abandonment of such ventures in Maine and Virginia, where no women had accompanied the men,
is proof that a common larder and fireside are not
the things for which men struggle against hardship,
disaster and death. But the street of Plymouth,
albeit made in the face of every trial of circumstance, was made by men for the women they loved,
and Plymouth has never been abandoned nor its
street untrod by the families and descendants of
these men and women.

The weeks of January drag by, spent by the men
ashore, many not returning to the ship at night when
the roof of the store-house was finished, both to save
the time of the trip back and forth and to guard
their belongings already there; so lights gleamed at
night from Plymouth, seen by the weary watchers
on the ship and the ship lights shone in the sight
of the builders, signals to one another yet seeming
to make the gloom of their situation more visible.

The violent storm which ushered in the month
caused the *Mayflower* to madly roll and tug at three
anchors necessary to hold her; in the midst of this
discomfort, the third birth occurred on the ship, but
the son of Isaac and Mary Allerton never knew the
world to which he came. One of the young men,

Richard Britteridge, also died about this time, and
so the burials began on the snow-covered hill.

The women had more to do, however, than look
towards the shore and long to land, for the life on
the ship was not an idle one for any of them while
health and strength lasted. As, one by one, illness
attacked them, those remaining well had many
added cares. Assisting Doctor Fuller, attending to
the wants of the families of those mothers who were
ill, preparing the food for the sick and for the men
who went daily ashore to work, keeping the children
safe and amused, and, above all, keeping their own
faith and hope alive went on as unendingly as the
swell of the sea beneath them.

By the end of the month, the house built to store
their belongings and to shelter some of them while
the others were being erected, was finished and was
also a hospital in its capacity of general or common
house, for numbers of the workers had to occupy the
beds as fast as they could be brought from the ship,
their brave fight against the odds overwhelming
many. The women had an hour of frightful suspense when, suddenly, before the eyes of some looking towards the land, flames leapt out and shouts
were heard. They were sure the dreaded event had
happened — that the Indians had attacked and van-
quished all ashore. But the later knowledge that no
Indians had appeared and no one was hurt, recon-
ciled them to the loss of the roof of the common
house from too great a fire in the chimney; it had
to be relaid — and then the joyful decision was made

that all who were able should come from the ship
on the next Sunday for a service in the common
house, which was to serve also as church and bar-
racks for a time.

The little ship of the Pilgrims, called only "the
shallop," and already proven staunch and true to
their needs, leaves the side of the *Mayflower* on this
wintry Sunday, with the women as passengers for
the first time, and sails over the mile or so of water
towards the landing. Some are using their greatest
efforts; some are too weak to come at all, and even
those still well are vastly different in looks and manner from their appearance at leaving old Plymouth
or even on that first Monday of enthusiasm at Cape
Cod. But all feel that a new era is dawning and
again the need calls out the latent spirit of sacrifice
inherent in every woman, on this occasion once more
requiring the putting aside of personal feelings of
sorrow or illness for the common good. From the
day when these women gave up their early associations and left their English homes to live in a
strange country among people with different customs and language, striving to preserve their own
during the twelve years of their sojourn, through
the time of their embarking at Delfshaven and later
sailing from Plymouth, when they saw cherished
possessions and loved members of their families left
behind, during the famous voyage with its heart-
rending conditions for them of wet, cold, poor food,
overcrowding, storms, anxiety, to the day they

landed, worn and exhausted with no homes to go to,
new hardships and dangers awaiting them, self-
sacrifice was in a continually ascending scale and,
for many, could go no further.

Some of the men are standing on the rock, watching the progress of the boat, some are grouped at
the Common House on guard, as ever, against a surprise from the unknown Indians. The governor, the
elder, several of the other men whose wives are in
the boat, two or three of the younger men we may
see in the grave group at the landing, but the light
of expectancy and contentment for this one hour at
least, glows in their faces. With costumes so similar
it is hard to distinguish where each woman is placed
in the shallop and to single out a special one for
whom a man may be looking. At the bow two or
three are grouped, waving to their welcomers, their
alertness seeming to be an urge to the little craft.
The eager children are held from crowding forward
as they near the shore. An instant of excitement,
the sailors making ready to fasten the boat, it
touches, is beside the rock; the woman who stood
foremost at the bow on the way over, has poised herself a second and sprung from the boat, catching at
the outstretched hands of the nearest man, to steady
her foothold on the slippery stone; the keen wind
and spray have dashed color in her cheeks, the brilliancy of sun on snow is reflected in her eyes — a
flashing triumph at being the first — it is Mary
Chilton. Someone has said that Plymouth Rock
began with her its fame, but for her and for the

other women, quickly following her to clasp the hands of the men, — as it had been for those men — it became for them the threshold into Plymouth Colony. Some of the women of the *Mayflower* have not gotten so far, and some of these scarce pass the threshold.

The service is held, as planned; once more they listen to the uplifting and strengthening words of their Elder. Afterwards some return to the *Mayflower*, but others remain with their husbands on shore.

The work on the other houses goes forward as rapidly as possible. All were built of squared logs, the crevices filled with clay, the roofs a thatch of the swamp grass, resembling their English cottages in this. The few windows have only oiled paper to resist the winter's storms. Each house is set on a plot of ground of its own on either side of the street — the location for each family being decided by lot. Yet building by men cramped with rheumatism and sciatica, or falling down from weakness as a prelude to illness and death is not a rapid business, and, for all that they planned at first to live as compactly as possible, without being crowded, the unattached young men to be part of the families — as they had been in Leyden — it soon became evident that many houses would not be needed.

In less than a week after the first visit of the women ashore, not all the prowess of Myles Standish, hero of war in Flanders, not all his own unending strength and endurance, could defend his Rose from the blight of illness nor shield his heart from the sharp stab of sorrow. She had dreamed of the new home in a land of fair skies, sunshine and flowers, not this region of snows; she knew how thin and white she was growing, but she knew that her husband had not ventured on any vain purpose, and willed to be brave for his sake. Her high resolves were not long tested however, ere she gained the reward of her faith.

Others soon followed her, and, having but crossed the threshold, Ann Tilly, Mrs. Martin, little Ellen More and Mary Chilton's mother were gone from the colony; another month and Mary Allerton, John Tilly's wife, Sarah Eaton and the sister-in-law of Doctor Fuller (Mrs. Edward Fuller), were numbered with them. Meanwhile, Susanna White had become a widow, and Elizabeth Tilly an orphan, with Mary Chilton, and soon Priscilla Mullins was added to these girls' forlorn state. Alice Rigdale and her husband; Thomas Tinker, his wife and child, needed not houses nor land in Plymouth. Two of the More boys and a number of the young men fell victims in the great mortality, and Sarah Priest, in Leyden, was a widow, though nearly a year passed before she knew it. A little later and Elizabeth Winslow slipped from the gentle hand clasp of Katherine Carver, to join her other dear friend, Rose Standish.

Thus twelve wives were swept away by this fatal epidemic, some from the *Mayflower*, some from the land. Even the comfort of graves bearing their names which should tell those who loved them, and others, that they had been with them, was denied them. But their monument is the hill by the sea-shore, on which their graves were made, and their remembrance shall last as long as mayflowers blossom.

From the time of the first anchoring of the ship (at Cape Cod) of the total of the twenty-five women and young girls, thirteen were released from their labors. It is indeed remarkable that even twelve should have survived. Into the hearts of those recovering from their own illness, the spirit of desolation must have entered for a time, as they struggled to their feet again, to grieve for those who were laid to rest under the snow and to take up the burdens of life once more. Many of the men had gone, too, but few of the children.

For the five elder women, life, even under the circumstances, still was worth while. The governor's wife had the loving care and interest of all but two of her household's original numbers; her husband, her young ward, her maid and John Howland; two of the other young men, as well as the little boy she cared for on the voyage, Jasper More, had gone. But deepest grief was not, as yet, her portion. Mary Brewster, too, was strengthened by the sight of her husband untouched by illness and apparently not weakened by the terrific work and strain he had been under, and her own two boys, soon helping as ably as before, and even Richard More, the sole survivor of his family, was already one of her's. For Eliza-

beth Hopkins and Eleanor Billington not one of
their own particular groups were gone. But
Susanna White had left only her own two children,
her nephew and her brother—and he, of course,
seemed to belong to each one as much as to her.

Humility Cooper and Elizabeth Tilly, Priscilla
Mullins and Mary Chilton were indeed the most
truly alone, each one being the sole representative of
her family.   -

On the five women the care and responsibility fell
heaviest, though the girls and even the children had
their share in the general division of labor. Each
served while there was nursing to be done. Cooking
was not only a duty but a serious problem in finding
the wherewithal to tempt failing appetites or keep
up the strength of the men and children. Who can
doubt that these women often went hungry that others might have more? Scarce wonderful that Mary
Brewster and Katherine Carver never regained their
full health again. The former took to her home and
mother love the homeless and motherless girls, sadly
missing her own daughters, so far away.

Gradually came a lessening of the strain of apprehension of unknown evils; the problem of the
Indians had been solved on the day that they heard
the word ''welcome'' from a strange voice, and, from
then on, mutual fear diminished between their immediate neighbors in the forest and themselves, and
visits from these strange people became frequent and
helpful as well.

The day of the making of another covenant was

one marked by color and animation in the doleful
monotony of those early months, for the women with
strength enough for interest. Their governor, with
all the formalities of his office, met and entertained
the sovereign of the savages, and the lively music of
the drum and trumpet, the firm footsteps of the
military guard quickened their spirits and brought
a sense of assurance. The green rug, on which roy-
alty sat, in one of the unfinished houses, must always
have brought back, to the woman who owned it, that
scene and its results — the lasting treaty of mutual
friendship and benefit. That other rug of modern
times, on which the Liberty Bell rested at the Pana-
ma-Pacific Exposition, in 1915, afterwards used at
celebrations connected with the great generals of the
World War, is interesting but not more important in
the historical part it has played than the rug which
we now see in fancy.

Also their defense from their fort was accomplished, the cannon being landed and dragged up
the greater hill, to the summit, and a strong building
erected there. Military preparedness began as soon
as the men were able to drill, under command of
Myles Standish, their chosen Captain.

Gradually, also, Spring came, the children found
arbutus and other early flowers, and were happy,
though their search might not take them far from
sound of the home voices, as the fearsome sound of
the wolves was a constant warning. Remember and
Mary Allerton and Damaris Hopkins played on the
beach with Constance, Elizabeth and Humility, and

gathered the bright shells in the warm sunshine till the pink of the shells and arbutus was reflected in their cheeks. The sailors, now that the connection between them and their erstwhile passengers was soon to end and their roughness softened by the common ills of the winter, were glad to tell tales to amuse the children, when lingering ashore.

And, so, with the April mildness on land and sea, came the last night when the lights of the *Mayflower* shone to them out of the darkness. On the morning of its departure, how visible the scene is to us. The women watch from places of vantage, in groups or singly, in company with some men or with the children clinging to them, from the hill beside the street, their wistful eyes following the battered sails out of the harbor, while the guns from the Fort ring out in parting salute the farewell to their ever-ready shelter, to the only connecting link between them and the rest of their race. Each one has been asked a question all have had plenty of time to consider well, if it were needed to repeat, "shall we, shall I go back?" Away with the *Mayflower* to a once familiar life from unfamiliar trials, from haunting memories to friends or relatives left on the other side of the sea? Each woman for herself has answered "No." The venture made in faith by those loved and gone from their sight, should not have been made in vain; the standard formed of high hope and courage should not go down while they were able in the light of that faith and remembrance to carry it forward.

Now only as a mirage can their ship be seen on the far horizon.

Susanna White, clasping her baby closer, stands near the place on the hill where the body of William, her husband, had been laid; not far away near the grave of Elizabeth, his wife, is Edward Winslow. Their eyes, though seeing each other, are viewing things far away. (Could a breath from the lindens of Leyden be wafted to them?) In that moment arose a consciousness of an unfelt emotion — hitherto drowned by selfishness in sorrow — pity.

Mutual shock and endurance was to continue for them all on this same day. To shake from them any idle reflections, the men worked steadily and vigorously for the remaining hours, on the new fields and planting of seeds, the elder, the doctor, the governor, each exerting every energy, as well as the other men and boys. The day proved unusually hot and the governor seemed to feel it greatly. Reaching his home, he lay down to rest, but while his family waited upon him in deep concern, he lost consciousness. Thus not only was the harbor dark that night, but a cloud hung over Plymouth and common anxiety on their governor's account caused the departure of the *Mayflower* to be almost forgotten. But the governor was worn out, not with that day's labor but by his labors, as has been said, "in three countries and on the sea, as counselor, agent, nurse, farmer, magistrate and man of God," and, in spite of their efforts and distress, consciousness did not

return ere he passed from them. In the pathetic
description, by his successor, "he was buried in the
best manner they could, with some vollies of shot
by all that bore arms," and his grave left smooth
and unmarked, as the others on the hill, that it
might not appear to any enemy that their numbers
were lessened. Though the office of governor was
filled, the first lady of the colony had no successor,
since the widower, William Bradford, was chosen.
Her anguish of grief was so intense, and her frail-
ness grew so perceptably, that it became evident her
stay with them was but transitory.

And again, as in Leyden, the doctor's sister kept
the home for him; but there were more members in
the family than in those by-gone days, for Susanna
had three little lads to care for now, and the doctor
three small nephews to play with. Let us follow the
bright rays of the sunset into their cottage on a May
evening. Supper is over, and now is little Peregrine's bedtime. His mother is gently rocking the
cradle, as she mends his brother's stockings, glanc-
ing now and then at the smiling but sleepy baby
and urging him in softest baby language to accompany the "sandman" without further delay; but
Peregrine's ambition seems to be to stay awake on
this bright particular evening and he coos and
laughs in response to his mother's admonitions. His
brother and cousin are romping just outside the
front door and Resolved runs in to get the cane that
had been his father's, to play horse with. Susanna

sits on a bench beneath the little square window, which swings open with its paper pane, and the breeze which enters plays with the soft, curly tendrils of her hair; beside her on the bench stands the little chest of drawers which has ever held her sewing articles and trinkets since William White gave it to her when they were married. A shadow falls across the light and men's voices come to her as her brother passes with a friend, returning from a stroll to enjoy a smoke by the cottage door. Twilight is fast failing now; the baby is at last asleep; Susanna softly puts away her sewing and goes into the living-room, adjoining, to light a candle at the fire-place; she then stands in the doorway to call in Resolved and Samuel, as she does each evening; she sees her brother and his friend on the doorstep bench, also quite a regular occurrence about this hour, and Edward Winslow rises in his courtly manner to receive her smile of greeting. In the few weeks since the sailing of the *Mayflower,* her pity and sympathy have unconsciously awakened an interest which is now slowly dawning in some wonderment upon her, while for Winslow he had already questioned himself if she would be willing to let him take William White's place, and if, on the other hand, she could fill the vacancy left at his hearth-stone by Elizabeth? He thought he knew the answer to the second question, but for the first sought her reply. That Edward Winslow, talented, aristocratic, of good family and of some wealth, should admire her, pictures Susanna for us almost as plainly as his

painted portrait represents him. We have not the
slight details of her features, but in fancying her
with the light brown hair, blue eyes and pink and
white skin of a young English mother in her twen-
ties, we cannot be far wrong; and for character, the
reflections of her life and times show us that which
certified the regard of all who knew her and gives
her to ours. Her good sense ever caused her acceptance of facts and prompt adjustment of her life to
the conditions imposed upon it by circumstances.
By her intelligence and resourcefulness she was
saved from the dissipation of despondency, devoting
her physical and mental energies to making the best
of the situation in which she found herself. With
courage she contemplated the present and took
thought of and measured the possibilities of the future. Her cheerfulness and adaptibility to the
inevitable in meeting her serious problems won her
a victory over them and greatly increased her own
pleasure in living and unquestionably added to the
pleasure of others. She had had advantages of comfortable circumstances always — more than some and
as much as few of the pilgrim women had; her
brother, her husband, were men of education and
breeding, such also the men of the families of her
nearest friends.

Edward Winslow, doing always the unexpected,
but always pleasing himself, soon found the opportunity of settling the question in his thoughts.
Shortly thereafter Mary Brewster again played con-
fident to a neighbor. When the bans were published

at the next Sunday service, announcing such an item of interest in the lonely, quiet existence of the community, any surprise was soon dissolved for most, by their regard for the principals. Before May was over, the simple ceremony took place, performed by the governor, as magistrate, as he himself has recorded, "after the fashion of the Low Countries," and the first bride of the colony appears before us. Anna Fuller whom we first knew in Leyden, there becoming Susanna White, now changes, as far as name goes, into the second Mistress Winslow of Plymouth and before her stretch long years of prosperity. And contentment and happiness? Yes, such as a woman like her will always seek and find.

Natural curiosity ever alert at a time of a wedding is sadly checked for us, by dearth of description or detail of this one, so full of an unusual interest. The old friend Mary Brewster, was surely witness for the bride, and her brother, the doctor; while the elder, as properly, was witness for the groom, and Isaac Allerton, doubtless, as assistant. But what repast Mary Chilton, Priscilla Mullins and Elizabeth Tilly, reinforced by the culinary skill of Mistress Hopkins, prepared for the newly married couple, or who were of the wedding guests who partook, or whether at her house or his, we have no record. We know simplicity was the keynote, as complying both with the Pilgrim opinion and the necessity caused by conditions. It was an important day for the bride and for the young girls, who were gladly stirred by the event into a remembrance of

romance and a brighter side of life, forgotten for
many a day. It even aroused Katherine Carver
from her lethargy of grief into a wondering attention when Elizabeth Tilly gave to Desire Minter all
the details in her possession, which we gladly would
glean also, if we could. However, the date appears
upon the page of Plymouth history like an illumin-
ated initial letter, for it marks the beginning of a
more normal life. The dark days since their arrival
which seemed emphasized only by sickness and death
and hunger and cold, had passed.

The summer thus ushered in, brought its herbs
for salad and medicine, its wild fruits and berries
of many varieties, its fish and game, also roses to
gladden their eyes, fragrant and colorful, and, owing to the friendliness and good understanding with
the Indians, the colonists might walk in the woods
round about their homes as in the highways of
England. The two Indians called Squanto and
Hobomok, who attached themselves permanently to
the colony, showed them many things of advantage
in the way of agriculture and home crafts which the
women were as glad to learn as the men.

About six weeks after their marriage, Susanna
Winslow bade her husband the first of the many
farewells she would experience in the coming days,
because of his frequent journeys in the cause of the
colony. He was now to seek the great Indian chief,
Massasoit, with whom the treaty had been made, a
few months before, and the governor had selected
him and Stephen Hopkins for this necessary visit.

The walk through the woods was long and tiresome and consumed more than a week, but the object of their journey was accomplished. Susanna Winslow and Elizabeth Hopkins, awaiting in some natural anxiety at home for their return, or news of them, must have been somewhat startled the day the governor sent them the message he had just received by an Indian runner, that their husbands were nearly starving and struggling homeward, exhausted. These two wives hastily despatched food by the Indian, to meet them at a certain place, and had an abundant supper in readiness on the rainy evening of their return.

Soon after this, the upsetting occurrence of a lost child came upon them, and Eleanor Billington had the sympathy of the mothers because one of her boys had been too venturesome in the woods and strayed away. He was found by the Indians miles from Plymouth and word being brought of this, the governor sent a boat to the place of the Indian encampment which brought the boy back, no worse for his adventure, so this excitement passed. Expeditions among the Indians became necessary, both of forceful and peaceful intent, which made recurring anxiety for the women, until the men had safely returned.

At the close of the summer, once again sorrow filled their hearts, as one more of their number went from the friends who loved her. It was the only happiness left for Katherine Carver to follow her husband out of this world, which no longer con-

tained anything of interest to her and the future no
hope strong enough to relieve her broken heart. So,
lovely and lamented, she was laid to rest on the hill
by the shore, where so many others of their brave
and fair were sleeping. This left but two of the
married women who had left Leyden together:
Mary Brewster and Susanna Winslow. But the
number of the girls remained complete.

The first anniversary of their sailing from old
Plymouth, came and went. The survivors of that
day's company on the ship must have observed it
with many thoughts. These September days were
busy ones, indeed, as preparations to meet the coming winter began. Their Spring planting had been
successful in all except peas, and their harvest of
corn was abundant. The wild grapes were made
into wine, the corn pounded into meal, each household a veritable hive of workers; while the wear and
tear on their clothes must be repaired and new garments made, or purchased when strictly necessary,
from the supply stored in the Common House.
But an interval occurred in this routine and it
may be introduced to us by a picture of the living-
room in the Brewster house, by candle light, which
contains all the women of the colony in earnest discussion. This conclave is caused by the recent suggestion of the governor that in view of the fact of
their successful harvest, and renewed health, a
period of recreation should be planned and enjoyed
by all; games, feasting, mirth and frolic, a combina-

tion of festivities of both England and Holland
with which they were familiar, and not only were
preparations to be for themselves but for guests —
Chief Massasoit and many of his warriors were to
be invited, with no doubt at all of their acceptance.
Many of the men had been hunting that day to provide the game, and the results were enough to last
a week. It was not questions of what to provide,
but how much of everything would be needed, and
which of them would prepare and roast the wild
turkeys, who boil the fish, who make sauces and side
dishes or cook vegetables, who bake, who make the
salads, and all the other necessary plans for cooks
who are hostesses, and hostesses who are cooks. The
problem has a familiar appearance to many of us
in our own day. Favorite receipts were compared,
and whoever excelled in a certain thing was to have
charge of that supply. All were good cooks so it
was a case of friendly emulation and rivalry in this
novel experience, with which each housekeeper retired that night, after they had talked and planned
to their satisfaction. More than a hundred to be
provided for over a three day period, and eleven
women and young girls to see it through; even the
littlest girls, Remember and Mary Allerton and
Damaris Hopkins had to help, and of course the
men did their share in keeping the great fires burning and dressing the game, and the boys in carrying
water from the brook. Every iron kettle, every long
and short legged pot and pan, every wooden bowl
and leathern bottle, every pewter dish, with hooks,

spits and trivets were in use; wooden cups or gourds to drink from, and knives and napkins. The only forks were the long-handled iron ones for cooking purposes, their use for the table was not known, their service was supplied by napkins and spoons.

The Indians arrived and encamped around the street, thoughtfully bringing a large supply of venison to add to the bill of fare. The cooks and waitresses in whitest of linen caps, kerchiefs and aprons, with short woolen skirts and buckled shoes, had many steps to take to serve the banqueters seated at the great tables erected in front of the houses; and when the men were having their contests of shooting or games, they cleared away or looked on at the entertainment as they could. They and the children, in sampling the products of their cooking or taking a mouthful, now and then, were kept from being hungry in the midst of plenty by being too busy to eat.

The long shadows of the third day saw the end of the event. And was the first American "block party" a success? We may say that it was. And were the women tired? We will agree to that also. But the men were pleased, the children happy, and one recovers quickly from the fatigue of gratifying achievement. Thus was their public thanksgiving celebrated, by order of the governor.

On a November day some weeks later, household tasks were going as usual; many of the men were gathering the last of the harvest, others getting in the winter's supply of wood. We may see Mistress

Brewster in her kitchen distilling herbs and witch-hazel for domestic medicines, as was the custom of each housewife, that Dr. Fuller's supply might not be too freely drained. She has the help and company of Mary Chilton this afternoon — both unconscious of any special interest that the day may bring to them especially, before its close, yet the unexpected was as often happening then as now. Priscilla and Elizabeth had taken Desire Minter on a search for more sassafras, hoping to entertain and amuse the listless girl, who, since Mrs. Carver's death, seemed to grow each day more unhappy. The two Marys are talking of the return voyage of the *Mayflower* — how long it might have been or how short — and if their friends in England and Holland had received the many letters and messages taken back by the Captain. Suddenly they are startled by the sound of the gun from the fort! Another shot! They are in the street now and likewise every woman and child — it is the signal for assembly — and the men may be seen hurrying from the woods and fields. The Governor accompanied by the Captain and an Indian runner are rapidly descending the hill from the fort, both looking especially determined. The news is soon in possession of all. A ship has entered Cape Cod harbor — seen by the Indians and word brought at once to Plymouth! Surprise and suspense were but some of the feelings this news aroused. They had been seven months without sight or sound of the world beyond their little settlement and its woodland neighbors.

It would have to be Spring before a friendly ship
could be expected to find them (for newcomers
could not live in comfort or be of use till then) and
as England and France were on far from friendly
terms, this might be a ship of the latter nationality,
seeking them with hostile intent. But preparedness
was ever their daily thought and ability to cope with
any emergency. Thus the Captain's little army of
defense, twenty men, was soon marshalled and ready
— none without a gun in hand — to protect their
women, children and homes to the last man.

Mary Brewster sees her husband in the front rank,
of course. He can fight as ardently as pray, if
necessary, and while wishing that an enemy might
be converted and enjoy life, if that were impossible,
then no question of who should fire first. The Captain had no weaklings in his command, even the boys
and younger men were heroes with such leaders.
Their eyes sharpened by expectancy and uncertainty, soon discern the stranger's sails, even as the
lookout from the fort calls out the fact that it is in
view. Intently they wait and watch, when, behold,
before their astonished eyes, the flag of England is
flung out in greeting! Relief and amazement run
a race in their minds. The ship is smaller than the
Speedwell. The first boat puts out, making straight
for the men drawn up on the seashore. In their in-
credulity they can scarce recognize, can scarce
believe, what they see: Robert Cushman grasping
the hands of Brewster and Bradford; John Winslow
seizing his brother Gilbert's shoulders; Jonathan

Brewster being sprung upon by his brothers, from the ranks, and then Thomas Prence just behind him.

Such confusion and laughter, such embraces and tears of joy as the women, realizing the situation, come running down the street to meet the crowd coming from the water's edge.

And in another boat come two women, friends from Leyden, the widow Ford and her children and Mistress Basset. The relief of the newcomers was quite equal to that of the Plymouth people, but for a different reason. Not finding any signs of habitation in the first harbor of their search, they feared that all survivors had died or been killed by Indians, and as in their long voyage of four months they had consumed about all of their provisions, they feared starvation for themselves. All were in good health, with good appetites and spirits and as soon as their apprehension was dispelled, at sight of their friends and their plentiful supply of food, gaiety reigned. The problem of housing for these thirty-five newcomers was finally settled by nightfall, each housekeeper putting up with some crowding to take in several, and the Common House once more giving shelter. What welcome of friends and relatives, what interest at news from others, the ensuing hours saw; what joyful supper parties that evening!

Thus the isolation of Plymouth was broken. The sails of the *Fortune* had brought them once again the touch of the outside world.

By daylight, another young lady had joined the colony, and Martha Ford opened her eyes, on the

first morning of her life, in Plymouth. Just why
her mother should have come across the ocean at
this time is not clear to us. She was a widow and
evidently of some means to be able to bring all her
children with her. We may suppose, without
stretching the bounds of probability, that her husband had been preparing to bring his family to the
new colony, and that, after his sudden death, she
carried out the plans.

The *Fortune* remained two weeks, and lively
weeks to get her well laden with the first exports of
the colony, furs, lumber and sassafras making a rich
invoice. Letters were written — letters of enthusiastic description; letters of encouragement to join
the life of the New World; letters of advice, and letters replying to those received, for many words of
sympathy had been sent in response to the dreary
news brought back by the *Mayflower*. There was a
particular letter from the governor (one of sympathy, also) to Mistress Alice Southworth, in London, since Robert Cushman brought the news of her
recent widowhood.

Robert Cushman had come especially as emissary
from the merchants who had underwritten the Pilgrims, and to see for himself in what condition they
were, for report at home. He was so pleased with
what he experienced, however, that he planned a
permanent stay at a future day, and left his young
son, who had accompanied him, with the governor.

So the *Fortune* was ready to sail, and by her
departure, was to make one more break in the ranks

of the women, since Desire Minter chose to go back
in her, to her friends in England, under charge of
Robert Cushman. Her health and spirits had so
failed that it was considered the best thing for her;
thus another blank was made in the life of Elizabeth
Tilly, who had found in Desire a dear friend — and
in whose heart she was never forgotten. Perhaps
Desire already forsaw that her place would soon be
taken and knew that she would leave little Elizabeth
in good hands. As the *Fortune* sailed out of the
harbor, we may see John Howland near Elizabeth
with his protective look and ready, encouraging
smile.

This little ship did not receive benefit from her
name, for fortune proved unkind. A French man-
of-war, lying near the coast of England, captured
her and took all on board prisoners to a French
island, where for more than a fortnight they were
detained. However the ship and passengers were
then released and reached England — but the valuable cargo and letters were spoils of war. So Alice
Southworth never received the governor's letter,
but the fact of its having been sent was reported to
her by her friend, Robert Cushman. Indeed the
various items of news he brought were of interest to
many.

But Desire, if she had only written of her experiences, or caused them to be written! Her experiences
as a woman of the *Mayflower*, as a woman of Plymouth Colony, her experiences in leaving the latter
for an English home — with her war adventure as

an extra detail. What material she had and of what
value for the world to read. She would have been
a rival historian of Bradford and Winslow, for
posterity. But of course such a thought never
occurred to her. She was a woman — and a woman
could not be independent in the society of that day,
which was an exclusively masculine society and with
a system by which feminine conduct was judged
from a masculine point of view. About two hundred
and fifty years elapsed before any other point of·
view was deemed possible. And Desire Minter was
far from being the first of her sex to question. In
due time word was brought to Plymouth that she
had reached her friends, and, later on, that her brief,
but not uneventful life was over. Somewhere Eng-.
lish roses bloom o'er her grave; an interesting pil·
grimage, if its location were known, as a remem-·.
brance of the first woman of the *Mayflower* and of
Plymouth Colony to return to her early home.

Meanwhile, before Plymouth knew aught of what
had happened to the *Fortune,* much happened
there. While pleasure in the company of the newcomers lasted, supplies did not, and their bubble of
joy was soon broken. The *Fortune* brought no food,
and thirty-odd extra people, mostly men, to provide
for, was a serious problem. So their second winter
was a hard one to get through, with little to eat —
half rations only — and resultant weakness (though
fortunately no sickness) scarce enabled them to improve their condition. Nevertheless, owing to the
threatening attitude of some of the distant Indians,

a protecting wall of lumber was built around the town. The street ran from the rock to the battlement on the greater hill, but some houses were erected at a different angle which indicated another street for the near future — to be called the Highway — and the square came into view.

In Spring, the women, in addition to household duties, helped plant, the children also — though for them more of a pleasure than for their mothers, struggling with the problems of supply and demand in food and clothes.

On an April day, after the planting, an episode occurred which brings before us for the first time, a woman not hitherto distinctly in the picture. The Indian squaws occasionally came to Plymouth and were a help or a bother, according to their personality, to the women of the colony. One, however, had such agreeable characteristics that she was considered a desirable member of the community. Her husband, Hobomok, was the colony's trusted interpreter and permanent resident. On this day, we see the mothers of the smallest children, Susanna Winslow, Martha Ford and Elizabeth Hopkins, assembled in Mistress Hopkins' big kitchen, learning from Hobomok's wife the craft of moccasin making; the soft foot-coverings were both comfortable and warm for the babies. But the lesson is interrupted and Hobomok takes his wife away, saying that the governor wants her. The surprise of the women is lessened only by apprehension when they later learn that she had been sent on a mission which none of

them could have performed, nor was a man of theirs
able to cope with its delicacy, not even Hobomok.
This peculiar circumstance was caused by Squanto,
their other trusted interpreter and friend. He had
stated that all was not well with their Indian allies
and that Massasoit was treacherously planning with
the Narragansetts to exterminate them. The quali-
fications of Hobomok's wife were at once apparent
to the men in consultation over this news, which
Hobomok insistently declared could not be true. She
was instructed, therefore, under guise of a casual
visitor, to go to Massasoit's camp and learn what
she could. Her return was anxiously awaited. She
accomplished her errand in a most satisfactory and
creditable manner, and her information relieved
them of alarm.

Another year passed, with a not very succesful
harvest; uncertain Indian affairs, and the arrival of
boats bringing letters, even visitors but no supplies
or friends or families — the Merchants and even
Robert Cushman seemed to fail them.

Some of the boats brought men whom they supported for a time from their scanty supply, who had
come out to establish another colony on the coast and
who requited their kindness by ingratitude and
scorn for a settlement having women. Another boat,
however, was more acceptable as proving they had
friends in need, though unknown, for by it word was
brought of a massacre of Virginia colonists by the
Indians. From this same kind-hearted ship captain,
John Huddleston, Edward Winslow — who visited

him to extend the colony's thanks for the warning — was able to procure some provisions, of which they were greatly in need, and thereby increased their bread allowance to a quarter of a pound ·a day. From this warning also they proceeded to build a stronger and larger fort, one part being planned for a place of worship.

A trading ship coming in, made them pay exorbitantly for their needs seeing how greatly they lacked them. On this ship, however, was a gentleman who was returning to England from Virginia. He made the acquaintance of the Plymouth people while the ship was in the harbor, and that he was a welcome visitor to the Brewster household is told by a letter he later sent to Governor Bradford saying how he had enjoyed Mr. Brewster's books. A man of like tastes, evidently, and ·his passing acquaintance a ·pleasant incident to them.

The autumn and winter were punctuated by trips taken by the governor and some of the other men, with Squanto, in search of camps where the Indians would sell corn, as their own harvest was far from being enough to keep them until the next. On one of these expeditions, Squanto died.

As planting time approached, in view of the fact that the next harvest must produce a much greater amount, to avoid the dangers of starvation which they were then enduring, the governor, in consultation, decided to divide the land into personal holdings, instead of all lands being worked for and held by the community. This new plan quickly grew

increased enthusiasm for planting and culture, since
emulation and friendly contests for success began.
Mary Chilton and Humility Cooper were each given
an acre, and the attention those acres received was
not less than any other. To work in one's very own
soil was pleasure as well as profit, discounting the
fatigue.

At this time, also, the women had a particularly
choice bit of satisfaction. No less than the total
disestablishment and wreck of the colony which the
men had come to plant who had accepted hospitality
from the Plymouth people, when they arrived, and
so discourteously returned it by ridiculing a settlement which contained women. Appeals for help
from them were received, and with usual generosity
were granted, to enable them to keep their lives from
starvation and the Indians, and to leave that country.

Plymouth had but six matrons; and the young
woman who had been maid to Mrs. Carver, and four
young girls, Priscilla, Mary, Elizabeth and Humility,
with Remember Allerton and Constance Hopkins
fast leaving childhood in the responsibilities of this
difficult life. With so many single men the widow
and the girls could have a half dozen at command in
an instant, while Mary Brewster had four strong
right arms to rely on, her husband and three sons;
Susanna Winslow the hands of her husband, brother
and brothers-in-law, Gilbert and John, at need. Remember and Constance had each a brother to call
upon and the other two married women, husbands

and sons. Nevertheless, no one would care to deny
that the twenty-four hours of the day of these loyal
and efficient members of the company were not as
heavily laden as those of the men, nor that their
efforts in sustaining the struggling community were
not as valuable in the final results.

"They made the home and kept the hearth fires
    burning;
They spun and wove and tilled the barren soil;
They met each day's return with patient trusting
    And murmured not through all the weary toil."

THE BRIDE SHIP.

THE BRIDE SHIP.

Massasoit was ill — very ill, and a Dutch ship had run aground near his encampment. This news, brought by runners, caused Winslow to again leave his family and penetrate the forests to visit the Chief, as he was looked upon as a special friend of Massasoit, and could speak Dutch. It was about a year from the time when Hobomok's wife went over the trail on her diplomatic errand. The Dutch ship had gotten away, but Massasoit was decidedly ill. Among Winslow's talents was skill in doctoring and nursing, so with some remedies and food he had carried with him, he was able to improve the condition of the Chief. Massasoit's delight and gratitude manifested themselves in an important piece of information, which was that an Indian conspiracy was in the making against Plymouth. With this startling revelation Winslow returned. The matter was soon concluded, for their Captain, as he believed preparation and prevention were better than cure, took a picked company and the offensive, and came back with the head of the bold ringleader. This salutary but grewsome object caused the women to look elsewhere than the point on the battlements of the fort where it was displayed. However the warning had its effect — discontented Indians became mild in terror of the Sword of the White Men,

as they called Myles Standish. The picked company
in this event was composed of several of the young
men who were specially, if secretly, favored by Priscilla, Mary and Elizabeth.

Ships and more letters, one bringing truly joyful
news that, at last, some of their own people would
come in the next ships sent out by the Merchants.
This cheer was sorely needed, but as they were just
managing to keep from starvation by the fish as
almost their only food, they wondered how they
could supply the newcomers with a living. The
prospect was indeed dreary, as a protracted drought
had wilted their cherished crops hopelessly. Another ship, bringing a rather important naval official in
charge of fishing activities on the coast, came in.
This officer, Captain Francis West, called Admiral
of New England, made but a short stay, but long
enough to fill them with anxiety as he told them he
had spoken a ship at sea, had boarded her, found
her bound for this port, and sailed in company with
her until in a violent storm they lost sight of her.
He supposed she had already come in, and, finding
she had not, feared some mischance.

These summer days were dark for them, starving,
with hopes of a harvest blighted by drought, and
now distress for the possible loss of the ship bringing their loved ones. In this deepest gloom, which
proved the fore-runner of dawn, they set apart a
day of prayer, in humility and distress, by their
faith's steady flame. Under the glaring sun, the
day began — but at evening the sun set in clouds

and the rain came for which they prayed. The corn, the fruit was saved.

Sweet and soft was the air of the summer morning some few weeks after this; birds sang joyously and a silver mist hung over the sea as Plymouth awoke to the new day. The women seemed more light-hearted than of late, shown by snatches of song now and then as they pursued the common tasks of the household. An indefinable feeling which had come to them that since the answer to their prayer for rain had been given by many refreshing showers, the one in supplication for the safety of the ship and their expected dear ones could not be in vain and all would yet be well, gave them more enjoyment of life notwithstanding a breakfast of boiled clams was all they could prepare for their families. The smoke from the chimneys rose over the thatched roofs, pointing seaward. Some of the men came forth from their homes, on their way to the day's labors, and cheerily greeted one another, stopping to speak of the weather and prospects of plenty.

Mary Brewster stands in her door-way, arranging the sprays of the wild rose trained beside it — the showers had revived it and it looked its best. She had planted and tended it, hoping for the day when her daughters might smile at her beside its blossoms. Priscilla joins her in admiring it, both thinking of Fear and Patience on the longed for ship. They speak of this being the first ship to come having a woman's name, and that she was bringing so many women.

John Alden stops on his way past with a morning greeting. What man more anxious than he for the arrival of the *Anne*, though his bride-to-be is not on the ship. Through many months Priscilla has heard love's voice, sweet and low, tender and strong, and though for one reason and another it seemed best to wait, she has now promised to marry him when the uncertainty about the ship is over, for she could not leave dear Mistress Brewster, who had so mothered her, in the suspense concerning her own daughters, nor be selfish in thinking of her own affairs when the universal anxiety was so great.

They too, talk of the weather, of the breeze from the southwest, and glance at the chimney's long finger of smoke pointing, pointing to the sea. Half unconsciously they look in that direction and watch the thinning fog as it seems to form in patterns like Flemish lace, as Priscilla says. Now it has parted and the sun's brilliancy streams through making a jewelled pathway on the water. Quickly Priscilla grasps Mary Brewster's hand and flings out her arm in the direction the smoke has been pointing. Against the pink and golden morning sky there is a ship, coming slowly, slowly, into the harbor, flinging before her wreaths of pearly foam. The *Anne!*

"Then from their houses in haste came forth the
    Pilgrims of Plymouth,
Men and women and children all hurrying down to
    the sea shore."
Never again did the Pilgrims of Plymouth expe-

rience the thrill of that moment at the arrival of any ship, and only once before had the feeling approached it — at the arrival of the *Fortune*. Though some emotions were similar in each case, such as relief and joy, the circumstances were dissimilar. The relief was for themselves, for their own welfare, in the first case, in the second their relief was doubled, as the welfare of those on the ship was the chief thought. The first joy was coupled with surprise at its unexpectedness, the second with thanksgiving at the fulfillment of a great hope and anticipation.

Fathers and husbands, brothers and friends jumped into boats to put off to the *Anne* to see and greet at the earliest possible moment those of whom they had been thinking and dreaming for so long. Here is Richard Warren, Doctor Fuller and Francis Cooke, of the first division, Jonathan Brewster and Thomas Prence, of the second, off in the first dash. The governor's boat takes also his assistant, Isaac Allerton, and Captain Myles Standish. Those on the ship, crowding along the rail, see the boats coming to them over the laughing wavelets, and recognizing one after another of the men as they come alongside, laugh in reply as they wave.

There has been written some charming verses descriptive of the arrival in this country of the foreign girls who married members of the A. E. F. of the recent war. The conclusion fits well with that scene of nearly three hundred years ago:

"They loved our heroes well enough
    To leave all else besides
And make America their own,
    So welcome home the brides."

Yes, and wives, too. The ship's band, if there had been one, might well have played the tune of "Sweethearts and Wives," while Plymouth's drum and fife could have replied with "Haste to the Wedding," or "Here Comes the Bride."

When the excitement had subsided a little, in a few days time, the Brewster girls had the interesting event of a wedding in their home, for their old friend, Priscilla married the young man of her choice, whom they had never seen, until they came to Plymouth. There was little wherewith to make a wedding feast, but, at least a health could be given the bride and bridegroom in the elderblow wine, made a year before.

Indeed the great shock to the newcomers was the condition of affairs in the colony — the thinness, paleness and weakness of all, from want of sufficient food. The governor recalls for many a day the embarrassment felt by the Pilgrims that so little could be offered to the new arrivals, only fish and cold water. But the *Anne*, unlike the *Fortune*, brought some supplies and necessaries, so the passengers were not a drain upon the colony as in the case of the *Fortune*, but, rather a great help.

Following the example of John Alden, Francis Eaton took to himself a wife, thereby adding another to the number of married women among the original company. He wedded the only woman who has been without a name in the history of the *Mayflower* and of the colony, perhaps the only woman in history who, being mentioned several times, has always been nameless. Of course she had a name and was called by it by her contemporaries, but seek as we may, she is designated only for us as "Mrs Carver's maid." For Francis Eaton she stayed, when she might have returned with Desire Minter; for him and his baby boy, left motherless, in the first winter, who had been looked after by plain but kind-hearted Eleanor Billington.

A passenger by the *Anne* whom we know, the wealthy widow, Mrs. Alice Southworth, brought her maid — but she was Christian Penn, and she married Francis Eaton for his third wife in after years, as the second Mrs. Eaton (we are glad to give her a name for once), did not live long.

The *Anne* stayed at Plymouth over a month — a witness of the several marriages which she had brought about, directly and indirectly.

Alice Carpenter — the lovely English girl, going with her family into voluntary exile in Leyden, marrying there and afterwards living, a prosperous matron of London, as Alice Southworth, then crossing the sea, a widow, to become a bride again, this time of a Colonial governor, living thereafter as Alice Bradford, an adornment of the community about her and a great factor in its peace and progress — weaves one of the bright threads of romance through the story of the women of Plymouth. The governor's marriage to the charming widow was indeed an important event in the life of the village.

Somewhat of a surprise to all but a few, was the announcement of the coming marriage of the Captain to an old friend, who had come out in company with Mrs. Southworth, for the same reason, in answer to a proposal of marriage, by letter. Then followed another wedding, of special interest to all the first comers by the *Mayflower* and to many of the recent arrivals, that of big John Howland with little Elizabeth Tilly, as she always seemed to her old friends, though quite grown up now and nearing seventeen. John Howland had patiently waited, as other men. Thus, by the coming of the *Anne*, bringing her own dear daughters, after three years of separation, Mary Brewster was able to smile at the departure of two of her loving daughters of adversity, to homes of their own. In this practical and primitive life, no honeymoons could be thought of. Plymouth, itself, then lay within the radius of a quarter of a mile and there was not another civilized habitation in hundreds of leagues, so the only wedding journey of these *Mayflower* girls, Priscilla and Elizabeth, was from Elder Brewster's doorway to their own new homes; one down, one up the street. We know that these girls had in addition to the loving interest of Mary Brewster, the affectionate encouragement of Susanna Winslow and the warm friendship of their girl companions of Leyden and of Plymouth, Fear and Patience Brewster, Mary Chilton and Humility Cooper — priceless wedding gifts — nor lacking was the regard of the governor's wife, a contemporary bride and old friend of Leyden days.

Of these marriages we have not a sketch in the written history of those days, except in the new book brought by the *Anne* for the colony's records, and the first entries, most appropriately, are these. And that the *Fortune* might be represented in the weddings of this season, as well as the *Mayflower* an *Anne*, the widow, Mrs. Ford, proceeded to take a second husband, in the person of Peter Brown, one of the sturdy and loyal men of the colony, who had come in the *Mayflower*.

The doctor's young wife, Bridget; Richard Warren's daughters, as well as their mother, and Hester Cooke and Juliana Morton, all arrivals by the *Anne*, hardly realized at first the sombre background of the life against which these marriages shone out for the first comers. To them it seemed they had arrived in a land of weddings and happiness — though lack of feasting and trousseaux was somewhat evident. Another interested on-looker, is the aunt of Remember and Mary, Isaac Allerton's sister, whom we knew in Leyden as Sarah Priest, but, widowed the first winter after her husband arrived at the new home he was to prepare for her, she nevertheless came to Plymouth with a new husband, whom she had recenly married in Leyden, and now she is Sarah Cuthbertson. She brought the little sister of the Allerton children, Sarah, who had been left in her care, but did not give up charge of her.

The augmented motion and sounds on Plymouth's

street, under the September sky was apparent.
Many women had come; numerous children were
there; the men's families were forming new households; strangers getting accustomed to one another
and surroundings; friends renewing old ties — the
newcomers feeling a bit lost, nevertheless.

The life, such as it had been, for the *Mayflower*
passengers was over. That time, within the three
years from their departure on the *Speedwell* from
Delfshaven, to their welcome of the *Anne*, at Plymouth, was a thing apart.

BENEATH THE PINES OF PLYMOUTH.

BENEATH THE PINES OF PLYMOUTH.

The *Anne,* laden with lumber, furs and mail, sailed in September, carrying also an important passenger; Susanna Winslow had to spare her husband for a time, while he went to England on the colony's business and his own affairs. However, her cares now were somewhat lessened by the coming in the *Anne* of a young women, named Mary Becket, to assist in her household labors. Since his other aunt had come, by the *Anne,* to live in Plymouth, little Samuel Fuller went back to the doctor's house to grow up. Bridget Fuller came with the baby, who was too delicate to make the voyage in the *Mayflower,* now three years old, and the doctor's sunny gentle spirit rejoiced.

Following the *Anne* came a small ship called *Little James,* which was to remain for the colony's use. It proved of little use and great expense, after all, but it brought other Leyden friends, as well as strangers from England. Thus Plymouth grew, and this autumn saw about a hundred and eighty persons instead of the handful who had struggled for life and a home in the wilderness for the past three years.

The new plan of individual division of the land with its planting and care proved its wisdom; the crops ripening rapidly, foretold an abundant har-

vest; the lightening of hearts and the promising
outlook caused the governor to proclaim a day of
public thanksgiving. It was not after the manner
of that of two years previously, as conditions were
different, but more in remembrance of the day of
supplication held in July. The dreaded visitor fam-
ine, was gone, never to return to the firesides of
Plymouth — although. for some awful hours it
seemed possible. On a wintry night, too great a
fire on the hearth of one of the new houses, caused
that house, and those nearest, to be consumed by
flames and to threaten the Common House where
their trading supplies and harvest were stored.
Well that the Captain had prepared his original
company to fight possible fire as well as possible
hostile attack, for by those men was that tragedy
averted, as, in the excitement and confusion, the
majority of the new-comers were more of a hin-
drance than help. The women must have felt that
if cares and labors were somewhat decreased, responsibility and uncertainty were increased through the
added numbers to the town.

That winter was the gayest Plymouth had ever
known. Families had been so lately reunited that
the satisfaction and joy of the occasion still caused
effervescence of spirits, and, too, there were many
more young people who never had to live through
the hard and perilous times which the first group
experienced. These all had either homes to go to or
loving friends to shelter them until homes were
built; no sickness to contend with and plenty to eat.

Where the comforts of all the men had depended more or less on a few women, now the hands of many women made all tasks lighter, and there was time for more social intercourse, which though in simplest form was sufficient then for relaxation and pleasure. No wonder happy voices were carried on the winter winds and light footsteps echoed on the street. Neighborliness being ever a characteristic of the Pilgrims, there was a constant exchange of goodwill and kindly attentions between the households. They had not needed Robert Cushman's admonition in his discourse to them, before returning in the *Fortune*, "There is no grief so tedious as a churlish companion and nothing makes sorrows easy more than cheerful associates. Bear ye therefore one another's burdens and be not a burden one to another," but they did not ignore it.

We may glance in the houses, on a frosty evening, and see who are sheltered within their cosy brightness and warmth. The governor's house has a large and merry party to hold, for he and his wife are entertaining for the winter, her sister, Juliana, with husband, George Morton and all the little Mortons: Patience, Nathaniel, John, Sarah, Ephraim and baby George; also a regular member of the family, Thomas Cushman. No wonder Christian Penn was in demand.

In the Brewster home, across the way, the Elder and his wife have also lively company, with three sons, the dear daughters, and Mary Chilton and Humility Cooper and Richard More. Thomas

Prence, John Winslow, Philip de la Noye and half
a dozen more of the young men drop in of an evening, with four attractive girls and charming hostess
to welcome them, and even an older man occasionally, as when Isaac Allerton brings his daughter over
to join in the fun; though he appears only to talk
to the Elder he glances at one of the girls, sometimes. Patience has her little flax wheel at one side
of the room under a candle bracket and the whir
of the wheel makes a background for the voices.
Thomas Prence is beside her mightily interested in
the spinning, as the product is for his sweetheart's
hope chest. The Brewster girls have brought a
supply of new linens to their mother, from Holland,
and indeed all the housekeepers are well supplied
with this necessity, but constant usage wears out
the best made and so more must be in readiness,
therefore spinning is a regular occupation, especially
for those with a wedding in mind.

Susanna Winslow has company, also, this evening, for her brother, the cheerful doctor, and his
young wife have been having supper with her and
her young brothers-in-law. John has gone over to
the Brewster's, but Gilbert, his handsome, rather
discontented face lit by the fire, sits near the hearth,
smoking, with the doctor and another man, for
Sarah Cuthbertson has come in for an evening's
gossip with her old friend, Anna, bringing her new
husband. The three women have much to talk of —
matters both grave and gay — and the new-comers
from Leyden are doing most of the chatter, Susanna

well pleased to listen, commenting occasionally on the narration of who had married or moved away and such items of interest as would accumulate in three years, with infrequent opportunities of communication.

John Howland and his Elizabeth go in the doorway of the Alden's house for a social call — and find Francis Cooke and his wife, Hester, there, also, and soon after, the Captain and his wife, Barbara, enter, and there is laughter and chat, while the women's fingers ply the knitting needles, for even in recreation moments the women can seldom afford to be wholly idle. Hester is an old Leyden friend to Priscilla and Elizabeth, though not of English birth, while Barbara is a new friend to them all, Hester having made her acquaintance on the sea voyage which brought them both to Plymouth. Francis Cooke had a comfortable house awaiting his wife and children, and Hester, naturally, quite fitted in with the first comers.

In the large house of the Hopkins, we see a number of the youngest inhabitants of Plymouth having a very jolly time — Giles and Constance being responsible. Here are Mary and Bartholomew Allerton, John and Jane Cooke, Patience Morton and Thomas Cushman, Ann and Sarah Warren, William Palmer and Samuel Jenny, even Jacob Cooke and Damaris Hopkins are admitted, also Mercy Sprague, Samuel Fuller, Resolved White and Sarah Annable, for at these children's parties the early hours kept could not rob even the youngest of much sleep. We know how many of the future marriages in Plymouth came from this gay group. Stephen Hopkins and his wife have gone out themselves and we see them in the home of Richard Warren, whose wife and daughter Mary, having gotten the youngest girls, Elizabeth and Abigail, in bed are glad to welcome company. Two of their fellow passengers in the *Anne* are also present, one being Robert Bartlett, whose interest in Mary began on their ocean voyage, which has a very modern sound. The other visitor is Ellen Newton, who came out with these friends, and is soon to marry John Adams, who preceded her in the *Fortune*.

Here is another gathering at the home of John and Sarah Jenny, who, with their three children, arrived on the *Little James*, they are of the old Leyden company; also we see here Stephen Tracy and Triphosa, his French wife and their little girl, Sarah, who has come to have a frolic with her playmates, Abigail and Sarah, while the parents are absorbed in their own affairs; they are soon joined by William Palmer (who came with his son in the *Fortune*) and his wife, Frances, a passenger in the *Anne*. The happy-go-lucky, or unlucky, household of the Billingtons is evidently satisfied with its own family this evening.

And to look further we see other homes whose inmates are strangers to us, though not to all of our earlist acquaintances, such as Francis and Anna Sprague, whose little girl, Mercy, is at the Hopkins, this evening; Anthony and Jane Annable, their oldest child we have also seen at the party but Sarah and Hannah are at home; Ralph Wallen and Joyce, his wife, Edward and Rebecca Bangs, with two children romping at home; Robert Hicks with Margaret and three children; also Mr. and Mrs. Edward Burcher, Mr. and Mrs. Thomas Flavell and Mr. and Mrs. William Hilton and little boys (all of the latter arrived by the *Anne*) besides numerous single men of the *Fortune, Anne* and *Little James,* who are quite welcome at the different houses. With so many young men, the girls had numbers to choose from, as each would have been glad for a wife and home of his own. Light refreshments add to the social hour we see, possets and manchets with home-brewed ale, and nuts, or the beverage made of roots, flavored with sassafras, similar to modern root beer, and popcorn — both the latter Indian additions to their knowledge. The possets and manchets are little cakes, the former sometimes called "sweet shrub" made of flour, sugar and spice, while manchets are flour, made without the spice and baked brown like our cookies.

Having thus seen who is who in Plymouth by the lights of the houses, "shining like stars in the dark and mist of the evening," we will observe some passing events, from this time, which were of interest to the women, either for themselves or members of their families or friends.

This happy winter passed into their history, and spring coming found the Plymouth people with hearts more in tune to the joy and hope of its opening buds and bird songs than ever before.

On a March day, the first ship of the season
from England came into view. If one has ever lived,
in modern times, far from native land and many
dear friends, as on island possessions, for instance,
in civil or military life, with ships coming safely
to harbor, the only chance of communication with
the outside world, bringing letters, packages of gifts
or a friend or two, perchance, with weeks or months
of interval between sight of a ship from overseas,
one may easily comprehend just how the women of
Plymouth felt when a ship was coming in. And
though the women did not write or receive letters
very often, in those days, yet they heard the contents
of those which frequently came to their husbands
and could think and talk of the tidings for many a
day.

The *Charity* brought Susanna Winslow's husband
home to her and to his welcoming friends. His mission had been eminently successful and proved the
adage of "If you want a thing done well, do it yourself," for Winslow knowing each need of the colony,
brought back the proper supplies for trade with the
Indians or the fishing ships, and adequate selection
of clothing for all. Having a wife, he knew what
to buy for the women, and what the children needed,
besides special commissions in way of books or
household comforts as they existed, at that time,
elsewhere. The colony was not rich — either as a
whole or by individual wealth — but though bearing
a heavy debt to the Merchants, they had to live

while every effort was being made to reduce the
original, and the Merchants were usually willing to
add to their obligation, especially since their exports were so marketable. Also some of the families
had personal credit in England, even though for
several years the results of their trade went to reduce the common debt, and the only personal gain
allowed in Plymouth was from selling the products
of their own lands to one another. Corn was legal
tender, nothing else was needed or of greater value
to them or the natives, until a later date. Therefore
the Elder, the Governor, the Captain, could rejoice
in more books, the women in the last word of costume
detail from London or Leyden suitable to their
present situation. We are quite sure that Mary
Chilton, Patience Brewster and the other girls, as
well as the young brides, were just as particular
about the set of a broad brimmed hat, or the ribbons
on a velvet hood, as interested in whether white neck-
wear had bows or tassels to fasten it, and if silver
shoe buckles were engraved or plain, as any woman
of today in her up-to-date appearance.

In addition to the many personal interests connected with Edward Winslow's return, he had purchased several head of cattle, and the children
watched with greatest curiosity — and some alarm
to those who had never seen such creatures — the
approach of the small boats from the ship with ropes
trailing behind attached to the horns and necks of
the cows, swimming valiantly to their new home.
Their familiar appearance brought an increased

home feeling to the women. From that day milk
was never lacking for beverage, butter, and cheese;
goat's milk was no longer their only supply.

And of great interest to many was a certain book
which Winslow had written and had printed that
winter, in London, called "Good News From New
England." This publication which threw the picture of themselves and their surroundings sharply
before the eyes of many on the screen of public intelligence, in England, was a factor in their life
thereafter by its results. Business for the colony
was not concluded at the time Winslow wished to
return to Plymouth, and, as he brought letters re-
questing his further presence, to continue these
matters, the governor agreed to his leaving them
again, and Susanna could do nothing but consent
also.

The *Charity* remained for fishing, throughout the
summer, which was crowded with events of moment.
In response to appeals from the Pilgrims in Plymouth to the Merchants in London that their pastor,
John Robinson, be sent to them with others of their
number from Leyden, the Merchants had made ex-
cuses. The *Anne* brought affectionate letters from
Robinson but not his longed-for presence. To their
great surprise, therefore, in company with Winslow,
on the *Charity*, there came a stranger whom the Merchants had decided should be the colony's religious
head. In vain had Winslow argued and pleaded for
Robinson, knowing what a disappointment this
would be. This minister brought his wife and

children and at first seemed well disposed toward
the Pilgrims, so they accepted what they could not
help and allowed him a seat on the Council board —
for now there were several assistants to the governor
— and requested him to act as associate with their
elder, but although he declared himself a convert to
the Separatist church, they did not admit him to the
position of their pastor. A more acceptable companion on this home-coming of Winslow's was a
clever and likable young carpenter, who did them
good service.

In the early summer, Ellen Newton married John
Adams, which was of interest to those who had
crossed with her in the *Anne,* and kindly observed
by others. In midsummer, two new comers brought
rejoicing and pleasure to many. In the governor's
family arrived the baby who received the name of
William, which had also been given to his father,
grand-father and great-grandfather. Into John and
Priscilla Alden's home came Elizabeth, called the
first born daughter of the Pilgrims. As one writer
has expressed it, ''She was destined to outlive every
individual then in the colony and to survive the
colony itself by twenty-five years.''

In August, just about a year from the time of the
arrival of the *Anne,* another of her passengers became a bride, making the eighth in the colony during
the twelve-month. This wedding was of special interest, not only because it was the first in a prominent family, but because of the popularity of the
bride and the groom and the affection and esteem

in which the parents were held. Plymouth rejoiced
when Patience Brewster married Thomas Prence,
and her mother felt that she then had all that heart
could wish for. With tall, affectionate sons and loving daughters, one going to a home of her own, but
not away, and, beside her, the handsome lover of her
youth as her devoted husband, sharing her feelings
on this important day; a home with all comforts
then obtainable; among admiring friends as of old,
Mary Brewster sighed in happy content. Plymouth
had returned to her the pleasures of Scrooby without its later uncertainties and trials. And Patience,
a reflection of her mother's early fairness and charm,
was as radiant a bride as New England's sun ever
lighted on a wedding day. Her young husband was
to steadily advance in the esteem of the colony and
in material position, reaching the important place of
governor in a few years. Thus destiny had woven
for her life a beautiful pattern, with childhood in
Scrooby, girlhood in Leyden, womanhood in Plymouth, with love and tender care to lighten all her
days. A bright particular star in the galaxy of
women of Plymouth colony who were not of the *Mayflower* company, but who found their life's fulfillment there.

Plymouth society had grown enough to be no
longer the one and indivisible association welded together by common experiences and mutual interests,
as it was at first. With the advent of those unconnected with the original pioneers and their objects,

who came as friends of the Merchants or as adventurers to a new but firmly established country, caring nothing for its interests, rather hoping to throw over what the first comers had won by their courage and faith (of firm government and laws, freedom of conscience and liberality for those of differing views, and united labor for prosperity and peace) came a change; a division was felt between the group with the anarchist spirit and that comprising the original element. Regretting this, but forced to acknowledge it by definite unpleasantness between them, the first families began to live within their own circle as much as possible. Stirring scenes took place, as autumn began, and the women had much to discuss. The governor was forced to make the issue and in upholding law and order to dismiss certain members of the community, though their families were allowed to stay and were cared for until new homes could be procured elsewhere. Chief among these disturbers of Plymouth's peace were a group who had come in the *Anne,* under leadership of one, John Oldham, and the hypocritical minister, Lyford, who was a sad disappointment to these charitably inclined people. The recital of this experience has been given in many of the writings which concern the men of Plymouth — the "Pilgrim Fathers," so often mentioned. The element of unrest being removed, other persons, not harmful but formerly indifferent only, became loyal supporters of the commonwealth; so calmness again settled over Plymouth when the first snow flakes draped the rugged pines, standing as sentinels or guardians for this little world, between the wilderness and the sea.

The winter was much like the one preceding it, with two new young housekeepers and the prospect of other brides. Susanna Winslow was again without her husband, and Gilbert had decided to revisit his old home — accompanying his brother to England, never to return. Matchmakers would gladly have mated him with one of the colony's belles. One wonders, even at this distant day, why this eligible young bachelor did not marry, what woman touched his heart? Pity he had not asked Desire to stay; perhaps it was she that was the something Plymouth lacked for him; or did he admire Mary Chilton's graces of mind and person, yet leave her for his brother John's happiness? Fancies play around a possible answer to this passing question among the many love stories that we know in Plymouth, which culminated for the principals, as fairy tales, in subsequent happiness.

Grey days and golden passed over Plymouth, each one finding the women busy with the successive round of household duties and industries, not ended with the sunset gun as the men's labors might be. Let us look at a list of occupations which kept them from idleness in each season of the year: candle-making, pickling eggs, preserve and cordial making, distilling of herbs, ale or beer making, manufacture of soap, laundrying, dying cloths and yarns, braiding mats of rushes, sweeping and sanding floors, cleaning wooden and iron utensils, scouring and

polishing pewter, brass and silver articles, pounding
corn, butter and cheese making, cooking, weaving,
spinning, sewing, drying wet shoes by placing hot
oats in them, or clothes — storm soaked — by blazing logs on the hearth (for umbrellas and overshoes
were then unknown) and teaching the boys and
girls. It was not until a later day that there were
schools for the children, and as it had been in England, so in their new home, their learning was ob-
tained from their elders. Some had brought what
books they could; nearly all brought Bibles in several languages, Psalm-books and Catechisms, and
before long, the almanacs proved a most useful
factor in home education.

Moments of recreation and rest were evidently
somewhat rare, but no less enjoyable, lighter occupations serving the purpose at home or when visiting. Can we not see them on many a winter evening
by the firelight of blazing cedar logs and candle glow
from the dips made in the autumn, with the fine em-
broidery and knitting in which the women of their
day and training took such pride; or placing the
stitches in the samplers which were to take the place
of pictures on the bare walls, also making designs
in colored threads upon the sets of curtains for
beds or windows; meanwhile talking together of past
days in their old homes — of the friends left there
whom they were hopefully expecting to join them,
showing keepsakes and telling their personal value
to amuse one another.

Doubtless their greatest peace and pleasure came

from singing songs as they had done in Pastor Robinson's house, looking out on the beautiful old garden in Leyden. The book from which they sang has been described in the poem we all know:
"The well-worn psalm book of Ainsworth
Printed in Amsterdam, the words and music together,
Rough-hewn, angular notes, like stones in the wall of a church-yard
Darkened and overhung by the running vine of the verses."
Such was the book, the delight of the Pilgrim women, for in that country of few books, not only did its pages afford their only music, but the annotations formed both a dictionary and encyclopedia of useful knowledge; things temporal and things spiritual were explained, scientific, historical and religious information was dispensed therein. Truly a library in a single volume.

Spring again, and the day of Edward Winslow's return found the town in excitement and the women decidedly disturbed. John Oldham had come suddenly amongst them, for no other purpose than to revile and insult the authorities. They had imprisoned him and were later getting rid of him in a chastened mood, when Winslow and the captain of the ship, which had brought him unnoticed into the harbor, walked up the street. John Oldham surprised them yet again, at a later day, but then returned to make amends and apologies, and to offer services, which the authorities were able to accept. And this man, with the upsetting propensities, met

a violent death at the hands of Indians in Massachusetts bay — his boat was rescued and his death
avenged by Captain John Gallup, Senior, of Boston.
This event has been called the first naval engagement
of American history, and in it were the seeds of the
Pequot war.

As John Oldham's boat put out from the harbor,
and the boats from the *Jacob* landed the colony's
supplies and Winslow's belongings, the unpleasantness was soon forgotten in welcoming him and the
popular captain, William Pierce, now an old friend,
by his frequent visits to Plymouth with various
ships. One special parcel Edward Winslow delivered with care to the governor's wife. It was a
gift to her of a package of spices from her old friend,
Robert Cushman, in London.

The bountiful summer was enjoyed in "peace and
health and contented minds." We may think of the
women in their gardens tending lovingly the plants
grown from seeds carefully brought from other
gardens, far away, where memories must have been
tended as well as flowers. Those who would, might
join the children and dogs in walks on the sea
shore and in the woods, bringing to their homes
decorations in the form of flowers and shells. One
writer has said, "The first ornaments of the houses
were probably the periwinkle shells, their memory
deserves to be cherished like the arbutus flower
among the things that awaken Pilgrim memories."

The first quickly built dwellings were now solidi-
fied into comfortable houses, various rooms being

added from time to time, with furniture colony-made
or imported; the ground plots around them were
kept attractively, some of them being washed by the
bubbling waters of Town Brook, as it flowed past,
and most of them enclosed with palings or wooden
walls, against which fruit trees and vines were
trained, as in kitchen gardens of the old country.
Sometimes at day's close, it was possible to watch or
partake in the old English game of stool-ball, a
distant cousin of croquet.

An evening in late summer beautifies the landscape with its serene light. Through the garden behind the house, Mary Brewster walks with her
daughters. They come toward the brook and pause
to enjoy their surroundings. From the woodland
across the stream the purple and golden flowers
of the season bend toward them in the lightest of
airs; the robins fly from bush to tree, preparing to
rest. We seem to feel with them the remembrance
of another scene of a summer evening long passed,
when these three walked down through the grounds
of Scrooby Manor to Ryton Stream to say farewell.
But Town Brook does not see the same expression
of sadness and uncertainty among them as Ryton
saw; the long shafts of illuminating light reveal
countenances where only satisfaction and tranquility
dwell.

The kitchen at the Winslow's presents a lively
scene this autumn morning. The Mistress and Mary
Becket are in the depths of preparations for a feast

and not an ordinary one. Susanna is registering great cheerfulness and Mary decided efficiency. Two important causes may be found both for the feast and good spirits. First, the master of the house returned yesterday from a somewhat hazardous but extremely successful trading trip far up the coast. The principal men of the old set were with him, so several other wives were also rejoicing at the return. The great quantity of beaver would make who would, a fur coat for the coming winter, like those the Indian women wore so comfortably. And as for Mary — why George Soule had told her last evening that she was the only woman for him, and indeed she would not be as long making up her mind on that subject as Mary Chilton had been in making up hers on a like matter. All of which shows that an elaborate cooking program was a small matter this morning. And the feast? Why, it is to be a supper party in compliment to Mary Chilton and John Winslow who have recently become engaged. The date hinged on Edward Winslow's return, but it had been thoroughly planned when he left. George Soule had been shooting one day and brought home a number of plump birds and a pair of wild turkeys.

These two are not the sole occupants of the kitchen, for others come and go. George Soule keeps up the noble fire by adding great oak sticks to the andirons in the mammoth fire-place and adjusting the multitude of hooks and chains and cooking utensils as they are needed. From the crane, big iron kettles exhale delicious odors, while numerous skillets hold different important positions, the contents of each cooking at its appointed degree of heat, while on the high mantle shelf above, the hour glass is watched and turned. As the great oven door is opened, what fragrance! Simmels, buns, biscuits and pastry and what besides! Enter an Indian with a bag of oysters specially ordered, since none are in Plymouth waters; they are to be baked in individual scallop shells, in the old, yet familiar way, with breadcrumbs and butter. Mrs. Hopkins comes with the kindly object of showing just how she manufactures on rare occasions her wonderful dish called "Hennes in Brette." The hens must be scalded and cut in pieces, fried lightly with pork, spice and crumbs, basted with ale, and colored gold with saffron. The turkeys are stuffed with beechnuts and will be roasted on the spit. A plum pudding is bubbling in one of the kettles, and dumplings of flour in another, to garnish the chicken dish; pumpkin pies are made and standing aside, so too, loaves of brown and white bread. Vegetables await their turn — samp, onions, parsnips, turnips, peas; the succotash is mixed, composed of corn, beans and meat. A ham is boiling, likewise clam chowder. Mary pulls a pan out of the oven — the nokake is done to a turn!

Edward and John Winslow have thoughtfully been asked for dinner by Mrs. Bradford — there could hardly be much chance for them at home, this day. Afternoon comes on apace and there is much for the last part for Susanna and the last moments for Mary and Hobomok's wife, who will help in the evening. The leg of mutton, rarest treat, with cucumber sauce, or couch, for the mutton to rest on is certainly perfection; the cucumbers, sliced and parboiled have drained, then butter fried, now, with condiments, onion, mutton gravy and lemon juice they are simmering gently, occasionally tossed about. A poloc, or stew of small birds, smothered with rice, onion and herbs, adds another to the wonderful combination of fragrance. And now come the partridges — a broth of boiled marrow bones, strained and put in an earthen dish with wine and spices is the delectable fluid in which they are cooked, the birds having been stuffed with whole peppers and marrow. Salad, cranberry tarts, grape jelly, pudding with strawberry sauce, and a marvelous sufflet, rich, frothing and crisp, (a pound roll of butter enlarged to half a dozen times its original size, from being turned on a long rod resting on the fire hooks, continuously dredged with flour and eaten as soon as possible.) Late in the day, Mrs. Warren comes in to direct the making of her special dish, another of the rarities, called cheese cake; boiled milk with beaten eggs has been cooling and curdling since last evening, it is now strained and to it added butter, mace, rose-water and wine, currants and syrup. Pastry forms are waiting to hold this combination for a few seconds in the oven. Elderblow wine (made by the old French receipt the women had learned on the Continent, of sugar, fruit, blossoms and yeast), cider, spiced ale and some of the excel-

lent wine which Edward Winslow brought on his
return from England, are to help digest this marvelous menu — and of great interest are the first apples from the Winslow's new orchard, likewise honey
from Plymouth bees, a recent industry.

Truly a feast—yet when it was ready, Susanna
met her guests with smiles, and renewed the admiration in the heart of her prospective young sister-in-
law. Those who partook of this supper and lived to
tell the tale were the old friends, of course, for Mary
Chilton was ever a favorite and one of the *Mayflower*
girls, so none of that list could be omitted, (Captain Standish on a mission in England, was missed),
and now that there was so large a younger set coming on to take the place of those who had married,
many of them must be invited, besides the recent
brides and bridegrooms, themselves, and one or two
of John Winslow's joyous and special friends of the
Fortune who might still be fancy free, but could not
be omitted on that account. That this invigorating
occasion was a success there is no doubt, and marked
a crest of the life of those first five years of the
Pilgrims in Plymouth.

Days go on, no matter how bright, they may not
be held. In a few years, changes — as ever.

We may look at a scene on another crisp autumn
morning. It is Sunday and there is stillness in the
town. Suddenly the drum rolls and people come
from their houses to assemble for the morning worship in the fort. The guard has formed in front of

the house of Captain Standish. Led by a sergeant, in rows of three abreast, followed by the Governor, the Elder, and the Captain, all wearing cloaks and carrying arms, they march silently up the hill. The rest of the population who may be going to the service this morning are ready to proceed also, for, unlike the severity of the rule from which these people fled, church attendance was expected but not compulsory. There are extra colors and numbers this morning. The town is entertaining a distinguished guest whose visit is to mark that tide in their affairs which, owing to their readiness to take at the flood, is to lead them on to fortune. Plymouth frequently entertains strangers, but this rotund, handsomely dressed gentleman, with the sharp eyes seeing all about him, with his several retainers and trumpeters, who walk on each side of him, though no notes are sounded this morning, is of more importance than any whom Plymouth has received. He represents the first foreign mission for commercial and personal benefits, and is the Secretary of the Dutch colony, five hundred miles to the southward, Isaac de Rasieres.

The intercourse already satisfactorily begun by negotiations culminating in this visit, was to be of mutual benefit for many years. The boat from Manhattan became a regularly welcomed bearer to Plymouth women of bright materials for clothes, sugar and other necessaries — in time quite the rival of a boat from England — the payment for these was by home grown tobacco, therefore nearly as interesting a crop as corn. Even the latter was to be replaced by something else as a medium of exchange through the visit of Monsieur de Rasieres. Wampum, familiar word to us, but strange to Plymouth people, was to make an important and permanent appearance, and to prove that shells on the shore were as a gold mine at the feet of the Pilgrims.

The ceremonious assent to the fort is accomplished, the congregation taking their places — the women on one side of the room, the men on the other, according to custom. To the visitor all is strange, new and interesting. We rejoice in the days he spent in Plymouth, for the advantage which came to the Pilgrims and for the legacy which came to us in the form of his written accounts of his visit.

As William Davidson, experienced statesman and courtier, in a long ago visit to Scrooby, opened a door of destiny through which it was appointed that William Brewster was to lead this people into a new world of liberty, so by this visit of Isaac de Rasieres, travelled man of the world, to Plymouth, another way was opened by which they were to reach, also prosperity and prominence. The portraits of these two men should hang as companion medallions in the hall of Pilgrim memory, as doubtless they did in the mind of William Brewster, himself having as much worldly experience as either, with the personal attractions of each; loved friend of one, respected acquaintance of the other.

At this time, the rather difficult role of step-mother was being played in three of the households. We know the families quite well, and are particularly interested in the women. The eldest in the position is Elizabeth Hopkins. If the part did not come easily to Stephen Hopkins' second wife, the responsibilities of it are now lessened, since Constance has recently added to the list of *Mayflower* brides by marrying Nicholas Snow and going to a home of her own. An impression seemed to prevail that Mistress Hopkins was rather jealous of her predecessor's son, Giles, on account of her own son, Caleb, yet it is through Giles only, that the name has been carried down to the present. Her four girls, Damaris, Deborah, Ruth and Elizabeth, made a lively home for any brother. Oceanus, born on the *Mayflower,* did not live beyond babyhood. The women of that day were just as human as of this, and amid all her fine qualities, if there was a little flaw, it no doubt came of her very fondness for her husband.

Across the street, in the governor's house, Alice Bradford has three boys to share the love and interest with her own, and the devotion of four. We have already seen one of them, Thomas Cushman, left by his father with Governor Bradford, until he should return to live in Plymouth — but Myles Standish, returning from his mission to England, had brought with other regretful tidings, the knowledge that Robert Cushman would not come again. Another fatherless boy, whom we have had but a glimpse of, is Nathaniel Morton, nephew to Alice Bradford.

George Morton lived but a short time as resident of Plymouth, leaving his wife and family alone in the new house, but the governor took Nathaniel to bring up as a son, and Juliana Carpenter Morton married again. The third boy is also fatherless in actual sense; he has recently come to Plymouth, but to the most loving mother and affectionate step-father boy could desire, for this is Constant Southworth come from London to his new home in the governor's house in Plymouth, as his mother had done, whom he strongly resembles in looks. And the fourth boy? He is not fatherless, but has only lately come to renew both the acquaintance and affection of his parent, being John Bradford, from Amsterdam, youngest of the quartette, and seeing him we are reminded of his girl mother, the governor's first wife. This group is soon to be added to by Thomas Southworth, whom his mother is expecting from England. We can imagine these boys having a pretty good time in the loving home of the Bradfords, and among them grew up the three babies, half brothers and half sister to John Bradford and the Southworth boys — only one girl to amuse and tease them through the years of childhood, the governor's daughter, Mercy. Although step-mother to but one, the part had no chance for prominence with Alice Bradford, in being at the same time aunt to one, friend to another and mother to five. Perhaps it was because of this masculine element at home, that Mistress Bradford was known for her special interest in the young girls of the colony — daughters of her neighbors and playmates of her Mercy, such advantages and accomplishments as she had, she taught them. No wonder she welcomed her husband's suggestion of having her youngest sister, Priscilla Carpenter, come from England to make her home with them.

Another woman, of the style and character of Alice Bradford, the third and youngest step-mother, making such a success in her position as to prove her the good angel of the family into which she came, is Fear Brewster — now Mrs. Isaac Allerton. She already had the love of Bartholomew, Remember and Mary — quite grown out of childhood, but they must have been as surprised as the rest of the society of Plymouth that their father could win her for his wife, as he was so much older than she and always seeming rather preoccupied and self-satisfied. It speaks well for him that such was the case and that her attachment and loyalty never wavered through the brief years of her married life — and that it was a shield to him from public criticism or censure is well known. This not only places her before us. against a background of esteem for herself, but in a reflection of the high regard and affection in which her father was held. Before matrimonial trials confronted her daughter, Mary Brewster, loved and loving, finished her pilgrimage; the lack of her presence affected many lives, her absence was an abiding sorrow. Love of wealth seems suddenly to have overtaken Isaac Allerton which made everything else of small importance. The pursuit

of it took him constantly and for long periods away
from home, so his wife had little of his company.
His talents were of use to the colony, at times, in
England, but he seemed to really care very little
for his old friends. Nevertheless, it was he who
completed the arrangements which closed the connection between the original settlers of Plymouth
and the Merchant Adventurers in London. Plymouth, thereby, paid all its indebtedness for assistance
given and went its way alone. He also procured
patents for increased land holdings for the colony,
especially in Maine. His complete indifference to
anything but his own ends was, perhaps, never better
shown than when he returned from one of his trips
to England, bringing, as secretary, a man who was
already too well and unfavorably known by Plymouth and the surrounding settlements, called Morton of Merry Mount, who had been sent to England
the year before, as an undesirable. That Allerton
could bring this man to his home, into the society
of his wife and daughters, made Plymouth gasp —
and Plymouth refused to stand it. The secretary
was dismissed, and business affairs again called Isaac
Allerton away. On one of his trips he took his son
to visit in England, and Bartholomew did not return to Plymouth.

About this time, two girls of the *Anne* added to
the procession of brides: Mary Warren marrying
Robert Bartlett and Jane Cooke marrying Experience Mitchell.

Passengers and letters came on the ships continually, both to Plymouth and the other settlements that were growing likewise. Persons desiring to come to the New World, took what ship they could and landed where the ship took them. Plymouth having boats could always send for their own voyagers and mail whenever word was received that a ship had come from the other side, though not to their harbor. Thus, one day, a letter came to Humility Cooper, which changed the quiet current of her life as it seemed to be running in Plymouth. Relatives in England wanted her to return. This was a surprise to her and to her good friends, but, half wanting to stay and half wanting to go, Humility prepared for leave taking. Henry Sampson, her cousin, was now grown up — she need feel no special reluctance — but she was Elizabeth Howland's last link with her childhood's days. As Edward Winslow was sailing shortly for England, on business for the colony, Humility said farewell to the ten years of *Mayflower* and Plymouth association and went back under his care.

During her husband's absence, Susanna Winslow's brother, Doctor Fuller, was also from Plymouth. The new colonies of Salem and Massachusetts Bay, just starting, met with the same devastating illness that had befallen the *Mayflower* passengers, and, as they were so unfortunate as to lose their doctor among the first victims, they appealed to Plymouth—and no appeal to Plymouth was ever in vain. Doctor Fuller went to Salem and the Bay and had great success in curing many, though nearly exhausting his supply of medicines.

During this year, and the next, all the old friends
still in Leyden, who had waited so long to come,
were brought over at Plymouth's expense and there
was great satisfaction that distance no longer divided them. But the saintly Robinson was not among
them. Five years earlier, the Pilgrim men and
women grieved to learn that he would never come to
them — his earthly labors having ceased. His wife
and oldest son became his representatives in Plymouth.

Intercourse between Plymouth and the newly established colonial neighbors became frequent, leading to interchange of visits and even of residence.
The newcomers were duly sensible of what they
owed to the Plymouth settlers, who had blazed the
way.

The opening of their second decade in the New
World showed great contrasts to those Plymouth
women who remembered what the first year and
those immediately following had been. Now, they
were able to see and hear of the experiences of
others, close at hand, with much in common. The
ships from England were no longer their only connection with the outside world nor their only source
of supplies, other than food. Massachusetts Bay and
Salem were glad to exchange commodities, as well
as Manhattan, but, being so much nearer, grew more
interlocked with the life and interests of Plymouth.

The ceremonial visit by the Governor and Assistants of Plymouth to the Governor of the Bay and

his wife, with the return of like courtesies by Governor Winthrop to Governor and Mrs. Bradford were brilliant incidents. Soon fashions, not clothes, and luxuries, not necessities, for the home were frequent thoughts to the women, instead of almost forgotten or sternly repressed instincts. Though they had not fashion books, some sent for garments and hats from the old country and the fortunate possessors lent these new fashioned articles as models for their neighbors. A very taking way of introducing styles to the colonists was by dressed dolls, or "babies" as they were called, that displayed them in careful miniature. During recent seasons this idea has been re-introduced, as may be seen in some of the shop windows in our cities. We learn that, withal, there was sometimes a shortage of sugar, which strikes a responsive chord in the memory of housewives three hundred years later.

If the arrival of the first cows was a never-to-be forgotten joy to the women of the *Mayflower* and of the *Anne*, the entrance of horses into Plymouth life was elation. The pleasure of owning a horse while it was a novelty for their circumstances, must have aroused the same feeling as the acquirement of an automobile has in families of our day; when not an owner, to have a special object of ambition, if a possessor, then a willing recipient of neighborly admiration. The advantage of a horse to a woman, then, was to ride on a pillion behind a male member of the family to meeting or to visit (until carriages came, much later), or else, if quite accomplished, to

ride alone, often with children, baskets, or even a
spinning wheel, as well, on the back of the amiable
friend of the family.

Ere long, life took on the virility and color we
associate with that spectacular period known as
Colonial. Naturally, Plymouth now began to over-
flow its first boundaries. As the children of the
families and worldly possessions increased, many
made summer homes where the cattle could have
greater range and families more room. These new
houses were built quite in the manner of bungalows,
for occupancy between frosts. Winters saw the
Plymouth residences occupied again. Gradually,
however, the summer homes became permanent, being made habitable for winter also, and edifices for
the religious services were erected. By another
decade Plymouth Colony comprised several towns,
outgrowths of the original. The new brides could
make a wedding journey if they pleased, and some
went away altogether to make their new homes. The
governor's wife was especially interested in two of
the weddings at this time — that of her sister, Priscilla Carpenter and her niece, Patience Morton.
The former was soon a widow, and, like her sisters,
married again. Patience became the mother of
Thomas Faunce — a link between two centuries —
the identifier, in his old age, of Plymouth Rock,
telling to his and other generations what his parents
had told to him, having learned from the first
comers.

Governor Bradford insisted that if the office he

had held so long was an honor and satisfaction, others should share it, if it was a care and duty, others should experience its responsibilities also; his health had been somewhat undermined by the efforts he had given to guide the temporal affairs of the colony throughout the years since he succeeded Governor Carver, and he absolutely declined a re-election. Edward Winslow, having returned from England, was chosen.

Thus Susanna became the first lady of Plymouth; easily pictured wearing the dainty white satin, lace trimmed slippers, or the white satin cape, actually to be seen now, in Plymouth, visible magic means of carrying us back to her days from the present. Alice Bradford smilingly relinquished her position to her friend and devoted her efforts to restoring her husband's health. Yet this twelve-month contained more of trial, anxiety and annoyance than the colony had experienced in many a year; it could not have been other than a sorrowful memory to Susanna.

Early in the spring a strange swarm of large noisy flies came out of the ground — ate the young green things, and disappeared. Such had never been seen by the colonists and the Indians foretold sickness. This prophecy proved all too true and during the summer and autumn a devastating fever swept away a score or more of men, women and children; some were of the new comers from Leyden, but the weight of the sadness was among the old families. Gentle Fear Brewster Allerton was laid

to rest beside her mother, on Burial Hill, leaving her
baby boy, Isaac, to her sorrowing father's care, who
was spending the summer with his two unmarried
sons on their farm in the country. Isaac Allerton's
sister, Sarah Cuthbertson, was also a victim to the
infection, likewise her husband. While Susanna
Winslow was mourning these two friends, her
brother, the doctor, after fighting the disease for the
help of others, succumbed. This shock and loss to
the colonists was felt not only in Plymouth — while
in Plymouth grief was deep. This educated,
Christian gentleman was sadly missed for many a
year. What he was to the people can be easily
imagined. His widow and children were devoted
to his memory; in after years, the son, Samuel,
studied for the ministry and married a granddaughter of Elder Brewster; the daughter, Mercy, married Ralph James; but his profession was carried
on in the Old Colony, after a time, by his nephews —
his namesake Samuel — whom we have known of
since the Pilgrims' emigration from Holland — and
Matthew, who came later to Plymouth.

The business affairs of the Colony became complicated in their trade on the Connecticut River, both
because of the Dutch and Indians. At home, Roger
Williams, whom they had befriended, acted in a
very unpleasant manner, so they were glad when he
left them. Notwithstanding the clouds over-shadow-
ing them, this year's return of the trade in furs was
noteworthy, and as election time drew near, it was
decided that it would be best for Edward Winslow

to go again to England on their foreign business; therefore Thomas Prence was elected Governor and Susanna was again left alone with her children. The White boys were now sturdy, manly lads, a comfort and joy to Susanna and the admiration of their small brothers and sister, the Winslows. Another brother-in-law, Kenelm, was a visitor in her home, and appearances indicated that he would remain as a permanent resident of Plymouth.

Several marriages occurred before a year closed. Ann Warren became Mrs. Thomas Little and her sister, Sarah, became Mrs. John Cooke, Jr.

Recently a family of four girls had come to the colony with their father, William Collier, a wealthy merchant from London; from among them one of the Brewster boys selected his wife and Sarah Collier went as Love's bride to the Duxbury home to try to bring cheerfulness to the three lonely men there and to help care for little Isaac Allerton, his mother's legacy to her family, until he should grow up. Remember Allerton married also, and was one of the girls who went away from Plymouth to a new home in Salem, leaving her sister Mary, to give their father such attention as he needed in his rare visits home.

At this time, in Boston, eggs were three cents a dozen, milk one cent a quart, butter six and cheese five cents a pound, so housekeepers not caring for the somewhat higher prices in Plymouth, could send for butter or cheese at least, if they did not make it themselves, and felt economically inclined.

In the early part of the new administration, when
Patience Brewster Prence was mistress of the execu-
tive mansion (which was the Governor's own house,
whichever one it was), certain affairs concerned two
of the Plymouth women mightily, Priscilla Alden
and Barbara Standish, but particularly the former,
which was caused by the interference in Plymouth's
affairs by Massachusetts Bay, through misrepresen-
tation. John Alden putting into Boston from a trip
to the Kennebec trading station, was held there and
imprisoned until Plymouth should explain its connection with a shooting incident in which two men
were killed at the station. The ship was allowed to
return to Plymouth bringing the news of this cool
proceeding, which, we can imagine made John Alden's wife anything but cool, and we can also think
that the Governor was not allowed to delay in getting John Alden home to his family. To do so,
Captain Myles Standish was dispatched to Boston,
with the facts of the unpleasant incident at the
trading station, which were so different from the
representation which the Bay authorities had received that John Alden was immediately set at
liberty. We can appreciate the feelings of both
Barbara and Priscilla as they looked for the return
of the ship again. Barbara anxious for the success
of her husband's efforts to release the husband of
her friend, and Priscilla both indignant and wor-
ried. However, the incident was happily concluded,
though more than Priscilla were indignant in Plymouth.

Later in the year, news came from London which caused the heart of Susanna to burn with indignation in her turn, and for the same cause concerning her husband as had agitated Priscilla. Through the old jealousy of the Church authorities, on trumped up charges concerning the business on which Winslow went to England, which was in behalf also of the Bay, he was held for many weeks in the Fleet Street prison. Fortunately friends were able to release him — but it was some time before he was able to return to his family in Plymouth.

Meanwhile Eleanor Newton Adams and Priscilla Carpenter Wright, both made widows by the epidemic of the previous year, became wives again. The marriage of the former, who had been left quite well off, was of special interest to Susanna since she became her sister-in-law, Mrs. Kenelm Winslow, the third Mrs. Winslow of Plymouth and Marshfield, as all had summer places in the latter suburb of Plymouth——Careswell, the Edward Winslow place, soon became a permanent abode, handsome of style and proportions.

This year saw sorrow once more fall on the members of the old families — bound together by the powerful ties formed in the old days — and many more, for at its close, the Governor's wife was taken by death — and Patience Brewster Prence's short, happy life was over. The religious convictions of the Pilgrims did not admit of undue mourning for their loved ones, since they regarded the departed not as victims to death, but as victors through death,

and the lives of those remaining must go on. Hearts
were true, nevertheless, and even in their wills the
men sometimes especially requested to be laid beside
the graves of their wives and daughters.

The following year, April, brought a marriage
ceremony performed by Captain Standish, as assistant, which was of interest to many — that of
Samuel Fuller, loved for his own admirable qualities
as well as for being the nephew of their Doctor of
happy memory. His bride was one of the girls who
had helped in the new settlement of Scituate, founded by her father and other men from Kent, in England. In spite of all his pretty playmates in Plymouth, Samuel found this girl of old England was
the one to receive his heart. But Jane Lothrop took
him from Plymouth to the newer township.

In August a furious storm broke over Plymouth
and the surrounding land and sea, inflicting great
damage and terrifying the women and children. It
wrecked many ships, killed cattle and blew roofs
from many of the houses and knocked others to
pieces in Plymouth, and uprooted quantities of great
trees; the evidences of it were prominent for many
years in the blemished beauty of the great pines
which withstood the hurricane, still remaining the
sentinels of Plymouth.

When Edward Winslow returned, he again served
as Governor, and one of the weddings of that year
was Mary Allerton's. She was last but one of the
Mayflower girls to marry — Damaris Hopkins'
marriage to Jacob Cooke completed the list. Mary's

courtship had begun in childhood's days, when
Thomas Cushman, in the house across the street, had
waited for her to grow up — while growing up himself and pursuing his studies with the other boys in
the Governor's family. At the time of her marriage
the rumblings of the Pequot war were beginning to
be heard, which soon broke, owing to the mistakes of
the Bay Colony, causing the old time fears to return
to Plymouth women for the safety of their men and
themselves. Under Captain Standish, the Plymouth
men played their valiant part, and Thomas Stanton,
the interpreter for Massachusetts, and Captain John
Gallup did their full share to redeem the situation.

Richard Church had not long before come from
the Bay Colony to visit Plymouth, but meeting
Elizabeth Warren decided him to remain permanently, in spite of displeasure from the Bay authorities, who missed him. He was one of the
Plymouth fighters in this Indian disturbance, as his
and Elizabeth's son, Benjamin, was in the greater,
bloodier war of a later time — King Philip's — when
the Pilgrim's good friend, Massasoit, was dead.
Plymouth tried to settle down to its own affairs after
this, and had plenty to attend to.

A lovely June day seemed ushering in another
summer when an unknown experience marked that
year as one to date by even as the one of the great
storm. That morning some of the principal men
were meeting to discuss important questions, and in
the street and about the doorsteps many of the
women were talking of their own or public affairs,

when a violent though brief earthquake shook them from their balance, and catching hold of whatever was nearest, they heard the crashing and falling of things in their houses. The children were frightened and began to cry, and all the women who were indoors came running out, fearing the houses would fall. The men were no less concerned and the streets presented a lively scene. Another shock was soon felt but less severe, and that was the end. Indians came hurrying into the town with their experience to relate; the quake was felt far inland and at sea. What with the frightful storm, the alarming Pequot trouble and this terrifying experience, all within a comparatively short time, the nerves of the women must have been more on edge than for many a day.

The young people of Marshfield and Duxbury, married and single, clung closely to their friends and associations of Plymouth and their amusements were shared in common. Weekly lecture day, a diversion of sober character, was nevertheless gladly welcomed as a means of enjoyable intercourse, going or returning. Maple sugar making, Training day, corn husking, apple bees were occasions for merry gatherings, the sequence found in the frequent weddings. Dancing became popular, though frowned on in some quarters, but it could not be repressed in an age when the desire for physical activity and excitement was as natural as now. Some of those early dance names such as High Betty Martin, Constancy, Orange Tree, Rolling Hornpipe, The Ladies

Choice, compare with our recent names of Hesita-
tion, Fox Trot, One Step.

The Coast Road from Boston, though never more
than a few feet wider than the old Indian trail,
came to mean to the dwellers in the various town-
ships of Plymouth such an artery of connection to
the life of all as the Great North Road had been to
the inhabitants of the little villages, Scrooby and its
neighbors, long ago homes to the elder members of
the Colony.

The coldest winter Plymouth has ever known has
frozen the harbor to a solid mass over which ox
teams and sledges have been driven for several
weeks, an astonishing and interesting sight and one
may walk over the ice to Duxbury as well as by the
land. One afternoon bright with the lengthening
daylight of the season, sees a pleasant picture in the
old parlor of Governor Bradford's house, for he is
again Governor, by urgent request of the community. A cheery fire blazes up the wide chimney and
there is gay chatter to the tune of the crackling logs.
Mistress Alice Bradford, now a grandmother (her
son, Constant Southworth having married Elizabeth
Collier and having a little Alice) has invited several
of her daughter's special friends to spend the day.
So we see Mercy, a delightful reproduction of her
mother and father both, as hostess to nine merry
girls: Mary Brewster, Betty and Sally Alden, from
Duxbury, Mary Cooke, Mercy Fuller and Deborah
Hopkins of Plymouth, Lora Standish of Duxbury

and Desire and Hope Howland. Elizabeth Tilly
had given charming companion names to her older
daughters, her first born having been named in
remembrance of Desire Minter, her dear friend.
Desire was now at the age of her mother when she
had married — that mother seeming always as an
older sister, being still young herself in spite of the
cares of a large family — but it was more than a
year later before Desire decided to marry, and be
the first bride, though not the eldest, of this pretty
group. The girls of this generation never having
experienced the world's hardships and vicissitudes
that had been their mother's portions, having been
carefully and lovingly brought up in comfortable,
cheerful homes, were not anxious to leave them for
the first time, even with love to point the way.
However, Desire was beginning to listen to the im-
portunities of her dashing young lieutenant — in
later years known as Captain John Gorham, who
was to lead the 2nd Barnstable Company under
command of Major William Bradford, Mercy's
brother, into fame, at the Great Swamp Fight in
Philip's War. The swift knitting needles click in
Desire's hands as she stands by the frame-work of
the western window, leaning to watch the progress
of the sampler which is being worked by a lovely
girl who is sharing the broad window seat with
another, who has evidently completed her sewing,
having just folded it and put it into a bag hanging
from her arm. This young beauty is Betty Alden —
eldest of the family of John and Priscilla. She too,

is eagerly watching the stitches that are to tell the
worker's admirers and friends, from that day to
this, that the sampler was made by Lora Standish,
only and much beloved daughter of the Pilgrim's
Captain. That piece of handicraft is the only speci-
men of their work that we know of and may look at
today as if we had seen it when its stitches were
being placed, among the group we are picturing of
Plymouth Colony's first-born daughters — the first
native generation of Colonial girls of New England.
On a seat by the hearth, Mary Cooke and Mercy
Fuller have a book between them and are reading
aloud snatches of receipts for making perfumes, or
poetry, or jokes — this is not a monthly magazine
as we might fancy from our own experience, but a
yearly periodical, welcomed by every household —
Pierce's Almanac, printed in Cambridge, its contents holding much that is similar but much that
is different to the magazines we know.   Leaning
over the high back, smoothing the soft hair of Mercy
Fuller, is Hope Howland. Bonny as her sister is,
somehow Hope reminds us more of little Elizabeth
Tilly of Leyden. Mercy Bradford is placing little
cakes with a pitcher of cider on a big center table
and lights one or two bayberry candles in wooden
holders that stand upon its polished top and twinkle
on it or in the shining pewter dishes and cups. At
the window towards the street, Deborah Hopkins
and Mary Brewster, granddaughter and namesake of
our first Mary Brewster, are looking out — evidently some one is expected. The last rays of the win-

ter sun, the flashing fire and the glowing bayberry flames, strive to light for one more instant this appealing picture. There is sound of footsteps in the cold air outside — stamping and laughing — the brothers and sweethearts have arrived to take the girls home but first to have some slight refreshment at the hands of Mistress Bradford and Mercy. Cloaks are brought and velvet hoods tied snugly over hair both light and dark, surrounding the pink cheeks and sparkling eyes of all the happy girls who have spent the day with Mercy Bradford and her mother.

The snowflakes of winter have turned to falling apple blossoms and spring has awakened the violets in the flower beds under the windows of William Brewster's library. The fragrance of these and other blossoms is borne through the white curtained windows open to the warm air, mingled with the saltness of Duxbury marshes. The library comprises four hundred books, the largest and most valuable in America. Whether it is or no, matters not, the books are the solace of their owner, who while enjoying his farm life and appreciating the companionship of his son's families and Isaac Allerton, Jr., his grandson, dwells much within himself. To keep the books dusted and the Elder's chair in just the right place, Mrs. Love Brewster has often the assistance of her nieces, Jonathan Brewster's daughters. This bright morning sees Mary, one of the girls in the winter's frolic at Mercy Bradford's, attending to these matters. A boy is

deep in study by a bookshelf, and Mary, playfully
sweeps her duster across his book as she works — it
is her cousin, Isaac — preparing for entrance into
the new College at Cambridge. Up the road a horse
comes at a lively pace and Samuel Fuller has arrived to join with Isaac in reading the precious
books, though his father left him some of his own.
The owner of the library glances through the
window and smiles and nods to the young people —
Mary seeing him, runs out to enjoy with him the
sunshine and to pat the horse tied near the door.
Possibly William Brewster recalls from the past a
spring morning when another lad rode a horse, to
acquire knowledge from books — but he says nothing as Mary slips her arm in his.

This decade flashes many another change before
our eyes. In a few years the first church building
has been erected in Plymouth, with Richard Church
as architect and builder, as seems appropriate. Its
bell rings out for many a year, succeeding the roll
of drums to summon worshipers. Many of the girls
marry and the younger children succeed to their
pleasures. Mercy Bradford has gone to live in Boston as Mercy Vermayes. Her mother's loneliness is
partly relieved by the coming to her of her remaining sister in England, Mary Carpenter. This sister
is rather notable among the women of Plymouth, in
that she never married. Her attractions were not
less than her sisters'; indeed, from what was said of
her, quite an appropriate companion for the governor's wife, her sister, Alice. Another exception to

the general rule may be noted, and another spinster
of the colony named Elizabeth Pool, daughter of Sir
William, who coming as Plymouth's boundaries expanded, and possessing wealth, property and intelligence, remained unwon. These two esteemed women, one a resident of Plymouth town, the other,
one of the founders of the new township of Taunton, are an interesting contrast. Miss Carpenter
lived quietly, uneventfully, until ninety years old;
of a religious frame of mind and given to kind deeds,
unknown, through her retiring nature. Miss Pool
seems much more modern in her career. She erected
iron works and was altogether enterprising and a
promoter of advancement for her settlement. She
brought over a minister for the church in Taunton,
so had a thought for religion, also, not only for herself but for others. A record states "she died
greatly honored, in 1654 aged 66."

Edward Winslow was again governor for a brief
period and then made another trip to England, at
the request of the authorities of the Bay, as they
had recognized his great abilities as a negotiator of
business interests and there were some affairs press-
ing on the Bay Colony which he undertook to
remove. This was to the regret of the Plymouth
people who were reluctant to have him go from
their own affairs. He left Susanna and his children,
almost grown now, in comfortable Careswell, and
there, for several years, his wife awaited his return.
Not that the Bay or his own affairs took very long,
but England herself needed him, as it seemed, and

he agreed to a diplomatic mission to an island
colony. Loving Plymouth and loving England he
was not destined to rest in either; his grave was
made in the ocean he had crossed so often. Susanna
had parted from her husband for the last time.

Other deaths among the first comers saddened the
Pilgrims. Elizabeth Hopkins closed her long and
honorable career as one of the women of Plymouth.
Her husband soon followed her. In this year perhaps its greatest blow fell on Plymouth when their
leader in spiritual and often advisor in temporal
things passed from among them. No words can more
fittingly describe the beautiful end of his earthly
life than those of the governor. There is no greater
record of loyalty and affection than that shown in
the nearly fifty years between his followers and himself. While his fame, as William Bradford said, is
more enduring than a marker at his grave — which
he lacks, in company with so many — such words as
the governor wrote of him and such work as Con-
stantino Brumidi has made to represent him, serve
to keep it vigorous through the centuries. (In the
President's room at the Capitol in Washington,
Brumidi has painted Elder Brewster as typifying
Religion.)

When Mary Chilton Winslow moved to Boston, it
could not have seemed more strange or different
than Plymouth had come to be to her by that time.
Except the Aldens, the Howlands and her sister-in-
law, few remained who had been her companions
and friends on the *Mayflower* and in building the

colony. Her husband had become a prosperous merchant in the West India trade and perhaps Boston seemed a necessary relief to them. Their position became at once prominent and important and her life flowed happily onward for many years. In one of her daughters, Myles Standish, Jr., found his fate, and upon their marriage likewise settled in Boston.

Meanwhile Susanna Winslow continued in eminence of circumstance, to live at her beautiful home in Marshfield. Her boys, Resolved and Peregrine, had married and made homes of their own but remained devoted to her. Josiah, her youngest son, reproducing in a marked degree the look and manners of his talented father, remained with her. As he grew into the handsome, courtly man, whom all admired, she must have smiled as she looked sometimes at the little shoes he had worn as her baby and which she carefully kept with other treasures — such as the cradle in which she had rocked all her boys and little girl. That little girl was now Mrs. Robert Brooks of Scituate.

In the heyday of Plymouth's prosperity a gentleman in England, long interested in colonial life by the reports of it which had found their way to him in his comfortable ancestral home, planned a visit to see life across the sea. With his young daughter, Penelope, Mr. Herbert Pelham came to the Old Colony. The spirit of adventure in them both and the interest they found in their new surroundings caused them to linger for a period beyond the length of a casual visit in their temporary home in Marsh-

field. To the men, the companionship of Herbert
Pelham was a delight, and seeing her father's pleasure, Penelope, with her own various employments,
did not long for home. Her's is the last romance
we may notice as closely connected with the women
of our special interest in Plymouth colony, even
as that of her mother-in-law, was the first. Penelope Pelham, with her high-bred manner and aristocratic face, made the only permanent impression on
the heart of Josiah Winslow and we can easily fancy
that in making her bead bag, Penelope had plenty
of time to decide that for him she would renounce
all thought of returning to her home, and remain a
colonial woman. The bead bag, her dressing-case
and her portrait are other links connecting us to
those vivid lives of our chronicle.

Soon Josiah Winslow was called to the place occupied by his father, for a time, and by William Bradford for many years — when the great governor had
left it vacant, forever — so Penelope became the
first lady of the land in her adopted home and
Susanna closed her life's history in the first place
which had been hers so often in the colony — first
mother after the *Mayflower* found harbor, first bride
of Plymouth and now mother of the first native
born governor of New England. Truly the foot-
prints of Anna Fuller, since we found them first
in Leyden, have led us along a colorful pathway.

The records we find of her brilliant daughter-in-
law show her a character after Susanna Winslow's
own type. The second mistress of Careswell lived

there for many happy years ere she and her family were forced to flee from it under the fearful scourge of Philip's War.

Thus on through its seventy years of shadow and sunshine, heroic daring, splendid achievement and independence, we may follow the fascinating records of Plymouth Colony — especially as those records are tinted even faintly by the foot-prints and finger-touches of its women.

As the first death on the *Mayflower* at anchor was that of a woman, Dorothy Bradford, so the last survivor of the original *Mayflower* company was a woman, Mary Allerton Cushman, who saw all of the life with its chances and changes of which we read.

Through the years we may well believe that the women of the *Mayflower* who became the women of Plymouth, and their children, whether in newer homes or remaining in the old, looked back to the early days of their privation, when by their anxieties, their sorrows, their economies, their endeavors, their fearlessness and faith, the foundation of their colony was laid.

We may well echo their thoughts as they remembered some of Elder Brewster's words on their first Thanksgiving Day, which one orator has expressed as "Generations to come will look back to this hour and these scenes, this day of small things and say, 'Here was our beginning as a people. These were our fathers and mothers. Through their trials we inherit our blessings. Their faith is our faith, their hope our hope, their God our God.'"

A CHAPLET OF ROSEMARY.

A CHAPLET OF ROSEMARY.

BURIAL HILL no longer bristles with the guns of the Pilgrim's fort but is thickly studded with the graves of the generations who in turn walked on Plymouth's first street below. One traversing this way and recalling the scenes it has witnessed, must be indeed insensitive not to feel the thrill that comes from treading on hallowed ground. Particularly must this be experienced by the descendants of the women we would honor.

We know that upon Cole's Hill, Burial Hill and in the old burying grounds at Duxbury and Marshfield are the graves of many of the women of Plymouth, and some lie elsewhere, yet the exact location of how few is positive.

The second wife of Governor Bradford requested in her will that she might be laid as near her husband's grave as might be. Their family plot is easily found. By another will, that of Captain Myles Standish, we may know where two of the women of his family rest — since his own grave is located and his request was to lie beside his two dear daughters — one his son's wife Mary, the other his own lovely Lora, whose early death caused him much sorrow. At Marshfield, in the family burying ground, Susanna Winslow rests. A stone in the center of the town of Taunton marks the grave of Elizabeth Pool. A tablet at Little Compton, has been erected to the memory of Elizabeth Pabodie, John and Priscilla Alden's eldest daughter; she lived her later years in this place. Mary Chilton Winslow lies beside her husband, in King's Chapel Burying Ground, Boston; their names are marked upon a slab at the gate in Tremont Street. Elizabeth Tilly Howland, after she became a widow, went to live with her daughter, Lydia Brown, in Swansea and there died; her husband's grave on Burial Hill is known, but she was not brought back to rest beside him. The grave of Mary Allerton, who lived to such a great age and saw the foundations of twelve of the thirteen colonies which formed the nucleus of the United States, is indicated by a monument erected to her and her husband on Burial Hill.

We would willingly make a pilgrimage to visit each known spot, regretting, the while, that there were so many we might not include. Yet upon all we may place the same unfading, if invisible, wreath of the leaves that signify remembrance.

Descendants of the women of Plymouth are now estimated to number more than a million. It is for them especially to rejoice in the results of artist's brush, writer's pen or sculptor's tool that have been produced in efforts to recall to all the world that epoch in its history in which these women lived, by portraying the events of which they were a part.

Thus we have such pictures as Jacob and Albert Cuyp's painting of the "Departure of the Pilgrims from Delfshaven." J. G. Schwartz's picture of

"The Pilgrim Fathers' First Meeting for Public Worship in North America." "The Embarkation of the Pilgrim Fathers," painted by Charles W. Cope, hangs in the British House of Parliament. "The Sailing of the Mayflower," a painting in the audit house, Southampton, England — no more appropriate setting could be found for that portrayal. Charles Lucy has called his picture "Departure of the Pilgrims," it is in Pilgrim Hall, Plymouth — that Memorial temple. Robert W. Wier's painting of "Embarkation of the Pilgrims" hangs in the nation's Capitol, while Edgar Parker's copy of it is in Pilgrim Hall. A. Gisbert has given us his idea of the "Landing of the Pilgrim Fathers at Plymouth Rock," and the "Landing of the Pilgrim Fathers" is the title taken by Henry Sargent. "The Mayflower in Plymouth Harbor," is portrayed by W. F. Halsall, and Granville Perkins has visualized "The Mayflower at Sea," while Linton has engraved this subject. George H. Boughton has made charming and familiar reproductions of the Pilgrim men and women, and many another artist's ideal has been depicted in the variations of the subject.

Fiction, verse and chronicle with the themes of the voyage and the Plymouth home of the Pilgrims have been produced by many able pens. Skillful historians, essayists, orators have done justice to the men; the events entering into their lives, the courage and valor which each day brought forth, have been recorded with emphasis and unflagging zeal. We are indeed glad and appreciative of the constant narration of the facts with which we have become familiar. At the same time, the regret comes to us that of the women so little has been said; that the balance of the two groups of the colony builders has not been better kept.

Of the Fathers we are accustomed to hear, but our gratitude salutes those who occasionally mention the Mothers and Daughters. They were two characteristic notes in the making of that Pilgrim score but because the latter was more lightly struck it has been too lightly regarded. Nevertheless, we rejoice that we know as much as we do of the women, and in the knowledge that increasing recognition is being given them.

Recently a plan was made that a chime of bells should be placed in the tower of the Pilgrim Monument at Provincetown and dedicated to the Women of the *Mayflower* by their descendants. More recently still, Henry H. Kitson has modeled a statue of a Pilgrim Woman for erection at Plymouth, in their memory. We may recall here the noble monument erected by the nation to the Pilgrims. In this design a woman is the exalted figure who holds the book and gazes over the sea. Also of the four important though lesser figures, two are women. Hon. John D. Long has said of the heroic figure, "Her eyes look toward the sea. Forever she beholds upon its waves the incoming *"Mayflower,"* she sees the Pilgrims land. They vanish, but she, the monument of their faith remains and tells their story to the world," which, as another has said, "in romance of

circumstance and charm of personal heroism . . .
is pre-eminent.''

Well may be seen the qualities of heart and mind
reproduced in countless of their descendants who
have carried on the influence of their personality
and work, deepening its roots down through the
years. ''The light they kindled has shone to many,
in some degree to our whole nation.'' In proof of
this is a relation of some who have claimed descent
from a Pilgrim of the *Mayflower* or of Plymouth.
This will comprise Presidents of the United States,
presidents of universities or colleges, jurists, dip-
lomats, writers, artists, military and naval men of
all our wars, governors of states, church dignita-
ries, physicians, scientists, senators, representatives,
signers of the Declaration of Independence, makers
of the Constitution. It is difficult to begin, more so
to pause, in such a list.

Annie A. Haxtun has said of one to be mentioned,
''John Tilly's spirit of adventure has fallen upon
one, at least of his descendants, General A. W.
Greely, the Arctic explorer, watched over by the
God of his Pilgrim forefathers, was saved by the
naval relief expedition to do good to the country,
which is his on a claim of more than two centuries.''
It is John and Hope Chipman, daughter of John
and Elizabeth Tilly Howland, who are also ancestors of General Greely; and it may here be said that
it is partly through his suggestion that the subject
of this work was projected (in the smaller form of
its first appearance); the other descendant likewise

responsible was Mr. William Lowrie Marsh, of Washington, D. C., founder of the Society of Mayflower Descendants in that city; the ancestors of Mr. Marsh were William and Alice Bradford.

John and Priscilla Alden, William and Mary Brewster, Richard and Elizabeth Warren and Francis and Hester Cooke have as their descendants those who have been Presidents of the Republic: John Adams and John Quincy Adams, Zachary Taylor, Ulysses Simpson Grant and William Howard Taft. Also from the Aldens have descended President Wheelock of Dartmouth College and President Kirkland of Harvard.

Bishop Soule of the Methodist Church is in line of descent from George Soule and his wife.

Descendants of Giles Hopkins and Catherine Wheeldon have added distinction to the family. Stephen Hopkins, great grandson of the original, again made the name famous by placing it among the signers of the Declaration of Independence, while his brother, Ezekiel, became the first admiral of our national navy. At the present time it is important through Colonel Thomas S. Hopkins, a veteran of the Civil War, past Governor-General of the General Society of Mayflower Descendants and a prominent lawyer and resident of Washington, D. C.

In Washington, also, Mr. Ernest W. Bradford, an able patent lawyer, continues the eminence of the name of his ancestors. Washington, likewise, is the residence of Mr. A. A. Aspinwall, historian of that city's Society of Mayflower Descendants, representing John and Elizabeth Howland.

A descendant of Francis and Hester Cooke is Major General Leonard Wood, at present Governor-General of the General Society of Mayflower Descendants.

The late Hon. Levi P. Morton, one time governor of New York State and Vice-President of the United States, was descended from the Hopkins and Cooke as well as Morton families.

From John and Priscilla Alden have come the poets William Cullen Bryant and Henry Wadsworth Longfellow, and the first Bishop of the Episcopal Church in America, Samuel Seabury; also the Revolutionary War Generals, Joseph and James Warren, the former of Bunker Hill fame, the latter President of the Congress of Massachusetts and husband of Mercy Otis, writer and patriot. Benjamin Church on whom the mantle of Myles Standish fell as Plymouth's military leader, was the son of Elizabeth Warren and Richard Church.

In line of descent from Mary and William Brewster is a family of North Carolina, interesting in three generations, Chief Justice Richmond Mumford Pearson, Hon. Richmond Pearson, Envoy Extraordinary and Minister Plenipotentiary of the United States to Persia, Captain Richmond Pearson Hobson, a hero of the Spanish American War.

From them also is Donald Grant Mitchel, author, Lieut. Alden Davidson, an aviator in the World War died for his country; as his name implies, John and

Priscilla Alden were his ancestors. A great great granddaughter of theirs was Faith Robinson; she married Governor Trumbull of Connecticut, George Washington's "Brother Jonathan" which name gradually became a synonym for a typical American. She gained fame for giving her scarlet cloak at a church collection for the army, in which she was decidedly interested, having three sons as officers. Her fourth son was the famous artist. Mrs. May Alden Ward, author, was a descendant in a recent generation.

From Mary (Allerton) and Thomas Cushman came America's famous tragedienne, Charlotte Cushman; also Mr. Cushman K. Davis, Governor of Minnesota, who made the speech of dedication at the ceremonies connected with the Cushman Monument on Burial Hill.

From Constance Hopkins and her husband Nicholas Snow, Robert Treat Paine, signer of the Declaration of Independance, and Robert Treat Paine, poet were descended.

In the convention which framed the Constitution John Tilly and the Howlands were represented by their descendant — through Desire Howland and Captain John Gorham — Nathaniel Gorham, who, as a member, was several times requested by General Washington to occupy the chair.

From this same group came Bishop Philips Brooks. As it is said, John Howland came to this country in the capacity of secretary to Governor John Carver, one, at least, of his and Elizabeth's descendants filled that position toward another celebrity. Edward Herbert Noyes, journalist and traveller, first returned to the land of his ancestors as private secretary to Hon. John Lothrop Motley, historian and diplomatist, United States Ambassador to the Court of St. James. Rev. Thomas Clap, fourth President of Yale College, was also of the line of Howland, while his wife, Mary Whiting, was descended from Governor Bradford and his wife.

From Mary Chilton and her husband John Winslow, comes Mrs. Robert Hall Wiles, of Chicago, past President of the National Society of United States Daughters of the War of 1812 and now serving as President-General of the National Society Daughters of Founders and Patriots of America. From Mary and John Winslow, also, came Lieutenant Sturdevant, another young aviator of the World War, killed over-seas in the service of his country.

For another repetion of the exact name of his ancestor there is Doctor Myles Standish, a noted occulist of Boston. In the medical profession also Doctor Stuart Clark Johnson of Washington and Doctor Ira Hart Noyes of Providence, the first from John and Priscilla Alden, the second from John and Elizabeth Howland, both answering the call of duty to country in the World War, to serve over-seas.

Two residents of Washington are Hon. William S. Washburne — United States Civil Service Commissioner and Mr. Frank Herbert Briggs of the Court of Claims — descended respectively from Francis

and Hester Cooke, and the Brewster, Bradford and
Alden families.

The late Henry Billings Brown, Associate Justice
of the Supreme Court of the United States was
another descendant of John and Elizabeth Howland
while the late Seth Shepherd, Chief Justice of the
Court of Appeals of the District of Columbia, was
another representative of the line of William and
Mary Brewster. Mr. A. Howard Clark, who was
editor of the magazine of the Smithsonian Institution, was a descendant from the Brewsters, Hopkins and Howlands. The name of Howland Davis
tells plainly why he has done so much for present
day Plymouth and the Society of Mayflower Descendants.

In the United States Senate are three prominent
descendants of the Pilgrims. The ancestors of Senator Henry Cabot Lodge of Massachusetts, chairman
of Committee on Foreign Relations, are John and
Elizabeth Tilly Howland. The Senators from New
York and Vermont, Hon. James Wolcott Wadsworth, Jr., and Hon. Carroll Smally Page, are
descendants respectively from Giles and Catharine
Hopkins and William and Mary Brewster.

A descendant in the person of William Wallace
Case, has visited Scrooby and brought from there a
piece of oak once a part of the old Manor house,
home of his ancestors, William and Mary Brewster
— this priceless relic has been made into the gavel
used by the Governor of the District of Columbia
Society of Mayflower Descendants.

In hundreds of cities and towns and villages of the nation there are other and equally consistent representatives of the glorious names of their Plymouth ancestors. As we have seen the men in all the branches of service to their country, the women may be compared no less favorably in what they have rendered. In their nation's wars, they have ever been faithful, and their efforts as beneficial to the men and cause as were those of their ancestors of their own sex, whose work was as the mortar in the solid foundation wall of the nation they helped to build. Someone has said that always in the history of mankind the woman has been at her best when she has felt herself most needed. Every reason then for her to attract as she appears in pioneer days, in those of the Revolution or War for the Union and in the World War, unfailingly illustrating, unconsciously or not, the age old motto of *Noblesse Oblige*.

In hamlet or city, women descendants of Plymouth women upheld the honor of their men and country in Red Cross, Government Loans or "Y." work during the World War. In the Sanitary Commission and Nursing Units of the Civil War the women's spirit was the same, and in 1776 when their days were nearest to the pioneer women, the women of the Revolutionary War inheriting the courage and self-forgetfulness, matched the heroism of the men. Thus each generation of women has met the crisis actuated by the same unanimity of purpose and devotion — from each in turn their successors have caught the falling torch, assuring that they

shall not have lived and worked in vain. And they
may sleep in peace.

The American women of today must meet the
challenge of the women of 1861, 1776 and 1620. She
must bear comparison with them in fundamental
things. Patriotism, firmness, thrift, decision and resourcefulness, characteristics which are their heritage. As someone has said, "We are living in the
tomorrow for which they wrought. We are to do
today with all fidelity each bit of work which lies
at our hands. This will make our next day brighter
and by so much, set the world forward."

The mission of the *Mayflower* company was to
open the way for a successful colonization of the
New World. Its mission was faithfully performed.
In studying the details and circumstances relating
to the immortal voyage and settlement of Plymouth
— particularly in relation to the women, vested today with supreme interest and in a glamour
peculiarly their own, we must feel that that nobility
of life may be ours as well as theirs and that it may
illuminate the difficult life of today and make it
worthy to be the fruit of the tree of Liberty they
helped to plant, in tears and smiles.

Realizing the heavy debt that we owe to the men
who were led to undertake the settlement of Plymouth we owe an equal if not greater debt to the
women who had the courage and spirit to enter with
them into the great and epoch making adventure.
These make the shrines which we would visit. It is
with reverence that we view not only the soil which

first they trod but every spot associated with them.

If history as some one has said is in its unchange-able essence a tale, then this particular history is a tale that cannot be too often told or heard, not mere-ly to hold our attention to the past but by its light to look forward with a thrill to the future, to the tasks and service for civilization, under the Provi-dence by which the women of the *Mayflower* and the women of Plymouth were upheld. This will be the best memorial we can give these women all through the years; the remembrance that cannot fade.

Mothering and Motherhood in Ancient Greece and Rome

EDITED BY LAUREN HACKWORTH PETERSEN
AND PATRICIA SALZMAN-MITCHELL

Mothering and Motherhood in Ancient Greece and Rome

University of Texas Press AUSTIN

This book has been supported by an endowment dedicated to classics and the ancient world and funded by the Areté Foundation; the Gladys Krieble Delmas Foundation; the Dougherty Foundation; the James R. Dougherty, Jr. Foundation; the Rachael and Ben Vaughan Foundation; and the National Endowment for the Humanities.

Requests for permission to reproduce material from this work should be sent to:
    Permissions
    University of Texas Press
    P.O. Box 7819
    Austin, TX 78713-7819
    www.utexas.edu/utpress/about/bpermission.html

♾ The paper used in this book meets the minimum requirements of ANSI/NISO z39.48-1992 (R1997) (Permanence of Paper).

LIBRARY OF CONGRESS CATALOGING-IN-PUBLICATION DATA

Mothering and motherhood in ancient Greece and Rome / edited by Lauren Hackworth Petersen and Patricia Salzman-Mitchell.
    p.   cm.
    Includes bibliographical references and index.
    ISBN 978-0-292-72990-2 (cloth : alk. paper) — ISBN 978-0-292-73923-9 (e-book)
    1. Motherhood—Greece—History.   2. Mothers—Greece—History.
3. Motherhood—Rome—History.   4. Mothers—Rome—History.
I. Petersen, Lauren Hackworth, 1965–   II. Salzman-Mitchell, Patricia, 1969–
    HQ759.M8786   2011
    306.874′30938—dc23

                                        2011034997

To mothers, past, present, and future

Contents

Illustrations

Acknowledgments

We are grateful to the Women's Classical Caucus for sponsoring the 2007 APA/AIA Annual Meeting paper session "Motherhood in the Ancient World," which provided the impetus for this volume. Four of the ten essays in this collection are revised and expanded versions of papers delivered at that session; they are authored by Angela Taraskiewicz, Anise Strong, Prudence Jones, and Genevieve Liveley. The remaining six scholars were commissioned by the editors: Mireille Lee, Yurie Hong, Angeliki Tzanetou, Antony Augoustakis, Patricia Salzman-Mitchell, and Margaret Woodhull. The contributors were all selected with an eye toward diversity in approaches to ancient mothering and motherhood, in regard to questions, evidence, chronology, and methodology.

This volume would not be possible without the kind assistance of a number of individuals and institutions. The following were instrumental in assisting us with the acquisition of images and reproductions rights: Dr. Nikolaos Kaltsas, Director, and Dr. Rosa Proskynitopoulou, Deputy Director, the National Archaeological Museum, Athens; Professor Dimitrios Pantermalis, the Acropolis Museum, Athens; Marisa Marthari, Director of the 21st Ephorate of Antiquities, Athens; Dr. P. J. Chatzidakis at the Archaeological Museum of Delos; Konstantinos S. I. Kissas, Director of the 37th Ephorate (Corinth Archaeological Museum); Carol A. Stein, then Acting Director of Publications, the American School of Classical Studies at Athens; Ioulia Tzonou-Herbst, Assistant Director, Corinth Excavations; Professoressa Jeanette Papadopoulos, then Soprintendente *ad interim* della Soprintendenza Speciale per i Beni Archeologici di Napoli e Pompei; Dottoressa Beatrice Basile, Director of the Museo Archeologico Regionale Paolo Orsi–Siracusa; Dr. Gian Luca Zanzi, the Ara Pacis Museum;

Chris Linnane, Harvard Art Museums; Dr. Elena Stolyarik, the American Numismatic Society; Dr. Ulrich Sinn; Glynnis Fawkes; Richard Huxtable; Fototeca Unione, American Academy in Rome; the British Museum; Bibliothèque nationale de France; Musée du Louvre; Deutsches Archäologisches Institut, Athens; the ever-helpful staff at Art Resource, New York; and George Freeman and Stephen Petersen, for assistance with some of the digital images.

It has been a true pleasure to work with the University of Texas Press. The two anonymous readers for the press provided valuable criticisms and suggestions for the individual authors. We would like to extend a special thank you to Kerri Cox Sullivan, for her judicious editing, and to Jim Burr, sponsoring editor at the press, for his unwavering support of this project. And finally, the editors would like to express their heartfelt gratitude to their families: Patricia, to her husband, Ken Mitchell, for his constant support and to her children, Alex and Luciana Mitchell, for their smiles and inspiration; and Lauren, to Stephen, Miles, and Stella, who showed great patience throughout the stages of this project.

[ONE]

Introduction

THE PUBLIC AND PRIVATE FACES

OF MOTHERING AND MOTHERHOOD

IN CLASSICAL ANTIQUITY

Lauren Hackworth Petersen and Patricia Salzman-Mitchell

Friend, I have not much to say; stop and read it.
This tomb, which is not fair, is for a fair woman.
Her parents gave her the name Claudia.
She loved her husband in her heart.
She bore two sons, one of whom
she left on the earth, the other beneath it.
She was pleasant to talk with, and she walked with grace.
She kept the house and worked in wool. That is all. You may go.

EPITAPH, ROME, *CORPUS INSCRIPTIONUM LATINARUM* I².I2II
(= *CIL* 6.15346); LEFKOWITZ AND FANT (2005), NO. 39

I would very much rather stand three times
in the front of battle than bear one child.

EURIPIDES, *MEDEA* 250–251; TRANS. WARNER (1944)

Many women at the nation's most elite colleges say they have already
decided that they will put aside their careers in favor of raising
children. . . . [And they] say they will happily play a traditional
female role, with motherhood their main commitment.

STORY (2005)

Women and motherhood. Given their very definitions, these two nouns are inextricably intertwined, as a woman's primary role has traditionally been defined vis-à-vis her ability to reproduce and/or care for offspring. (Try "men" and "fatherhood"—the

impact of the pairing of the words is simply not as vivid.) While images of ancient women, in either literary or visual testimony, have received ample scholarly attention, the diverse, if sometimes conflicting, roles of women as mothers in ancient sources—for both Greece and Rome—have received relatively little focused and sustained treatment. This is not to suggest that discussions of ancient mothers have been neglected in scholarship. It is widely known, for example, that the mothers of classical antiquity could wield enormous influence, as the reproductive bodies of society and, in many cases, of culture. Impressive and inspiring, recent studies have delved into the constructions of ancient Greek and Roman mothers,[1] who are typically placed within discourses of archetypal female behavior for the respective societies—as paragons of female virtue and, by extension, as good mothers (e.g., Claudia from the epitaph above), or as the polar opposite (e.g., Medea, who murders her own children). Furthermore, scholarly interest in ancient families has, by necessity, brought to the fore the roles of mothers in shaping civic and personal identities.[2]

But not all mothers and acts of mothering can be easily categorized. There is still much ground to cover in revealing the complexities of ancient mothering. To this end, this volume brings together scholars whose expertise in a diverse range of areas permits us to explore notions of motherhood from new perspectives, with many tackling topics that have yet to be discussed with respect to motherhood and others challenging existing scholarship. In examining different kinds of representations of mothers from Greece and Rome, the authors explore the multilayered dimensions of motherhood. This collection also seeks to demonstrate that the notion of motherhood was not uncontested territory, but rather could be fraught with tension and contradictions. Even today, pointed discussions on the competing roles placed on mothers in modern society persist and reveal just how challenging—and precarious—motherhood can be. It is our hope, then, that the essays in this book not only contribute to our knowledge of motherhood in the ancient world, but can also be inserted into larger, current debates on motherhood, such as the conflict mothers may feel in choosing between work and family life and the controversies surrounding appropriate forms of rearing and feeding children (e.g., breast or bottle). This book thus intimates links between the lives of ancient mothers and the various roles of women in modern Western society and ideology.

Although the themes approached by the essays ahead are wide-ranging, they together explore how mothering and motherhood—while traditionally located in the private, domestic sphere of Greek and Roman life—were

topics that found plenty of exposure in the public domain and were even deployed to political (dis)advantage. To this end, this study reveals how ancient motherhood—in both reality and rhetoric—was negotiated along a continuum of private and public. This public–private dynamic is but one theme that is touched upon throughout this collection. In this regard, some essays focus on motherhood as largely private, that is, as an emotional, intimate experience, but also as physical work, as work of the body on public display. These contributions include Mireille Lee's on pregnancy and Greek dress, Angela Taraskiewicz's on Greek rituals of incorporation, Yurie Hong's on embryology in Greek discourse, Anise Strong's on Greek and Roman prostitute mothers, and Patricia Salzman-Mitchell's on images of breast-feeding in Greek and Latin literature. In contrast, the pieces by Angeliki Tzanetou on citizenship and motherhood in Greek drama, Prudence Jones on the public uses of Cleopatra's own motherhood, and Margaret Woodhull on imperial mothers and their Roman monuments explore the ramifications of public, if not politicized, displays of motherhood; the private experiences of these mothers are subsumed in the name of ideology. Genevieve Liveley's piece straddles these two facets of mothering, unveiling the contradictions of a character like Venus, an intimate and sexual mother, and yet a deity recognized as having tremendous political importance for the Augustan regime. In a similar vein, Antony Augoustakis' discussion of motherhood in Flavian epic reveals how the constructions of motherhood could address ideals of Romanness and otherness not only in Roman Italy, but also in peripheral societies beyond the peninsula as the empire underwent expansion (see too Jones on this topic).

These private/public faces of motherhood resonate as well in issues concerning modern motherhood, and are especially crystalized in the dilemmas mothers with careers face: should a recent mother disclose in a job interview that she has young children, for example? Should she ask for a place to pump or breast-feed in her workplace? Does the public display of motherhood help or harm a mother in a position of power, such as a political candidate today (for example, Sarah Palin's 2008 bid for the U.S. vice presidency as the mother of an infant)? While talking about or showing that one has young children may be useful in certain situations (such as getting through a line for children or people with strollers in an airport), it might be detrimental for a woman who aspires to be CEO of a company. Also, the question of whether to conceal or reveal publicly the motherly body (in pregnancy or lactation) is of pointed concern for modern mothers. Generally speaking, the essays here confront these types of issues, al-

beit in an ancient context, and in so doing, reveal the common ground some modern mothers share with their ancient counterparts. Mothering, it would seem, was to be intensely private, and its place on the public stage oftentimes met with contestations and frustrations.

IDEALS AND REALITIES OF MOTHERHOOD

A related thematic thread running through these essays is the potential misfit between the realities of mothers on a day-to-day basis and the ideals of motherhood as presented in ancient visual and verbal testimony. For example, it is widely recognized that motherhood could bestow honor on Greek and Roman women. Both literary and archaeological sources indicate that to have borne children and raised them well was considered a virtue, if not a necessity. Of the many Greek written sources, two examples will suffice in suggesting how pervasive prescriptions were for women to aspire to motherhood. In Xenophon's famous and oft-cited dialogue, from the fourth century BCE, Ischomachus describes to Socrates his method for training his wife, a method that he presents as "natural" and ordained by the gods:

> "It is important then, when the provisions are brought into the home, for someone to keep them safe and to do the work of the household. A home is required for the rearing of infant children, and a home is required for making food out of harvest. Similarly a home is required for the making of clothing from wool. Since both indoor and outdoor matters require work and supervision," I said, "I believe that the god arranged that the work and supervision indoors are a woman's task, and the outdoors are the man's. . . . With this in mind the god made the nursing of young children instinctive for woman and gave her this task, and he allotted more affection for infants to her than to a man." (Xenophon, *Oeconomicus* 7.21–7.24)[3]

This passage firmly places women and mothers in the private sphere, more specifically, inside the home. To be a proper Greek woman, according to Xenophon, is to be a mother working industriously inside the house.

Also from the fourth century BCE, Hippocrates provides advice for treating virgins afflicted with hysteria, that is, his advice is for young females who fell decidedly outside the ideals of Greek womanhood (on ac-

count of being virgins *and* afflicted with a disease). Nonetheless, his recommendation is straightforward enough—become pregnant, and, by extension, enter motherhood:

> My prescription is that when virgins experience this trouble, they should cohabit with a man as quickly as possible. If they become pregnant, they will be cured. If they don't do this, either they will succumb at the onset of puberty or a little later, unless they catch another disease. (Hippocrates, *On Virgins* = 8.466–470)[4]

Hippocrates thus suggests that a sick woman can be healed by becoming a mother, a notion that conforms suspiciously well with Greek thought about the proper roles of women in society, despite the very real physical and emotional demands of motherhood that must have taken some toll on an already fragile woman.

Greek vases adorned with scenes of domestic life, including images of mothers tending to their children, celebrate motherhood and seem to affirm the literary tradition. A red-figure, fifth-century BCE Greek vase depicts a private scene of domestic harmony (fig. 1.1), for example, in which a mother, seated on a high-backed chair (*klismos*), hands her child to her nurse-servant, who will tend to the child. To the left stands a loom, a symbol of female domestic activity and virtue. Behind the mother stands a man, perhaps the husband or an older child.[5] It is tempting to read this picture as a slice of everyday Greek life, precisely because it offers a glimpse of a mother and mothering (the nurse-servant). But it is also important to bear in mind that this pot comes from a funerary context and was likely a tomb gift intended to honor the deceased female with the trappings of motherhood and domesticity, and thereby virtue.

In a somewhat similar vein, a red-figure, fifth-century BCE *chous* (squat jug) depicts a playful scene in which a mother (or caregiver) gently lifts a child so that he can grab a bunch of grapes (fig. 1.2). Although a vessel like this is typically used in an Athenian festival (the *Anthesteria*), it may have also been offered as a funerary gift for a child, as many such objects were found in tomb settings.[6] The image, if of a mother and child, would thus depict the very centrality of mothers in both rituals and the daily lives of children; and if from a funerary context, the mother has been, in a sense, buried with her child.

Much of our knowledge of the lives of mothers in Rome comes from the realm of commemoration. From a relatively modest context, a husband

FIGURE 1.1. *Family scene in a domestic setting, red-figure hydria (kalpis), attributed to the circle of Polygnotos, ca. 430 BCE. Harvard Art Museums, Arthur M. Sackler Museum, Bequest of David M. Robinson, 1960.342. Photo: Michael A. Nedzweski, © President and Fellows of Harvard College.*

records the virtues of his wife in a second- or third-century sarcophagus inscription:

> Of Graxia Alexandria, distinguished for her virtue and fidelity. She nursed her children with her own breasts. Her husband Pudens the emperor's freedman [dedicated this monument] as a reward to her. She lived 24 years, 3 months, 16 days.[7]

251

FIGURE I.2. *Woman (mother or caregiver) and child, Attic red-figure* chous,
*ca. 420 BCE. Erlangen, Universität Erlangen-Nürnberg I321. Photo: van Hoorn (1951),
fig. 251.*

Pudens praises his young wife as having borne and lovingly raised their children; the image he projects of his wife is of the genuine, intimate, and selfless bond a mother nurtures with her own offspring. Here we observe the private experience of nursing made public by a male. The evocation of the female body in the act of breast-feeding is poignant as a sign of female virtue and, by extension, the family's good name.

The theme of female virtue as directly connected to motherhood is also apparent, for example, in Roman writings of the Augustan period. In Propertius (4.11) the honorable Roman matron Cornelia speaks "from her grave," as a woman proud to have had three children:

> et tamen emerui generosos vestis honores,
>   nec mea de sterili facta rapina domo.
> et bene habet: numquam mater lugubria sumpsi;
>   venit in exsequias tota caterva meas.
> tu, Lepide, et tu, Paulle, meum post fata levamen,
>   condita sunt vestro lumina nostra sinu.
> filia, tu specimen censurae nata paternae,
>   fac teneas unum nos imitata virum.
> (63–68)

Yet I lived long enough to earn the matron's robe of honour, nor was I snatched away from a childless house. So all is well: never as a mother did I put on mourning garb; all my children came to my funeral. You, Lepidus, and you, Paullus, my consolations after death, in your embrace were my eyelids closed. Daughter, born to be the model of your father's censorship, do you, like me hold fast to a single husband.[8]

This passage, and indeed the entire poem, is particularly striking not only because it provides direct testimony of the expectations Roman society had of mothers, but also because it clearly reflects the then-current Augustan ideology concerning morality and the family.[9] The Augustan sets of laws regarding marriage—which we know as the *Lex Julia et Papia Poppaea* and to an extent also the *Lex Julia de adulteriis*—are outstanding and unusual in the ancient world, as they interfere with and legislate directly on matters of motherhood and mothering. An experience that is generally performed in the privacy of the family is here brought out into the public and even political domain. Indeed, a whole system of rewards and penalties was involved in these laws. For example, families that did not conform to the Augustan ideology suffered in matters of inheritance.[10] Likewise, women

who complied with it were liberated from the oppressive *tutela muliebris*.[11] If a freeborn woman had three children or a *libertina* four, she was free from the guardianship of a male. Further, as in the case of Cornelia, they were granted the honor of wearing the *stola*.[12] The inheritance situation of mothers who bore many children was also greatly improved by the Augustan legislation.[13]

Often, however, the realities of motherhood were far removed from the ideals depicted on pots, written in stone, or presented in literary, medical, and legal discourses, suggesting that motherhood was not as unproblematic as some of these ideologically charged testimonies imply. For example, maternal death in childbirth was a much more common occurrence than today.[14] Grave *stelai* of Greek women who died in childbirth offer vivid reminders of the physical and emotional hardships that many mothers and their families endured. On a fourth-century BCE *stele*, a woman in distress leans back on a *kline* (small bed or couch) (fig. 1.3). A female supports the dying woman from behind, while an older man holds her right hand as he bids her farewell. The pose, loosened garments, and accentuated belly all work together to inform viewers that the seated woman who is commemorated here has tragically died in childbirth.[15] The suffering and hardship of motherhood are depicted in stone for public display in the cemetery to memorialize a woman as mother, commemorating what would otherwise remain an intensely private, domestic scene.

As maternal death in childbirth was of significant concern, so too was the high child mortality rate in the Greek world (with survival rates at roughly one in three).[16] As John Oakley has argued, the emotional toll of losing a child is given greater visual expression for mothers, however, than for fathers, which is not to imply that Greek fathers did not mourn the loss of their own children but that conventions dictated that they did so less freely than mothers. Illustrating Oakley's point is a late fifth-century BCE white-ground *lekythos* (slender oil or perfume vessel), upon which a young boy is depicted in Charon's boat (fig. 1.4).[17] Before the youth departs the world of the living and crosses the river Styx, he reaches out to his mother, who stands grieving at the shore. She, too, attempts to touch her child one last time, but that effort is only in vain. Although the father is seen standing in the background, the story told here is of the grief of the mother at the premature loss of her son.

All of these images of mothers come from and/or represent the private world of the fairly well-to-do, that is, of established, traditional families. In fact, many essays within this volume confront evidence that reveals the various dimensions of mothering and motherhood, but usually within pre-

FIGURE 1.3. *Woman dying in childbirth, Attic grave* stele, *ca. 330 BCE. Harvard Art Museums, Arthur M. Sackler Museum, Gift of Edward W. Forbes, 1905.8. Photo: Junius Beebe, © President and Fellows of Harvard College.*

scribed (normative) maternal patterns of ancient Greece and Rome. Much more difficult to locate are the lives of mothers who lived humbly and thus left little record of their existence. Paradoxically, these mothers, whose presence was commonplace in the ancient world, are rarely the subject in ancient writings and art. For example, the private life of the prostitute-mother

is elusive, although Strong's essay in this volume provides us with methodologies for thinking about these mothers in ancient Greece and Rome. Much is still to be gained by thinking about the lives of slave-mothers in the Roman world, whose own children (*vernae*)—or those of others—they could rear, should the master not break the already fragile mother–child bond by selling the slave-mother or -child to another household. Slave-mothers are notoriously silenced in the archaeological record and literary texts, but the exploitation of slave-mothers' productive and reproductive capacities has received recent, much-needed attention.[18] Telling, too, is the evidence from an *ergastulum* (slave prison) at Chalk, Kent; within the floor were cut three pits that held the remains of three infants. These remains have a story to tell about motherhood, a story that we can at best only imagine.[19] Vivid and haunting, too, are the bodies left in the wake of Pompeii's destruction. One pair is typically read as a mother clutching her child

FIGURE 1.4. *Parents (father at far left and mother, gesturing to her son, to the left of the boat) bid farewell to deceased son, who stands in Charon's boat and reaches back (see image at right), Attic white-ground lekythos, ca. 430 BCE. National Archaeological Museum, Athens, inv. no. 16463. © Hellenic Ministry of Culture and Tourism/ Archaeological Receipts Fund.*

FIGURE 1.5. *Plaster casts of mother and child, 79 CE. Pompeii. Photo: Lauren Hackworth Petersen (with the permission of Ministero per i Beni e le Attività Culturali—Soprintendenza Speciale per i Beni Archeologici di Napoli e Pompei).*

one last time—a gesture made permanent through plaster casting (fig. 1.5). This mother's remains provide only a limited view into the lived lives of mothers, even if that view rests largely in our own desires to see real mothers in the material record.[20] It is our hope that the authors here offer ways to advance even further discussions of the lesser-known testimonies of ancient motherhood.

Although women themselves left little trace of their own existence, the study of ancient mothers, mothering, and motherhood can be accomplished through the lens of (elite) men—that is, through male-authored words, rituals, and artifacts. This lack of direct evidence from a female perspective is not prohibitive. Indeed, the contributors to this volume attempt to get behind the rhetoric to explore, on one hand, everyday realities of motherhood and, on the other hand, the constructions of motherhood used to fulfill social and political agendas. This is not to suggest two mutually exclusive categories. Rather, this volume examines different aspects of motherhood and reveals that despite the very real marginalization of women in nearly all aspects of ancient life, mothering and motherhood were sites for both private/self- and public/civic definition in ancient Greece and Rome. From mother

as healer, lover, devoted parent, and family member, to mother as murderer and enemy of the state, mothers could also be viewed as cooperative and/or antagonistic within their respective societies. The authors thus seek to expose the complexities that the idea of mothering could engender and how the private world of women and children in the household negotiated with public and political displays of motherhood on civic monuments, within cemeteries, and in the thought-worlds of the ancients.

ON ANCIENT MOTHERHOOD

Different work on aspects of motherhood in either Greece or Rome has added much to our current state of knowledge, although no one study attempts the chronological and geographical breadth and the diversity of approaches that this collection of essays offers. Nonetheless, the individual authors of this volume are deeply indebted to earlier groundbreaking work on motherhood in ancient societies, even as each contributor strives to advance conversations on ancient mothers in new and exciting directions. What follows is a brief outline of some of the more salient and influential works on the subject.

Critical for any study of Greek and Roman mothers are the outstanding studies by Nancy Demand and Suzanne Dixon. Demand's *Birth, Death, and Motherhood in Classical Greece* (1994) carefully illuminates many issues surrounding pregnancy, as well as the female role in reproduction in the Greek world. Demand's review of the medical texts, specifically *Epidemics*, and the attention she gives to childbirth are particularly insightful and have informed essays within this volume. In addition, focusing on women as child-bearers for the *polis* and the family, Demand explores their roles in the state and male control of women's reproductive lives, an important theme that many of the authors in this edited volume bring to the fore.

Most notable in studies of Roman motherhood are two books by Dixon, *The Roman Mother* (1988) and *The Roman Family* (1992). In *The Roman Mother*, Dixon explores crucial issues regarding the place of motherhood within the Roman family: its legal implications; the official encouragement of motherhood; and the more specific relations of the Roman mother with her sons, daughters, and infant children; it also provides some insight on substitute or surrogate maternity. *The Roman Family*, though focusing on the family more generally, provides some key insights on the roles of mothers and their children in ancient Rome. Each volume offers excellent overviews of motherhood in Roman society, and they are both innova-

tive regarding Roman attitudes toward young children, which are unavoidably interlinked with the question of maternity and a topic that had been somewhat understudied. Dixon's approach is developed primarily from a historical and legal perspective.

More recently, the theme of Roman mothers was the focus of an issue of *Helios* (Sept. 2006).[21] The five articles, by leading scholars of ancient women, present mothers from a largely literary perspective, thereby complementing Dixon's work as well as the contributions on Roman mothers presented here. Another timely and enlightening volume on the subject is *Madres y maternidades: Construcciones culturales en la civilización clásica*, edited by Rosa María Cid López (2009). This collection of essays explores motherhood as a stereotype created by men to assert their own power and legitimize their superiority over women. While there are some points of contact between this volume and our current work, the texts and material approached in each collection are fundamentally different. Finally, a significant study in the area of Latin literature is Augoustakis' book on mothers in Flavian epic, *Motherhood and the Other: Fashioning Female Power in Flavian Epic* (2010), a topic that will be newly addressed in this volume by the author.

A number of books focus on specific aspects of mothering. For example, Patricia Watson's *Ancient Stepmothers: Myth, Misogyny, and Reality* (1995) concentrates on the figure of the stepmother in myth and the historical reality of fifth-century Athens and Republican and early Imperial Rome. Because Watson's book addresses aspects of mothering and its surrogacy, its methodologies are useful for thinking about acts associated with mothering. Likewise, a thought-provoking, recent addition to this growing body of work on ancient mothering is Sabine Hübner and David Ratzan's *Growing Up Fatherless in Antiquity* (2009). Given that about one-third of children in the ancient world grew up fatherless and thus were raised by single mothers, stepmothers, or other relatives, this study sheds light on the everyday lives and responsibilities of motherhood in Greece and Rome (while also participating in debates on modern families). Meanwhile, Aline Rousselle's *Porneia: On Desire and the Body in Antiquity* (1988) also deserves mention here. Although her book is not focused on motherhood per se, in her discussions of the female body Rousselle makes sharp observations about the bodies of mothers, their lives, and the expectations laid on them.

It is our desire that this collection of essays will also complement recent scholarship on childhood in antiquity, namely Jenifer Neils and John Oakley, eds., *Coming of Age in Ancient Greece: Images of Childhood from the Classical Past* (2003), Beryl Rawson, *Children and Childhood in Roman Italy*

(2003), Jeannine Uzzi, *Children in the Visual Arts of Ancient Rome* (2005), and Ada Cohen and Jeremy B. Rutter, eds., *Constructions of Childhood in Ancient Greece and Italy* (2007). These texts, among others, are fundamental in shedding some light on the rather understudied topic of the relationship of mothers with their young children.

ORGANIZATION OF THE VOLUME

Mothering and Motherhood in Ancient Greece and Rome builds on these pioneering studies, among others, by focusing on topics and problems related to mothering in antiquity that have been left largely untouched, such as relations between prostitutes and their daughters, dress in pregnancy and motherhood, and specific religious rituals involving mothers. The collection of essays deals in its first half with considerations of motherhood in ancient Greece; the second half of the volume is dedicated to evidence derived from Rome. While the essays are organized loosely by chronology, the contributors variously navigate the perceived dichotomy between the private world of motherhood as physical and social work inside the house and the public displays of motherhood as political asset.

The first two essays, by Lee and by Taraskiewicz, explore the important transition from maiden to mother in the Greek world, that is, the rituals of pregnancy and childbirth. Here we see the overlapping interaction between transformations in the female body and the female's transformations in the social sphere. Novel in her approach, each author makes judicious use of visual and material evidence, in addition to making cross-cultural comparisons. Their essays also reveal some of the Greek anxieties surrounding pregnancy and childbirth, alongside the rituals designed to reintegrate mothers into their households and, by extension, society.

Despite rituals meant to recognize the transformed body of females and mothers, not all mothers and acts of mothering were perceived as ideal. Hong examines three Hippocratic treatises and explores how the physiological process of birth is actually coded as a violent struggle between mother and child. The author identifies the maternal body as the physical point of origin for potential familial conflict and highlights cultural ambivalence regarding the nature of a mother's relationship both to her child and to her household.

That the private lives of mothers could be made part of public discourse is also evident in the pieces by Tzanetou, Strong, and Salzman-Mitchell. Tzanetou explores representations of motherhood in Greek trag-

edy from the vantage point of female citizenship in classical Athens. This essay focuses on the woman on stage and her social and political relationships as a mother; it emphasizes the civic implications of maternal agency in tragic poetry through the oftentimes highly charged characters of Praxithea, Aithra, Creusa, Clytemnestra, and Medea. But what might we know of actual mother–child relationships? Strong's essay begins with the premise that one of the only means of understanding ancient familial relationships is to examine atypical familial structures. In an innovative study on the private lives of marginal mothers, Strong analyzes the figure of the mother-prostitute. Her essay explores the dynamics of both the economic and the emotional relationships between prostitute-mothers and their children and offers a fascinating alternative to the conventional narrative of the ancient family. Salzman-Mitchell offers a study on women's use of their bodies in the work of motherhood and explores ideologically loaded images of breast-feeding in Greek and Latin literature. She offers interpretations for what seem to be conflicting views of breast-feeding in the ancient world, as an act that is both nurturing and virtuous, and also potentially destructive.

Turning to Rome, the last four essays explore the extent to which ideals of Roman motherhood were deployed for exclusively political gain. The essays by Jones and Liveley focus on the precarious moment when Octavian/Augustus asserted his *imperium*, with motherhood as a central component of his political campaign. Specifically, Jones investigates the similarities in the political uses to which both Cleopatra and the Romans put motherhood as a way to explain the advantage Octavian gained by suppressing this important aspect of Cleopatra's self-presentation (in Egypt) to Roman audiences. Meanwhile, Liveley examines both textual and visual *exempla* to extrapolate models of good and bad mothering in Augustan Rome. In particular, she focuses on the tensions and paradoxes between mother and lover, and maternal and erotic love.

The concluding essays focus on mothers on the periphery and mothers in the center of the empire, while building on themes presented by Jones and Liveley. Augoustakis addresses the role of non-Roman mothers in Flavian epic poetry and explores the dynamics of a renegotiated Romanness through the representation of otherness. Back in Rome, the concluding essay by Woodhull carefully examines how ideals of motherhood were inscribed on the cityscape of Rome, beginning with the radical transformation of the urban space begun under Augustus and moving through the second century. We see here emphatic public displays and uses of motherhood created for political advantage.

Whereas most studies of women tend to engage either literary or visual source material—one to the exclusion of the other—we hope that readers find that one of the merits of this book, which focuses solely on mothering and motherhood in classical antiquity (rather than on women more broadly), lies in its interdisciplinarity. The essays also span a broad chronological range, covering an expansive period from the Homeric age in Greece to late imperial Rome. In addition, the authors consider different kinds of mothers—from the mythical to the real, from empress to prostitute, and from citizen to foreigner—to expose both the mundane and ideologically charged lives of mothers and the attendant discourses of motherhood in ancient Greece and Rome. Rituals, dress, legal and medical texts, literary testimony, art, and architecture are all brought together in various ways to reveal the centrality of motherhood in ancient Greece and Rome, despite the virtual absence of overt female participation in the public and political spheres of ancient life.

So, where do we go from here? There is, to be sure, much work still to be done. For example, we hope to encourage further research on highly visible female figures such as Cleopatra and Julia Domna, who are often studied in their political/public roles but not commonly seen as mothers who mothered. Regarding the latter, Julia Domna was the biological mother of co-emperors Geta and Caracalla and the recipient of numerous titles, all naming her as an imperial mother figurehead in no uncertain terms: *Mater castrorum*/Mother of the Military Camps; *Mater senatus*/Mother of the Senate; *Mater Augustorum*/Mother of the Emperors; *Mater patriae*/Mother of the Native Land; and *Mater populi Romani*/Mother of the Roman People.[22] On the reverse of one coin, minted in ca. 200 CE, Julia Domna's biological motherhood is presented for political gain (fig. 1.6). She appears at the center of the coin with her two sons, each shown in profile facing her. The legend—*felicitas saeculi*, a slogan of sorts for the Severan dynasty—ended up being utterly false, as Caracalla murdered his own brother so as to claim the throne for himself. As Natalie Kampen has shown, the attempts to publicize and politicize Julia's motherhood as a harbinger of happy times concealed the very instability of family and dynasty at this point in history.[23] Moreover, this visual campaign was a public one; we have yet to ask what actual motherhood might have meant in daily life for this particular mother.

While previous discussions of ancient motherhood have focused on the mother's role in society and the family, more recently studies of the female body have been in the ascendance. These studies, however, tend to focus on

FIGURE I.6. *Coin,*
reverse: *Julia Domna
with Caracalla and
Geta, ca. 200 CE.
New York, American
Numismatic Society,
1959.228.33. Photo:
Courtesy of the
American Numismatic
Society.*

ideals of femininity and womanhood rather than on the woman as mother. With this book we hope to stimulate research that focuses on the centrality of the female body in the task of mothering. In addition, there is a relative paucity of work on the lives of mothers from an archaeological perspective, a need that some of the essays will begin to fulfill. It is our goal that this book will also identify opportunities to delve into relatively humbler expressions of the lived lives of mothers, such as epitaphs, which can perhaps help us to identify working mothers and maybe even slave-mothers.

As readers move through the essays, it will be important to bear in mind that the rhetorical and visual constructs of motherhood were surely contested, with ideals often masking the realities and complexities of motherhood in the classical world. In spite of the relative silence of ancient mothers themselves, the contributors to this volume, by undertaking new and often un- or understudied topics, seek to expose some of the many facets of ancient motherhood, both lived and imagined. In so doing, they invite us to think further about how motherhood made the woman—a statement that has at least some resonance even today.

NOTES

1. For example, Dixon (1988); Rousselle (1988); Demand (1994); Hallett, Gold, Lateiner, and Newlands (2006); Burns (2007); Cid López (2009); Augoustakis (2010).

2. Lacey (1968); Rawson (1986) and (1996); Dixon (1992); Saller (1994); Pomeroy (1997); Rawson and Weaver (1997); George (2005); and now Kampen (2009).

3. As translated in Lefkowitz and Fant (2005), no. 267.

4. As translated in Lefkowitz and Fant (2005), no. 349.

5. On this vase, see, for example, Neils and Oakley (2003), 230; Lewis (2002), 16–17; Masser (1995); Williams (1993), 93–94.

6. Lewis (2002), 156. On *choes* and their funerary contexts, see van Hoorn (1951), 49; Hamilton (1992); and Ham (1999).

7. *Corpus Inscriptionum Latinarum* 6.19128. *Graxiae Alexandriae / insignis exempli / ac pudicitiae / quae etiam filios suos / propriis uberibus educavit / Pudens aug. lib. maritus / merenti vix ann XXIIII m III d XVI.* As translated in Lefkowitz and Fant (2005), no. 251.

8. Translation by G. P. Goold (1990).

9. For an excellent overview of the official encouragement of motherhood, in the Augustan period in particular, and of the figure of the mother within imperial families, see Dixon (1988), chap. 4, and now Milnor (2005), esp. chap. 3.

10. The literature on this topic is vast. See, for example, Csillag (1976), 148; Mette-Dittmann (1991); Severy (2003); and Milnor (2005).

11. For a discussion of the *tutela* and inheritance, see esp. Gardner (1986).

12. Csillag (1976), 167–168; Treggiari (1991), 69.

13. Treggiari (1991), 69.

14. Demand (1994), 71–86.

15. On this *stele*, see, for example, Oakley (2003), 186–187; Stewart and Gray (2000); Demand (1994), 124.

16. Oakley (2003), 163 and 192, n. 1.

17. Oakley (2003), 173–174. On mourning children, see also Golden (1988).

18. Roth (2007), 1–24, esp. 17.

19. Webster (2005), 166–168.

20. Of course the interpretation of these casts as mother and child cannot be proven unless DNA evidence were to establish a blood relationship. The reading of affecting gestures as indicating familial relationships has been a preoccupation for observers since the nineteenth century (Eugene Dwyer, personal communication). See now Lazer (2009), 249–258, esp. 252.

21. With articles by Hallett, Gold, Lateiner, and Newlands (2006).

22. On Julia Domna, see most recently Kampen (2009), 82–103; Levick (2007), both with excellent bibliographies. On the titles given to Julia Domna, see esp. Levick (2007), 93, and Langford-Johnson (2005).

23. Kampen (2009), 82–103.

WORKS CITED

Augoustakis, Antony. (2010). *Motherhood and the Other: Fashioning Female Power in Flavian Epic*. Oxford: Oxford University Press.

Burns, Jasper. (2007). *Great Women of Imperial Rome: Mothers and Wives of the Caesars.* London: Routledge.

Cid López, Rosa María. (2009). *Madres y maternidades: Construcciones culturales en la civilización clásica.* Colección alternativas 32. Oviedo: KRK Ediciones.

Cohen, Ada, and Jeremy Rutter, eds. (2007). *Constructions of Childhood in Ancient Greece and Italy.* Princeton: Princeton University Press.

Csillag, Pál. (1976). *The Augustan Laws on Family Relations.* Budapest: Akadémikai Kiadó.

Demand, Nancy. (1994). *Birth, Death, and Motherhood in Classical Greece.* Baltimore: Johns Hopkins University Press.

Dixon, Suzanne. (1988). *The Roman Mother.* Norman: Oklahoma University Press.

———. (1992). *The Roman Family.* Baltimore: Johns Hopkins University Press.

Gardner, Jane. (1986). *Women in Roman Law and Society.* London: Routledge.

George, Michele, ed. (2005). *The Roman Family in the Empire: Rome, Italy, and Beyond.* Oxford: Oxford University Press.

Gold, Barbara. (2006). "How Women (Re)act in Roman Love Poetry: Inhuman She-Wolves and Unhelpful Mothers in Propertius's Elegies." *Helios* 33.2:165–187.

Golden, Mark. (1988). "Did the Ancients Care When Their Children Died?" *Greece and Rome* 35:152–163.

Goold, G. P. (1990). *The Elegies of Sextus Propertius.* Loeb Classical Library. Cambridge, MA: Harvard University Press.

Hallett, Judith. (2006a). "Introduction: Cornelia and Her Maternal Legacy." *Helios* 33.2:119–147.

———. (2006b). "Fulvia, Mother of Iulius Antonius: New Approaches to the Sources on Julia's Adultery at Rome." *Helios* 33.2:149–164.

Ham, Greta. (1999). "The Choes and Anthesteria Reconsidered: Male Maturation Rights and the Peloponnesian Wars." *Bucknell Review* 43:201–221.

Hamilton, Richard. (1992). *Choes and Anthesteria: Athenian Iconography and Ritual.* Ann Arbor: University of Michigan Press.

Hübner, Sabine, and David Ratzan, eds. (2009). *Growing Up Fatherless in Antiquity.* Cambridge: Cambridge University Press.

Kampen, Natalie. (2009). *Family Fictions in Roman Art.* Cambridge: Cambridge University Press.

Lacey, W. K. (1968). *The Family in Classical Greece.* Ithaca, NY: Cornell University Press.

Langford-Johnson, Julie. (2005). "Mater Augustorum, Mater Senatus, Mater Patriae: Succession and Consensus in Severan Ideology." Ph.D. diss., Indiana University.

Lateiner, Donald. (2006). "*Procul est parentes*: Mothers in Ovid's *Metamorphoses*." *Helios* 33.2:189–201.

Lazer, Estelle. (2009). *Resurrecting Pompeii.* London: Routledge.

Lefkowitz, Mary, and Maureen Fant. (2005). *Women's Life in Greece and Rome: A Sourcebook in Translation.* 3rd ed. Baltimore: Johns Hopkins University Press.

Levick, Barbara. (2007). *Julia Domna, the Syrian Empress.* London: Routledge.

Lewis, Sian. (2002). *The Athenian Woman: An Iconographic Handbook*. London: Routledge.

Masser, N. (1995). "Images de la famille sur les vases attiques à figures rouges à l'époque classique (480–430 av. J.C.)." *Annales d'histoire de l'art et d'archéologie* 17:23–38.

Mette-Dittmann, Angelika. (1991). *Die Ehegesetze des Augustus: Eine Untersuchung im Rahmen der Gesellschaftspolitik des Princeps*. Stuttgart: Steiner.

Milnor, Kristina. (2005). *Gender, Domesticity, and the Age of Augustus*. Oxford: Oxford University Press.

Neils, Jenifer, and John Oakley, eds. (2003). *Coming of Age in Ancient Greece: Images of Childhood from the Classical Past*. New Haven: Yale University Press.

Newlands, Carole. (2006). "Mothers in Statius's Poetry: Sorrows and Surrogates." *Helios* 33.2:203–226.

Oakley, John. (2003). "Death and the Child." In Jenifer Neils and John Oakley, eds., *Coming of Age in Ancient Greece: Images of Childhood from the Classical Past*, 163–194. New Haven: Yale University Press.

Pomeroy, Sarah. (1997). *Families in Classical and Hellenistic Greece*. Oxford: Clarendon Press.

Rawson, Beryl. (1986). *The Family in Ancient Rome: New Perspectives*. Ithaca, NY: Cornell University Press.

———, ed. (1996). *Marriage, Divorce, and Children in Ancient Rome*. Oxford: Clarendon Press.

———. (2003). *Children and Childhood in Roman Italy*. Oxford: Oxford University Press.

Rawson, Beryl, and Paul Weaver, eds. (1997). *The Roman Family in Italy: Status, Sentiment, Space*. Oxford: Clarendon Press.

Roth, Ulrike. (2007). *Thinking Tools: Agricultural Slavery between Evidence and Models*. London: Institute of Classical Studies, School of Advanced Study, University of London.

Rousselle, Aline. (1988). *Porneia: On Desire and the Body in Antiquity*. Trans. Felicia Pheasant. Oxford: Blackwell.

Saller, Richard. (1994). *Patriarchy, Property, and Death in the Roman Family*. Cambridge: Cambridge University Press.

Severy, Beth. (2003). *Augustus and the Family at the Birth of the Roman Empire*. London: Routledge.

Stewart, Andrew, and Celina Gray. (2000). "Confronting the Other: Childbirth, Aging, and Death on an Attic Tombstone at Harvard." In Beth Cohen, ed., *Not the Classical Ideal: Athens and the Construction of the Other in Greek Art*, 248–274. Leiden: Brill.

Story, Louise. (2005). "Many Women at Elite Colleges Set Career Path to Motherhood." *New York Times*, Sept. 20, A1 and A18.

Treggiari, Susan. (1991). *Roman Marriage*. Oxford: Clarendon Press.

Uzzi, Jeannine. (2005). *Children in the Visual Arts of Ancient Rome*. Cambridge: Cambridge University Press.

Van Hoorn, G. (1951). *Choes and Anthesteria*. Leiden: Brill.

Warner, Rex, trans. (1944). *The Medea*. Reprinted in David Grene and Richmond Lattimore, eds., *Euripides* I (1955). Chicago: University of Chicago Press.

Watson, Patricia. (1995). *Ancient Stepmothers: Myth, Misogyny, and Reality*. Leiden: Brill.

Webster, Jane. (2005). "Archaeologies of Slavery and Servitude: Bringing 'New World' Perspectives to Roman Britain." *Journal of Roman Archaeology* 18:161–179.

Williams, Dyfri. (1993). "Women on Athenian Vases: Problems of Interpretation." In Averil Cameron and Amélie Kuhrt, eds., *Images of Women in Antiquity*, 92–106. Detroit: Wayne State University Press.

TWO

Maternity and Miasma

DRESS AND THE TRANSITION
FROM *PARTHENOS* TO *GUNĒ*

Mireille M. Lee

As well articulated by Robbie Davis-Floyd, pregnancy is a rite of passage.[1] Being "both a state and a becoming,"[2] pregnancy represents a liminal period in a woman's life. Although certainly a physiological phenomenon, women's experiences of pregnancy are very much culturally determined. Davis-Floyd notes that in the United States prior to World War II, pregnancy was rarely discussed and pregnant women were generally secluded in their homes.[3] Today, American women remain engaged in most aspects of their personal and professional lives throughout their pregnancies; as a result, their personal experiences of pregnancy are squarely in the public sphere. But although pregnancy has "come out of the closet," in the words of Davis-Floyd, it is still laden with taboo as society attempts to reconcile its contradictions: "the pregnant woman, neither childless nor mother, public proof of a sexuality properly kept private, walking representative of nature in a culture that seeks to deny nature's power . . . still crosses too many categories for comfort."[4] American women navigate the liminal period of pregnancy by means of various "rituals": visits to the doctor or midwife; medical tests such as ultrasound and amniocentesis; reading books about pregnancy and birth; childbirth education classes; the baby shower.

Women also negotiate the liminality of pregnancy by wearing special-purpose maternity garments.[5] Such garments are necessary on a functional level; since modern "international-style" garments are typically cut and sewn to fit the body, maternity garments are designed to accommodate the changing shape of the pregnant woman. But maternity dress has important psychological and ideological functions as well. According to Jennifer Musial: "Once a woman chooses to wear said attire, she publicly announces her pregnancy, and, in effect, her embodied experience becomes public dis-

course."[6] In this way, pregnancy may be seen as a kind of performance, and maternity dress a sort of costume. A basic tenet of dress theory is that the dressed body both reflects and constructs individual identity.[7] But when identity is in flux, as during pregnancy, the relationship between dress and the body becomes problematic. In her study of the iconography of maternity dress in popular culture, Musial argues:

> As a liminal body, pregnant corporeality is threatening because it refuses categorization. This potentially transgressive embodiment is diffused through maternity wear, either through infantilizing or matronizing the wearer.[8]

In other words, the pregnant woman, no longer a child but not yet a mother (for first pregnancies, at least), is made to fit acceptable social categories by means of her dress.[9]

Certainly women's experiences of pregnancy were different in antiquity from what they are today; likewise, maternity dress was conceived differently. This essay considers the visual, literary, and epigraphic evidence for maternity dress in ancient Greece, from the Archaic to the Hellenistic periods, in order to reconstruct its social functions. It will be seen that in antiquity, as today, maternity dress was an essential element in the construction of new motherhood, both for the individual woman and for her community.

IMAGES OF PREGNANT WOMEN IN ANCIENT GREEK ART

Visual representations of pregnant women are relatively rare in ancient Greek art.[10] Because of the draped arrangement of Greek garments, the identification of a female figure as pregnant is not always secure.[11] In general, the images can be classified into three broad categories: votive plaques of the Archaic and Classical periods; Classical and Hellenistic terracotta figurines; and late Classical funerary reliefs depicting women in childbirth.

Votive Plaques

The best preserved of the polychrome wooden plaques discovered in a cave near the village of Pitsà in the northern Peloponnese depicts four women who are approaching an altar and are accompanied by three

FIGURE 2.1. *Wooden votive plaque from Pitsà, ca. 540–520 BCE. Athens, National Archaeological Museum, inv. 16464. © Hellenic Ministry of Culture and Tourism/ Archaeological Receipts Fund.*

younger males, the smallest of whom leads a sheep to sacrifice (fig. 2.1). All the figures are depicted wearing vivid blue and red garments. The first three women wear the garments typical of adult women in this period: belted *peploi* with *himatia* draped over their shoulders and arms.[12] The figure at the far left is completely enveloped in a blue *himation*, her extended hands discernible beneath the cloth. Unfortunately, the plaque is broken at this point, and it is unclear whether the garment covered her head as well. Matthew Dillon has identified this scene as a pregnant woman sacrificing to the nymphs.[13] Nymphs, named by inscription on the plaque, were often worshiped by women seeking their protection during childbirth.[14] Whether the draped woman is indeed pregnant is debatable; certainly no distinct "baby bulge" is discernible, though it may be masked by her draped garment.

A late Archaic marble votive relief from the Athenian Acropolis depicts what appears to be a family sacrificing a sow to Athena, perhaps in celebration of the *Apaturia*, a three-day festival during which children were enrolled in their father's *phratry* (fig. 2.2).[15] Two young boys (perhaps twins?) bring the sacrificial victim; a young girl follows, standing between a *himation*-clad man and a woman wearing *chiton* and *himation* (both adult figures are cut off at the top). The woman's *chiton* protrudes away from her body below the belt in an unusual manner, and some scholars have interpreted this figure as pregnant.[16] The effect is not realistic, and one wonders whether the sculptor intended instead to show the woman postpartum, as might befit a festival establishing a young child's legitimacy.

FIGURE 2.2. *Votive marble relief to Athena, ca. 490 BCE. Athens, Acropolis Museum, inv. 581.* © *Hellenic Ministry of Culture and Tourism/Acropolis Museum.*

A fragmentary marble votive relief from the sanctuary of Artemis-Eileithyia on the island of Delos depicts a standing female accompanied by a male figure leading a sacrificial animal (fig. 2.3). The woman performs a gesture of adoration toward the goddess (partially preserved in a joining fragment). Her unbelted garment billows away from her body, leading the excavator to interpret the scene as a pregnant woman praying to the goddess for "une heureuse délivrance."[17] A second votive relief from the same sanctuary depicts a woman, also wearing an unbelted garment, holding an offering for the goddess. The excavator suggests that the object in her hand may be a necklace of the type pregnant women dedicated to the goddess Eileithyia.[18]

A successful birth is commemorated in a marble votive relief in the Metropolitan Museum of Art dating to the late fifth century BCE (fig. 2.4).[19] In the center of the plaque, the exhausted mother is shown slumped on a stool. Her garments are in disarray, reflecting her recent ordeal, and her right breast is visible.[20] The midwife stands behind her, supporting the mother with one hand and holding the swaddled infant in the other. The left side of the relief is broken, but a standing female divinity is preserved, along with the hand of a male divinity; perhaps they are Hygieia and Asklepios, whom the woman thanks for their protection.[21]

The votive plaques show women in the presence (actual or implied) of a female divinity from whom each seeks protection, either for herself or for her child. Whether the women can be identified as pregnant (or recently pregnant) is not secure on the basis of physiognomy alone. Likewise, the types of garments they wear, *chitones* and *himatia*, are indistinguishable from those worn by other adult women. On the other hand, the draping and girding of their garments may indicate "maternity" dress. The woman

FIGURE 2.3. *Marble votive relief from the sanctuary of Artemis-Eileithyia, Classical period. Delos Museum, inv. A 3154. © Hellenic Ministry of Culture and Tourism/Delos Museum.*

FIGURE 2.4. *Marble votive relief, late fifth century BCE. New York, Metropolitan Museum of Art, inv. 24.97.92. © The Metropolitan Museum of Art/Art Resource, NY.*

on the painted plaque from Pitsà is completely enveloped by her *himation*, while her female companions wear their *himatia* draped in the conventional way. The woman on the relief from Delos is not so well preserved, but it is clear that her garment is unbelted so that it billows away from her body in an unusual manner. The dress of the adult woman on the relief from the Athenian Acropolis is identical to that of other adult women (belted *chiton* surmounted by *himation* draped over shoulders and arms), perhaps an

indication that she is, in fact, no longer pregnant, but has recently given birth.

Terracotta Figurines

Terracotta figurines representing pregnant women date primarily to the Classical and Hellenistic periods.[22] It is possible to identify at least three different types: votive figurines; so-called Tanagra figurines; and figurines representing comic characters from ancient Greek drama.

The votive figurines comprise the most cohesive group in terms of their iconography and function.[23] Most are represented without garments, and are hence easily identifiable as pregnant.[24] Because they were excavated from sanctuary contexts, it is likely that these figurines were dedicated in an effort to manage the risks and discomforts of pregnancy. Although no garments are indicated among this group, they are not entirely "naked" either. Figure 2.5, for example, wears a cord above the abdomen and below the breasts, in the center of which is a small indentation representing an amulet, either for the protection of the pregnant dedicator or to help bring about a beyond-term birth.[25]

The "Tanagra" figurines (e.g., fig. 2.6) include both dressed and undressed examples. Unfortunately, the archaeological context is unknown for many of the figurines, which were popular among collectors during the nineteenth century.[26] Although the authenticity of many Tanagra figurines is suspect, properly excavated examples are typically funerary offerings; perhaps the pregnant examples were buried with women who had died during pregnancy or childbirth. In most cases, the woman can be clearly identified as pregnant on account of her protruding abdomen; some figures also gesticulate toward or touch the belly.[27] Figure 2.6 has been identified by some as wearing a special abdominal binder.[28] On closer inspection, however, it is clear that she has lifted her garment to reveal her legs, creating a mass of fabric over the abdomen.[29]

A series of terracotta figurines depicting actors from Middle Comedy may be identifiable as "pregnant" on account of their padded bellies (e.g., fig. 2.7). Since these figurines represent male actors dressed as fictional characters from Greek drama, they are not the best source for actual maternity garments worn by real women. The identification of "pregnancy" among these examples is likewise debatable; caricatures or grotesques of obese, naked women have been identified as aging *hetairai* (courtesans),[30] and it may be that the dressed figurines should likewise be interpreted as old women.[31] In either case, their dress is not distinctive in any way.

FIGURE 2.5. *(Right) Terracotta votive figurine, Hellenistic period. Paris, Musée du Louvre, inv. CA 5231. © 1970 Musée du Louvre/Pierre et Maurice Chuzeville.*

FIGURE 2.6. *(Bottom left) Terracotta figurine, Hellenistic. Athens, National Archaeological Museum, inv. 12884. © Hellenic Ministry of Culture and Tourism/Archaeological Receipts Fund.*

FIGURE 2.7. *(Bottom right) Terracotta figurine, third century BCE. Corinth Archaeological Museum, inv. MF-12046. © American School of Classical Studies at Athens, Corinth Excavations, I. Ioannidou and L. Bartzioti; and Hellenic Ministry of Culture and Tourism/Archaeological Receipts Fund.*

Funerary Reliefs

Another potential source for information about maternity garments is a series of funerary monuments of the fourth century BCE depicting scenes of childbirth (e.g., fig. 1.3 in this volume).[32] Whether intended to commemorate a woman who had died in labor, or the attending midwife,[33] the conventional composition includes the woman reclining on a *kline* (small bed or couch) surrounded by standing female figures who support her under the arms; sometimes an older male figure (her husband? father?) clasps her hand or bows his head in mourning. The reclining woman is not represented with a protruding abdomen to indicate pregnancy, but with the slightly rounded belly of an ideal *gunē*, that is, a woman who has given birth. Her garments are indistinguishable from those worn by other adult women (primarily the *chiton* and *himation*), though they are unbelted at the waist and often slip off the shoulder, sometimes revealing one or both breasts.[34] While it cannot be established whether these garments were worn during the pregnancy, or represent special garments worn during labor (or, indeed, are idealized images that reflect neither), like the garments depicted in the votive plaques and figurines, they are represented as unbelted. Throughout Greek literature, laboring women are described as having loosened garments and unbound hair.[35]

Although representations of pregnant women are rare in Greek art, they are consistent in all media from the Archaic to the Hellenistic periods. The garments worn by pregnant women do not appear to be different in structure from those worn by other adult women; they are simply worn unbelted to accommodate the woman's growing abdomen.[36] Traditional Bedouin dress, which is draped and pinned exactly like the ancient Greek garment conventionally known as the *peplos*, offers a good ethnographic parallel.[37] Not only is this garment adaptable to a woman's body throughout her pregnancy, but the shoulder-fasteners facilitate breast-feeding.[38]

The absence of special maternity garments would have allowed women to conceal their pregnancies, at least in the early months. Likewise, protective amulets worn next to the body, underneath garments, would not have been visible to the community. But if pregnant women were not always immediately identifiable by their dress, the liminal period of pregnancy was nevertheless strictly regulated by the community by means of ritual.

As in many cultures, including our own, pregnancy in ancient Greece was constructed as a dangerous, liminal period, both for the mother and for the community. While in modern America, pregnant women negotiate their pregnancies by means of various secular "rituals," in ancient Greece they sought divine protection, as reflected in the votive plaques and figurines discussed in the previous section, as well as the use of magical amulets.[39] But the participation of pregnant women in ritual was highly regulated, on account of fear of pollution. "Maternity garments" play an important role in ritual, symbolizing the protection of the mother and her unborn child, as well as the community as a whole.

While the visual and archaeological evidence demonstrates that pregnant women visited Greek sanctuaries dedicated to female divinities associated with childbirth, the textual sources are ambivalent about their presence in other religious contexts. Aristotle suggests that pregnant women be required to visit the sanctuaries of divinities associated with childbirth (*Politics* 1335b12–16), but some sanctuaries prohibited pregnant women. Expectant and nursing mothers were banned from the mysteries of Despoina at Lykosura, for example, and pregnant women (and animals about to give birth) were not allowed to visit the hill in Arcadia that was believed to be the birthplace of Zeus.[40] In these cases, the prohibition seems to stem from a conflict of categories: those expecting a child should not participate in rites of fertility or visit a mythical birthplace.

According to Robert Parker, "the pregnant woman was not herself polluting, but it is interesting that she was particularly exposed to pollution by others."[41] The notion that pregnant women were not considered a source of pollution is surprising given that they exist between social categories, as discussed above. From a structuralist perspective, perhaps pregnant women were not polluting because they do not menstruate.[42] On the other hand, it seems likely that pregnant women, if not actually polluting, were a *potential* source of pollution, given the very real dangers associated with pregnancy and childbirth.[43] Hence, the concern that pregnant women were "particularly exposed to pollution by others" may in fact mask a concern for the protection of the community from potential pollution.

Whether pregnant women were viewed as a source of, or in need of protection from, pollution, their votive dedications indicate a certain vulnerability during this period of tremendous physical and psychic transition. The women's garments may be a further reflection of this vulnerability; their garments completely envelop them, creating a visual, if not a

physical, barrier between the pregnant body and the community.[44] On one hand, the fabric conceals the swelling abdomen of the pregnant woman; on the other hand, it comprises a layer of protection from external dangers. Given the important ritual function of garments in the cult of Artemis in particular (see below), this enveloping garment may symbolize the protection of the goddess, both to the community and to the wearer herself. From a phenomenological perspective, the pregnant woman would have sensed the protection of the goddess in the fabric touching her skin.

Importantly, such an enveloping garment would have actually concealed the liminal status of the pregnant woman from the community (unlike modern maternity garments, which often seem to "broadcast" a woman's pregnancy). As the pregnant woman is in between social categories, her social role is erased, in part by means of the concealing garment. The transitional period of pregnancy would have been especially fraught for first-time pregnancies, when the woman was no longer a *parthenos* but not yet a *gunē*. Given the particular dangers associated with the transition from maidenhood to motherhood, pregnant women supplicated the goddess with one thing over which they did hold control: their dress.

MATERNITY DRESS AND THE CULT OF ARTEMIS

Within the Greek pantheon, Artemis was the special protector of women and girls, especially at critical transitional periods such as menarche and childbirth. Although several divinities received garments as dedications, the cult of Artemis was unique in the very personal nature of such offerings.[45] According to the Hippocratic *Peri parthenion* ("On the Diseases of Virgins"), the traditional remedy for delayed menarche was for the girl to dedicate her most splendid garments to Artemis.[46]

Various literary and epigraphic sources confirm the practice of dedicating garments to Artemis following childbirth. Several epigrams in the *Palatine Anthology* (e.g., 6.146, 6.201–202, 6.270–274) describe offerings made by new mothers grateful for a successful delivery. Euripides' *Iphigenia among the Taurians* concludes with an *aition* for the dedication of garments at the sanctuary to Artemis at Brauron, in rural Attica:[47]

And you, Iphigenia, in the holy meadows of Brauron must serve this goddess as her temple warder. When you die, you will lie buried here, and they will dedicate for your delight the finely woven garments which women who die in childbirth leave behind in their houses. (1462–1467)[48]

Although the garments themselves have not survived, inscribed *stelai* recording the inventories of the sanctuary illustrate the significance of such dedications.[49] The garments are listed according to type, including variations of *chitones* and *himatia*, but also several that are otherwise unknown to modern scholars. Descriptive categories include fabric, color, decoration, and form of garments, as well as their condition.[50] The names of the dedicators were also listed when known.[51]

On the dedications at Brauron, one scholar remarked: "It must all have looked something like a large women's clothes store at an end-of-season clearance sale."[52] But the care with which the garment-dedications were recorded suggests their careful organization, the monetary value of the garments, and the social and ritual significance of the women's dedications. The high status of the dedicators themselves has been established by means of prosopography.[53] Yet despite their wealth (or rather, the wealth of their husbands, by whom they are identified in the inscriptions), women deliberately chose to dedicate ephemeral garments as opposed to more lasting monuments such as sculptures. Lin Foxhall and Karen Stears suggest that women dedicated garments because they were their particular property, passed down from mother to daughter via *pherne* ("trousseau").[54] Certainly women in ancient Greece were ideologically associated with all kinds of textiles, whether or not they wove them themselves.[55] But offerings of garments that had been worn by the dedicators themselves would have carried special significance, particularly if they had been worn during pregnancy and birth, as suggested by some of the literary and visual sources.[56]

THE ECHINOS RELIEF

Remarkable pictorial evidence for the dedication of garments to Artemis following childbirth has come to light in the form of a late fourth-century votive relief from her sanctuary at Echinos, at Lamia in northern Greece (fig. 2.8).[57] The goddess, in larger scale than her devotees, stands on the right side of the frame, behind an altar. She is identifiable by her torch, and also the quiver of arrows once visible behind her left shoulder. She wears an over-girded *peplos*; a second garment draped over her shoulder partially obscures a *stele* against which she leans. Approaching the altar from the left is a young boy leading the sacrificial victim, a horned cow or young steer. He is followed by a female figure wearing an over-girded *peplos* with her hair pulled back into a bun. She holds an infant, presumably a girl on account of the drapery and hairstyle, who extends her arms toward the goddess. Be-

FIGURE 2.8. *Marble votive relief, ca. 300 BCE. Lamia, Archaeological Museum, inv. AE 1041. Drawing by Glynnis Fawkes.*

hind this figure is a female attendant holding a small jug and bearing a basket on her head containing fruits and cakes as dedications. At the far left of the scene, a standing female figure wears a garment (*chiton?*) so voluminous it drapes on the ground, with a mantle drawn over her head so that her face is obscured. (Sadly, the relief is broken at exactly this point, so that it is unclear to what degree her facial features were originally visible.) The woman extends one hand from beneath the garment in a gesture of adoration toward the goddess; in the other hand she holds a *pyxis*, perhaps containing incense.[58] At the top of the frame, in very low relief, articles of clothing are rendered as if hanging from a clothesline. From right to left it is possible to identify: a sleeveless *chiton* or chemise; a sash or belt with fringed ends; two fringed textiles, one wider than the other, perhaps worn as draped *himatia* or even *peploi*; a tunic with short sleeves; and a pair of low boots or shoes.

Although scholars agree that the relief depicts a sacrificial scene in honor of Artemis, and that the garments on display represent dedications in her sanctuary, the specific identities of the dedicants, and the motivation for the sacrifice, have been variously interpreted. The original publication identified the central figure holding the infant as the young mother, and the larger, draped, figure behind as her mother or mother-in-law.[59] Alternatively, Yvette Morizot interprets the standing draped figure as the mother (and therefore the dedicator of the plaque); she is represented in larger scale than the others, wears luxurious garments that completely envelop her body as a reflection of her *aidos* (modesty), and is accompanied by servants, including a wet-nurse who carries the infant.[60] Although most have identified the scene as the presentation of the infant to the goddess, in order to se-

cure her continued protection, Morizot suggests that the mother is the central figure in the ritual; the sacrifice marks the end of her lying-in, and her ritual purification (implied by the *pyxis* containing incense) prior to her reincorporation into society as an adult *gunē*.[61] In this light, the garments in the background are not generic decorative elements identifying the sanctuary as that of Artemis; they refer specifically to the successful pregnancy and childbirth of the dedicant, brought about by the goddess, to whom she gives thanks.

The dedication of maternity garments to Artemis symbolizes the successful management of miasma in the transition from *parthenos* to *gunē*. The mother-to-be was removed from society during the liminal period of her lying-in, during which time she was both polluted and polluting of all who entered the household.[62] Following the birth, purity was restored by means of ritual, and the new mother was reincorporated into society (a topic presented fully in the following essay).[63] The anxieties surrounding this significant social and psychic transition from maidenhood to motherhood are nonetheless managed by means of dress. Garments worn during the period of pregnancy and childbirth symbolized the protection of the goddess. Following her successful birth, the new mother dedicated these garments as a gesture of thanks, but also to reflect her new social role, which required new garments.

NOTES

Thank you to the editors for the invitation to participate in this project, and to Glynnis Fawkes for her excellent drawing. I am grateful to Vanderbilt University for financial support to reproduce the images. This essay is dedicated to Chloe, who teaches me about motherhood every day.

1. Davis-Floyd (1992), 22–43.
2. Davis-Floyd (1992), 23.
3. Davis-Floyd (1992), 25.
4. Davis-Floyd (1992), 25.
5. Maternity dress is surprisingly understudied and undertheorized, despite the recent surge of scholarly interest in motherhood and in dress across cultures. For recent approaches to motherhood, see the first essay in this volume. For good introductions to the interdisciplinary field of dress studies, see Eicher et al. (2008) and Roach-Higgins et al. (1995). The *Berg Encyclopedia of World Dress and Fashion*, edited by Eicher (2010), is now the essential reference.

6. Musial (2004), 128.

7. For the dynamic relationship between the body and dress, see Entwistle (2001).

8. Musial (2004), 128.

9. It will be seen that in ancient Greece dress was also employed to "sanitize" (Musial [2004], 130) the pregnant body, though in a different way.

10. Dierichs (2002), esp. 71–102; Gourevitch and Grmek (1998); Gourevitch (1988). See also Speert (2004), 49–50, 60–61, and 64, although several of his identifications are suspect (see below). Interestingly, images of mothers nursing infants are likewise nearly absent from Greek art; see Bonfante (1997), and now Patricia Salzman-Mitchell in this volume.

11. As noted by Gourevitch and Grmek (1998), "Parfois, il est difficile de choisir entre grossesse et obésité, voire hydropisie" (314).

12. The term *peplos* is highly problematic, but is retained here for ease of discussion. A pinned, woolen garment appears in early Greek sculpture and vase painting, disappears during the Archaic period, and then reappears in the early Classical period. Literary sources are unclear as to the name of this garment. It was identified as a *peplos* by scholars in the nineteenth century. See Lee (2005).

13. Dillon (2002), 228. The figure is not identified as pregnant in Jennifer Larson's comprehensive study of Greek nymphs; see Larson (2001), 232–233, and fig. 5.1.

14. Dillon (2002), 229; Larson (2001), esp. 5, 131–134, 183, 238.

15. Palagia (1995).

16. Lehmann-Hartleben (1926), 20; recently revived by Neils (2003), 145 and fig. 5.

17. Demangel (1922), 78. The excavator dates the relief to the Classical period on the basis of style.

18. Demangel (1922), 85–86, fig. 18.

19. Demand (1994), 89, and pl. 1; Van Straten (1981), 100, and fig. 43.

20. In sculpture of the Classical period, women's breasts are sometimes exposed accidentally as a result of the action of the wearer. See Cohen (1997), 70–72.

21. Interestingly, the iconography of the new mother is identical to that of women who died in childbirth, as depicted on funerary monuments of the same period (see fig. 1.3 of this volume, and below). In contrast to the funerary images, the success of the birth here in fig. 2.4 is confirmed by the depiction of the swaddled infant.

22. Schematic terracotta groups from Cyprus representing birthing scenes date as early as the seventh century BCE; Gourevitch (1988), 47.

23. Van Straten considers figurines representing pregnant women a subset of the anatomical votives dedicated to Asklepios and other divinities as a request (or thanks) for healing; see esp. Van Straten (1981), 98–100.

24. Though at least one scholar has suggested a diagnosis of dropsy; see Van Straten (1981), 99, n. 172.

25. Gourevitch (1988), 44 and 46, discusses such amulets, which were used by both the Greeks and the Romans, but does not identify an amulet cord on this figu-

rine. For birthing amulets specifically, see Hanson (2004); for ancient uterine magic generally, see Aubert (1989).

26. Jeammet (2007).

27. An excellent example of the undressed type is Paris, Musée du Louvre, D 198, illustrated in Gourevitch and Grmek (1998), 313, fig. 246, and Gourevitch (1988), 43.

28. For example, Speert (2004), 61, fig. 2-33.

29. Indeed, many of the Tanagra figurines wear garments that seem to emphasize the abdomen, even if they are not identifiably pregnant.

30. See especially Thompson (1954), 90–91.

31. This is very likely the case for Speert (2004), fig. 2-13, a figurine of a woman holding a child from the Staatliche Museen, Berlin. Her sagging breasts and protruding belly, together with her wrinkled face and bent posture, identify her as an old nurse, not a pregnant woman.

32. See esp. Stewart and Gray (2000); Demand (1995); Vedder (1988).

33. Demand (1995).

34. A few later examples are belted under the breasts, as was the fashion in the late Classical and Hellenistic periods.

35. Aubert (1989), esp. 444 and n. 48; 449 and n. 59. A unique late Classical limestone group in the Metropolitan Museum of Art has the same iconography as the funerary reliefs, and may also have had a funerary function. See Dierichs (2002), fig. 44; Vedder (1988), pl. 25.2.

36. Soranus of Ephesos (second century CE) describes the use of abdominal and breast-binders by pregnant women, but these are adaptations of everyday dress in the Hellenistic and Roman periods, not special: *Gynecology* 1.55; 2.6 [70b]; 2.8 [77]; 2.24 [93] (Temkin [1991]). Speert (2004) discusses maternity garments. See Soranus on the binders, though Speert's identification of such garments in the visual sources is erroneous: see 60–61, and figs. 2-33, 2-38.

It is possible that garments worn during pregnancy were differentiated from regular garments by means of color or decoration, which has not been preserved in the visual sources. On the other hand, the blue *himation* of the woman in the Pitsà plaque does not distinguish her from the other worshipers.

37. For the *peplos*, see Lee (2005), esp. 61, fig. 5.6 for the traditional Bedouin garment.

38. Specialized nursing garments seem to be absent also from ancient Greek dress, though see the unique Archaic limestone *kourotrophos* from the cemetery at Megara Hyblaea in Sicily, whose garment features strategically placed openings through which she suckles twins. Boardman (1995), 162–163 and fig. 174. For breast-feeding in Greek and Roman literature, see Salzman-Mitchell in this volume.

39. Above, n. 25, and below, n. 41.

40. Parker (1983), 49.

41. Parker (1983), 49. The perceived vulnerability of pregnant women is suggested also by their use of magical amulets to protect against complications during pregnancy, including miscarriage. See Aubert (1989), 426.

42. For Greek attitudes toward menstruating women see Cole (2004), 108–111.

43. Cole (2004), 106–108, 113.

44. A similar argument has been made recently in reference to women's veiling practices: Llewellyn-Jones (2003), 189–214.

45. For dedications of garments to Artemis, see most recently Morizot (2004); Foxhall and Stears (2000); also Dillon (2002), 19–23; Cole (1998), 36–39; and Demand (1994), 87–91. For a general overview of dedications of garments in Greek sanctuaries see Lee (1999), 218–269.

46. Delayed menarche was thought to cause suicidal tendencies, in particular a desire for strangulation. The author of the *Peri parthenion* denounced the practice of dedicating garments to Artemis, in favor of quick marriage and defloration. See esp. King (1998), 75–88, with earlier references.

47. On the extra-mural character of Artemis sanctuaries, see Cole (1998).

48. Translation by Kovacs (1999).

49. The so-called Brauronion inscriptions recovered from the Athenian Acropolis are generally acknowledged to be copies of those discovered at Brauron, which remain unpublished. The primary publication of the Athenian inscriptions is Linders (1972), now supplemented by Cleland (2005). Though the inscriptions date to the middle of the fourth century BCE, they presumably reflect a long-standing practice.

50. A few garments are identified as "new," presumably meaning unworn. Articles described as *rhakos* are not, as previously suggested, menstrual "rags" dedicated by girls at menarche, but rather older dedications that had become tattered over time. For discussion, see Linders (1972), 58–59.

51. Some garments were inscribed by means of weaving; others were stored inside a case tagged with the name of the dedicator.

52. Van Straten (1981), 99. As a rejoinder, Dillon (2002) suggests: "it is more probably a Parisian boutique which should be imagined . . . clothes draped over statues, some in boxes, some hanging in racks, all meticulously recorded from year to year in the inventories published at Athens" (21).

53. Osborne (1985), 154–172, discussed in Demand (1994), 90; and Dillon (2002), 22.

54. Foxhall and Stears (2000), 11–12.

55. The literature on the association between women and textile production is extensive. For an overview, see Papadopoulou-Belmehdi (1994).

56. The Brauronion inscriptions list garments that are unlikely to have been used as maternity dress, including men's and children's garments and several identified as "half-woven." Although the specific occasions for the dedication of these garments are not recorded, it is clear that women were the primary producers and dedicators of all types of garments.

57. The primary publication of the relief, now in the Lamia museum (inv. no. AE 1041), is Dakoronia and Gounaropolou (1992). For further discussion, see esp. Morizot (2004); also Dillon (2002), 231–233; Cole (1998), 34–35.

58. Morizot (2004), 162.

59. Dakoronia and Gounaropolou (1992), 220, 221–222; accepted by Cole (1998), 34–35.

60. Morizot (2004), 162–163. Dillon (2002) likewise identifies this figure as the mother on the basis of her larger scale, and also the shape of her body, noting "it is not long since she had her baby" (232). As discussed above in the context of the votive reliefs, the voluminous garments obscure the shape of the woman's body, so that it is difficult to tell if a woman is represented as (recently) pregnant.

61. Morizot (2004), 168–169.

62. Parker (1983), 49–50.

63. For the restoration of purity following childbirth, see Parker (1983), 50–52.

WORKS CITED

Aubert, Jean-Jacques. (1989). "Threatened Wombs: Aspects of Ancient Uterine Magic." *Greek, Roman, and Byzantine Studies* 30:412–449.

Boardman, John. (1995). *Greek Sculpture: The Late Classical Period*. London: Thames and Hudson.

Bonfante, Larissa. (1997). "Nursing Mothers in Classical Art." In Ann O. Koloski-Ostrow and Claire L. Lyons, eds., *Naked Truths: Women, Sexuality, and Gender in Classical Art and Archaeology*, 174–196. London: Routledge.

Cleland, Liza. (2005). *The Brauron Clothing Catalogues: Text, Analysis, Glossary, and Translation*. BAR International Series 1428. Oxford: Joan and Erica Hedges.

Cohen, Beth. (1997). "Divesting the Female Breast of Clothes in Classical Sculpture." In Ann O. Koloski-Ostrow and Claire L. Lyons, eds., *Naked Truths: Women, Sexuality, and Gender in Classical Art and Archaeology*, 66–92. London: Routledge.

Cole, Susan Guettel. (1998). "Domesticating Artemis." In Sue Blundell and Margaret Williamson, eds., *The Sacred and the Feminine in Ancient Greece*, 27–43. London: Routledge.

———. (2004). *Landscapes, Gender, and Ritual Space: The Ancient Greek Experience*. Berkeley: University of California Press.

Dakoronia, Fanouria, and Lukretia Gounaropolou. (1992). "Artemiskult auf einem neuen Weihrelief aus Achinos bei Lamia." *Mitteilungen des Deutschen Archäologischen Instituts, Athenische Abteilung* 107:217–227.

Davis-Floyd, Robbie. (1992). *Birth as an American Rite of Passage*. Berkeley: University of California Press.

Demand, Nancy. (1994). *Birth, Death, and Motherhood in Classical Greece*. Baltimore: Johns Hopkins University Press.

———. (1995). "Monuments, Midwives, and Gynecology." In Philip J. van der Eijk et al., eds., *Ancient Medicine in Its Socio-Cultural Context*, 1:275–290. Amsterdam: Rodopi.

Demangel, Robert. (1922). "Fouilles de Délos: Un sanctuaire d'Artémis-Eileithyia à l'est du Cynthe." *Bulletin de Correspondance Hellénique* 46:58–93.

Dierichs, Angelika. (2002). *Von der Götter Geburt und der Frauen Niederkunft.* Mainz: von Zabern.

Dillon, Matthew. (2002). *Girls and Women in Classical Greek Religion.* London: Routledge.

Eicher, Joanne B., ed. (2010). *Berg Encyclopedia of World Dress and Fashion.* Oxford: Berg.

Eicher, Joanne B., Sandra Lee Evenson, and Hazel A. Lutz, eds. (2008). *The Visible Self: Global Perspectives on Dress, Culture, and Society.* 3rd ed. New York: Fairchild.

Entwistle, Joanne. (2001). "The Dressed Body." In Joanne Entwistle and Elizabeth Wilson, eds., *Body Dressing,* 33–58. Oxford: Berg.

Foxhall, Lin, and Karen Stears. (2000). "Redressing the Balance: Dedications of Clothing to Artemis and the Order of Life Stages." In Moira Donald and Linda Hurcombe, eds., *Gender and Material Culture in Historical Perspective,* 3–16. New York: St. Martin's Press.

Gourevitch, Danielle. (1988). "Grossesse et accouchement dans l'iconographie antique." *Dossiers histoire et archéologie* 123:42–48.

Gourevitch, Danielle, and Mirko D. Grmek. (1998). *Les maladies dans l'art antique.* Paris: Fayard.

Hanson, Ann Ellis. (2004). "A Long-Lived 'Quick-Birther' (*okytokion*)." In Véronique Dasen, ed., *Naissance et petite enfance dans l'Antiquité,* 265–280. Göttingen: Vandenhoeck and Ruprecht.

Jeammet, Violaine, ed. (2007). *Tanagras: De l'objet de collection à l'objet archéologique.* Paris: Musée du Louvre.

King, Helen. (1998). *Hippocrates' Woman: Reading the Female Body in Ancient Greece.* London: Routledge.

Kovacs, David. (1999). *Euripides: Trojan Women, Iphigenia among the Taurians, Ion.* Cambridge, MA: Harvard University Press.

Larson, Jennifer. (2001). *Greek Nymphs: Myth, Cult, Lore.* Oxford: Oxford University Press.

Lee, Mireille M. (1999). "The Myth of the Classical *Peplos*." Ph.D. diss., Bryn Mawr College.

————. (2005). "Constru(ct)ing Gender in the Feminine Greek *Peplos*." In Liza Cleland, Mary Harlow, and Lloyd Lewellyn-Jones, eds., *The Clothed Body in the Ancient World,* 55–64. Oxford: Oxbow.

Lehmann-Hartleben, Karl. (1926). "Athena als Geburtsgöttin." *Archiv für Religionswissenschaft* 24:19–28.

Linders, Tullia. (1972). *Studies in the Treasure Records of Artemis Brauronia.* Stockholm: Svenska Institut Athen.

Llewellyn-Jones, Lloyd. (2003). *Aphrodite's Tortoise: The Veiled Woman of Ancient Greece.* Swansea: Classical Press of Wales.

Morizot, Yvette. (2004). "Offrandes à Artémis pour une naissance: Autour du relief d'Achinos." In Véronique Dasen, ed., *Naissance et petite enfance dans l'Antiquité,* 159–170. Göttingen: Vandenhoeck and Ruprecht.

Musial, Jennifer. (2004). "Fashioning Pregnancy: The Maternity Dress in Clothing Catalogues." In Sandra Weber and Claudia Mitchell, eds., *Not Just Any Dress: Narratives of Memory, Body, and Identity*, 127–136. New York: Lang.

Neils, Jenifer. (2003). "Children and Greek Religion." In Jenifer Neils and John H. Oakley, eds., *Coming of Age in Ancient Greece: Images of Childhood from the Classical Past*, 139–161. New Haven: Yale University Press.

Osborne, Robin. (1985). *Demos: The Discovery of Classical Attica*. Cambridge: Cambridge University Press.

Palagia, Olga. (1995). "Akropolis Museum 581: A Family at the Apaturia?" *Hesperia* 64:493–501.

Papadopoulou-Belmehdi, Ioanna. (1994). "Greek Weaving; or, The Feminine in Antithesis." *Diogenes* 42 (167): 39–56.

Parker, Robert. (1983). *Miasma: Pollution and Purification in Early Greek Religion*. Oxford: Oxford University Press.

Roach-Higgins, Mary-Ellen, Joanne B. Eicher, and Kim P. Johnson, eds. (1995). *Dress and Identity*. New York: Fairchild.

Speert, Harold. (2004). *Obstetrics and Gynecology: A History and Iconography*. 3rd ed. New York: Parthenon.

Stewart, Andrew, and Celina Gray. (2000). "Confronting the Other: Childbirth, Aging, and Death on an Attic Tombstone at Harvard." In Beth Cohen, ed., *Not the Classical Ideal*, 248–274. Leiden: Brill.

Temkin, Owsei, trans. (1991). *Soranus' Gynecology*. Baltimore: Johns Hopkins University Press.

Thompson, Dorothy B. (1954). "Three Centuries of Hellenistic Terracottas." *Hesperia* 23:72–107.

Van Straten, Folkert T. (1981). "Gifts for the Gods." In Hendrik S. Versnel, ed., *Faith, Hope, and Worship: Aspects of Religious Mentality in the Ancient World*, 65–151. Leiden: Brill.

Vedder, Ursula. (1988). "Frauentod-Kriegertod im Spiegel der attischen Grabkunst des 4. Jhs. v. Chr." *Mitteilungen des Deutschen Archäologischen Instituts, Athenische Abteilung* 103:161–191.

[THREE]

Motherhood as Teleia

RITUALS OF INCORPORATION

AT THE KOUROTROPHIC SHRINE

Angela Taraskiewicz

It is widely recognized that the female developmental trajectory in ancient Greece was incremental and involved a battery of ritual events that guided female children through a series of role statuses from *parthenos* (maiden), to *nymphē* (bride), to *gunē* (mature female).[1] Ritual evidence for passage through the first two statuses is abundant. At kourotrophic sanctuaries (sites concerned with the nursing and rearing of children) *parthenoi* were introduced to the prospects of their marriageability.[2] In the ritual events surrounding marriage *nymphai* were separated from their natal families and transferred to new homes, new families, and husbands.[3] However, attainment of mature female status was not complete until they gave birth to a surviving child.[4] Medical, juridical, and folkloric testimony all bear witness to the provisional nature of the transfer evinced in the *enguē*, the formal betrothal of the bride, where her father handed her over to the groom "for the plowing of legitimate children."[5] Just as the *enguē* anticipated the eventual offspring of the union, the rituals following childbirth secured that union by integrating the *lechō* (postpartum mother) into her home following the birth of her child.

This essay examines the ritual process by which the betrothed bride ascended to her adult female status and attained permanent attachment to her conjugal home. I begin by reviewing evidence for the intermediate nature of the bride's status. Next, I examine the ritual mechanisms that served to resolve her ambiguous state. Votive inventories from kourotrophic sanctuaries throughout Greece preserve dedications that indicate a well-established history of childbirth rituals.[6] These votives, viewed with a mind to the dangers associated with pregnancy and parturition, are divisible into three distinct types. The first set concerns protection of the woman and child throughout pregnancy, birth, and the postpartum period. The second

set marks the termination of the ambiguous status of *lechō*, and the third serves to incorporate both mother and child into her conjugal home and community following birth. By reading childbirth dedications as indicative not only of the infant at the beginning of its social career, but of the bride at the culmination of hers, this essay reconstructs an incorporation ritual for the *nymphē* that marked her "social return from childbirth,"[7] effected her permanent integration into her conjugal family, and conferred on her the *teleia* appropriate to Greek femininity.[8]

BRIDAL INSTABILITY

The suggestion that the *teleia*, or fulfillment, attributed to the Greek *gunē* was merely hailed, not accomplished, by the wedding ceremony comes from legal, medical, and religious sources. In her study of Athenian lawsuits, Virginia Hunter has demonstrated that only the birth of children could solidify a bride's status within her new household, and failure thereof often led to her return to her natal family for remarriage.[9] Likewise, in her study of Greek gynecological texts, Helen King has shown that the biological transformation of the female was thought to begin at *menarchē* and to conclude at first *lochia*, the discharge after the birth of the first child. "Ideally," King explains, "the temporal gap between *parthenos* and *gunē* would be short; the Greek process of becoming married, extended from the betrothal to the birth of the first child, would cover it, and the term *nymphē* would be applied to those in the 'latent period' stretching from marriageable to married."[10] Finally, as Sarah Iles Johnston has demonstrated, Greek beliefs surrounding *aōrai*, or women who have died prematurely, emphasize their failure to have given birth to surviving children: "The *aitia* [explanatory myths] deliver the same message that a Greek woman heard from other sources: her goal in life was to become a mother."[11]

The ambiguity of the bride's status seems to have resulted in a corresponding low position in her conjugal household prior to the birth of her first child. This low position arises from a number of factors. First, the bride's intense attachment to her natal hearth causes a corresponding grief when she is transferred to her conjugal hearth. Such melancholy is captured in a fragment from Sophocles' *Tereus*, where Procne declares:

> In childhood, in our father's house we live the happiest life, I think, of all
> mankind; for folly always rears children in happiness. But when we have
> understanding and have come to youthful vigour, we are pushed out and

sold, away from our paternal gods and from our parents, some to foreign
husbands, some to barbarians, some to joyless homes and some to homes
that are opprobrious. And this, once a single night has yoked us, we must
approve and consider happiness.[12]

Secondly, the bride seems to have been viewed as a foreigner in her new
household. Medea claims that a woman feels like a ξένος, or foreigner, arriving at a strange hearth:

A woman, arriving among new customs and laws [ἤθη καὶ νόμους],
must be clairvoyant, for she didn't learn at home [οἴκοθεν] how best to
interpret [χρήσεται] her bedmate.[13]

The birth of a child was thought to help mitigate this rift. As the dissimu-
lating Clytemnestra states, a child acts as "the keeper of the pledges, both
mine and yours."[14]

This same sentiment is echoed by Eratosthenes in Lysias 1, *On the Murder of Eratosthenes*:

When I decided to marry and had brought a wife home, at first my attitude toward her was this: I did not wish to annoy her, but neither was
she to have too much of her own way. I watched her as well as I could,
and I kept an eye on what was proper. But later, after my child was born,
I came to trust her and handed all my possessions over to her, believing
this was the greatest possible proof of affection.[15]

The juridical context of Eratosthenes' speech suggests that such views were
widely held. Lysias hopes to exonerate his client by manipulating the jury's
expectations in this way. The sentiment, voiced by both male and female
speakers, is that brides were thought to constitute a threat to the integrity
of the household, were regarded with suspicion prior to bearing children,
but thereafter were held to be more invested, and hence more trustworthy.

Comparative ethnography confirms these ancient testimonies. John
Campbell describes the subordinate status of a new bride among the Sara-
katsani in terms that suggest an openly hostile environment for the *nymphi* up to the birth of her first child.[16] Loring Danforth, whose fieldwork
was conducted in Greek Macedonia, emphasizes that "a daughter-in-law is
an outsider, a *xeni*, in her family of marriage," and that hostility from her
mother-in-law could wreak havoc on the fragile psyche of the new bride.[17]
Sydel Silverman, studying the life-cycle of women in rural Umbria, ob-

serves that the period extending from a woman's engagement to the birth of her first child is the most stressful of all the role transitions she faces.[18] Finally, Roger and Patricia Jeffrey report that in rural north India there is a specific term (like *nymphē* or *nymphi*) for the prepartum bride: *bahū*. The *bahū*'s place in her conjugal home is described as one of abject submission, hard labor, beatings, and verbal abuse if she does not comply with the demands of her husband and mother-in-law. However, following the birth of her first child she is accorded a new status, that of *jachā*, a term used to describe the parturient mother in the forty-day postpartum period.[19] In all of these cases, the birth of the couple's first child serves to end the period of the bride's socio-psycho liminality.[20]

FERTILE DANGERS

As Nancy Demand has demonstrated, ensuring conception, delivery, and the survival of a child presented formidable odds to women. Because of their young age at marriage many brides were simply not mature enough to conceive. If they did conceive, the risks associated with childbirth were very high. Finally, even if they did not themselves die in childbirth, the odds that their child would survive were still low. Demand estimates that "at least half of all newborns failed to reach maturity," and that a "30–40 percent mortality rate [might be expected] in the first year of life."[21] As such statistics imply, we find considerable evidence for anxiety throughout the childbirth process, a topic explored in detail in the following essay, by Yurie Hong. Literary and epigraphic sources attest that oracles were often consulted regarding failure to conceive,[22] and prayers to cure sterility at the sanctuary of Asklepios at Epidauros were only exceeded by prayers associated with vision.[23] Due to the high risks and anxiety associated with pregnancy, Edith Hall has argued that "dramatic enactment of the effect of births on the *oikos*, whether with tragic or comic consequences, constituted a form of collective social *couvade*."[24]

In order to protect themselves against the considerable dangers associated with fertility, pregnancy, and childbirth, women employed a variety of apotropaic charms and amulets. Figurines representing the Egyptian childbirth deity Bes[25] have been found in large numbers in sanctuaries associated with childbirth (figs. 3.1 and 3.2). The Bes figurines have been interpreted as images that have the power both to repel evil, with their exposed genitalia and ugly grimaces, and to nurture the infant, as figured in their exaggerated bellies.[26] The amulets are fabricated from a range of natural stones and

FIGURE 3.1. *Egyptian Bes. British Museum AN55663000I.* © *Trustees of the British Museum.*

FIGURE 3.2. *Samian Bes with cakes.* Photo: Ulrich Sinn.

manufactured objects, including jasper, aetites, Samian stone, pierced seal-stones, scarabs, and coral.[27] As Susan Wise points out, many such charms would have been unremarkable, consisting of nothing more than a pierced stone, and it is likely that many of them went unnoticed, or have remained unpublished, by excavators who were focused on recovering more valuable objects.[28] The first-century CE medical writer Dioskourides reports that a jasper amulet was worn on the thigh during childbirth.[29] Items so intimately associated with the *lechō* may have been deposited as terminal offerings comparable to the dedication of toys in age-grading rituals. Their close proximity to the pollution of the birth may also have required their disposal afterward, as a votive type of *katharmata*, ritual off-scourings.[30]

In addition to charms that were worn to divert childbirth demons, there are other votives present in the temple inventories and sanctuary deposits that appear to have been associated with easing labor. Such items include keys (figs. 3.3 and 3.4), *zonai* (belts), and dress-pins. The presence and significance of keys at childbirth sanctuaries has only recently been recognized.[31] This is because many of these keys, known as "spike keys" or "pressure keys" (e.g., figs. 3.4 and 3.7), have been mistaken for hooks or iron

FIGURE 3.3. *Bronze key. Photo: Waldstein,* AH *II, 299, no. 2262.*

FIGURE 3.5. *Maiden using spike key, Attic red-figure hydria. Berlin 2382. Photo: H. Diels,* Antike Technik *(1914), pl. 6.*

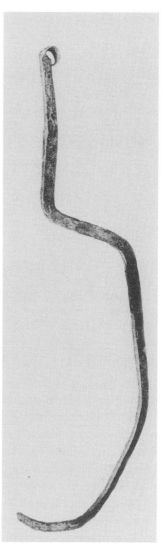

FIGURE 3.4. *Spike key. Photo: Waldstein,* AH *II, 324.*

spits. A fifth-century Attic hydria (fig. 3.5) depicts how such keys were used, however. The status of keys as childbirth dedications is attested by the second-century Roman grammarian Festus, who writes: "It was the custom for women to dedicate a key to signify an easy delivery."[32] That this was also the case in Greece is suggested by the fact that Iphigeneia was called *kleidouchos,* "the one who holds the keys" at Brauron,[33] and by a fourth-

FIGURE 3.6. *Argive coin*, obverse: *head of Hera, fourth century BCE. Luynes 2297. Photo: Bibliothèque nationale de France.*

FIGURE 3.7. *Argive coin*, reverse: *spike key with garland, fourth century BCE. Luynes 2297. Photo: Bibliothèque nationale de France.*

century BCE coin from Argos depicting Hera on the obverse, and a spike key on the reverse (figs. 3.6 and 3.7).[34]

As another metaphor for the opening of the womb, garment fasteners of all kinds were popular as thank-offerings following a successful childbirth.[35] The importance of the act of loosening *zonai*, or belts, in childbirth is suggested by the fact that *lyzizonos*, belt-loosener, is a common cult epithet for Artemis and Eileithyia.[36] In Pindar's *Olympian 6*, Evadne is said to "have laid down her purple- and saffron-colored girdle" prior to giving birth to Iamus.[37] Soranus recommends those assisting in childbirth "loosen . . . girdles, as well as free the chest of any binder, though not on account of the vulgar conception, according to which womenfolk are unwilling to suffer any fetter, but also to loosen their hair."[38] Images of women in labor on funerary *stelai* and *lekythoi* confirm this practice (see figs. 1.3 and 2.4 in this volume).[39] F. T. van Straten suggests that a dedication of a *zonē* to Artemis in thanks for a successful childbirth may be depicted on a fifth-century Attic *lekythos* (fig. 3.8).[40]

Jens Baumbach argues that the wide distribution of metal garment fasteners at childbirth sanctuaries is reflective of this same practice (figs. 3.9 and 3.10).[41] Between seven and eight hundred dress-pins were found at

FIGURE 3.8. *Belt-loosening, Gela lekythos, fifth century BCE. Syracuse 21186. Photo: Museo Archeologico Regionale Paolo Orsi–Siracusa (with the permission of the Assessorato dei Beni Culturali e dell'Identità Siciliana).*

FIGURE 3.9. *Belt clasp, seventh century BCE. Photo: Payne,* Perachora *I, pl. 44.*

FIGURE 3.10. *Phrygian belt clasp. Samos. Photo: Gösta Hellner, DAI, neg. D-DAI-ATH-1969/794.*

Argos, along with more than one hundred bronze fibulae.[42] Although dress-pins occur in other contexts (such as graves and sanctuaries of male deities), Yngve Flognfeldt estimates that 84 percent of known examples were dedicated in the sanctuaries of female deities.[43] In addition to dress-pins, belt clasps have been found at both Perachora and Samos.

Worldwide, childbirth rituals focus on concepts of opening and loosening the womb.[44] Claude Lévi-Strauss, in his analysis of a Cuna incantation to facilitate childbirth, argues that such images evoke, through symbolic imagery, a corresponding physiological response:

> The shaman provides the sick woman with a *language*, by means of which unexpressed, and otherwise unexpressible, psychic states can be immediately expressed. And it is the transition to verbal expression—at the same time making it possible to undergo in an ordered and intelligible form a real experience that would otherwise be chaotic and unexpressible— which induces the release of the physiological process, that is the reorganization, in a favorable direction.[45]

For Lévi-Strauss, a woman's belief in her mythic tradition combines with the sympathetic ideas of release to provide an effective therapy. Literary and iconographic sources provide evidence that similar birthing practices were employed in antiquity. One recalls the images of constriction and release associated with Alcmena's difficult labor with Heracles, where Lucina sits outside the house with crossed legs and clasped hands until she is tricked into letting go her grip.[46]

TOWARD *TELEIA*

It would be surprising if an event like this, invested with so much social importance and subject to so much anxiety, would stand without any ritual intervention. Explicit references to ritual practices surrounding pregnancy and childbirth are quite fragmentary, however. Robert Parker assembles the epigraphic testimony in his classic discussion of miasma, the Greek beliefs surrounding pollution and purification.[47] We know that the Greeks considered childbirth polluting. Women were forbidden, for instance, to give birth inside of sanctuaries.[48] Fragments from the Cyrene cathartic law suggest that anyone who entered a house where a birth had taken place would retain that pollution for three days. However, the duration the mother herself remained polluted is not clear. Parker suggests that while her capacity to pass on contagion was likely lifted in time for the *amphidromia* on the fifth/seventh day, her complete purification and reintegration process probably extended longer.[49] Medical texts suggest a period of 30–40 days, during which the *katharsis* associated with lochial bleeding could run its course.[50] It has been suggested that statues of dog figurines found at Perachora support literary testimony that dog sacrifice was part of the purification process of women emerging from childbed.[51]

That parturient women brought an end to their confinements with a visit to a sanctuary and a sacrifice, which included some sort of cake dedication, is suggested by a number of inscriptions. A late fifth-/early fourth-century BCE inscription from Delphi which catalogues the festival calendar of the Labyad phratry makes a reference to "one who should accompany a *lecho*," the woman emerging from childbed.[52] The phrase "to accompany a *lecho*" requires some interpretation. In my translation I follow Parker, who describes this inscription as referring to "sacrifice by a λεχώ."[53] Since side A of the same inscription includes references to special cake sacrifices called *daratai*, "on the occasion of marriages or for children," it is conceivable that one accompanied a *lecho* who made sacrifices of *daratai* when she emerged from her confinement.

Further contemporary evidence for such a ritual is provided by a fragment of Antimachus of Colophon's *Artemis*.[54] The hexameter fragment reads: ὄφρ' ὑπὸ μ[ὲν] Λαθρίαι θύσηι λόχια τριθ[άλεια]ι[55] (that I may sacrifice *lochia* on behalf of thrice-blooming Lathria). V. J. Matthews points out in his discussion of this passage that these *lochia* are likely bread sacrifices, a reading supported by Hesychius, who reports, s.v. λόχια, that they are "ἄρτος τῇ 'Αρτέμιδι γενόμενος καὶ ... ἁδροὺς ἀστάχους ἔχουσα," or "bread for Artemis made of ripe corn." Matthews further sup-

ports the reading that the *lochia* here refer to bread by citing Hesychius, s.v. ἄγρωστις, "which is a plant and a type of bread called *lochia*." He adds that "trithalia" is an epithet for Artemis which is indicative of her kourotrophic identity "as the goddess responsible for the thriving growth of children."[56]

A first-century CE inscription from Miletus that describes the auction of the priesthood of Asklepios includes a list of public officials and private individuals who are required to perform sacrifices in the sanctuary.[57] Parker and Dirk Obbink label these requirements as "θύοντω rules," and suggest that their purpose was "to increase the priest's income by forcing particular classes of person to sacrifice in the shrine."[58] Most often they require public officials of various types to perform regular sacrifices, but they also stipulate that certain classes of private individuals sacrifice on certain occasions: "Piety becomes obligatory, and even (in principle) legally enforceable."[59] Such regulations would increase the value of the priesthood on auction by in effect taxing the commonest rituals of civic life. Thus, among the host of Milesian civil servants we find an unlikely group, women described as "walking out the *lochia*," presumably representing its termination, and tying their *zonai*, or girdles.[60] The inclusion of "women walking out the *lochia*" in this list suggests that the ceremony, at least in first-century Miletus, was prominent, frequent, and socially significant, since it contributed substantial revenues to the priesthood of Asklepios. This balanced phrase referring to the women is instructive. As we have seen, the loosening of the girdle was equated with the onset of labor; the ritual tying of it would neatly signify that the transition to motherhood had been accomplished.

As we have already seen, a number of inscriptions associate bread sacrifice with childbirth. In addition to those already mentioned, Delian inscriptions mention that a baker, ἀρτοκόπος, was employed during the festival for Eileithyia.[61] Obviously, such perishable dedications have not survived, but a number of sanctuaries associated with childbirth preserve terracotta replicas of cakes as well as bread-baking figurines (figs. 3.11 and 3.12; see also fig. 3.2).[62]

An elaborate terracotta from the Argolid of unknown provenance depicts a bakery scene (fig. 3.13). Moving around the circle from the top of the image clockwise, we see various women depicted in bread-baking. The one to the right of the oven appears to be stoking the fire with her right hand while cradling an infant in her left; the next figure appears to have a large amount of dough ready to be made into cakes; the next seems to carry a platter of formed cakes, while the next two are engaged in forming the loaves. Finally, the sixth figure (fig. 3.14), who is the tallest, and distinguished by a high and elaborate *polos*, may be a goddess, and perhaps is

FIGURE 3.11. *Terracotta cakes. Photo: Frickenhaus, DAI, neg. D-DAI-ATH-1973/ 1957*

FIGURE 3.12. *Female figure holding cake. Photo: DAI, neg. D-DAI-ATH-Tiryns 121.*

Hera.[63] This figure has suffered some damage, but the position of her right arm suggests she is nursing another infant that she holds at her breast.[64] At her feet lies an animal that may be a dog. Although the provenance of this terracotta is unknown, its state of preservation suggests that it was part of a funerary deposit. Kourotrophic statues are commonly found in childbirth sanctuaries and graves.[65] Whatever the original dedicatory context, this particular group is significant because it correlates bread-making with kourotrophy and links the iconography of these two common types of terracotta votive.

As presented in the previous essay, a fifth-century dedicatory plaque to Artemis from Echinos, which depicts a *lechō* performing the type of sacrifice described by the inscriptions, provides the most detailed image of what the dedications of a postpartum mother would have looked like (see fig. 2.8 of this volume).[66] In this group, Artemis stands at the far right side of the relief, taller than the other figures in stature, holding a torch, and wearing her quiver. She stands near a column, which indicates the scene is inside a temple. Just to her left, and standing before her, a small male figure, a boy or servant, leads an ox to slaughter at an altar. Behind him stands a

FIGURE 3.13. *Argive bread-baking figurine, ca. 530 BCE. EAM 5573. Photo: National Archaeological Museum, Athens, © Hellenic Ministry of Culture and Tourism/Archaeological Receipts Fund.*

FIGURE 3.14. *Detail, Argive bread-baking figurine, ca. 530 BCE. EAM 5573. Photo: National Archaeological Museum, Athens, © Hellenic Ministry of Culture and Tourism/ Archaeological Receipts Fund.*

female figure with a bare head who holds a child in her arms and extends it toward the goddess. This figure may be the child's mother. If so, the fact that her head is not covered, and that the infant is unswaddled, may indicate they have both passed out of the dangerous postpartum period.[67] The child reaches out energetically toward the goddess.

Behind the mother, a female servant, also small in stature, carries an offering tray on her head, and she balances it with her left hand. On the offering tray, conical shaped honey-cakes appear with pomegranates, apples,

grapes, and myrtle.[68] In the servant's right hand she carries a vessel, perhaps an *askos*, which she will use to pour a libation.[69] To the far left of the plaque and bringing up the rear of the procession is a veiled woman, taller in stature than the other participants, but slightly smaller than the goddess. She holds her right hand up in adoration, and in her left hand she holds a small *pyxis*. The figure does not show any attributes to identify her as a priestess, and because of her stature, Fanouria Dakoronia and Lukretia Gounaropoulou suggest that she is the donor of the plaque and is likely to be either the mother-in-law or mother of the new *gunē*.[70] Behind the group, a clothesline displays a range of garments that have evidently been dedicated to the goddess.[71] Hanging from left to right we see a pair of shoes, a short *chiton* with short sleeves, two bedsheets, a *zonē*, and a *peplos* trimmed with fringe.

So how did the *nymphai* who were fortunate enough to become *lechoi* and to survive childbirth ascend to the status of *gunaikēs*? I reconstruct the rituals surrounding childbirth as follows. From the moment of her presentation to her conjugal hearth in the *katachysmata*, where she was showered with fruits, nuts, and coins, the Greek bride and her potential fertility were guarded with great anxiety. Throughout pregnancy, labor, and the postpartum period she made use of *apotropaia* to ward off divine envy. During labor she loosened her clothing and hair, and as a result she often dedicated relevant garment fasteners to childbirth sanctuaries following a successful birth. Both amulets and fasteners served as appropriate terminal offerings suggesting that the status of *lechō* had been left behind, and that the new status of *gunē* had been attained.

Successful childbirth, however, did not ensure the survival of the infant. The period of confinement following birth served to protect mother and child in their most vulnerable period. Epigraphical sources suggest a gradual lessening of pollution that coincided with a gradually increasing sphere of movement for mother and child. Early rituals occurred within the home and inscribed a widening circle of movement from childbed to the hearth in the *amphidromia* on the fifth or seventh day,[72] to the naming ceremony of the *dekatē* on the tenth.[73]

These essentially private rituals seem to have culminated in a journey to a childbirth sanctuary after a period of around forty days.[74] At that time, final purification rituals may have been performed publicly, such as the dog sacrifice common to Hekate,[75] or fumigation through the burning of incense, either of which could have served to end the period of pollution experienced by the mother following the birth. The preponderance of *pyxides* found in childbirth sanctuaries may have served as containers for such

incense.[76] Following such purification rites, the child was presented to the *kourotrophos* for protection, and both mother and child may then have been formally entered into the husband's phratry. Dedications to the childbirth deity would have been made at this time.

Disentangling the rhetoric of dedications is complex since it is often difficult to distinguish attitudes of dread at divine hostility from expressions of pious gratitude.[77] However, three distinct types of dedication seem to emerge from the array common to most childbirth sanctuaries. First, there are the terminal offerings: dedications like amulets, apotropaic figurines, and garment fasteners, which seem emblematic of the surpassed role status. Secondly, there are *agalmata*, dedications of fine clothing and jewelry.[78] Such offerings are usually considered thank-offerings, but they seem more intended to appease potential hostility than to express thanks. In keeping with Johnston's arguments regarding the vulnerability of women throughout pregnancy and childbirth, such *pars pro toto* offerings, like Polycrates' ring,[79] seem to have been dedicated to prevent envious goddesses and spirits from harassing the parturient mother and her newborn.[80] Third, there are first-fruits dedications, particularly hearth cakes, but also fruits, flowers, and animal sacrifice. As part of a celebratory feast which coincided with the public presentation of the child at the childbirth sanctuary, this last category of dedications seems to have served to reintegrate mother and child into the community following their confinements.

Since the dedication of cakes was not limited to childbirth sanctuaries, the importance of their inclusion here requires some comment. According to Artemidorus in his *Interpretation of Dreams*, the Greeks associated children with bread, and mothers with ovens: "The hearth signifies life and the wife of the dreamer"; "To light a fire which burns brightly in the hearth or in the oven signifies the begetting of children, for the hearth and the oven are like a woman . . . and the fire in them foretells that the woman will become pregnant."[81] The use of bread as a symbol for future progeny also figures in the Athenian wedding ritual described in Zenobius 3.98:

> It was the custom of the Athenians at their weddings that a child with both parents living be crowned with thistles mixed with the fruit of live oak, and carrying a winnowing basket [*liknon*] full of bread he would say: "I escaped that bad, I found the better." They indicated how they rejected the wild and ancient diet, and discovered domestic nourishment.[82]

The dedication of hearth cakes at the time of the presentation of the child would recall the wedding ritual, as well as mimic the ritual of the *amphi-*

dromia, this time extending the circuit of the cake from hearth, to family, to the kourotrophic goddess herself.

All of this ritual work—deflecting danger, releasing the womb, putting aside the ambiguous self of betrothal and pregnancy—culminates in the woman's procession to the kourotrophic sanctuary. The movement from the intimate space of the bed to domestic hearth in the *amphidromia* integrates mother and child into their household; the movement from their threshold to the public kourotrophic sanctuary and back introduces them both to the community. Likewise, the sharing of hearth cakes with intimates, peers, and finally the local kourotrophic goddess mirrors their spatial progress, establishing commensality with a gradually widening sphere of associations. Upon her return home the mother is transformed into a new social being, a *gunē*.

But how should we understand the implications of that new status? Seen in ritual terms, attainment of motherhood is the prerequisite to attaining adult female status, but it is not its equivalent. Above all, the surviving child serves to anchor the woman in her new home. As Clytemnestra explains, the child is "the keeper of pledges." Deborah Lyons has argued that the security of this position was critical to a *gunē* because "once she is established in her marital household, a woman may lay claim to a new economic (and affective) power as wife and mother, no longer allowing herself to be exchanged as a passive object."[83] Furthermore, motherhood and marriage grant her parity with other adult women in her community. This parity opens new possibilities for sociality and qualifies her for those religious festivals open only to *gunaikēs*, such as the *Thesmophoria*.[84]

I suggest that it is this moment of integration into home and community that has been the aim of the long chain of rituals that began with a woman's betrothal. At the end of her journey, recrossing the threshold of her home, babe in arms, a cautiously optimistic *gunē* must be imagined, one who has triumphed in the most challenging contest open to her: *teleia*, at last.

NOTES

I am grateful to the editors for organizing the 2007 APA panel in which this paper first appeared and for inviting me to contribute to this volume. Their comments and suggestions, as well as those of fellow panel members, have contributed greatly to its clarity and coherence. I would also like to thank the two anonymous readers from the University of Texas Press and Kerri Cox Sullivan for their careful reading and incisive questions.

1. Cole (2004) and (1984); Redfield (2003); Dowden (1989); Perlman (1989); Sourvinou-Inwood (1988); King (1983); Calame (1997) and (1999); Kondis (1967).

2. At Brauron: Jeanmaire (1939), 260; Cole (1984), 238–244; Clinton (1988); Faraone (2003). At Athens: Burkert (1966). At Patras: Redfield (1990).

3. Detienne (1974), 66; Loraux (1995), 25; Calame (1999), 127.

4. King (1983), 10; Demand (1994), 11–26; Hunter (1993); Johnston (1995); Ferrari (2003), 38.

5. The formula occurs several times in Menander with slight variations: ἐγγυῶ παίδων ἐπ᾽ ἀρότῳ γνησίων τὴν θυγατέρ᾽ ἤδη μειρακιόν σοι προῖκά τε δίδωμι ἐπ᾽ αὐτῇ τρία τάλαντα (*Dyscolus* 842) Cf. *Misumenus* 444; *Fragmentum dubium* 5; *Fragmenta* 151, line 444. Redfield (2003), 43.

6. Hall (2006), 61–62; Wise (2007), 9–10; Lyons (2007).

7. Van Gennep (1960).

8. Although *teleia*, or fulfillment, is often associated with marriage, the intermediate status of the bride seems to contradict this interpretation. The prenuptial ritual (variously attested as a libation, a bath, or a collecting of sacred water) was called the *proteleia*, and was frequently associated with the nymphs, Artemis, Hera, Zeus, and others. Cf. Larson (2001), 111. However, the term *proteleia* seems to indicate that the attainment of fulfillment is pending. Similarly, *teleia* frequently occurs as a cult epithet of Hera: in Athens (Aristophanes, *Thesmophoriazusae* 973–976; Aeschylus, *Eumenides* 213–214), and in Plataia (Pausanias 9.2.5–4.30). Yet as we shall see, Hera is just as frequently associated with childbirth in cult as with marriage, suggesting the two events are linked, *contra* Clark (1998). Cf. Caldwell (2007), who argues that a similarly drawn-out process served to integrate the Roman *sponsa* into her conjugal home: "While Roman girls could be propelled into marriage at a very early age, it is equally important to remember that familial anxiety about girls' movement into marriage, combined with the state's emphasis on marriage as a venue for the production of legitimate children, created a lengthy period of transition for females rather than a moment in time. In law, the female achievement of 'adult' status, in terms of agency, might in fact be considered the acquisition of the *ius trium liberorum*, which freed a woman from the requirement of guardianship (*tutela mulierum*)" (220).

9. Hunter (1993), 108, citing Isaeus 3.36; Harrison (1968), 109. Demand (1994), 17, citing Lysias 1.6–7.

10. King (1983), 112.

11. Johnston (1995), 368–369.

12. Sophocles, fr. 583; trans. Hugh Lloyd-Jones (Loeb edition [1996]).

13. Euripides, *Medea* 238–240.

14. Aeschylus, *Agamemnon* 877: ἐμῶν τε καὶ σῶν κύριος πιστωμάτων.

15. Lysias 1.6–7; trans. Freeman (1946).

16. Campbell (1964), 64–65.

17. Danforth (1991), 103–105, emphasizes that both the alienation of the bride from her natal support system and the failure of her husband to defend her can aggravate her instability.

18. Silverman (1975), 319–320.

19. Jeffrey, Jeffrey, and Lyon (1989), 28–31, 43–61.

20. Van Gennep (1960), 48.

21. Demand (1994), 17–24.

22. Wise (2007), 72, citing Euripides, *Ion* 404–406, 422–424; Plutarch, *Life of Theseus* 3.5, Apollodorus 3.15.5. Inscriptions at Dodona: *Syll.*³ III 1160; Parke (1967), II.5, II.7. II.8, II.9, II.11. Inscriptions from Epidauros: Edelstein, Edelstein, and Ferngren (1945), T423, case no. 31, p. 235; T423, case no. 34, p. 236; T423, case no. 39, p. 237; T423, case no. 42, p. 237; T426, pp. 239–240.

23. Corvisier (1985), 121, 161–165.

24. Hall (2006), 94.

25. For a summary of Bes' kourotrophic identity in Egypt, see Andrews (1989), 39–40. Sinn (1983), 88–89, demonstrates that Bes retains his kourotrophic function in Greek sanctuaries, although the iconography of the god becomes somewhat Hellenized.

26. Baumbach (2004), 29–30; Sinn (1983), 89–90. Sanctuaries in which Bes figurines have been found include Perachora, the Argive Heraion, the Samian Heraion, the Aphaia sanctuary on Aegina, the Athena sanctuaries at Kamirus and Lindos, the Artemision at Ephesus, and the sanctuaries of Demeter and Kore in Catania, Gela, Selinus, and Tocra.

27. Baumbach (2004), 26–27, n. 179, lists the following sanctuaries as yielding amulets: Perachora, Athena Lindia, Aphrodite at Miletus, Artemis at Ephesos and Sparta, Aphaia on Aegina, and Eileithyia at Inatos on Crete.

28. Wise (2007), 224.

29. Dioskourides, *De materia medica* 5.142.

30. Parker (1996), 18, quoting Plato: "Of the kind of division that retains what is better but expels the worse, I do know the name . . . every division of that kind is universally known as purification" (*Sophist* 226d).

31. Baumbach (2004), 81–82, who lists Argos: *AH* II, 324, nos. 2714–2722, nos. 2723–2728; Aegina: Furtwängler (1906), 391, no. 11; and Delphi: Rolley (1984), 279, no. 68. Wise (2007), 224, lists Olympia: *Olympia* IV, 190–191, no. 1204; Perachora: *Perachora* I, p. 190, pl. 86.28; Delphi: *FdD* V.i, p. 214, nos. 757–758, pl. 215, fig. 941; and Athens: Aleshire (1989), 155; Harris (1995), 266–267.

32. Festus, *De verborum significatione* III, s.v. *clavim.*

33. Wise (2007), 225; cf. Simon (1986), 358, n. 10.

34. Imhoof-Blumer (1871), pl. II, no. 64.

35. *Zonai* dedicated to Artemis and Aphrodite in the *Palatine Anthology* are identified as being dedicated for a safe delivery: Wise (2007), 221, n. 415: *Palatine Anthology* 6.59, 201, 202, 272, 6.210; Brauron: *IG* II² 1514.7–18. Belt clasps have been found at both Perachora (*Perachora* I, 138ff., pls. 44–45) and Samos: Baumbach (2004), 160; Jantzen (1972), 48–53.

36. See Wise (2007), 46, who lists Hesychius, s.v. Λυσίζωνος; schol. Apollonius Rhodius, *Argonautica* I.288; *Orphic Hymn* 2.7 and 36.5; Theocritus 17.60.

37. Pindar, *Ol.* 6.37–39.

38. Soranus 2.6.1. Cf. Theocritus 17.60.

39. Wise (2007), 232–252, esp. 239–240.

40. Van Straten (1981), 91, pl. 30. Syracuse 21186: Beazley, *ARV*² 993.80. Van Straten notes that it is not clear whether this vase depicts a premarriage ritual or a childbirth ritual. Although it is normally interpreted as the former (cf. Oakley and Sinos [2002], 14; Parker [2007], 242, n. 106), there is nothing on the vase itself which so identifies the scene (cf. Van Straten [1981], 91, n. 127; Wise [2007], 221, n. 414).

41. Baumbach (2004), 32–37, 61, 92ff., 160.

42. Kilian-Dirlmeier (1984); Strøm (1995), 71–76; Wise (2007), 218.

43. Flognfeldt (2009), 79.

44. Wise (2007), 86, n. 71, identifies parallels. See also Jacobson (1980), 81; Gélis (1991), 95; Lefèber and Voorhoeve (1988), 33.

45. Lévi-Strauss (1963), 198.

46. Ovid, *Metamorphoses* 9.292–324.

47. Parker (1996), 48–73.

48. *IG* II² 1035.10; Pausanias 2.27.1,6; *LSA* 83; Antoninus Liberalis, *Metamorphoses* 19.3.

49. Parker (1996), 51–52.

50. Parker (1996), 55, n. 87, citing *LSJ*, s.v. κάθαρσις IIa; Hippocrates, *De natura pueri* 18, *De natura mulieris* 72; Aristotle, *Historia animalium* 583a.

51. Such sacrifices are common to Hekate, who was associated with both brides and childbirth. Cf. Hadzisteliou Price (1978), 123, 159, 192; Pingiatoglou (1981), 93. Nine dog figurines were excavated at Perachora (*Perachora* I, 228, n. 162). Baumbach (2004), 27–28, notes several other attestations of dog sacrifice in a childbirth context: Aphrodite Genetyllis at Colias in Attica; Eilioneia at Argos (to secure an uncomplicated birth). See also Wise (2007), 93–94; and Johnston (1997), 211, n. 32.

52. *LSCG* 77, 12–22. Also published in Homolle (1895); Schwyzer (1923), no. 323; and Rhodes and Osborne (2003), no. 1. As printed in *LSCG*, no. 77D: καἴ κ'αὐτὸς θύηι ℎιαρήιον καἴ κα λεχοῖ παρῆι [κ]αἴ κα ξένοι Ϝοι παρέωντι ℎιαρήια θύοντες καἴ κα πενταμαριτεύων τύχηι· αἱ δέ τι τούτων παρβάλλοιτο τῶν γεγραμμένων, θωεόντων τοί τε δαμιοργοὶ καὶ τοὶ ἄλλοι πάντες Λαβυάδαι πρασσόντων δὲ τοὶ πεντακαίδεκα.

53. Parker (1996), 52, n. 74.

54. Matthews (1996), 15, following Apollodoros, dates Antimachus's *floruit* to the period following the Peloponnesian War.

55. Antimachus of Colophon, fr. 107, as printed in Matthews (1996), 277–281. Also published by Wyss (1936), no. 182.

56. Matthews (1996), 280–281.

57. *LSA* 52B. Sokolowski (1955) claims that the inscription pertains to the auction of the priesthood, and as such describes payment due for sacrifices.

58. Parker and Obbink (2000), 427.

59. Parker and Obbink (2000), 428.

60. *LSA* 52B 10–11: καὶ αἱ τὰ λοχῖα ἐκπορευόμεναι καὶ ζωννύμεναι.

61. Linders (1994), 77.

62. *Perachora* I, 67–99, pl. 16.6; Argos: *AH* II, 43, no. 267; 18, no. 24; 42, no. 267, 268. *Tiryns* I, 63–79; Samos: a Bes figurine supporting a tray of cakes on his head: Sinn (1983), 90, pl. 3. For a comprehensive list of sanctuaries with cake dedications and a list of names of sacrificial cakes see Brumfield (1997), 167–171.

63. Bell (1981) 81–82, and Hadzisteliou Price (1978) 180, both suggest that the *polos* indicates the divine status of a kourotrophic figure.

64. Kourouniotis' drawing, (1896), pl. 11, no. 1, suggests such an interpretation.

65. Wise (2007), 159; Neils and Oakley (2003), 224.

66. Dakoronia and Gounaropoulou (1992).

67. Wise (2007), 170–171.

68. Dakoronia and Gounaropoulou (1992), 221, n. 24.

69. Dakoronia and Gounaropoulou (1992), 221, n. 26, identify the vessel as an *askos*, noting that pottery vessels such as *oinochoai* and *prochoi* are more typical for pouring libations, while the *askos* was used for liquids poured drop by drop.

70. Dakoronia and Gounaropoulou (1992), 222–223.

71. Cf. the description and interpretation of this scene in Mireille Lee's essay in this volume.

72. Hamilton (1984), 243–251; Parker (1996), 51.

73. Demosthenes 39.20; Aristophanes, *Birds* 494–495; Isaeus 3.69–71.

74. Such a journey following a long period of confinement has numerous parallels in the childbirth rituals of traditional societies. Ancient Israel: Leviticus 12; Bulgaria: van Gennep (1960), 45–46; China: Walsche (1908), 646; Turkey: Delaney (1991), 68–71.

75. Such sacrifices to Hekate are common; she was associated with both brides and childbirth: Plutarch, *Questiones Romanae* 68; Pausanias 3.14.9. Cf. Hadzisteliou Price (1978), 123, 159, 192; Pingiatoglou (1981), 93; Wise (2007), 93–94. Baumbach (2004), 27–28, identifies attestations of dog sacrifice at the following sanctuaries: Hera Akraia at Perachora, Aphrodite Genetyllis at Colias in Attica, Eilioneia at Argos (to secure an uncomplicated birth).

76. Incense is said to be presented to Eileithyia in Olympia (Pausanias 2.20.1–6), and also in Hermione (Pausanias 2.35.11). Dakoronia and Gounaropoulou (1992) suggest the *pyxis* on the Echinos relief may have served to contain incense, although *comparanda* normally depict an incense-burner (222, n. 30).

77. *Pace* Burkert's remarks on offerings in general: "Ubiquitous, as far as I can see, is the association of religion with anxiety; even if the aspect of dread seems to recede somewhat into the background in certain forms of Greek religion, it is always present . . . the loss involved is worth so much less than that which is preserved. The 'offering' turns into a bait to manipulate and to fool a powerful pursuer" ([1987], 14–15).

78. Jewelry of all types, especially finger rings, is common at childbirth sanctuaries and attested to in the inscriptions. Wise (2007), 217, reports that bracelets, earrings, necklaces, and rings are listed in the Delian inventory as stored in the Eileithyaion.

Baumbach (2004), 38, and Pintiatoglou (1981), 51, report jewelry was found in a cave sanctuary of Eileithyia at Inatos on Crete. Perachora likewise possesses an enormous inventory of jewelry; Baumbach (2004), 37–38.

79. Versnel (1977), 30–31, identifies hair, statues, clothing, and jewelry as likely *pars pro toto* offerings and describes Polycrates' actions in Herodotus 3.40 as a kind of substitution sacrifice (32–37).

80. Goddesses are notoriously envious of mortals in childbirth. In the *Homeric Hymn to Delian Apollo*, Eileithyia is given a necklace by Iris to help Leto in her delivery (104). That ghosts may be appeased by such offerings is suggested in the story Herodotus tells about Periander and the ghost of his dead wife, Melissa. In this case, Melissa is not harassing anyone, but she is refusing to help Periander find a lost treasure. Periander's solution was to take all the women of Corinth out to the sanctuary of Hera, probably Perachora, and dedicate their clothing to her (5.92).

81. Artemidorus 1.74, 2.10.

82. Redfield (1982), 193.

83. Lyons (2003), 95.

84. Burton (1998) argues that women's commensality, particularly at all-female religious ceremonies, contributed substantially to their sociality outside the household. Likewise Cohen (1990), 225, explains that exclusion from public rituals was the penalty faced by a woman taken in adultery who is "excluded from that sphere of life which is the equivalent of politics for men."

WORKS CITED

Abbreviations

AH I = Ch. Waldstein, *The Argive Heraeum* I (1902).
AH II = Ch. Waldstein, *The Argive Heraeum* II (1905).
FdD II = R. Demangel, *Le sanctuaire d'Athèna Pronaia: Topographie du sanctuaire*, Fouilles de Delphes, École française d'Athènes II (Paris, 1926).
FdD V = P. Perdrizet, *Monuments figurés: Petits bronzes, terres-cuites, antiquités diverses*, Fouilles de Delphes, École française d'Athènes V (Paris, 1908).
IG = D. M. Lewis, *Inscriptiones Graecae* (Berlin, 1981).
LSA = F. Sokolowski, *Lois sacrées de l'Asie Mineure* (Paris, 1955).
LSCG = F. Sokolowski, *Lois sacrées des cités grecques* (Paris, 1969).
LSJ = H. G. Liddell, R. Scott, and H. S. Jones (eds.), *A Greek–English Lexicon*, 9th ed. with suppl. (Oxford, 1996).
Olympia IV = A. Furtwängler, *Die Bronzen und die übringen kleineren Funde von Olympia* (Berlin, 1890).
Perachora I = H. Payne, *The Sanctuaries of Hera Akraia and Limenia: Architecture, Bronzes, Terracottas* (Oxford, 1940).

*Syll.*³ = W. Dittenberger, *Sylloge Inscriptionum Graecarum*, 3rd ed. (Leipzig, 1915–1924).

Tiryns I = A. Frickenhaus, *Die Hera von Tiryns* (1912).

Aleshire, Sara. (1989). *The Athenian Asklepion: The People, Their Dedications, and the Inventories.* Amsterdam: Gieben.

Andrews, Carol. (1989). *Amulets of Ancient Egypt.* Austin: University of Texas Press.

Baumbach, Jens David. (2004). *The Significance of Votive Offerings in Selected Hera Sanctuaries in the Peloponnese, Ionia, and Western Greece.* Oxford: Archaeopress.

Beazley, John. (1963). *Attic Red-Figure Vase-Painters.* Oxford: Clarendon Press.

Bell, Malcolm. (1981). *Morgantina Studies* I: *The Terracottas.* Princeton: Princeton University Press.

Brumfield, Allaire. (1997). "Cakes in the Liknon: Votives from the Sanctuary of Demeter and Kore on Acrocorinth." *Hesperia* 66.1:147–172.

Burkert, Walter. (1966). "Kekropidensage und Arrhephoria: Vom Initiationsritus zum Panathenäenfest." *Hermes* 94:1–25.

———. (1987). "Offerings in Perspective: Surrender, Distribution, Exchange." In Tullia Linders and Gullög Nordquist, eds., *Gifts to the Gods: Proceedings of the Uppsala Symposium*, 43–50. Uppsala: University of Stockholm.

Burton, Joan. (1989). "Women's Commensality in the Ancient Greek World." *Greece and Rome* 45.2:143–165.

Calame, Claude. (1997). *Choruses of Young Women in Ancient Greece: Their Morphology, Religious Role, and Function.* Trans. D. Collins and J. Orion. Lanham, MD: Rowan and Littlefield.

———. (1999). *The Poetics of Eros in Ancient Greece.* Trans. Janet Lloyd. Princeton: Princeton University Press.

Caldwell, Lauren. (2007). "*Nuptiarum Sollemnia?* Girls' Transition to Marriage in Roman Jurists." In Maryline Parca and Angeliki Tzanetou, eds., *Finding Persephone: Women's Rituals in the Ancient Mediterranean*, 209–227. Bloomington: Indiana University Press.

Campbell, John K. (1964). *Honour, Family, and Patronage: A Study of Institutions and Moral Values in a Greek Mountain Community.* Oxford: Clarendon Press.

Clark, Isabelle. (1998). "The Gamos of Hera: Myth and Ritual." In Sue Blundell and Margaret Williamson, eds., *The Sacred and the Feminine in Ancient Greece*, 13–26. London: Routledge.

Clinton, Kevin. (1988). "Sacrifice at the Eleusinian Mysteries." In Robin Hägg, Nanno Marinatos, and Gullög Nordquist, eds., *Early Greek Cult Practice*, 69–80. Stockholm: Aström.

Cohen, David. (1990). *Law, Sexuality, and Society: The Enforcement of Morals in Classical Athens.* Cambridge: Cambridge University Press.

Cole, Susan Guettel. (1984). "The Social Functions of Rituals of Maturation: The Koureion and the Arkteia." *Zeitschrift für Papyrologie* 55:233–244.

————. (2004). *Landscapes, Gender, and Ritual Space: The Ancient Greek Experience.* Berkeley: University of California Press.

Corvisier, Jean-Nicolas. (1985). *Santé et société en Grèce ancienne.* Paris: Economica.

Dakoronia, Fanouria, and Lukretia Gounaropoulou. (1992). "Artemiskult auf einem neuen Weihrelief aus Achinos bei Lamia." *Mitteilungen des Deutschen Archäologischen Instituts, Athenische Abteilung* 107:217–227.

Danforth, Loring M. (1991). "The Resolution of Conflict through Song in Greek Ritual Therapy." In Peter Loizos and Euthymios Papataxiarchis, eds., *Contested Identities: Gender and Kinship in Modern Greece,* 98–113. Princeton: Princeton University Press.

Delaney, Carol. (1991). *The Seed and the Soil: Gender and Cosmology in Turkish Village Society.* Berkeley: University of California Press.

Demand, Nancy. (1994). *Birth, Death, and Motherhood in Classical Greece.* Baltimore: Johns Hopkins University Press.

Detienne, Marcel. (1974). "Orphée au miel." In J. LeGoff and P. Nora, eds., *Faire de l'histoire,* vol. 3, 56–75. Paris: Gallimard.

Diels, Hermann. (1914). *Antike Technik.* Leipzig: Teubner.

Dowden, Ken. (1989). *Death and the Maiden: Girls' Initiation Rites in Greek Mythology.* London: Routledge.

Edelstein, Emma J., Ludwig Edelstein, and Gary Ferngren. (1945). *Asclepius: A Collection and Interpretation of the Testimonies.* 2 vols. Baltimore: Johns Hopkins University Press.

Faraone, Christopher. (2003). "Playing the Bear and the Fawn for Artemis: Female Initiation or Substitution Sacrifice." In David B. Dodd and Christopher A. Faraone, eds., *Initiation in Ancient Greek Rituals and Narratives: New Critical Perspectives,* 43–68. London: Routledge.

Ferarri, Gloria. (2003). "What Kind of Rite of Passage Was the Ancient Greek Wedding?" In David B. Dodd and Christopher A. Faraone, eds., *Initiation in Ancient Greek Rituals and Narratives: New Critical Perspectives,* 27–42. London: Routledge.

Flognfeldt, Yngve Thomassen. (2009). "Sanctuaries and Votive Offerings from the Early Iron Age: A Comparative Study of Votive Offerings from the Peloponnese." M.A. thesis, University of Bergen.

Furtwängler, A. (1906). *Aegina: Das Heiligtum der Aphaia.* Munich: Verlag der K. B. Akademie der Wissenschaften in Kommission des G. Franz'schen Verlags.

Gélis, Jacques. (1991). *History of Childbirth: Fertility, Pregnancy, and Birth in Modern Europe.* Trans. Rosemary Morris. Boston: Northeastern University Press.

Hadzisteliou Price, Theodora. (1978). *Kourotrophos: Cults and Representations of the Greek Nursing Deities.* Leiden: Brill.

Hall, Edith. (2006). "Childbearing Women: Birth and Family Crisis in Ancient Drama." *The Theatrical Cast of Athens: Interactions between Ancient Greek Drama and Society,* 60–99. Oxford: Oxford University Press.

Hamilton, Richard. (1984). "Sources for the Athenian Amphodromia." *Greek, Roman, and Byzantine Studies* 25.3:243–251.

Harris, Diane. (1995). *The Treasures of the Parthenon and Erechtheion.* Oxford: Oxford University Press.

Harrison, A. R. W. (1968). *The Law of Athens.* Oxford: Oxford University Press.

Homolle, Théophile. (1895). "Inscriptions de Delphes." *Bulletin de Correspondance Hellénique* 19:5–69.

Hunter, Virginia. (1993). "Agnatic Kinship in Athenian Law and Athenian Family Practice." In Baruch Halpern and Deborah W. Hobson, eds., *Law, Politics, and Society in the Ancient Mediterranean World*, 100–121. Sheffield: Sheffield Academic Press.

Imhoof-Blumer, Friedrich. (1871). *Choix de monnaies grecques du cabinet de F. Imhoof-Blumer.* Winterthur.

Jacobson, D. (1980). "Golden Handprints and Red-Painted Feet: Hindu Childbirth Rituals in Central India." In Nancy Falk and Rita Gross, eds., *Unspoken Words: Women's Religious Lives in Non-Western Cultures*, 73–93. San Francisco: Harper and Row.

Jantzen, Ulf. (1972). *Ägyptische und orientalische Bronzen aus dem Heraion von Samos.* Samos VIII. Bonn: Deutsches Archäologisches Institut/R. Habelt.

Jeanmaire, Henri. (1939). *Couroi et courètes: Essai sur l'éducation spartiate et sur les rites d'adolescence dans l'antiquité hellénique.* Lille: Bibliothèque Universitaire.

Jeffery, Patricia, Roger Jeffery, and Andrew Lyon. (1989). *Labour Pains and Labour Power: Women and Childbearing in India.* London: Zed Books.

Johnston, Sarah I. (1995). "Defining the Dreadful: Remarks on the Greek Child-Killing Demon." In Marvin Meyer and Paul Mirecki, eds., *Ancient Magic and Ritual Power*, 361–387. Leiden: Brill.

———. (1997). "Corinthian Medea and the Cult of Hera Akraia." In James J. Clauss and Sarah Iles Johnston, eds., *Medea: Essays on Medea in Myth, Literature, Philosophy, and Art*, 44–70. Princeton: Princeton University Press.

Kilian-Dirlmeier, I. (1984). *Nadeln der frühhelladischen bis archaischen Zeit von der Peloponnes.* Prähistorische Bronzefunde XIII.8. Munich: Beck.

King, Helen. (1983). "Bound to Bleed: Artemis and Greek Women." In Averil Cameron and Amélie Kuhrt, eds., *Images of Women in Antiquity*, 109–127. Detroit: Wayne State University Press.

Kondis, I. D. (1967). "Artemis Brauronia." *Archaiologikon Deltion* 22:156–206.

Kourouniotis, Konstantinos. (1896). "Πήλινα ἀρτοπεῖα." *Archaiologikē Ephemeris*: 201–216.

Larson, Jennifer. (2001). *Greek Nymphs: Myth, Cult, Lore.* Oxford: Oxford University Press.

Lefèber, Yvonne, and Henk W. H. Voorhoeve. (1998). *Indigenous Customs in Childbirth and Childcare.* Antwerp: Van Gorcum.

Lévi-Strauss, Claude. (1963). "The Effectiveness of Symbols." In *Structural Anthropology*, 186–205. Trans. Claire Jacobson. New York: Basic Books.

Linders, Tullia. (1994). "Sacred Menus on Delos." In Robin Hägg, ed., *Ancient Greek Cult Practice from the Epigraphical Evidence*, 71–79. Stockholm: Svenska Institutet i Athen.

Loraux, Nicole. (1995). *The Experiences of Tiresias: The Feminine and the Greek Man.* Trans. Paula Wissing. Princeton: Princeton University Press.

Lyons, Deborah. (2003). "Dangerous Gifts: Ideologies of Marriage and Exchange in Ancient Greece." *Classical Antiquity* 22:93–134.

———. (2007). "The Scandal of Women's Ritual." In Maryline Parca and Angeliki Tzanetou, eds., *Finding Persephone: Women's Rituals in the Ancient Mediterranean,* 29–51. Bloomington: Indiana University Press.

Matthews, V. J. (1996). *Antimachus of Colophon: Text and Commentary.* Leiden: Brill.

Neils, Jenifer, and John H. Oakley. (2003). *Coming of Age in Ancient Greece: Images of Childhood from the Classical Past.* New Haven: Yale University Press.

Oakley, J. H., and R. Sinos. (1993). *The Wedding in Ancient Athens.* Madison: University of Wisconsin Press.

Parker, Robert. (1996). *Miasma: Pollution and Purification in Early Greek Religion.* Oxford: Clarendon Press.

———. (2007). *Polytheism and Society at Athens.* Oxford: Oxford University Press.

Parker, Robert, and Dirk Obbink. (2000). "Aus der Arbeit 'Inscriptiones Graecae' VI. Sales of Priesthoods on Cos." *Chiron* 30:415–447.

Perlman, Paula. (1989). "Acting the She-Bear for Artemis." *Arethusa* 22:111–133.

Pingiatoglou, Semeli. (1981). *Eileithyia.* Wurzburg: Königshausen and Neumann.

Redfield, James. (1982). "Notes on the Greek Wedding." *Arethusa* 15.1/2:181–201.

———. (1990). "From Sex to Politics: The Rites of Artemis Triklaria and Dionysos Aisymnëtës at Patras." In David Halperin, John Winkler, and Froma Zeitlin, eds., *Before Sexuality: The Construction of Erotic Experience in the Ancient World,* 115–134. Princeton: Princeton University Press.

———. (2003). *The Locrian Maidens: Love and Death in Greek Italy.* Princeton: Princeton University Press.

Rhodes, P. J., and Robin Osborne. (2003). *Greek Historical Inscriptions: 404–323 B.C.* Oxford: Oxford University Press.

Rolley, C. (1984). "Autre objets de metal." In *L'antre corycien* II. Bulletin de Correspondance Hellénique, suppl. 9. Paris: École française d'Athènes.

Schwyzer, Eduard. (1923). *Dialectorum graecorum exempla epigraphica potiora.* Leipzig: Hirzel.

Silverman, Sydel F. (1975). "The Life Crisis as a Clue to Social Function: The Case of Italy." In Rayna R. Reiter, ed., *Toward an Anthropology of Women* (New York: Monthly Review Press, 1975), 309–321. Originally published in *Anthropological Quarterly* 40.3 (1967): 127–138.

Simon, C. G. (1986). "The Archaic Votive Offerings and Cults of Ionia." Ph.D. diss., University of California, Berkeley.

Sinn, Ulrich. (1983). "Zur Wirkung des ägyptischen 'Bes' auf die griechische Volksreligion." In *Antidoron: Festschrift für Jürgen Thimme,* 87–94. Carlsruhe: Müller.

Sourvinou-Inwood, Christiane. (1988). *Studies in Girls' Transitions: Aspects of the Arkteia and Age Representation in Attic Iconography.* Athens: Kardamitsa.

Strøm, Ingrid. (1995). "The Early Sanctuary of the Argive Heraion and Its External Re-

lations: The Greek Geometric Bronzes." In Sored Dietz, ed., *Proceedings of the Danish Institute at Athens*, 1:37–127. Aarhus: Aarhus University Press.

Van Gennep, Arnold. (1960). *The Rites of Passage*. Trans. Monika Vizedom and Gabrielle Caffee. Chicago: University of Chicago Press.

Van Straten, F. T. (1981). "Gifts for the Gods." In H. Versnel, ed., *Faith, Hope, and Worship: Aspects of Greek Religious Mentality*, 65–141. Leiden: Brill.

Versnel, H. S. (1977). "Polycrates and His Ring." *Studi Storico-Religiosi* 1:17–46.

Walsche, W. G. (1908). "Birth (Chinese)." *Encyclopedia of Religion and Ethics*, 2:645–646. New York: Charles Scribner's Sons.

Wise, Susan. (2007). "Childbirth Votives and Rituals in Ancient Greece." Ph.D. diss., University of Cincinnati.

Wyss, Bernhard. (1936). *Antimachi Colophonii reliquiae*. Berlin: Weidmann.

[FOUR]

Collaboration and Conflict

DISCOURSES OF MATERNITY IN

HIPPOCRATIC GYNECOLOGY AND EMBRYOLOGY

Yurie Hong

The uterus . . . is termed mētra, *because it is the mother of all the embryos borne of it or because it makes mothers of those who possess it.*

SORANUS, *GYNECOLOGY* I.6; TRANS. TEMKIN (1956), 8

Within any culture, motherhood is defined in biological and social terms. To varying degrees, a mother may be identified as a woman who has given birth to a child and/or one who bears the primary responsibility for its upbringing. On the whole, ancient Greek sources tend to express intense ambivalence about women's birthing and rearing of children. While positive representations of mothers do exist,[1] the majority of our sources reflect great anxiety about the nature of a mother's relationship to her husband and child[2] and the overall risks and benefits of reproduction for men and women alike.[3] Ancient medical writing echoes this ambivalence and gives voice to a similarly complex range of responses to the female body and the physiological phenomena of pregnancy and childbirth. While ancient gynecological and embryological texts focus on the *biological* processes by which women become mothers, cultural discourses on the *social* institution of motherhood reveal how those processes are articulated and understood. This essay looks at how Greek medical writing constructs the maternal body and the maternal–fetal relationship in narratives of conception, gestation, and childbirth.

MATERNAL MEDICINE

Composed primarily during the fifth and fourth centuries BCE, the sixty or so treatises contained in the Hippocratic corpus comprise the ear-

liest set of Greek medical writing that survives.[4] About ten of these treatises are devoted specifically to "women's diseases" and detail the impact of menstruation, conception, pregnancy, and birth on the female body.[5] This narrow focus indicates that a woman's ability to bear children was a primary medical and social concern and that motherhood was viewed as an integral part of a woman's social identity and physical well-being.[6]

As previous scholars have shown, theories about female physiology and anatomy were heavily influenced by the notion that women's bodies were fundamentally different from and inferior to men's.[7] That difference was thought to stem from women's reproductive capacity, which was viewed as governing women's physical and mental disposition. Hippocratic doctors believed that the womb could become oriented in different directions, causing menstrual blood to be expelled inside the woman's body, where it would putrefy and lead to infections or tumors. They also believed that if the womb became dehydrated, it could move throughout the body in search of moisture, pushing up against the woman's organs, suffocating her, and driving her mad.[8]

As scholars have observed, these theories often were used to justify women's exclusion from the public arena.[9] They also provided medical support for upholding traditional gender roles by promoting the salutary effects of pregnancy and childbirth:[10] Women who have had sex with men, conceived, and given birth are said to be healthier and less prone to suffer from menstrual problems.[11] Frequently, sexual intercourse is itself prescribed as part of the treatment or as a test to determine whether the patient has been cured. The recommendation for the woman to "have intercourse with her man"[12] and the refrain "if she becomes pregnant she will be healthy"[13] demonstrate the degree to which a woman's good health was thus perceived to be contingent on the fulfillment of her social role as a sexual partner and reproducer of the household.[14]

However, while the Hippocratic writers operated within a cultural framework that took these roles for granted, their main concern was to identify and treat the bodily conditions to which women were subject, that is, to follow the theory and practice of medical expertise.[15] But not all medical writers weighted these goals equally or in the same way. Some were more dedicated to theory and others to therapy, and the approach a medical writer adopted could play a significant role in the resulting image of the maternal body.[16] This effect can be seen in narratives of pregnancy and birth contained in the two types of "women treatises" in the corpus: 1) gynecology, which focuses on treating disorders related to menstruation, pregnancy, and birth, and 2) embryology, which seeks to elucidate the internal

processes of conception and fetal development.[17] While both sets of treatises subscribe to the same physiological principles, each develops its own goals and adopts a rhetoric of reproduction that casts the maternal body in different, often conflicting, lights.[18]

Diseases of Women (*DW*) 1 is the most comprehensive gynecological and obstetrical treatise in the corpus.[19] The text takes a primarily therapeutic approach and catalogues and suggests treatment for such conditions as uterine displacement and problems with menstruation (1–9), inability to conceive (10–20, 22–24), gestational complications (21, 25–32), difficult births (33–34, 68–70), abnormal lochial flow, or afterbirth (35–41), and uterine complications after birth or miscarriage (42–67, 71–73). It concludes with a list of additional recipes and therapies (74–109).

As this outline of its contents makes clear, the treatise has two overlapping goals: to treat women's conditions and to achieve positive reproductive outcomes.[20] The repeated references to a woman's potential to conceive, even when conception is not the issue at hand, highlight the extent to which preservation of women's fertility constitutes the treatise's overarching concern.[21] It is important to emphasize, however, that its primary goal is to remedy women's physical ailments, and childbirth figures as just one aspect of this overall aim. When the fetus is mentioned, it is often treated as a secondary figure whose impact on the maternal body is described in terms of mechanical processes.

This focus on female disorders can be viewed negatively, as constructing women's bodies as flawed and in need of constant medical intervention.[22] However, it can also be seen as validating women's bodily experience by acknowledging the pain of menstrual cramping, the discomfort of pregnancy, and the very real dangers involved in childbirth. The litany of potential complications demonstrates, quite dramatically, the fact that birth was a serious business for both mother and child and underscores the potential costs involved in becoming a mother.

By contrast, the embryological treatises, *On Generation* and *On the Nature of the Child*, take a much more theoretical approach.[23] Accordingly, the characterization of the maternal–fetal relationship shifts. Originally transmitted as a single text, *On Generation* and *On the Nature of the Child* were also most likely composed by the same author as *Diseases of Women* 1.[24] Unlike that treatise, *On Generation* and *On the Nature of the Child* limit their discussion of reproduction to conception, gestation, and birth, and focus almost exclusively on the fetal, rather than the maternal, body. In contrast with the more woman-centered perspective of *Diseases of Women* 1, this approach envisions mother and child as two separate entities.[25] The treatises'

methodological interest in one over the other leads to the emergence of a model of conflict and dominance that amplifies over the course of the narrative.

In this essay I argue that medical accounts of conception, gestation, and birth contain a shadow narrative about motherhood that is inflected with anxieties about maternal or fetal harm, the potential instability of maternal allegiances, and possible fluctuations in the power dynamics of the household. Given their shared authorship, these three treatises provide valuable insight not only into the ways in which medical writing engages with cultural constructions of motherhood, but also into the ways in which different modes of intellectual thought and argumentation shape the images of motherhood and mother–child relations. I will begin by examining the rhetoric of the embryologies' narrative of pregnancy and birth before turning to corresponding passages in the gynecologies.[26]

CONCEPTION: DUELING MODELS
AND THE BATTLE OF THE SEXES

On Generation contains the fullest account of the production of male and female seed and the mechanical processes of conception.[27] As early as the sixth century BCE, medical and scientific thinkers posited the following theories on the nature of the seed:[28]

1. Pangenesis (seed was composed of elements derived from the entire body)
2. Seed was the foam of agitated blood
3. Encephalo-myogenesis (seed was derived from the head or brain via the spinal marrow)

Rather than introducing a new theory of conception, the author of *On Generation* synthesizes several preexisting hypotheses into one coherent narrative.[29] He asserts that for men, seed is derived from the "most potent" (τὸ ἰσχυρότατον) part of each humor in the body. Derived from the foam of blood agitated during sexual intercourse, the seed collects in the head and is "diffused from the brain . . . into the spinal marrow," passing "via the testicles into the penis" and stimulating the growth of facial and body hair as it goes (*Gen.* 1.1–3). In addition to debates on the nature of seed, the respective contributions of mother and father to the developing fetus was a favorite topic of discussion. The author's statement that "a sim-

ilar process" of seed production occurs in women constitutes an additional attempt to reconcile two mutually exclusive arguments about the process of reproduction.[30]

While women's centrality in reproduction is taken for granted in mythical examples of goddesses, such as Gaia and Hera, who manage to reproduce parthenogenically,[31] scientific debates about whether and to what degree women played a role in the physical generation of the fetus tend to assume the primacy of the father. Some thinkers believed in what is called the one-seed theory (in which fetal material derived only from the father), while others subscribed to the two-seed theory (which attributed fetal material to both parents).[32] The most notorious example of the one-seed theory occurs in Aeschylus's *Eumenides*, where Apollo famously denies that mothers are truly parents of the children they bear:[33]

The woman who is called *the "mother" of the child is not the parent*,
but rather a *nurse* of the newly sown embryo.
He who impregnates generates [the child], while *she, as a stranger for a*
stranger,
preserves the shoot if the god does not harm it in some way.
(*EUMENIDES* 658–661)

According to this model, the father is the real parent of the child, whereas the mother is characterized as a "stranger" (ξένη) to the household. While a woman may house, nourish, and give birth to the child, she is biologically unconnected to its physical being. This construction of the maternal–fetal relationship provides a vivid example of the notion that women were perpetual outsiders whose loyalty to their husbands and children was always in question. This embryological theory, especially as represented here, undercuts assumptions of women's centrality to birth and reflects an ideological privileging of the father in reproduction as well as in society.

The one-seed theory was not, however, the one most commonly held by the Hippocratic writers.[34] The author of *On Generation* asserts emphatically that *both* male and female emit seed and contribute to the child's physical makeup (*Gen.* 4.1, 6.1).[35] The two-seed theory likely arose, or at least became more widely accepted, from the simple fact that children sometimes resemble their mothers or maternal family members, in addition to the fact that only women give birth. While the two-seed theory also reflects a desire to affirm paternal importance, in contrast to the one-seed theory it does not do so at the expense of the mother. Reproductive contribution is not viewed necessarily as a zero-sum game.[36] What is innovative about this au-

thor's approach is that while he subscribes to the two-seed theory, he none-theless incorporates aspects of the one-seed theory in his discussion of how fetal sex is determined. The dominance of the father in the one-seed theory is replaced by a seemingly more collaborative model of conception. The at-tempt to synthesize multiple strands of scientific discourse, however, results in an increasingly vivid rhetoric of conflict and dominance that unfolds in the narrative of gestation and birth to follow.

With the assertion that women, too, emit seed, the author moves on to discuss the determination of fetal sex, taking a similarly eclectic approach to preexisting intellectual debates. His central argument is that women and men both emit seed "derived from the whole body" and that both par-ents may emit two types of seed at any given time: a "stronger," male-determining, seed or a "weaker," female-determining, one. He further re-marks that "strong" seed will result in a boy "because the male is stronger than the female" (*Gen.* 6.1). The conflation of fetal sex with seminal potency is consistent with common cultural assumptions about the relative strength and weakness of men and women outside of the womb.[37] Preexisting as-sumptions about gender and social relationships are thus mapped onto the qualities of biological matter and its various interactions. At the same time, the fact that women may produce "strong," male-determining seed while men may produce "weaker," female-determining seed allows for the possi-bility that the child's sex may have been designated by either parent.

The idea that "stronger" or "weaker" seed determined fetal sex was the one-seed theory's explanation of how a fetus made up of purely paternal material may become male or female.[38] The application of this idea, in con-junction with the theory of pangenesis, to the two-seed model explains the problem of maternal resemblance that the one-seed theory failed to address. The author then states that because seed is drawn from all parts of the body, both mother and father will contribute to each of the child's attributes:

> And so it is sometimes the case that a daughter will bear a closer resem-blance to her father than to her mother in the majority of her character-istics, while at other times a boy will resemble his mother more closely than his father. (*Gen.* 8.2)

Compared to the one-seed theory of parentage, the two-seed model re-flects a relatively egalitarian view of gender roles in reproduction because it at least recognizes the mother's potential contribution to each aspect of the child.[39] This particular synthesis of the one-seed and two-seed models con-tains the potential for a rhetoric of parental complementarity and coopera-

tion. The author says that if both parents emit "strong" seed, the combined mixture will result in a boy, while "weak" seed emitted by both will result in a girl. Thus, parental material may be collaborative in determining fetal sex if they contribute the same type of seed. The stage seems to be set for a fifty-fifty chance of parental consensus as to the child's sex. This potential, however, is never fully realized, and the interaction between maternal and paternal seed is quickly characterized in terms of conflict.

ἢν γὰρ πολλῷ πλέον τὸ ἀσθενὲς σπέρμα ἢ τοῦ ἰσχυροτέρου, κρατεῖται τὸ ἰσχυρὸν καὶ μιχθὲν τῷ ἀσθενεῖ ἐς θῆλυ περιηνέχθη· ἢν δὲ πλέον ᾖ τὸ ἰσχυρὸν τοῦ ἀσθενέος, κρατηθῇ τε τὸ ἀσθενές, ἐς ἄρσεν περιηνέχθη. (*Gen.* 6.2)

If the weak seed is much greater in quantity than the stronger seed, the strong seed is overpowered and, having been mixed with the weak, results in a female. But if the strong seed is greater in quantity than the weak, and the weak is overpowered, [the mixing] results in a male. (emphasis mine)

The language of strength, weakness, and overpowering is fairly emphatic. This is in part due to the author's incorporation of the final, and most crucial, Hippocratic theory, the principle of *prevalence* (ἐπικράτεια)—the idea that all opposing elements (for example, heat/cold, wet/dry) will compete with the other for dominance. The principle of prevalence establishes conflict as the primary mode of interaction between the parents' seed, identifying male and female as polar opposites fighting for dominance.[40] Furthermore, the author then states that the negotiation of maternal and paternal material applies to all of the child's physical characteristics. Thus, even if both partners contribute "strong" seed that results in a boy, characteristics drawn from each parent's body will struggle with one another to determine whether the boy inherits, for example, the father's nose and the mother's ears.

The narrative of conflict thus develops along a number of axes:

1. Gender (male-determining vs. female-determining seed)
2. Potency (strong vs. weak seed)
3. Parentage (mother's seed vs. father's seed)

Not only does the principle of prevalence establish conflict as the main interactional mode, but its incorporation into the two-seed theory suggests

the unsettling possibility of the maternal seed (weak or strong) prevailing over the paternal. Thus, not only does the blending of these theories reflect cultural assumptions about gender difference, but it also provides fertile ground for the expression of broader anxieties about the implications of an oppositional relationship in the context of the family.

Combining the theory of seminal bi-potency and the principle of prevalence marks a crucial transition in *On Generation*. The polarities that describe biological *material* shift to denote the *interactions* of that material. When both parents emit seed of the same strength or weakness, "potency" refers to the *quality* of the biological material. When maternal and paternal seed do not correspond, however, "potency" refers to the *ability* of one to overpower the other. This is an important shift. "Strength" and "weakness" as descriptors of physical *qualities*—that is, levels of concentration—become descriptors of physical *interactions*. This shift—from seed concentration to seed interaction—sets the following discussion of gestation and birth along a narrative trajectory of opposition and relational conflict. The resulting conceptual framework further shapes the characterization of the mother's relationship not only to her partner but also to the fetus developing within her.[41]

GESTATION AND FETAL "GENDER":
LIKE FATHER, LIKE (FETAL) SON

As *On Generation* moves on to fetal gestation, it emphasizes the motif of polarity and conflict. This oppositional framework provides the intellectual and rhetorical foundation for the author's explication of fetal development and has a profound impact on the way that the maternal–fetal relationship is characterized.

Discussing the possible reasons for the birth of small or sickly children, the author asserts that "the womb is to blame because it is narrower than it should be," offering the analogy that "if someone were to put a growing cucumber . . . into a narrow vessel, it would equal the hollow of the vessel [in size]" (*Gen.* 9.3). The assumption that the woman's body or behavior is to blame for negative reproductive outcomes is a common one.[42] *Diseases of Women* I says that a woman will have difficulty conceiving or carrying a child to term if she "lifts a heavy weight," "receives a blow," "jumps about," "faints," "eats too much or too little," "becomes fearful and alarmed," or if her womb is "flatulent . . . flabby, too large, or too small" (*DW* 1.25).

In both gynecological and embryological accounts, the woman is figured as a potential cause of harm. Mother and child are thus set against one another. *Diseases of Women* 1, however, adopts a somewhat sympathetic attitude, adding that "some women abort unintentionally: for it requires much vigilance and skill to nourish an embryo in the womb and bring it to full term, and to survive [the bringing of] it [into this world] in childbirth" (*DW* 1.25).[43] It further states that if a woman is "sickly and bilious," her child will also be "weak and . . . bilious" (*DW* 1.26), and acknowledges that, while a mother may have a negative impact on her unborn child, the fates of both are usually linked: "When the woman is cared for, the embryo gets stronger, and the woman herself is healthy. But if she is not cared for, the embryo is aborted and she herself is in danger of acquiring a long-term disease" (*DW* 1.25).[44]

By contrast, *On Generation*'s cucumber analogy contains no such concessions and instead amplifies the opposition by saying that if the vessel is large, the cucumber will grow larger—not because the vessel's capaciousness will accommodate the cucumber's natural size, but because the cucumber "competes [ἐρίζει] with the hollow of the vessel" (*Gen.* 9.3). Thus, even a vessel large enough to accommodate the cucumber (that is, the fetus), is characterized as an obstacle with which it must contend.

The undercurrent of rivalry that animates the vessel-womb/cucumber-fetus relationship recalls the contest of parental seed—not only with regard to the concept of relative, competitive strength but because it builds on the dual assumption that male and female are opposites and that opposites will compete for prevalence. The womb is configured as a gendered space in which the battle of the sexes will determine the medical fates of mother and child.[45] Although the fetus itself is not explicitly gendered, the cucumber has specifically male connotations. Not only does it have a phallic shape, but it was used in treatments meant to remedy barrenness—a use no doubt influenced by its association with the penis, to which it is sometimes compared.[46] As mentioned above, sex and pregnancy were thought to remedy uterine displacement because the penis would straighten the mouth of the womb, semen would irrigate it, and the fetus would weigh it down.[47]

The penis and the fetus thus serve similar functions in correcting women's perceived wayward anatomy. Furthermore, as Ann Hanson has observed, the medical writers regularly assume that a normal or healthy fetus is a boy and identify it as a girl only if there are problems arising from the fetus's presumed weakness. A fetus that could successfully "contend" with the womb would, therefore, by default be male while a female

fetus would be more likely to be miscarried.[48] Given the Greek tendency to view scientific phenomena in terms of similarity and difference,[49] it becomes clear that in *On Generation*, what should be a gender-neutral discussion of where deformed or sickly babies come from is increasingly inflected with notions of generational and gendered conflict. In other words, the narrative of conflict implied in the competition of maternal and paternal seed shifts and broadens to then describe the relationship between not only mother and child, but implicitly mother and unborn son. The inseminating penis ("father") and the product of the insemination, that is, the fetus ("son"), are aligned against the maternal body.

By contrast, in *Diseases of Women* 1, the fetus behaves not so much like a penis or as a separate entity, but rather more like the uterus itself. In two nearly identical passages describing the cause of suffocation in women, the author describes how the womb and the fetus head toward the liver, occupy the breathing space around the belly, encounter phlegm flowing down from the head, and then "gurgle" as they settle back into place (*DW* 1.7, 32). The implicit analogy between fetus and womb elides the fetal body with the womb and hence the mother's body (cf. the assertion above that a bilious woman will give birth to a bilious child) and is representative of the treatise's general approach to viewing the fetus within the context of the maternal body.

On Generation, however, privileges the fetal body at the expense of the mother's. It is striking that despite his reliance on observation and analogy in explicating fetal development, the author makes relatively little use of the external signs of fetal growth provided by the maternal body.[50] For example, while he postulates that fetal differentiation is complete by thirty-five days for boys and forty-two days for girls, he does not address the possible corresponding differences in the date when a woman pregnant with either sex will begin to "show." Nor does he mention observable phenomena such as the swelling of belly and breasts as possible indicators of fetal development. By contrast, in *Diseases of Women* 1 he says that when "the fullness of the breasts and the belly collapse . . . and the breasts shrivel up and no milk appears, it is apparent that the child is either dead or is alive but weak" (*DW* 1.27). He also notes that pregnant women become pale and crave "strange foods" because blood is diverted to the belly (*DW* 1.34).

While both the gynecologies and embryologies subscribe to the same physiological principles, their differing priorities and methodologies view the fetus as aligned with or against the mother. Because gynecology is primarily therapeutic in its goals, the female body takes center stage in the

texts while the fetus is a supporting player. By contrast, in embryologies such as *On the Nature of the Child*, the maternal body disappears almost entirely.[51] The fetus becomes the protagonist of the story of childbirth while the mother is cast as a figure of secondary importance, one alienated from and potentially at odds with the child growing within her.

BIRTH AND THE "WAR IN THE WOMB"

This shift in focus from mother to fetus has great implications for the birth narrative to follow, where the implicit ideas of gender and conflict in the narratives of conception and gestation become much more vivid. According to *On the Nature of the Child*, birth begins when nutriment for growth provided by the mother's body is no longer sufficient for the child (ἡ τροφὴ καὶ ἡ αὔξησις ἡ ἀπὸ τῆς μητρὸς κατιοῦσα οὐκ ἔτι ἀρκέουσα τῷ παιδίῳ ἐστίν) (*Nat. Ch.* 30.5).[52] In response, the child's physical reaction to this failure of nutriment initiates the birth and causes labor pangs for the mother:

συμβαίνει τότε τῷ παιδίῳ κινεομένῳ καὶ ἀσκαρίζοντι χερσί τε καὶ ποσὶ ῥῆξαί τινα τῶν ὑμένων τῶν ἔνδον· ῥαγέντος δ' ἑνός, ἤδη οἱ ἄλλοι ἀκιδνοτέρην δύναμιν ἔχουσι . . . Ὁκόταν δὲ ῥαγέωσιν οἱ ὑμένες, τότε λύεται τοῦ δεσμοῦ τὸ ἔμβρυον, καὶ χωρεῖ ἔξω κλονηθέν· οὐ γὰρ ἔτι ἔχει σθένος τῶν ὑμένων προδόντων καὶ τούτων ἀπενεχθέντων οὐδ' αἱ μῆτραι δύνανται ἔτι τὸ παιδίον ἴσχειν· (*Nat. Ch.* 30.1)
[. . .]
Ὁκόταν δὲ χωρῇ τὸ παιδίον, βιῆται καὶ εὐρύνει τὰς μήτρας ἐν διεξόδῳ . . . ἐν δὲ τῆσι μήτρησιν ἐὸν ἐγκρατὲς μᾶλλον γίνεται ἐς τῶν ὑμένων τὴν κατάρρηξιν ἅμα δεκάτῳ μηνί . . . (*Nat. Ch.* 30.2)
[. . .]
ζητέον οὖν πλείω τροφὴν τῆς παρεούσης τὸ ἔμβρυον ἀσκαρίζον ῥήγνυσι τοὺς ὑμένας, καὶ λυθὲν τοῦ δεσμοῦ χωρεῖ ὁμοῦ ἔξω. (*Nat. Ch.* 30.9)

[Birth] comes about when the child tears some of the internal membranes with its hands and feet by moving and thrashing about. And when one [of these membranes] is torn, the power of the remaining ones is weakened. And when the membranes are torn, the fetus is freed from its bond,

and goes out in a rush; for no longer is there any strength [to hold it] once the membranes fail and have been carried away, nor does the womb have the power to restrain the child.

When the child emerges, it forces its way through the womb and widens it at the birth canal . . . [The fetus] becomes strong enough in the womb to tear up the membranes in the ninth month [of its gestation].

in search of more nutriment than is being provided, the infant tosses about until it ruptures the membranes and, released from its bond, it emerges all at once. (emphasis mine)

The maternal body is portrayed as restricting the fetus's growth, depriving it of food, and keeping it chained up (δεσμοῦ) until it develops enough physical force (βίη, δύναμις) to fight back and free itself by rupturing the uterine membranes with its hands and feet.[53] Mother and child are pitted against one another as the womb is unable (οὐδ' . . . δύναται) to control or manage the potency (δύναμις) of her empowered (ἐγκρατές) child, who causes the mother physical pain in labor and alters her internal landscape as it goes. The birth narrative thus describes a warlike scenario in which mother and child are cast as engaging in intrauterine violence.[54]

This coded struggle is further clarified by the author's subsequent comparison of human childbirth to the hatching of a chick from its egg:

Ὁκόταν ἐπιλείπῃ ἡ τροφὴ τῷ νεοσσῷ ἐκ τοῦ ᾠοῦ, οὐκ ἔχον ἀρκέουσαν . . . κινεῖται ἰσχυρῶς ἐν τῷ ᾠῷ, ζητέον τροφὴν πλείονα, καὶ οἱ ὑμένες περιρρήγνυνται, καὶ ὁκόταν ἡ μήτηρ αἴσθηται τὸν νεοσσὸν κινηθέντα ἰσχυρῶς, κολάψασα ἐξέλειψε. (*Nat. Ch.* 30.8)

When nourishment from the egg lessens [and] becomes insufficient for the chick . . . seeking more, [the chick] moves vigorously in the egg and the membranes are broken. And when the mother notices the chick's vigorous agitation, pecking at the shell, she hatches it.[55] (emphasis mine)

While the description of the birth of the human child is filled with violent words and active verbs, descriptions of the same natal phenomenon is more benign in the chicken world. The chick does not break chainlike membranes with its claws and beak. Rather, "the membranes are broken." Instead of reacting violently (βίηται), it simply "moves vigorously" (κινεῖται ἰσχυρῶς), and whereas the repetition of the word δύναμις in the human birth envisions the fetus overpowering the maternal body, this less aggres-

sive phrase indicates that the chick's struggles are not directed against its mother, who, upon noticing the chick in distress, helpfully pecks the eggshell and assists her offspring.[56] The hatching of the chick is represented as a collaborative process,[57] whereas the description of the human birth emerges even more clearly as an antagonistic struggle between mother and child.

While the analogy's primary function is to illustrate the notion that the failure of nutriment causes the child to move about and initiate its own birth, the hatching egg analogy sets the cultural paradigm of the nurturing, helpful mother (in the form of the hen) against that of the overbearing (human) mother who must be defeated if the child is to achieve independence. Given that chickens do not, in fact, engage in this behavior,[58] the inclusion of such a detail only heightens the difference in the characterization of the two mothers. One protects and nurtures her offspring, and one is at odds with it by the very nature of her own biology.

In light of the emerging pattern of a rhetoric of gendered conflict in the earlier competition between maternal and paternal seed and the fetus's competition with the womb, the battle between mother and child in birth emerges more specifically as one between mother and son. Given that female infants were thought to be weaker at birth than boys, it is difficult to envision this birth narrative, with its emphasis on strength and vigor, as describing the birth of a girl.[59] By contrast, due to their therapeutic orientation, the gynecologies only discuss difficult births, which leads to the implication that these births involved girls (or perhaps weak males).

The narrative of reproduction in the embryologies thus operates within a network of multiple axes of generational and gendered opposition: the conflict between mother and father, mother and child, and, implicitly, mother and son. As in the assumption that fetal harm was caused by the womb, such a construction of the mother–child relationship reflects the anxiety that the interests of mother and child might eventually be at odds with one another, however beneficial the relationship might have been at first. Despite the two-seed theory's acknowledgment of the mother's contribution, the overarching themes of competition and prevalence yield a family dynamic and mother–child relationship not unlike Apollo's definition of mothers in the *Eumenides* as biologically alienated from their children.[60]

The narrative of reproduction contained in *On Generation* and *On the Nature of the Child* is at war with itself, in its attempts to reconcile competing medical theories into a comprehensive one. Just as the author's account of conception integrates multiple, conflicting discourses and perspectives from the one- and two-seed theories, the birth narrative combines elements of the caring and the dangerous mother paradigms via the helpful chicken

analogy and the imagery of birth as war. In other words, the author's explication of the two-seed theory argues for a stronger mother–child connection than does the one-seed theory, but it also expresses a corresponding ambivalence about the enhanced potential for conflict that this biological intimacy entails.

It is not difficult to see how human childbirth could be understood primarily in terms of contentious violence while the hatching of a chick might not be. The hen and its egg are not physically attached to one another and pose no threat to each other's bodily integrity. The observation of blood and pain during birth as well as the very real risk of death for both mother and child would understandably have given rise to the analogy of birth as the domestic equivalent of a heroic struggle.[61]

Direct interpersonal conflict is not, however, the only way of envisioning birth. The treatise *Seven-Months' Child* states that "when the membranes are stretched out and the umbilical cord is extended, it causes pain for the mother. And then the fetus, released from its old bonds, becomes heavier" (3). Although this passage deploys vocabulary and physiological concepts similar to those found in *On the Nature of the Child*, it is not fetal violence but rather "the strained membranes and the extended umbilical cord" that cause pain. In contrast to *On the Nature of the Child*'s configuration of birth as the fetus's reaction to maternal restriction, the fetus's vigorous movements in *Eight-Months' Child* are said to be a demonstration of the fetus's renewed health and vigor following a period of sickness—one which is presented as a dangerous period for both mother and child.[62] In both instances, fetal movement and its effect on the maternal body are not articulated in terms that evoke interpersonal relations.

Similarly, in *Diseases of Women* I, a woman's discomfort in labor is due to fetal "convulsions" in addition to the fact that a constricted belly causes heartburn (*DW* 1.34). While this depiction of birth also subscribes to an active-fetus/passive-womb model, the author says that difficult births are the result of breech presentation and notes that "many times the women themselves, their babies, or both have died" (*DW* 1.33).[63] Thus, birth is characterized as a set of mechanical processes that can affect both mother and child in both positive and negative ways.[64] The physical intimacy of mother and child is viewed not as the precondition for parturitional violence, but as a mutual bond, with birth as an intense, yet shared, experience.[65] Acknowledging that maternal and fetal fates are often linked, *Diseases of Women* I gives the impression that for the most part bodily mechanics, rather than the mother and child themselves, are to blame when complications arise, and it expresses much concern over the life and health of the mother.

Indeed, grave *stelai* dedicated to women who died in childbirth provide ample evidence for the fact that giving birth was a dangerous business for both mother and child (e.g., fig. 1.3 of this volume). In an interesting twist, a funerary inscription for a woman named Socratea from Paros that dates to the second century CE reads, "The unstoppable Fury of the newborn infant took me, bitter, from my happy life with a fatal hemorrhage. I did not bring the child into the light by my labor pains, but it lies hidden in its mother's womb among the dead."[66] The tombstone, though inscribed from the perspective of the dead woman, would have been erected by the head of the household and therefore expresses publicly his own view of the death. In this case, the inscription engages in a discourse of fetal agency that results in harm to its mother.[67] Contrary to the more widespread trope of the harmful mother, here the fetus is viewed as the greater threat to the household because it is characterized as having caused the death of one of its central members. This inscription gives voice to the complexity of emotions surrounding childbirth, acknowledging that a child can be both an object of desire and a source of great anxiety. Because marriage was contracted for the production of legitimate children, motherhood was a way for women to gain status inside and outside of the household. Yet the pain of labor and the risk of death could not have been too far from anyone's mind.

There are two factors at work in the construction of maternal identity and relationships in the medical texts: preexisting cultural anxieties about women, birth, and family dynamics and the methodological focus and corresponding rhetorical strategy of any given treatise. Although written by the same author, *Diseases of Women* 1, *On Generation*, and *On the Nature of the Child* adopt divergent rhetorics of reproduction by capitalizing on different facets of broader cultural discourses on maternity. By inscribing the dynamics of gender onto reproductive processes, they express a range of anxieties about women and the institution of motherhood at the same time as they argue for a biologically cohesive family unit.

Building on the assumption of male–female difference and the notion that the interaction of opposites is a zero-sum game, the embryologies' emphasis on conflict affirms and validates a system whereby men must protect their own interests and those of their unborn children from the very bodies of the women who bear them. In the gynecologies, female biology and the mechanics of birth endanger the household by putting mother and child's lives at risk, thereby necessitating medical intervention. Both types of treatises simultaneously stoke and allay anxieties about reproduction by characterizing medical expertise and supervision as necessary to ensure individ-

ual and collective survival. In so doing, they not only capture the complex emotions and ambivalent attitudes surrounding childbirth and motherhood, but they also offer tantalizing glimpses into the experience of pregnancy and childbirth—the biological processes that, in turn, produce and reinforce a woman's social identity as a mother.

NOTES

I would like to express my gratitude for the support provided by Gustavus Adolphus College's Research, Scholarship, and Creativity grant and the assiduous work of my student research assistants, particularly that of Laura Luce. I would also express my deep appreciation to the following readers for taking the time to read earlier drafts of this paper: Ruby Blondell, Bronwen Wickkiser, Ann Hanson, Marilyn Skinner, David Leitao, Lawrence Bliquez, Mark Nugent, and Benjamin Crotty. Their thoughtful comments have been invaluable and have improved my work immeasurably. In particular I would like to thank Patricia B. Salzman and Lauren Petersen for their generous and insightful feedback. Finally, I am most grateful to Seán Easton and Emmet Easton-Hong for providing last-minute inspiration in the final stages of this project.

All translations are my own unless otherwise specified. Hippocratic texts are those of Littré (1839–1861), with the exception of *On Generation* and *On the Nature of the Child*, which have been edited by Joly (1970).

1. For ideological constructions of mothers as nurturing and self-sacrificing, see Aristotle, *Nichomachean Ethics* 1159a28–33, 1161b26–27, and Xenophon, *Memorabilia* 2.2.5. For vase paintings illustrating maternal–child bonding, see Keuls (1985), 110–113. See Loraux (1995), 23–43, on dying in childbirth as the female equivalent of dying in battle.

2. See Semonides, *On Women* and Hesiod, *Works and Days* 695–705 for the view of wives as an unavoidable curse. In Hesiod's *Theogony*, mothers repeatedly bear offspring who are a threat to their fathers (164–172, 468–472, 888–898); Medea kills her children in order to destroy Jason's household (*Medea* 816–817); and Clytemnestra murders Agamemnon as revenge for the sacrifice of their daughter (*Agamemnon* 1417–1418). See Murnaghan (1992) for additional examples of mothers as the source of both life and death.

3. Hesiod laments that wives and children are a drain on resources but are necessary for perpetuating the household (*Theogony* 590–612). Few data are available on maternal mortality rates, but these would likely have increased with the number of births. Morris (1987), 63, estimates that the ancient world had a population replacement rate of about five to six births per woman and that during prehistoric times 10–20 percent of women died giving birth. For tombstones that bear witness to the precariousness of childbirth, see Demand (1994), 155–166.

4. The specific number of treatises is difficult to pinpoint. *On Generation* and *On*

the Nature of the Child, for example, were originally composed as one continuous text but were treated separately in the manuscript tradition. Some later texts, such as *On the Nature of Women*, appear to be composites of earlier treatises. See Dean-Jones (1994), 10–13, for a helpful overview of the women treatises.

5. Most treatises assume a male patient. Some, such as *Epidemics* and *Aphorisms*, contain subsections on women or note responses to diseases that are perceived to be specific to women. For additional examples, see King (1998), 35.

6. Women are given to their husbands in marriage "for the plowing of legitimate children" (cf. Kock [1880–1888], Menander, fr. 720). Problems in conceiving seem to be a common reason for seeking treatment. The vast majority of texts assume that difficulty in conceiving is due to the woman. See Lloyd (1983a), 84 n. 101, however, for sources recommending adjustments to men's regimen.

7. See King (1998), 11–12, for ancient views of female anatomical difference and women's health as a distinct branch of medicine. See Dean-Jones (1991), 119, on the perceived relationship between female physical weakness and menstruation. Lloyd (1983a), 58–86, discusses the ways in which assumptions of male superiority influence the development of medical practice and theory. See Hanson (1992), esp. 32–33, on the way that embryological theories about the fetal origins of female weakness supported an interventionist approach to gynecology.

8. *Diseases of Women* (*DW*) 1.2. *On the Diseases of Virgins* says that girls beginning to menstruate are seized by desires to throw themselves down wells.

9. Women's flesh was thought to be spongier and moister than men's, a condition that would render women less capable of strenuous labor and more prone to illness (*DW* 1.1). As Dean-Jones (1991), 114–116, argues, such perceptions were taken as biological evidence that women's bodies were inferior to men's. Furthermore, the hazards of uterine displacement identified women as weak and in need of constant monitoring (King [1998], 36–39) and reinforced cultural notions of women as unstable and lacking in self-control (Dean-Jones [1992], 86–87). With regard to the theory of the wandering womb, in the later stages of pregnancy the uterus does indeed press up against the bladder and digestive organs and can cause great discomfort and irritability. Perhaps this suggested that the uterus had a similar effect on women even if they were not pregnant. See Dean-Jones (1991), 121–123, for a summary of scholarship on the wandering womb theory as possibly originating from observations of uterine prolapse, the lack of uterine space in the male body, women's own interpretation of bodily pain, the quasi-magical notion of the womb as an entity with a mind of its own, or mechanical principles whereby the dry would naturally be attracted to the wet.

10. Hanson (1990), 316–320. See also Hanson (1992), esp. 33, 48, and 59, on the way that Hippocratic medicine serves the broader interests of the *oikos* and the *polis*. This is not to imply that the goal of these treatises was simply to indoctrinate and oppress women. As Lloyd (1983a) notes, the treatises are genuinely concerned with treating women's conditions (85). Reproduction would certainly have been a central concern for women as well.

11. *On Generation* 4.3; *DW* 1.1.

12. *DW* 1.58, 59; *DW* 2.127, 135, 139; *On Barren Women* (*BW*) 220, 223.

13. *DW* 1.59; *DW* 2.135; *BW* 213, 220.

14. Occasionally the treatises recommend that a woman avoid sex because it will exacerbate preexisting medical conditions or interfere with the treatment: *DW* 1.76; *DW* 2.143, 149; *BW* 230. As Lloyd (1983a), 84–85, observes, such prescriptions are relatively rare, but they do indicate that enhancing fertility was not the *only* concern in these texts. Later, some medical writers, such as Soranus, viewed virginity as more healthful for both men and women. See Hanson (1992), 57.

15. This is also the case for men's diseases. For the ways in which men's bodies were also constructed as objects of medical inquiry and intervention, see King (1998), 9. While Hippocratic theories did generally relegate women to the category of "the other," as Hanson (1998) points out, "Hippocratics tried to cure diseases of women in accordance with the same mechanical principles applied to . . . men, for the mechanical paradigms enhanced their ability to intervene" (94).

16. Hanson (1992), 31–32, has shown the ways in which a medical writer's expectations and his treatise's own themes influence the characterization of gender difference.

17. Obstetrics is a specialization within the field of gynecology that deals specifically with pregnancy and childbirth. Like gynecology, it is primarily therapeutic and outcome oriented.

18. As Hanson (1995), 293–294, has observed, while gynecological and embryological treatises share the same assumptions about the nature and processes of the female body, the former focus more on therapy and practical application, while the latter emphasize theory. She thus argues that sexual asymmetry is less pronounced in the gynecologies than in embryologies because each had different goals in mind (293, 304–305): "The Hippocratic gynecologies [sought to bring] women's concerns in *paidopoiïa* within the compass of the written medical tradition, [while] the sophisticated embryologies . . . had the more grandiose aim of encompassing human life in all its stages within medical explanatory models" (294). My argument about the representation of maternal–fetal relations follows similar lines.

19. The physiological principles and therapeutic approaches in *DW* 1 are generally compatible with those of other gynecological treatises in the corpus. While the majority of my discussion will center on this treatise, the main arguments are meant to apply to the gynecologies more broadly.

20. A full translation of this treatise has not yet been published. Hanson (1975) and Lefkowitz and Fant (2005) provide selections.

21. Hanson (1990), 316.

22. For discussions of the way that the Hippocratic writers justified medical intervention into the female body, see Dean-Jones (1991); King (1998), 10–12, 36–39, 40–53; Hanson (1998), 93–94 and (1992), 31, 36, 56.

23. For the sake of clarity I will refer to them separately, as *Gen.* and *Nat. Ch.* Full translations are available in Lonie (1981) and Lloyd (1983b). On these treatises' canonical status, see Jouanna (2008) and Hanson (2008), 101, esp. n. 21, and 103–104.

24. The treatises date to the late fifth century or the early fourth century BCE and refer to one another explicitly at crucial points. See Lonie (1981), 43–54. Hanson (1991), 77, summarizes and refines earlier attempts to identify different layers of composition, or "viewpoints," that link these embryologies with specific gynecological treatises.

25. As Hanson (1995), 293, notes, unlike the embryological treatises, which view the fetus "as [a] prototype for mankind in his origins," the gynecological treatises instead view the fetus as a "potential cause of health or disease in women."

26. Despite all of its remedies aiding in conception, *DW* i contains only one short passage on the processes of conception itself, the significance of which I will address below.

27. The Hippocratic treatises overwhelmingly favor the term γονή, though γόνος is sometimes used with no discernible difference in meaning. The author's central point here is that women emit biological matter. I will use the more gender-neutral term "seed" for both male and female emissions, which should be thought of not as individual, quantifiable seeds but as maternal and paternal substances containing each prospective parent's "genetic code."

28. The list is adapted from Lonie (1981), 99–103.

29. Lonie (1981), 101.

30. The author is rather vague on this point and does not address the fact that women typically do not have testicles or facial hair. Here he is concerned primarily with the notion that women also emit seed generated from agitated blood.

31. Even Zeus, who gives birth to Athena and Dionysus, must first impregnate Metis and Semele, respectively.

32. Anaxagoras, Hippon, Diogenes of Apollonia, and some Pythagoreans subscribed to the one-seed theory. The two-seed theory is expounded by Alcmaeon, Parmenides, Empedocles, and Democritus, and in the Hippocratic treatises *On Regimen* i and *DW* i. Lonie (1981), 119.

33. See Goldhill (1984), 252–261, and Zeitlin (1996) for a detailed analysis.

34. Nor was it, by any means, the dominant view among pre-Socratics. See Lonie (1981), 119–120. Even in the *Eumenides*, the fact that the jury is split evenly and Athena's vote is necessary to break the tie is evidence of other cultural views on the matter.

35. The author foregrounds the woman in his discussion of bi-potential seed because this is the nonconventional part of his argument. Lonie (1981), 127–128.

36. As David Leitao (personal communication) has pointed out, the one-seed theory need not deny maternal contribution entirely. While one-seed theorists argued that the fetus derived from one (paternal) seed, menstrual blood may also be seen as contributing to the child's physical makeup later in the process. Subsequently, we see the way that scientific theory is again influenced by ideology in Aristotle (*De generatione animalium* 1.2.716a4–7, 2.4), who argues that women simply provide biological matter while the paternal seed is the real formative force.

37. The perceived differential in male and female bodily strength is used to substantiate theories about fetal development overall. Male fetuses were thought to be

fully developed by thirty days, while female fetuses required forty-two days (*Nat. Ch.* 18.1–7). See Lonie (1981), 190–194, and Hanson (2008), 97–99, for additional theories on the differential development of male and female embryos.

38. Lonie (1981), 127. Location of the embryo or fetus on the right or left side of the womb was another possible explanation.

39. The author asserts emphatically that a complete replica of one parent or the other cannot occur, thus foreclosing the possibility of a *de facto* one-seed model whereby the father's seed, for example, could completely overpower the mother's (*Nat. Ch.* 8.1). This argument imposes a theory of collaboration *and* conflict onto the process of conception. Even though the seeds emitted by the man and the woman are engaged in conflict, with one prevailing over the other, the prevailing parts together, regardless of their provenance, make up the whole. See Hanson (1992), 44–45.

40. See Lonie (1981), 129, for the concept of prevalence in the Hippocratic corpus. The use of social and political analogy to comprehend health and physiology goes back to Alcmaeon's theory that illness was the result of one or more opposing factors gaining sovereignty (μοναρχία) over others and upsetting the body's delicate equilibrium (ἰσονομία). Lonie (1981), 129–130.

41. For an illuminating example of a different rhetorical outcome, see Jouanna's (2008) discussion of the late treatise *On the Generation of Man*, which draws heavily on the Hippocratic treatises *On Generation* and *On the Nature of the Seed*. While *On the Generation of Man* uses the same argument about "stronger" and "weaker" seed, similarity is emphasized more heavily than competition of maternal and paternal elements: καὶ ἢν μὲν ἀπ᾽ ἀμφοτέρων τὸ σπέρμα ἰσχυρότερον ἔλθῃ, ἄρρεν γίνεται τὸ παιδίον ἢν δὲ ἀσθενέστερον, θῆλυ. 6.2 καὶ ἢν μὲν τοῦ ἀνδρὸς πλέον ἐπέλθῃ ἡ γόνος, ὅμοιον ἔοικε τῷ πατρὶ τὸ παιδίον ἢν δὲ τῆς γυναικὸς πλέον, ὅμοιον ἔοικε τῇ μητρί· ἢν δὲ ἴσῃ ἐπέλθῃ ἐξ ἀμφοτέρων, ἀμφοτέροις ὅμοιον ἔοικεν ("And if both contribute stronger seed, the child will be a boy, but if both contribute the weaker, then it will be a girl. Furthermore, if the seed from the man is more plentiful, the child will resemble its father; but if the seed from the woman is more plentiful, the child will resemble its mother; and if the seed comes from both in equal measure, the child will resemble both [parents]"; 6.1–2). The later text, *On the Generation of Man*, then, while importing many of the same Hippocratic theories about conception and gestation, does not adopt its characterizations of maternal–paternal and maternal–fetal relationships.

42. This remains true today. See Wood (2004) on the pervasiveness of hostile or judgmental terminology used to denote women's reproductive complications as well as countless studies that investigate the influence of maternal (but not paternal) behavior on negative reproductive outcomes; and see Daniels (1999) on the importance of paternal behavior.

43. This sentiment may reflect women's own expressions of self-blame when things go wrong.

44. Daniels (1999) analyzes contemporary medical and cultural discourses that pit maternal and fetal health against one another. She argues that the two are inter-

twined and that policies meant to promote fetal health must begin with concern for maternal well-being.

45. For additional ways in which the embryological treatises interpret the womb as a gendered space see Hanson (1992), 32–33, 44–45 and (2008), 98–99.

46. *Barren Women* 222 prescribes constructing a syringe-like apparatus with a cucumber "like a man's penis [in width]" (ὡς ἀνδρὸς αἰδοῖόν ἐστιν). In *DW* 2.144, a remedy for a prolapsed uterus includes hanging the woman upside down and leaving a large cucumber in her vagina. See also *BW* 222 for the use of a dry cucumber as a makeshift fumigation tube or syringe. See Hanson (2008), 98, on the way that medical writers "manipulate[d] gestation in such a way as to assert the primacy of the male."

47. *Nat. Ch.* 4.3 and *DW* 1.1. See also Hanson (1990), 319. See *DW* 2.133 and *BW* 221 for the use of tubes and probes generally for fumigation and for straightening the mouth of the uterus.

48. Hanson (2008), 98–99, 101–102.

49. See Lloyd (1966), 15–26, on pre-Socratic theories of opposites; and 345–360 on the medical writers' reliance on analogy.

50. In *DW* 1 descriptions of internal processes correspond to visible, external symptoms and describe the woman's experience of those symptoms. A displaced uterus, for example, will cause a woman to experience suffocation, while menstrual blood expelled inside the body will manifest as a tumor on the skin's surface.

51. The most frequently mentioned effects of pregnancy—nausea, fatigue, cravings, mood swings, back pain, the shape and location of the belly, etc.—are nowhere to be found. The author does describe the swelling of breasts during pregnancy but only to explain the internal, physiological process of lactation rather than the changes experienced by the pregnant woman herself (*Nat. Ch.* 21.2). For the tendency to erase the woman when focusing on the fetus, see Casper (1999), who notes that currently, "fetal treatment teams have emphasized pediatric surgery often at the expense of obstetrical perspective . . . the fetus has become the center of this new specialty . . . the health and well-being of the pregnant woman has [*sic*] often assumed a secondary role" (107).

52. In myth, maternal nurture is linked to the idea that nutriment provided may also be withheld. Cf. the *Homeric Hymn to Demeter*, in which Demeter (that is, goddess of the harvest), grieving at the loss of her daughter, withholds nutriment from her symbolic children, the mortals, who die without it.

53. See Lonie (1981), 216–218, for a discussion of the author's conception of δύναμις as an abstract power as well as a substantive force contained within the seed. See Lloyd (1966), 210–232, on the prominence of social and political metaphor in pre-Socratic cosmology, esp. 230 on δύναμις and 219–220 on κρατεῖν and its cognates. Lloyd (1966), 219, notes that "power (both physical force and political authority) and intelligence are often ascribed to cosmological factors." Lloyd (1966), 252–253, and *passim*, has also demonstrated that pre-Socratic theories, metaphors, and methodologies are closely interrelated with medical ones (for example, analogies of the human body and the cosmos).

54. Although these responses are clearly not meant to be seen as intentional on

the part of the mother and child, agency may exist without intention. Even a woman who wants her child may be seen as having a body that fights against it.

55. It is well established that chickens, like many other birds, frequently consume the eggshells of their hatched young, most likely as a way of replenishing calcium stores depleted during the laying process (Welty and Baptista [1988], 150). Hens, however, frequently eat unhatched eggs, for a number of possible reasons—nutritional deficiencies, stress, or simply taste—a common problem for those who raise chickens. See Jacob et al. (1997) and Luttmann and Luttmann (1976), 10.

Regardless of whether the ancient analogy is based on observed egg-pecking/-eating behavior, the important point is that hens, in reality, do not peck at eggs to *assist* in the hatching process but to *consume* the egg itself—an action that results in the death and/ or cannibalization of the potential chick. Therefore, contrary to the image of the helpful hen depicted in this analogy, the actual relationship of an egg-pecking hen with its chick is in fact far more troubling than the human mother's birthing relationship with her newborn (my thanks to Joel Carlin and Jon Grinnell of the Gustavus Adolphus College biology department for their assistance with this topic). On the pre-Socratics and medical writers' tendency to rely on flawed analogies and hypothetical experiments to make apparent that which would otherwise be difficult to prove, see Lloyd (1996), 357–360 and Lonie (1981), 77–86.

56. It is unclear whether the author knew of contractions, which could have been mentioned to strengthen his analogy. The womb might then have been viewed, like the hen, as helping the child emerge. See Hanson (2008), 103 and (1999), esp. 252–253, for a detailed discussion. *Contra* Lonie (1981), 244–245, Dean-Jones (1994), 212. Hanson argues that the Hippocratics viewed the uterus, like other bodily organs, as a passive receptacle and that the verbs περιστέλλεσθαι ("contract") and συνέλκεσθαι ("draw together") in *DW* 1.34 more accurately describe the uterus "collapsing around" the fetus rather than "contracting" to expel it.

57. The mother hen pecking at the egg and helping the chick hatch recalls the male-assisted birth of Athena from Zeus's head, which was broken open by Hephaestus's axe. My thanks to Ruby Blondell for this point.

58. This has been confirmed by an informal survey of biologists and chicken farmers. Given how fundamentally ingrained birthing practices are in nature, it is unlikely that chickens engaged in this behavior during the author's time and abandoned it during later periods (Joel Carlin, personal communication). See Lonie (1981), 77–86, on the use of analogy vs. experiment in medical argumentation as an instrument of persuasion.

59. Female fetuses were seen as weaker because the seed from which they were formed was wetter; Hanson (2008), 98. Hanson rightly observes that "[the Hippocratics] imagined the womb as a gendered space that replicated the experience of adults" (98).

60. For an additional example of this conflict-ridden family paradigm, see Herodotus's description of the Arabian vipers (3.109). The female viper is said to bite through the neck of the male viper during copulation, thereby killing him as he ejac-

ulates. Herodotus says that the female "pays recompense" (τίσιν . . . ἀποτίνει) for the deed because the offspring "avenge their father while still in the womb" (τῷ γονέι τιμωρέοντα ἔτι ἐν τῇ γαστρὶ) and eat through their mother by consuming her uterus (διεσθίει τὴν μητέρα, διαφαγόντα δὲ τὴν νηδὺν αὐτῆς). Sandwiched between two words for "womb," μητέρα suggests a pun on a third word for womb: μῆτραι. The emergence of these viper offspring from the μήτηρ after consuming her μῆτραι most vividly depicts birth as a zero-sum game. Birth is rendered as both an act of revenge and an act of survival, both of which depend on the annihilation of the mother in support of the father.

61. For the association of childbirth with battle, see Euripides, *Medea* 250–251, where Medea says she would rather die in battle than in childbirth, and *Iliad* 11.267ff., in which Agamemnon's pain at being stabbed in the thigh is compared to that of a woman in labor. For the equivalence of battle and childbirth see Loraux (1995), esp. 23–37. On the continuing characterization of mothers as either "heroic" or ignorant and selfish, a potential threat to the success of the fetal surgical endeavor, see Casper (1998), 168–203.

Warlike imagery continues to characterize pregnancy as a conflict of interests. A recent study, summarized by the *New York Times*, suggests that preeclampsia and other complications may arise due to maternal–fetal competition for nutrients on a genetic level: "A fetus does not sit *passively* in its mother's womb and wait to be fed. Its placenta *aggressively* sprouts blood vessels that *invade* its mother's tissues to *extract* nutrients. Meanwhile, . . . natural selection should favor mothers who could *restrain* these *incursions*, and manage to have several surviving offspring carrying on their genes. [Dr. Haig] envisioned pregnancy as a *tug of war*. Each side *pulls hard*, and yet a *flag* tied to the middle of the rope barely moves" (Zimmer [2006]; emphasis mine).

62. Hanson (2008), 97.

63. See also *Seven-Months' Child* 3 on the shared risk of premature births.

64. As outlined above, reproductive function is often represented as conferring health benefits on women by opening up their passageways and allowing for the proper drainage of fluids. Childbirth, however, is also acknowledged to be potentially disruptive to women's health. The author says that complications arising from excessive *lochia* can occur due to the rupturing of passageways from "the violence of the embryo's departure" and that the violence of birth can cause lesions (*DW* 1.39–40).

65. The treatise *Eight-Months' Child* posits that, during the eighth month of pregnancy, women suffer fevers due to the strain that the growing fetus puts on the uterine membranes and the pressure it exerts on her internal organs. Both mother and child could die from these fevers. That the fevers are precipitated by the fetus itself results in a narrative less inflected by a rhetoric of conflict and blame, emphasizing instead the symbiotic nature of maternal–fetal existence. See Hanson (1987), 595. For the social usefulness of the notion that certain infants were doomed, see Hanson (1987), esp. 600–602.

66. καί με πικρὰν νεαροῖο βρέφους ἀφύλακτος Ἐρεινύς / αἱμορύτο ιονόσωι τερπνὸν ἔλυσε βίον. / οὔθ ὑπ' ἐμαῖς ὠδεῖσι τὸ νήπιον εἰς φάος ἦγον, / ἀλλ' ὑπὸ

γαστρὶ φίλαι κεύθεται ἐμφθιμένοις (Kaibel [1878] §218). The inscription goes on to recount that she left behind a husband and two sons, a vivid reminder of both what could be gained through childbearing and what could be lost. Note the use of "Fury" ('Ερεινύς). In myth the Furies, or the Erinyes, were avenging goddesses who punished those guilty of killing blood relatives. The appearance of the term here is particularly evocative given the Furies' pursuit of Orestes for the murder of his mother, Clytemnestra. See the discussion of Aeschylus's *Eumenides* above.

67. For an interesting comparandum, see McDonagh (1996), who discusses pregnancy and abortion in accordance with legal concepts of consent and agency.

WORKS CITED

Brisson, Luc, Marie-Hélène Congourdeau, and Jean-Luc Solère, eds. (2008). *L'embryon, formation et animation: Antiquité grecque et latine, tradition hébraïque, chrétienne et islamique*. Paris: Vrin.

Cantor, David, ed. (2002). *Reinventing Hippocrates: The History of Medicine in Context*. Aldershot: Ashgate.

Casper, Monica. (1998). *The Making of the Unborn Patient: A Social Anatomy of Fetal Surgery*. New Brunswick, NJ: Rutgers University Press.

———. (1999). "Operation to the Rescue: Feminist Encounters with Fetal Surgery." In Lynn M. Morgan and Meredith W. Michaels, eds., *Fetal Subjects, Feminist Positions*, 101–112. Philadelphia: University of Pennsylvania Press.

Daniels, Cynthia. (1999). "Fathers, Mothers, and Fetal Harm: Rethinking Gender Difference and Reproductive Responsibility." In Lynn M. Morgan and Meredith W. Michaels, eds., *Fetal Subjects, Feminist Positions*, 83–93. Philadelphia: University of Philadelphia Press.

Dean-Jones, Lesley Ann. (1991). "The Cultural Construct of the Female Body in Classical Greek Science." In Sarah Pomeroy, ed., *Women's History and Ancient History*, 111–137. Chapel Hill: University of North Carolina Press.

———. (1992). "The Politics of Pleasure: Female Sexual Appetite in the Hippocratic Corpus." *Helios* 19.1/2:72–91.

———. (1994). *Women's Bodies in Classical Greek Science*. Oxford: Oxford University Press.

Demand, Nancy. (1994). *Birth, Death, and Motherhood in Classical Greece*. Baltimore: Johns Hopkins University Press.

Dunstan, G. R., ed. (1990). *The Human Embryo: Aristotle and the Arabic and European Traditions*. Exeter: University of Exeter Press.

Garofolo, Ivan, et al. (1999). *Aspetti della terapia nel Corpus Hippocraticum: Atti del IXe Colloque International Hippocratique (Pisa, 25–29 settembre 1996)*. Florence: Olschki.

Goldhill, Simon. (1984). *Language, Sexuality, Narrative: The Oresteia*. Cambridge: Cambridge University Press.

Halperin, David, John Winkler, and Froma Zeitlin, eds. (1990). *Before Sexuality: The Construction of Erotic Experience in the Ancient Greek World*. Princeton: Princeton University Press.

Hanson, Ann E. (1975). "Hippocrates: *Diseases of Women* 1." *Signs* 1.2:567–584.

———. (1987). "The Eight Months' Child and the Etiquette of Birth: *Obsit Omen!*" *Bulletin of the History of Medicine* 61:589–602.

———. (1990). "The Medical Writers' Woman." In David Halperin et al., eds., *Before Sexuality*, 309–337. Princeton: Princeton University Press.

———. (1991). "Continuity and Change: Three Case Studies." In Sarah Pomeroy, ed., *Women's History in Ancient History*, 73–110. Chapel Hill: University of North Carolina Press.

———. (1992). "Conception, Gestation, and the Origin of Female Nature in the Corpus Hippocraticum." *Helios* 19.1/2:31–71.

———. (1995). "*Paidopoiïa*: Metaphors for Conception, Abortion, and Gestation in the *Hippocratic Corpus*." In Ph. J. van der Eijk, H. F. J. Horstmanshoff, and P. H. Schrijvers, eds., *Ancient Medicine in Its Socio-Cultural Context*, 1:291–307. Amsterdam: Rodopi.

———. (1998). "Talking Recipes in the Gynaecological Texts of the *Hippocratic Corpus*." In Maria Wyke, ed., *Parchments of Gender: Deciphering the Body in Antiquity*, 71–94. Oxford: Oxford University Press.

———. (1999). "A Hair on Her Liver Has Been Lacerated . . ." In Ivan Garofolo et al., *Aspetti della terapia nel Corpus Hippocraticum*, 235–254. Florence: Olschki.

———. (2008). "The Gradualist View of Fetal Development." In Luc Brisson et al., eds., *L'embryon, formation et animation*, 95–108. Paris: Vrin.

Jacob, J. P., F. B. Mather, and H. R. Wilson. (1997). *Egg Eating by Chickens*. http://edis.ifas.ufl.edu/ps022 (accessed April 29, 2011).

Joly, Robert. (1970). *Hippocrate XI*. Paris: Éditions Belles Lettres.

Jouanna, Jacques. (2008). "La postérité de l'embryologie d'Hippocrate dans deux traités pseudo-hippocratiques de la médecine tardive: *Sur la formation de l'homme* et *Sur la génération de l'homme et la semence*." In Luc Brisson et al., eds., *L'embryon, formation et animation*, 15–41. Paris: Vrin.

Kaibel, Georg, ed. (1878). *Epigrammata Graeca ex lapidibus conlecta*. Berlin: Berolini.

Keuls, Eva. (1985). *The Reign of the Phallus: Sexual Politics in Ancient Athens*. New York: Harper and Row.

King, Helen. (1998). *Hippocrates' Woman: Reading the Female Body in Ancient Greece*. London: Routledge.

Kock, Theodor, ed. (1880–1888). *Comicorum Atticorum Fragmenta*. Leipzig: Teubner.

Lefkowitz, Mary, and Maureen Fant, eds. (2005). *Women's Life in Greece and Rome: A Sourcebook in Translation*. 3rd ed. Baltimore: Johns Hopkins University Press.

Littré, Emile. (1839–1861). *Oeuvres complètes d'Hippocrate*. 10 vols. Paris: Baillière.

Lloyd, G. E. R. (1966). *Polarity and Analogy: Two Types of Argumentation in Early Greek Thought*. Bristol: Bristol Classical Press.

———. (1975). "The Hippocratic Question." *Classical Quarterly* 25.2:171–192.

————. (1983a). *Science, Folklore, and Ideology: Studies in the Life Sciences in Ancient Greece*. Cambridge: Cambridge University Press.

————. (1983b). *Hippocratic Writings*. New York: Penguin.

Lonie, Iain M. (1981). *The Hippocratic Treatises: "On Generation," "On the Nature of the Child," "Diseases IV."* Berlin: de Gruyter.

Loraux, Nicole. (1995). *The Experiences of Teiresias: The Feminine and the Greek Man*. Princeton: Princeton University Press.

Luttmann, Rick, and Gail Luttmann. (1976). *Chickens in Your Backyard: A Beginner's Guide*. Emmaus, PA: Rodale.

McDonagh, Eileen L. (1996). *Breaking the Abortion Deadlock: From Choice to Consent*. Oxford: Oxford University Press.

Morgan, Lynn M., and Meredith W. Michaels, eds. (1999). *Fetal Subjects, Feminist Positions*. Philadelphia: University of Pennsylvania Press.

Morris, Ian. (1987). *Burial and Ancient Society: The Rise of the Greek City-State*. Cambridge: Cambridge University Press.

Murnaghan, Sheila. (1992). "Maternity and Mortality in Homeric Poetry." *Classical Antiquity* 11.1:242–264.

Temkin, Oswei. (1956). *Soranus' Gynecology*. Baltimore: Johns Hopkins University Press.

Welty, J. C., and L. Baptista. (1988). *The Life of Birds*. 4th ed. Fort Worth, TX: Saunders.

Wood, Summer. (2004). "Fertile Territory: The Moral Agenda of Intrauterine Plot Devices." *bitch magazine* 26:48–55.

Zeitlin, Froma. (1996). "The Dynamics of Misogyny: Myth and Myth-Making in Aeschylus' *Oresteia*." In *Playing the Other: Gender and Society in Classical Greek Literature*, 87–122. Chicago: University of Chicago Press.

Zimmer, Carl. (2006). "Silent Struggle: A New Theory of Pregnancy." *New York Times*, March 14, F1 and F6.

FIVE

Citizen-Mothers on the Tragic Stage

Angeliki Tzanetou

In one of the few books devoted to the important topic of mother-hood in ancient Greece, Nancy Demand offers a pessimistic account of the role accorded women as mothers in Athenian society.[1] Demand's assessment of women's roles as mothers is predicated on the vicissitudes that women faced in childbirth as well as the demands that the care and nurture of their offspring placed upon them. But Demand casts her net more broadly by approaching the realities of motherhood against the backdrop of Athenian laws and customs concerning sexual conduct, reproduction, and property. She finds that the regulation of these areas, which served the interests of the family and the city in concert with the male ideology of the *polis*, is closely allied with the negative valuation of women's contributions as mothers, not least by precluding their participation in the public realm.[2] From this, a dismal portrait of motherhood emerges, one which places women's oppression within the familiar norms of subordination and segregation.[3] Accordingly, reality and representation coalesce in attributing mothers a low stake in the affairs of the Greek city-state.

Recent scholarship on women, gender, and the family has begun to rethink aspects of women's marginality by conceptualizing the scope and types of agency ascribed to women under a more varied paradigm that acknowledges their membership in the community.[4] In line with the aim of this volume of presenting new assessments of motherhood and mothering in Greek and Roman society, I offer a view of motherhood derived from Attic tragedy, by sketching its civic potentialities, real and imagined, as they are represented in the extant plays. My goal here is twofold: first, to outline the evidence on motherhood derived from tragedy; and second, to delineate an argument concerning the civic import of motherhood, focusing on select examples of maternal agency.

The extant plays constitute the largest body of material on motherhood in Greek literature and thus prove an important resource for an overall evaluation of motherhood in the fifth century BCE. Tragedy provides fertile ground for examining the scope and limits of maternal authority by allowing us to look specifically at the interaction between the dramatic situations in which female characters are placed and the evolving realities of Athenian civic life that affected the lives of men and women in the *polis*. Seen in this light, the dramatic identity of mothers in tragedy proves distinct as compared to portraits of motherhood found in earlier poetry. For although mothers—such as Hecuba, who leads a group of Trojan women to Athena's temple to pray for her support in *Iliad* 6, or Jocasta, who mediates the conflict between Polynices and Eteocles in Stesichorus's *Thebaid*[5]—stand out as representative examples of the type of agency that women undertake especially during times of crisis, in tragedy such agency is both more pervasive and more consistently problematized.[6] Thus, while women and, mothers in particular, are wont to play a role especially in times of war in saving the city,[7] tragedy presents mothers as "good" or "evil" as judged against accepted social standards of womanhood in Greek society. Because of its predilection for deviations from the norm, tragedy cultivates the creation of terrifying portraits of motherhood in the guise of Medea, Agave, Clytemnestra, and Procne, to name only a few obvious examples.[8] But even characters such as Aethra, Praxithea, or even Jocasta—who do not act in vengeful or destructive ways—do not conform with the norms of motherhood in Athenian society; this is because the portrayal of maternal agency does not readily conform with women's access to speech and power in Athenian society.[9]

In this article, I evaluate one set of concerns that emerges from these diverse representations of motherhood in the plays by examining manifestations of female authority as civic expressions of motherhood in Athenian tragedy.

FROM PERIPHERY TO THE CENTER

The important recent body of work on women and gender in drama has called attention to the striking disjunction between reality and representation by highlighting women's marginality in Athenian society in contrast to the power female characters wield onstage. Since such power more often than not portends harm and destruction for the family and the city, the plays are seen as articulating expressions of gender ideology in line with

patriarchal norms.[10] Women's exclusion from citizenship places them at the periphery of civic action, which is undertaken by men alone at the heart of the city.

Perceptions of women's marginality and abjection carry over to the interpretation of their dramatic roles, since women's foray onstage invariably wreaks havoc and undermines political norms, deemed vital for the preservation of the civic body. As Nancy Rabinowitz argues, the plays mirror the prevailing norm of women's exclusion:

> In this cultural artefact (i.e., tragedy) through which Athens represented itself to itself, then, real women were abjected, alienated, excluded, as they were excluded from the ideological construction of the democratic city, even though they inhabited the physical city.[11]

Demand in particular takes the view that Pericles' citizenship law of 451/0 BCE further curtailed women's public standing by denying them access to civic power:

> The increasingly restrictive definition of citizenship status that went with the development of the [Athenian] *polis* thus brought with it suspicions that haunted male lives and fed men's obsession with the control of their womenfolk.[12]

Demand's interpretation highlights the ramifications of the law from the standpoint of feminist thinking, where the intersection between gender and citizenship becomes pivotal for assessing the type of agency ascribed to women in ancient societies. The claim, however, that as a result of this law women faced further scrutiny and oppression in part distorts the historical picture and invites reconsideration of the methodological premise upon which the analysis relies. For example, Cynthia Patterson has argued that there is no conclusive evidence to suggest that sexual control of women increased as a result of the law.[13] In line with this argument, it is worth examining further the implications of Demand's reading; her views on women's marginality come close to representing women as a subaltern group—a group that effectively stands outside the social and political power structures—thereby precluding the type of agency against which she reads their isolation from the civic body.

More recent work on this topic has begun to address the methodological limits of an approach to citizenship based on the legal formulation of citizenship alone and has suggested alternatives to analyzing civic member-

ship, for men and women, under broader and more flexible criteria. To begin with, the law delimited citizenship to a restricted group, seeking above all to preserve the purity of the civic body through both lines of descent, male and female.[14] Women's citizenship, though nominal in the eyes of the law, deserves to be addressed in this vein as a first step toward exploring the civic import of mothers in tragedy. This is not to say that the imaginary world of Greek tragedy affirms women's political stakes by giving them a civic voice. Rather, what this notion indicates is that positive and negative expressions of motherhood refract in a variety of ways the norms of conduct that defined and bounded women's position not only in the family but also in the city.

"Passive" or "latent" are terms frequently used to refer to women's citizenship. Thus, as Raphael Sealey explains, "latent citizenship" describes women's civic membership in the sense that Athenian women could transmit citizenship, even though they were barred from performing duties equal to those of their male counterparts.[15] Patterson, by contrast, advocates an alternative to the prevailing understanding of citizenship as a legal status. In her book on Pericles' citizenship law, Patterson has argued that the Athenians' understanding of citizenship is conceptually more capacious than the legal definition, and argues to this effect that Athenian citizenship is conceived actively in terms that denote participation. As she has shown, phrases such as μέτειμι or μετέχω τῆς πόλεως, which denote participation, are regularly employed to describe the Athenians' "shares" in their *polis*.[16]

More specifically, in addition to political "shares," which were strictly limited to men, men's and women's participation in the religious sphere constituted an additional facet of their civic membership, since many cults made citizenship a criterion for participation.[17] In addition, Patterson argues that the same terms that apply to citizenship are used to denote family membership.[18] Thus, consideration of the nonlegal aspects of citizenship offers an important counterpoint to the prevailing paradigm and furnishes the scope for defining female agency as a corollary of women's civic membership, not least by bridging the divide between the private and public spheres of activity. Seen in this light, women's inclusion in the civic body, for example, allows them access to property and inheritance. For however limited and secondary their claims to property may have been, compared to those of men, "only Athenians, male and female, could own a 'piece of Attica' and inherit Athenian land," as Patterson puts it.[19]

This more inclusive definition of citizenship is crucial for approaching the roles that mothers play in tragedy. It places women in civic space, cre-

ating the potential for exploring and imagining their agency as oscillating between their exclusion from and their inclusion in the public sphere. Second, the conceptual link between family membership and citizenship is especially germane for evaluating different varieties of civic action in tragedy, where the family always takes center stage. As a rule, family and kinship ties determine access to political power; the dynastic family rules over the city and its members subsume the functions allotted citizens under the democracy. Thus, tragedy conflates familial with civic identity and in the process mirrors or distorts the very norms and practices that inform the audience's experience.[20] For example, concerns over succession and inheritance are treated as part of exchanges that take place within the realm of the *oikos*, where women are ever-present, even when they do not participate directly in political decision-making. The plays implicate female characters in situations where they are seen as mediating conflicts (e.g., Jocasta in Euripides' *Phoenician Women*), partaking in deliberations (e.g., Aethra in Euripides' *Suppliant Women*), and even wielding power in the absence of a king (e.g., Atossa in Aeschylus's *Persians*; Clytemnestra in Aeschylus's *Agamemnon* [and also jointly with Aegisthus in Aeschylus's *Libation Bearers*, Sophocles' *Electra*, and Euripides' *Electra*]).

More importantly, women's civic participation can be more readily traced to their family membership than it can for men, whose political affiliations are drawn in more complex ways within the plays. In light of this argument, we can evaluate the types of authority which female characters wield as mothers onstage.

CONFIGURING MATERNAL AUTHORITY

Nicole Loraux's monograph on women and mourning has focused on the ways in which the figure of the vengeful mother in tragedy undermines maternal authority by endorsing cautionary attitudes toward female speech and lament, which are also inscribed into the ban on women's public mourning within the official venue of the state funeral.[21] As in her pioneering study on female citizenship, *Children of Athena*,[22] Loraux's *Mothers in Mourning* concentrates on the tropes of women's exclusion by discussing negative instantiations of maternal agency in tragedy. The present discussion seeks to amplify the scope of the civic discourse on motherhood by examining the ways in which the broad construal of women's citizenship contributes to an understanding of the roles that female characters discharged as mothers in tragedy.[23]

A critical question that arises in connection with the civic attributes
of motherhood concerns women's portrayal as figures of authority in the
plays. While such roles typically lie in the purview of fathers and kings, as
Mark Griffith has shown,[24] we are justified in asking whether women who
had fulfilled their civic duty by giving the state citizens are represented as
authority figures in front of the audiences of the dramatic performances
and whether civic discourse in drama takes stock of or underplays women's
merits and contributions. At first sight, this approach seems to run counter to the realities that permeated both real-life Athenian families and their
portrayals on stage, wherein the economic, legal, and political authority resided with the head of the family (*kyrios*). But in the Theater of Dionysus
women are given prominence and speak authoritatively by stepping in to
critique, confront, or correct male characters within the public sphere.

It is in this vein that I first discuss two examples, although these are
from comedy. Aristophanes portrays female characters claiming for themselves the authority normally reserved for men. Aristophanic women occupy male spheres of action such as the Assembly, mount schemes to save
the city from partisan politics, and intervene to end men's ineffective handling of war. The reversal of spheres of action is central to the comic fiction
of women in power. While the essential "topsy-turviness" of Aristophanes'
plays relies upon the reversal of the gendered division of space—women
in the *oikos* versus men in the *polis*—(and therefore precludes a serious engagement with women's claims), some female characters assert their civic
prerogatives in light of their contributions as mothers.[25] While such claims
do not suggest that Aristophanes intended to validate female citizenship in
its own right, the implied homology between male and female claims to
citizenship sharpens comic effect by aiming at realism.

Two brief examples from Aristophanes' *Women at the Thesmophoria*
(*Thesmophoriazusae*) and *Women in the Assembly* (*Ecclesiazusae*) exemplify
the ways in which comic fiction affirms women's "shares" in the city by
highlighting their contributions. In the parabasis of *Women at the Thesmophoria*, the women protest their exclusion from civic honors in the following way:

Χρῆν γάρ, ἡμῶν εἰ τέκοι τις ἄνδρα χρηστὸν τῇ πόλει,
ταξίαρχον ἢ στρατηγόν, λαμβάνειν τιμήν τινα,
προεδρίαν τ' αὐτῇ δίδοσθαι Στηνίοισι καὶ Σκίροις
ἔν τε ταῖς ἄλλαις ἑορταῖς αἷσιν ἡμεῖς ἤγομεν·
(832–835)

If a woman bears a son who's useful to the polis—a taxiarch or a commander—she ought to be honored in some way and to be given front-row seating at the *Stenia* and the *Skira* and any other festivals we women might celebrate.[26]

Such honors are due, they argue, to those who have given birth to the city's most distinguished civic officers and should be awarded to mothers at the (female) festivals such as the *Stenia* and the *Skirophoria*. The inversion here lies in women's wish to appropriate the honors which men held in the theater—specifically, the right of *proedria* (front-row seats) reserved for civic officials and generals in the Theater of Dionysus, from which women, except for priestesses, stood excluded.[27] More specifically, the women complain that even in their own festivals seats of honor were given according to the rank of their male kin.

The inversion of roles is rooted in the realities of men's and women's prerogatives, since the women claim such honors for themselves in the context of female religious festivals from which men were excluded. Women's claims to such honors were based on their standing as citizen-mothers—a precondition for their participation in the *Thesmophoria*.[28]

In *Women at the Assembly*, Praxagora singles out among women's other merits their role as mothers:

ταύταισιν οὖν ὦνδρες παραδόντες τὴν πόλιν
μὴ περιλαλῶμεν, μηδὲ πυνθανώμεθα
τί ποτ᾽ ἄρα δρᾶν μέλλουσιν, ἀλλ᾽ ἁπλῷ τρόπῳ
ἐῶμεν ἄρχειν, σκεψάμενοι ταυτὶ μόνα,
ὡς τοὺς στρατιώτας πρῶτον οὖσαι μητέρες
σῴζειν ἐπιθυμήσουσιν· εἶτα σιτία
τίς τῆς τεκούσης θᾶττον ἐπιπέμψειεν ἄν;
(229–235)

And so gentlemen, let us hand over governance of the *polis* to the women, and let's not beat around the bush or ask what they want to accomplish. You need to consider only two points; first, as mothers they'll want to protect the soldiers; and second, who could be quicker at sending rations to soldiers than the mothers who bore them.

Performed in 392 BCE, this next to last of Aristophanes' extant plays presents a far more subversive version of women in power than he gives us in *Lysistrata*, as the female characters in this play take over the Assembly, and

Praxagora puts forward a radical proposal for the organization of the state along the lines of a communist utopia.[29] Even so, women's claims to power are primarily constituted along the lines of the familiar topos of their primacy in managing the household (*oikos*).[30] Unlike the parabasis of the earlier play, the comic fiction here goes further, to imagine women's rule over the city.[31] The inversion of the spheres of action that men and women occupied in real life underscores precisely the opposite, namely, that women could never be regarded as civic actors. Even so, in this particular excerpt the civic attributes of motherhood—their giving sons to the state and their role as nurturers—also come to the fore by way of bolstering the legitimacy of women's claims to power and their critique of men's flawed handling of the war.

In staging female power, Aristophanic comedy takes stock of women's contributions not only to the familial but also to the civic life of the *polis*. Women's public voices are not the outcome of the reversal of their domestic arrangements alone, but further stem from their roles as citizens within the *polis*. As Jeffrey Henderson has argued, unlike tragedy, comedy insists on the realism of its *mimesis*, and hence women's claims to power must be regarded to some degree as "real" if the comic fiction is to be effective.[32]

MOTHERS OF THE STATE

While comedy presents women in power in line with the fiction of the inversion of male power, tragedy instead highlights an enduring ambivalence toward female power. Such ambivalence is typified by a dichotomy in the case of motherhood through examples of "good" versus "evil" mothers. As we have already seen, the law's specific formulation of Athenian citizenship for women created the potential for exploring and imagining their agency as oscillating between their exclusion from and inclusion in the public sphere. This dialectic is enacted in the plays that feature mothers as discharging duties in the public sphere that highlight their interventions—negative and positive—in critical areas such as war, succession, and governance.

Female characters, then, are not simply interlopers or neutral bystanders to the main action, but can provide critical input analogous to that of men. As such, these women characters' political contributions, even when positively construed, reflect their subordinate and secondary position, serving as they do in the role of advisor and intermediary. Thus, Aethra in Euripides' *Suppliant Women*, Praxithea in Euripides' *Erechtheus*, and Jocasta

in Euripides' *Phoenician Women* reflect quite precisely the scope and limits of maternal agency. Unfavorable examples of motherhood—embodied by Clytemnestra in Aeschylus's *Agamemnon* and Medea in Euripides' *Medea*—typify the negative instantiations of motherhood, as their agency openly resists the male political order by seeking to supersede or destroy it.³³

There are good reasons for examining the civic contours of motherhood in drama under a paradigm that sanctions women's membership. As noted, drama brings together the familial and civic spheres of activity and also highlights the performance of rituals as integral for the preservation of the community (i.e., marriage, sacrifice, cult), an area where women could legitimately claim participation.³⁴ But other factors contributed to the prominent roles that female characters discharge as mothers onstage. More specifically, the consolidation of Athens' democratic constitution at the height of Athenian imperialism elevated Athenian citizenship to a privileged status, setting those who could lay claims upon it apart from other groups—resident aliens and slaves as well as Athens' imperial allies.³⁵ By acknowledging women's "shares" in the city, Pericles' law, as we have seen, also set Athenian women apart from those barred from access to citizenship and property in Athens.³⁶

This background enables a fuller understanding of the ways in which tragedy begins to capitalize on the symbolic potential of women as participants in the city and on their authority to pronounce on moral and civic matters. In this regard, we find that plays that involve Athenian myths and characters, many of which date to the latter half of the fifth century, increasingly portray mothers as acting in concert with, or against, Athenian civic and practices. Among them, mothers like Praxithea in *Erechtheus* and Aethra in *Suppliant Women* use the authority vested in them as mothers to speak or act on behalf of the state. Praxithea, who assents to her daughter's sacrifice to save Athens in the battle against Eumolpus of Eleusis, offers an extreme instantiation of the mother of the state type:

εἰ δ' ἦν ἐν οἴκοις ἀντὶ θηλειῶν στάχυς
ἄρσην, πόλιν δὲ πολεμία κατεῖχε φλόξ,
οὐκ ἄν νιν ἐξέπεμπον εἰς μάχην δορός,
θάνατον προταρβοῦσ'; ἀλλ' ἔμοιγ' εἴη τέκνα   (25)
<ἃ> καὶ μάχοιτο καὶ μετ' ἀνδράσιν πρέποι,
μὴ σχήματ' ἄλλως ἐν πόλει πεφυκότα.
τὰ μητέρων δὲ δάκρυ' ὅταν πέμπῃ τέκνα,
πολλοὺς ἐθήλυν' εἰς μάχην ὁρμωμένους.
μισῶ γυναῖκας αἵτινες πρὸ τοῦ καλοῦ   (30)

ζῆν παῖδας εἵλοντ᾽ ἢ παρήνεσαν κακά.
καὶ μὴν θανόντες γ᾽ ἐν μάχῃ πολλῶν μέτα
τύμβον τε κοινὸν ἔλαχον εὔκλειάν τ᾽ ἴσην·
τῇμῇ δὲ παιδὶ στέφανος εἰς μιᾷ μόνῃ
πόλεως θανούσῃ τῆσδ᾽ ὑπερδοθήσεται.   (35)
καὶ τὴν τεκοῦσαν καὶ σὲ δύο θ᾽ ὁμοσπόρω
σώσει· τί τούτων οὐχὶ δέξασθαι καλόν;
(EURIPIDES, *ERECHTHEUS*, FR. 360, 22–37)

If our family included a crop of male children instead of females, and the flame of war was gripping our city, would I be refusing to send them out to battle for fear of their deaths? No, give me sons who would not only fight but stand out amongst the men and not be mere figures raised in the city to no use. When mothers' tears send children on their way, they soften many men as they leave for battle. I detest women who choose life rather than virtue for their sons, or exhort them to cowardice. And sons, if they die in battle, earn a common tomb and equal glory shared with many others; my daughter, though, will be awarded one crown for herself alone when she dies for this city, and will save her mother, and you, and her two sisters: which of these things is not a fine reward?[37]

By conceptualizing her civic duty as a mother as one of extreme sacrifice, Praxithea pledges allegiance to Athenian patriotic ideals,[38] as she proclaims in a militant tone her readiness to sacrifice her daughter, in the absence of male children (22–25). The speech provides a striking reversal of the stock rhetorical topos of the parent's refusing to accede to a sacrifice, as Praxithea attempts to persuade King Erechtheus to yield to Poseidon's demand to ensure Athens' victory against Eumolpus of Eleusis.[39] The effect is jarring, as Praxithea proclaims that as a mother her duty toward the city takes precedence over family and progeny alike.[40]

Beginning with the praise of Athenian autochthony, Praxithea further asserts her civic voice by juxtaposing the superior contributions that citizens made to the city against those of foreigners (fr. 360, 8–13). Praxithea comes close to earning the honors due women as mothers of the state, though unlike her comic counterparts, she articulates her obligations as a citizen in the idiom of Athenian male patriotic ideology. In this case, the civic idiom of motherhood therefore aligns the female perspective with male concerns about the preservation of the state. The effect is also ironic, though not in the manner that Philip Vellacott suggests when he claims that "this woman has so adopted what she conceived to be the masculine attitude that she has

become a monster."[41] Rather, Praxithea's endorsement of the sacrifice in this fragmentary play could be set against the broader context of the critique of civic salvation in Euripides' plays of voluntary self-sacrifice.[42] Praxithea thereby embodies an extreme example of civic motherhood, which stands out as anomalous, as she attempts to normalize the aberrant act of human sacrifice by bringing it in line with the standards of conduct that the city enjoined upon its female citizens.[43]

Aethra in Euripides' *Suppliant Women*, on the other hand, best exemplifies mothers' roles as civic intermediaries by interceding on behalf of the Argive mothers before Theseus, king of Athens. As the mother of the Athenian king, her agency articulates the civic implications of maternal authority within the Athenian paradigm. When she steps forward to advise Theseus, Aethra is careful to frame her civic agency in terms apposite to her gender. She calls attention to the discrepancy between Athenian gender norms that excluded women from public speech and her own decision in coming forth to speak:

> AI. εἴπω τι, τέκνον, σοί τε καὶ πόλει καλόν;
> ΘΗ. ὡς πολλά γ' ἐστὶ κἀπὸ θηλειῶν σοφά.
> ΑΙ. ἀλλ' εἰς ὄκνον μοι μῦθος ὃν κεύθω φέρει. (295)
> ΘΗ. αἰσχρόν γ' ἔλεξας, χρήστ' κρύπτειν φίλους.
> ΑΙ. οὔτοι σιωπῶσ' εἶτα μέμψομαί ποτε
> τὴν νῦν σιωπὴν ὡς ἐσιγήθη κακῶς,
> οὐδ' ὡς ἀχρεῖον τὰς γυναῖκας εὖ λέγειν
> δείσασ' ἀφήσω τῶι φόβωι τοὐμὸν καλόν.[44]
>
> (EURIPIDES, *SUPPLIANT WOMEN* 293–300)

AETHRA: Shall I say something, my son, that brings honor to you and the city?
THESEUS: Yes, for much wise advice can be heard even from women.
AETHRA: But the suggestion I have in my heart causes me to hesitate.
THESEUS: For shame—keeping good words from your near and dear!
AETHRA: I shall not hold my peace and then at some later time reproach myself for my present silence, nor, since it is a useless thing for women to be eloquent, shall I, out of fear, let go of the noble task that is mine.

Her renunciation of political quietism echoes one of the central tenets of democratic civic ideology.[45] Thus Aethra lays claims upon male tropes of speech, even as she seeks Theseus's permission, in order to establish her authority.

She next outlines a rationale in favor of Athens' intervention: It is Athens' duty, she argues, in sum, to ensure the right of burial for the Argive dead by leading a campaign against Thebes; military intervention is desirable and advantageous to protect the city's honor and hegemony (306–332). While her voice, like Praxithea's, lends support to Athens' imperial ideals, her intercession on behalf of the Argive mothers frames the civic implications of maternal agency in two additional ways. First, the action of the play underscores the authority vested in her as the mother of the Athenian king,[46] when she frames the suffering of the Argive mothers in terms that are consequential for Athens. Second, the play highlights women's civic membership in its own right. As recipient of the supplication of the Argive mothers, who stand barred from administering the final rites over their closest of kin, Aethra is charged with representing their rightful claims in a civic capacity.[47] Thus, Aethra brings the religious and moral imperatives of burying the dead to bear upon Theseus's decision by focusing on its consequences for Athens. Her intervention, moreover, does not run counter to the norms of women's civic duties, which lay in the care of the dead, as women were charged with and performed many of the rituals associated with funeral and burial.[48] Jocasta in Euripides' *Phoenician Women* (528–585) plays a similar role in mediating her sons' conflict, aligning her role as a mother with the political advice she dispenses, as she unsuccessfully attempts to thwart the impending death of her sons and the destruction of the city.

Euripides' *Ion* highlights the intersections between female citizenship and Athenian civic identity in the context of imperial ideology. In the wake of the Athenian defeat at Syracuse, Athenian imperial ideology began embracing claims of descent by way of strengthening the ties between Athens and the Ionian cities in the eastern part of her empire.[49] The shift toward Ionianism also informs the ideological register of the play, which enacts the Athenian foundational myth of the birth of Ion, son of Creusa and Apollo, as legitimate successor of Erechtheus, Athens' autochthonous king, and as founder of the four tribes of Attica. The play places female citizenship at the center, granting Creusa a pivotal role in resolving the problem of succession, as she alone is able to bestow Athenian citizenship upon Ion.

Ion's vexed standing as both an illegitimate son of Apollo and founder of the Ionian tribes frames the unstable relationship between mother and son, as Creusa—in ignorance of her son's identity—comes close to killing him before the recognition scene, which sets the action on a different course, thereby allowing her own identity as a mother to be drawn positively through recourse to her Athenian heritage.[50] The legacy of her rape

by Apollo is redefined through the awareness of the civic inheritance that she will bestow upon Ion—a recognition of women's ability to confer citizenship in the most absolute terms (reinforced in Creusa's case by her legal standing within her own *oikos* as *epikleros* [heiress]).[51] The significance of her civic standing is further enhanced in relation to that of Xuthus, her non-Athenian husband, who is altogether sidestepped and who accepts Ion as the rightful successor of the royal *oikos* of Athens. All these strands come together in Athena's speech at the end of the play:

λαβοῦσα τόνδε παῖδα Κεκροπίαν χθόνα
χώρει, Κρέουσα, κὰς θρόνους τυραννικοὺς
ἵδρυσον. ἐκ γὰρ τῶν Ἐρεχθέως γεγὼς
δίκαιος ἄρχειν τῆς ἐμῆς ὅδε χθονός,
ἔσται δ' ἂν' Ἑλλάδ' εὐκλεής.   (1575)
παῖδες γενόμενοι τέσσαρες ῥίζης μιᾶς
ἐπώνυμοι γῆς κἀπιφυλίων χθονὸς
λαῶν ἔσονται, σκόπελον οἳ ναίουσ' ἐμόν.[52]
(EURIPIDES, *ION* 1571–1578)

> Creusa, you are to take this child with you to Cecrops' land and establish him on the royal throne. As a descendant of Erechtheus, he has a right to rule over my land, and his fame will spread throughout Greece. For his sons—four from the one root—will give their names to the land and to the native tribes of the land, the inhabitants of my cliff.

Creusa's identity as daughter of the autochthonous king of Athens bestows upon her perhaps an even larger role than those ascribed to Praxithea and Aethra as citizen-mothers. Creusa's civic standing functions in two ways: first, it is critical for articulating Athens' right to rule. As David Rosenbloom puts it, "The mother–son bond between Kreousa and Ion is replicated in the political relation between Athenians and Ionians as metropolis and colony."[53] In this light, Creusa's anguish over the loss of her son further highlights the role that women served in securing the continuity of the family—a duty which the play articulates poignantly by interlacing the personal with the civic consequences of Creusa's responsibilities.[54]

As a counterpoint to the official representation of Creusa's charge as mother in Athenian political mythology, I mention briefly the portrait of Alcestis as wife and mother. In Euripides' play, Alcestis' last exchange with Admetus allows her, as Victoria Wohl has shown,[55] to establish not only

her authority, but also her subjectivity by making arrangements for the future of her children and her household, demanding that they not have a stepmother after she dies (Euripides, *Alcestis* 280–325). Admetus's accession to her final demands affirms not only her domestic and maternal authority, but also her political authority, as in her final moments she briefly gains control of the *oikos* over her husband.

BREAKING THE RULES

Mothers who do not appear to act in concert with the aims of Athenian civic ideology are represented in negative terms, as vengeful, nonnurturing, and harmful toward their offspring. Clytemnestra's and Medea's transgressions of their maternal roles engender acts of vengeance which have political consequences and destroy proper succession within the *oikos*. Negative and misogynistic representations of motherhood are indeed rooted, as Froma Zeitlin has shown, in myths of women's rule.[56] It is possible, however, that the absence of any positive valuation of women's contributions as mothers may also be partially the result of the fact that Pericles' citizenship law set clear criteria for configuring Athenian civic identity. Thus, the impact of the law arguably sharpened awareness of the civic relevance of motherhood. Accordingly, we find in tragedy that the scenarios that implicate women begin to address more directly their contributions, positive and negative, as citizens.

The *Oresteia*, performed in 458 BCE, depicts motherhood in adverse terms and offers an important counterpoint to the civic configurations of motherhood in later plays. The negative depiction of Clytemnestra's agency throughout the trilogy stems from her appropriation of male authority and in turn significantly undermines her portrait as a mother. Clytemnestra vindicates Agamemnon's murder by presenting her vengeance as an act of justice undertaken to punish Agamemnon for sacrificing her daughter. But her maternal vengeance has clear political motives, since she continues to wield political power in Argos openly by sharing the throne with Aegisthus (Aeschylus, *Agamemnon* 1431–1436). Her political aspirations distort the relationship with her surviving children, whose position in the *oikos* she undermines by excluding them from their inheritance. Orestes and Electra emphasize their bond and loyalty to their father; both view their mother as a political opponent and a tyrannical usurper and pray to Zeus to restore their status by returning their patrimony (Aeschylus, *Libation Bearers* 246–254). They express their estrangement from their mother in political terms:

οὕτω δὲ κἀμὲ τήνδε τ᾽, Ἠλέκτραν λέγω,
ἰδεῖν πάρεστί σοι, πατροστερῆ γόνον,
ἄμφω φυγὴν ἔχοντε τὴν αὐτὴν δόμων.
(AESCHYLUS, *LIBATION BEARERS* 252–254)

So you see both me and Electra here, children deprived of their father,
both exiles alike from our home.

Their alienation is a form of exile—different for each on account of their gender—Orestes is banished to Phocis to live with his father's guest-friend, Strophios, while Electra lends voice to her civic marginality by describing her diminished status as an internal exile that takes the form of confinement within the inner recess of the house (ἐγὼ δ᾽ ἀπεστάτουν / ἄτιμος, οὐδὲν ἀξία, μυχῶι δ᾽ ἄφερκτος πολυσινοῦς κυνὸς δίκαν: "But all the while I was kept sequestered, despised, accounted a worthless thing. Kenneled in my room as if I were a vicious dog" [*Libation Bearers* 445–446]).

Motherhood, I would argue, is negated in the strongest terms possible in the *Oresteia*, because of the anxieties surrounding the disruption of the proper succession of the *oikos*. The *Oresteia* is the best example of the intersection of familial with civic concerns and the need to subordinate the former to the latter to protect civic stability from the danger of tyranny. Orestes is able to reclaim his civic rights in Argos only after Athena and the court pronounce a verdict that exonerates the matricide. The overarching concern with reinstating Orestes in his patrimony undermines the contributions of mothers to procreation and by extension to the prosperity of the state.

Motherhood is never fully rehabilitated here. The only concession in that regard is the Furies' function as guarantors of fertility (Aeschylus, *Eumenides* 829–836, 907–909). But the Furies, who are perpetual virgins like Athena, are only charged with overseeing the proper function of the *oikos*. As such, they offer instead a partial acknowledgment of the place of the female principle within the *polis*. *Eumenides*, as many have argued, ends with an affirmation of patriarchal norms. The trilogy's negative assessment of Clytemnestra's maternal agency, however, is also filtered through the democratic norms of citizenship, introduced by Cleisthenes and supported under the radical democracy.

A concluding example of the negation of motherhood is Medea, whose extreme civic marginality as both a foreigner and an exile further distorts normative connections between motherhood and civic belonging. The play both intimates and eschews an easy identification of Medea's actions with

those befitting a political actor. For, unlike Clytemnestra, Medea is not after political power—although she fully understands its significance for Jason, who wishes to possess it at all costs. Viewed in this light, this domestic
tragedy takes on the character of political intrigue, as Medea's vengeance
harms the royal household in addition to her own.

The Athenian perspective, provided by the scene with King Aegeus,
serves a key role in this regard. Not only does it expose her plan for revenge, but it also, I would argue, clarifies the civic implications of Medea's
transgression of her maternal identity. Aegeus introduces Athenian views
on the significance of children politically and ideologically when he shares
with Medea his concerns for the survival of his own *oikos*. Medea's anticipated contribution as a foreigner in Athens is envisioned in light of Athenian norms that align motherhood with civic membership; Medea prom-
ises Aegeus that she will return the king's favor by helping him acquire an
heir, if he grants her asylum. As a result, this episode further engages the
audience's knowledge of Medea's actions later in Athens—her attempted
regicide against Theseus—and brings into sharper focus another facet of
Medea's maternal identity, her role as destroyer of the *polis*.[57] For by killing the princess and her children, Medea destroys any hope for familial and
civic safety alike.

Yet Medea's maternal portrait does not provide a straightforward affirmation of Athenian norms either. For one, her foreignness allows her role as
a mother to be drawn as the very antithesis not only of Athenian, but also
of Greek norms in general. Jason condemns her on these grounds, claiming
that no Greek woman would have dared to undertake such acts (1339–1341).
Nonetheless, Medea continues to lay claims on her rights as a mother. Pro-
claiming just before the murder that the children she gave birth to are dear
to her (1249–1250), she offers a far more chilling portrait of motherhood
than she does in her earlier monologue. And, in her semi-divine authority,
she continues to discharge her maternal duties in a civic capacity, taking
charge of the burial of her children and founding rites at the sanctuary of
Hera Akraia to memorialize their death and offering compensation for it.[58]

οὐ δῆτ᾽, ἐπεί σφας τῆιδ᾽ ἐγὼ θάψω χερί,
φέρουσ᾽ ἐς Ἥρας τέμενος Ἀκραίας θεοῦ,
ὡς μή τις αὐτοὺς πολεμίων καθυβρίσηι (1380)
τυμβοὺς ἀνασπῶν· γῆι δὲ τῆιδε Σισύφου
σεμνὴν ἑορτὴν καὶ τέλη προσάψομεν
τὸ λοιπὸν ἀντὶ τοῦδε δυσσεβοῦς φόνου.

αὐτὴ δὲ γαῖαν εἶμι τὴν Ἐρεχθέως,
Αἰγεῖ συνοικήσουσα τῶι Πανδίονος.   (1385)
(EURIPIDES, *MEDEA* 1378–1385)

Certainly not. I shall bury them with my own hand, taking them to the sanctuary of Hera Akraia, so that none of my enemies may outrage them by tearing up their graves. And I shall enjoin on this land of Sisyphus a solemn festival and holy rites for all time to come in payment for this unholy murder. As for myself, I shall go to the land of Erechtheus to live with Aegeus, son of Pandion.[59]

The transcendence of the norms that secure the continuity of familial and civic life by a figure who is as foreign, exotic, and supernatural as Medea perhaps provided Euripides with the freedom to explore the most extreme negation and affirmation of motherhood, one which profoundly challenged not only Athenian civic norms, but also the very perception of motherhood for audiences of the play, both ancient and modern.

This overview of select examples of motherhood in plays that mostly concern Athens has sought to establish an argument regarding the import of female citizenship for outlining the range of representations of mothers in tragedy. This is a first step toward establishing the parameters that define maternal authority in drama at large. As such, its validity must be further tested and analyzed within the context of plays that portray maternal agency within a wider range of settings, including the household and religion, as well as war and politics.

NOTES

1. Demand (1994).

2. Demand (1994), 121–154.

3. For a similar assessment, see Gould (1980). On women's social, legal, and political standing in Athens, see Schaps (1979); Just (1989), 13–104; Sealey (1990), 12–49. On segregation and sexual control, see Cohen (1989) and (1991), 133–170; Schaps (1998), 161–188.

4. Some representative examples include Foley (2001), on women as moral actors in tragedy; Patterson (1986), 49–67, (1998), and (2009), on female citizenship and the family; and Goff (2004), on women's religious and ritual agency.

5. See further Bremer et al. (1987), 128–172.

6. Much of the recent work focuses specifically on violence and revenge: Loraux (1998); McHardy (2005) and (2008). For a psychoanalytic perspective on aspects of motherhood and misogyny, see Zeitlin (1978) and Slater (1968).

7. Kearns (1990), 323–344, argues that women at such times become "unlikely saviors" and calls attention to the reversal of the prevailing hierarchies of periphery (women, foreigners, slaves) vs. center (citizen males).

8. For a brief survey on maternal figures, see Zeitlin (2008); on childbirth scenes in tragedy, see Hall (2006), 60–98.

9. On female speech in tragedy, see esp. McClure (1999).

10. Rabinowitz (1993) and Zeitlin (1996) suggest that the ends of the plays re-assert the structures of paternal authority and place women in their proper roles after they have acted in ways that distort prevailing male views.

11. Rabinowitz (2004), 46.

12. Demand (1994), 151.

13. Patterson (1996), 323.

14. On the nature and development of Athenians' views of themselves as citizens, see Lape (2010).

15. Sealey (1990), 14.

16. Patterson (1981), 164–165: "An Athenian, however, did not need to use either astos, politēs or Athēnaios to express his belonging to the city, his citizenship. He could simply say, 'I have a share in the city' (metechō tēs poleōs or metesti moi tēs poleōs). . . . In addition to material, judicial and political 'shares,' an Athenian would have considered his participation in his city's cults—and in the benefits which resulted from proper relationships with gods—as an essential part of his citizenship or his 'sharing in' Athens. Conversely, loss of citizenship, atimia, meant exclusion from all civic cults as well as from the assembly."

17. The implications of Patterson's reading for interpreting women's roles in religion and ritual are further discussed in Goff (2004), 160–226.

18. Patterson (2009), 58–59.

19. Patterson (2009), 59.

20. On the definition of family and civic identity in tragedy, see further Maitland (1992).

21. Loraux (1998). Though undeniably a strong strand of Athenian civic ideology highlighted the threat that women's mourning posed for the city, tragedy covers a broader spectrum of attitudes that highlights the intrinsic power of female lament to produce statements at once subversive and authoritative. See further Foley (2001), 19–56, and Dué (2006).

22. Loraux (1993).

23. For a discussion and reevaluation of the available theoretical approaches regarding women's civic exclusion, see Katz (1999).

24. The lucid typology offered by Griffith (2005) includes the following four categories: 1) the public, sociopolitical sphere; 2) the domestic sphere; 3) the religious sphere; and 4) the epistemological and cultural/literary field. I focus here mostly on

women's authority in the sociopolitical sphere, but the topic of maternal authority in tragedy is part of a larger project on motherhood in Greek literature.

25. In Aristophanes' *Lysistrata* 651, for example, women emphasize the giving of their sons to the state. Patterson (1994), 201–203, notes that women's civic shares are not simply rooted in comic fantasy, but stem from civic privileges distinct from those which foreigners and slaves possessed in Athens.

26. Text for Aristophanes is from Wilson (2007) and translations are from Henderson (1996).

27. See Maas (1972), 85; Connelly (2007), 205–213.

28. The *Stenia* and the *Skirophoria*, which also honored Demeter, were probably run by a female magistrate as well. See further Brumfield (1981), 156–181.

29. Sommerstein (1998), 8–22.

30. On the continuity between *oikos* and *polis*, see Foley (1982).

31. Cole (1994), 35.

32. See further Henderson (1996), 25–29.

33. Medea's revenge follows the pattern of tragic filicide identified by Loraux (1998) and discussed by McHardy (2005).

34. The contributions by Vernant and Vidal-Naquet (1990) and Seaford (1994) offer representative (though opposing) views on the social, political, and ritual contexts of drama.

35. On the social and political aspects of Athenian civic identity, see the contributions in Boegehold and Scafuro (1994), esp. Patterson's essay (1994) on the uses to which female citizenship is put in Apollodorus's *Against Neaira*.

36. Osborne (1997) makes the case that the citizenship law of 451/0 BCE increased the importance of civic identity for women.

37. Translation from Collard et al. (1995).

38. In this light, Praxithea's adoption of patriotic topoi from the Athenian funeral oration (e.g., praise of self-sacrifice [22–27], rejection of *philophychia* [30–31], placing collective over individual salvation [32–37]) stands as the type opposite to that of Loraux's mourning mother, silencing as she does the female point of view.

39. See further Wilkins (1990).

40. Praxithea's speech was cited by the orator Lycurgus in *Against Leocrates* 98–101. See further Collard et al. (1995), 148–155.

41. Vellacott (1975), 196.

42. Foley (1985); Mendelsohn (2002).

43. Her supreme civic loyalty is rewarded at the end of the play by Athena, who makes Praxithea her first priestess. See further Connelly (1996), 53–80.

44. Text is from Diggle (1981) and translation is from Kovacs (1998).

45. For a fuller discussion of Aethra's rhetorical manipulation of gender and political norms, see Mendelsohn (2002), 164–170.

46. Though we ought to note that Aethra is not an Athenian by birth, but by marriage. The play attempts to normalize the foreign origin of Theseus's mother by making her the wife of Aegeus. Despite this anomaly, Theseus speaks from an Athe-

nian perspective on citizenship, having earlier censured Adrastus for marrying a foreign bride (219–224).

47. Goff (2004), 318–322, reads Aethra's agency in positive terms, as viewed against the ritual background of the festival of the *Proerosia*. Goff notes that while the festival's main focus was agricultural fertility, its location at Eleusis also vividly evokes Demeter's and Persephone's separation and subsequent reunion. As Goff indicates, "Aithra's speech is facilitated by her ritual performance, in that she can be seen to espouse the cause of parent–child reunion invested both with the authority of Demeter and with the sign of fertility provided by the Proerosia" (322). Her discussion offers a counterpoint to Foley (2001), 21–55, who argues that the force of women's mourning is undercut by male politics.

48. Patterson (2006) and (2009).

49. Zacharia (2003); Rosenbloom (2011).

50. See further Saxonhouse (1986); Loraux (1993).

51. The precise rendering of *epikleros* is "with property," and it was used in reference to a daughter whose father had no male heirs; see further Just (1989), 95–98.

52. Translation from Waterfield (2001).

53. Rosenbloom (2011), 371. Though, as Dougherty has shown (1996), Creusa's rape by Apollo under his guise as Patroos, co-ancestor of Athenians and Ionians, refashions the myth of autochthony and Creusa's Athenian identity in accordance with the aims of the colonial narrative of the play. On Creusa's role as citizen-mother and on maternal inheritance in *Ion*, see Lape (2010), 95–96.

54. Lefkowitz (2007), 32–33.

55. Wohl (1997), 133–147.

56. Zeitlin (1978).

57. Sfyroeras (1994).

58. On the rites in the cult of Hera Akraia, see Johnston (1997).

59. Text is from Diggle (1984) and translation is from Kovacs (1994).

WORKS CITED

Boegehold, Alan L., and Adele Scafuro, eds. (1994). *Athenian Identity and Civic Ideology*. Baltimore: Johns Hopkins University Press.
Bremer, Jan Maarten, A. Maria van Erp Taalman Kip, and S. R. Slings. (1987). *Some Recently Found Greek Poems*. Mnemosyne Supp. 99. Leiden: Brill.
Brumfield, Allaire C. (1981). *Attic Festivals and Their Relation to the Agricultural Year.* Monographs in Classical Studies. New York: Arno.
Cohen, David. (1989). "Seclusion, Separation, and the Status of Women in Classical Athens." *Greece and Rome* 36:3–15.
———. (1991). *Law, Sexuality, and Society: The Enforcement of Morals in Classical Athens.* Cambridge: Cambridge University Press.

Cole, Susan. (1994). "Women and Politics in Democratic Athens: 2500 Years of Democracy." *History Today* 44.3:32–37.

Collard, Christopher, Martin J. Cropp, and Kevin H. Lee, eds. (1995). *Euripides: Selected Fragmentary Plays*, vol. 1. Warminster, England: Aris and Phillips.

Connelly, Joan B. (1996). "Parthenon and Parthenoi: A Mythological Interpretation of the Parthenon Frieze." *American Journal of Archaeology* 100:53–80.

————. (2007). *Portrait of a Priestess: Women and Ritual in Ancient Greece*. Princeton: Princeton University Press.

Demand, Nancy. (1994). *Birth, Death, and Motherhood in Classical Greece*. Baltimore: Johns Hopkins University Press.

Diggle, James. (1981). *Euripides Fabulae*, vol. 2. Oxford: Clarendon Press.

————. (1984). *Euripides Fabulae*, vol. 1. Oxford: Clarendon Press.

Dougherty, Carol. (1996). "Democratic Contradictions and the Synoptic Illusion of Euripides' *Ion*." In Josiah Ober and Charles W. Hedrick, eds., *Demokratia: A Conversation on Democracies, Ancient and Modern*, 249–270. Princeton: Princeton University Press.

Dué, C. (2006). *The Captive Woman's Lament in Greek Tragedy*. Austin: University of Texas Press.

Foley, Helene P. (1982). "The Female Intruder Reconsidered: Women in Aristophanes' *Lysistrata* and *Ecclesiazusae*." *Classical Philology* 77:1–21.

————. (1985). *Ritual Irony: Poetry and Sacrifice in Euripides*. Ithaca: Cornell University Press.

————. (2001). *Female Acts in Greek Tragedy*. Princeton: Princeton University Press.

Goff, Barbara. (2004). *Citizen Bacchae: Women's Ritual Practice in Ancient Greece*. Berkeley: University of California Press.

Gould, John. (1980). "Law, Custom, and Myth: Aspects of the Social Position of Women in Classical Athens." *Journal of Hellenic Studies* 100:38–59.

Griffith, Mark. (2005). "Authority Figures." In Justina Gregory, ed., *A Companion to Greek Tragedy*, 333–351. Oxford: Blackwell.

Hall, Edith H. (2006). *The Theatrical Cast of Athens: Interactions between Ancient Greek Drama and Society*. Oxford: Oxford University Press.

Henderson, Jeffrey. (1996). *Three Plays by Aristophanes: Staging Women*. London: Routledge.

Johnston, Sarah Iles. (1997). "Corinthian Medea and the Cult of Hera Akraia." In James J. Clauss and Sarah Iles Johnston, eds., *Medea: Essays on Medea in Myth, Literature, Philosophy, and Art*, 44–70. Princeton: Princeton University Press.

Just, Roger. (1989). *Women in Athenian Law and Life*. London: Routledge.

Katz, Marilyn. (1999). "Women and Democracy in Ancient Greece." In Thomas M. Falkner, Nancy Felson, and David Konstan, eds., *Contextualizing Classics: Ideology, Performance, Dialogue. Essays in Honor of John J. Peradotto*, 41–68. Lanham, MD: Rowman and Littlefield.

Kearns, Emily. (1990). "Saving the City." In Oswyn Murray and Simon Price, eds., *The Greek City from Homer to Alexander*, 323–344. Oxford: Clarendon Press.

Kovacs, David. (1998). *Euripides*, vol. 3: *Suppliant Women, Electra, Heracles*. Loeb Classical Library. Cambridge, MA: Harvard University Press.

———. (1994). *Euripides*, vol. 12: *Cyclops, Alcestis, Medea*. Loeb Classical Library. Cambridge, MA: Harvard University Press.

Lape, Susan. (2010). *Race and Citizen Identity in the Classical Athenian Democracy*. Cambridge: Cambridge University Press.

Lefkowitz, Mary. (2007). *Women in Greek Myth*. 2nd ed. Baltimore: Johns Hopkins University Press.

Loraux, Nicole. (1993). *The Children of Athena: Athenian Ideas about Citizenship and the Division between the Sexes*. Trans. Caroline Levine. Princeton: Princeton University Press.

———. (1998). *Mothers in Mourning: With the Essay on Amnesty and Its Opposite*. Trans. Corinne Pache. Ithaca: Cornell University Press.

Maas, Michael. (1972). *Die Proedrie des Dionysostheaters in Athen*. *Vestigia* 15. Munich: Beck.

Maitland, Judith. (1992). "Dynasty and Family in the Athenian City-State: A View from Attic Tragedy." *Classical Quarterly* 42:26–40.

McClure, Laura. (1999). *Spoken Like a Woman: Speech and Gender in Athenian Drama*. Princeton: Princeton University Press.

McHardy, Fiona. (2005). "From Treacherous Wives to Murderous Mothers: Filicide in Tragic Fragments." In Fiona McHardy, James Robson, and David Harvey, eds., *Lost Dramas of Classical Athens*, 129–150. Exeter: University of Exeter Press.

———. (2008). *Revenge in Athenian Culture*. London: Duckworth.

Mendelsohn, David. (2002). *Gender and the City in Euripides' Political Plays*. Cambridge: Cambridge University Press.

Osborne, Robin. (1997). "Law and the Democratic Citizen and the Representation of Women in Classical Athens." *Past and Present* 155:3–33.

Patterson, Cynthia. (1981). *Pericles' Citizenship Law of 451/0 B.C.* New York: Arno Classical Monographs.

———. (1986). "Hai Attikai: The Other Athenians." In Marilyn Skinner, ed., *Rescuing Creusa: New Methodological Approaches to Women in Antiquity* (*Helios* 13.2), 149–167. Lubbock: Texas Tech University Press.

———. (1994). "The Case against Neaira and the Public Ideology of the Athenian Family." In Alan L. Boegehold and Adele Scafuro, eds., *Athenian Identity and Civic Ideology*, 199–216. Baltimore: Johns Hopkins University Press.

———. (1996). Review of Nancy Demand, *Birth, Death, and Motherhood in Classical Greece* (1994). *American Journal of Philology* 117.2:323–325.

———. (1998). *The Family in Greek History*. Cambridge, MA: Harvard University Press.

———, ed. (2006). *Antigone's Answer: Essays on Death, Burial, and Commemoration in Classical Athens*. *Helios* Supp. 33. Lubbock: Texas Tech University Press.

———. (2009). "Citizenship and Gender in the Ancient World: The Experience of Athens and Rome." In Seyla Benhabib and Judith Resnik, eds., *Migrations and Mo-*

bilities: Citizenship, Borders, and Gender, 47–75. New York: New York University Press.

Rabinowitz, Nancy Sorkin. (1993). *Anxiety Veiled: Euripides and the Traffic in Women.* Ithaca: Cornell University Press.

———. (2004). "Politics of Exclusion/Inclusion in Attic Tragedy." In Fiona McHardy and Eireann Marshall, eds., *Women's Influence on Classical Civilization,* 40–55. London: Routledge.

Rosenbloom, David. (2011). "The Panhellenism of Athenian Tragedy." In David Carter, ed., *Why Athens? A Reappraisal of Tragic Politics,* 353–381. Oxford: Oxford University Press.

Saxonhouse, Arlene. (1986). "Myths and the Origins of Cities: Reflections on the Autochthony Theme in Euripides' *Ion.*" In J. Peter Euben, ed., *Greek Tragedy and Political Theory,* 252–273. Berkeley: University of California Press.

Schaps, David M. (1979). *Economic Rights of Women in Ancient Greece.* Edinburgh: Edinburgh University Press.

———. (1998). "What Was Free about a Free Athenian Woman?" *Transactions of the American Philological Association* 128:161–188.

Seaford, Richard. (1994). *Reciprocity and Ritual: Homer and Tragedy in the Developing City-State.* Oxford: Clarendon Press.

Sealey, Raphael. (1990). *Women and Law in Classical Greece.* Chapel Hill: University of North Carolina Press.

Sfyroeras, Pavlos. (1994). "The Ironies of Salvation: The Aegeus Scene in Euripides' *Medea.*" *Classical Journal* 90:125–142.

Slater, Philip E. (1968). *The Glory of Hera: Greek Mythology and the Greek Family.* Boston: Beacon Press.

Sommerstein, Alan H., ed. (1998). *The Comedies of Aristophanes,* vol. 10: *Ecclesiazusae.* Warminster, England: Aris and Phillips.

Vellacott, Philip. (1975). *Ironic Drama: A Study of Euripides' Method and Meaning.* Cambridge: Cambridge University Press.

Vernant, Jean-Pierre, and Pierre Vidal-Naquet, eds. (1990). *Myth and Tragedy in Ancient Greece,* vol. 2. Trans. J. Lloyd. New York: Zone Books.

Waterfield, Robin. (2001). *Euripides: Ion, Orestes, Phoenician Women, Suppliant Women.* Oxford: Oxford University Press.

Wilkins, John. (1990). "The State and the Individual." In Anton Powell, ed., *Euripides, Women, and Sexuality,* 177–194. London: Routledge.

Wilson, Nigel G. (2007). *Aristophanes Fabulae,* vol. 2. Oxford: Oxford University Press.

Wohl, Victoria. (1997). *Intimate Commerce: Exchange, Gender, and Subjectivity in Greek Tragedy.* Austin: University of Texas Press.

Zacharia, Katerina. (2003). *Converging Truths: Euripides' "Ion" and the Athenian Quest for Self-Definition. Mnemosyne* Supp. 242. Leiden: Brill.

Zeitlin, Froma. (1978). "The Dynamics of Misogyny: Myth and Mythmaking in the *Oresteia* of Aeschylus." *Arethusa* 11:149–184.

————. (1996). *Playing the Other: Essays on Gender and Society in Classical Greek Literature*. Chicago: University of Chicago Press.

————. (2008). "Intimate Relations: Children, Childbearing, and Parentage on the Euripidean Stage." In Martin Revermann and Peter Wilson, eds., *Performance, Iconography, Reception: Studies in Honour of Oliver Taplin*, 318–332. Oxford: Oxford University Press.

SIX

Working Girls

MOTHER–DAUGHTER BONDS

AMONG ANCIENT PROSTITUTES

Anise K. Strong

Perhaps the most difficult familial relationship to study in the ancient world is that of mothers and their daughters. For most respectable Greek and Roman families, this private bond is invisible to us, although it was presumably important both emotionally and educationally to the women involved. We have entire books about father–daughter, mother–son, and father–son relationships in the fields of both classical history and classical literature, but lack almost any source material or scholarship on the ubiquitous female–female parent–child relationship.[1]

This lacuna is not a problem unique to the ancient world. From antiquity to the present day, Western literature and historical texts, which tend to be male-authored, reveal little information concerning mother–daughter ties. While sexism may in part explain this lacuna, it is also important to bear in mind that men simply lacked knowledge about female–female relationships and their particular dynamics. The mother–daughter relationship, especially in somewhat gender-segregated societies such as those of ancient Rome and Greece, was fundamentally alien to male outsiders. As such, male-authored literary sources tend to depict dialogues between mothers and daughters as both hostile to males and focused on the female manipulation of male relatives and lovers.[2]

A rare exception of a positively depicted mother–daughter relationship in classical literature is that of Clytemnestra and Iphigenia in *Iphigenia at Aulis*; yet this play ends tragically, with Clytemnestra losing her daughter to her husband's sacrificial knife.[3] Even in this case, most of Iphigenia and Clytemnestra's conversations with each other concern either Agamemnon or Iphigenia's supposed marriage to Achilles. In the *Homeric Hymn to Demeter*, the relationship between Demeter and her daughter Persephone

is close and intimate, but again, the story told is one of bereavement and tragedy.[4]

In contrast, the limited historical evidence we have from antiquity, which comes primarily from legal cases and letters, suggests more positive and female-centered relationships between mothers and daughters. Their interactions tend to focus on issues of either economic or emotional support of each other, rather than on plots against their male kin.[5] These two distinct representations of mother–daughter bonds suggest a disparity between ancient male views of women and the actual lived experiences of those women.

While the public historical texts must be viewed through the potentially distorted lenses of male jurists and advocates, they still offer a door into the private "female sphere" of Greek and Roman women's interactions with each other. The characterizations of the women themselves are biased and untrustworthy as historical data, since the jurists and statesmen are attempting to win their cases, often by representing the mother or daughter in question as villainous and greedy. However, the technical details of law cases which detail interactions between women and their daughters are likely to be true or at least representative of actual social patterns. While such testimony must be carefully filtered, it offers a more accurate impression of women's daily lives than the purely literary imaginings of elite male authors.

Previous historical studies of ancient mothers, most notably the work of Suzanne Dixon, have focused primarily on the evidence of elites concerning respectable Roman matrons, which frequently disregards or minimizes female–female bonds. For instance, we have a significant amount of firsthand data about the families of the first-century BCE Roman statesman Marcus Tullius Cicero and the first-century CE Roman civil servant Pliny the Younger. However, Cicero's and Pliny's letters focus on the men's own relationships to their female kin rather than the interrelationships among their wives, mothers, and daughters.[6] We can only infer what Tullia thought about her mother, Terentia, or vice versa.

One of the only means of glimpsing such a mother–daughter relationship is therefore to examine atypical familial structures that lacked a central male figure as the focus of authorial attention. Perhaps the most common type of such a family was the household of a madam and her prostitute-daughter. We are constrained, as usual in the study of ancient women, by a reliance on male-authored sources, but we can still gain glimpses of how elite men perceived particular relationships. Specifically, this essay compares representations of madam–prostitute mother–daughter relation-

ships in plays and comic dialogues to those chronicled in legal cases. By examining this evidence, we can both study the male representation of female bonds and gain some sense of women's own view of prostitution and mother–daughter ties, as evidenced by the issues they valued deeply enough to fight for in court. While the literary mothers glamorize prostitution and advocate it as a lifestyle for their daughters, the historical mothers tend to seek respectable marriage for their daughters, and prostitution is represented as a desperate and bleak alternative for the economically desperate.

Given the paucity of source material overall about such relationships, my data set ranges from classical Greece to late Roman Egypt and across the Mediterranean. I focus on stories about the elite escorts or courtesans, known in the Greek world as *hetairai*, mainly because there are fewer records about the lives of poor streetwalkers, known as *pornai* to the Greeks and *scorta* to the Romans.[7] While most ancient prostitutes did not live in elegant houses or brothels with their mothers, tales of wealthy freelance courtesans were popular sources of entertainment. Meanwhile, male jurists frequently levied accusations of prostitution at female defendants or witnesses in ancient lawsuits. Despite the variety of source materials, the stereotypes of madam-mothers presented in the literary sources in particular are remarkably consistent across time and culture, largely because they draw on earlier literary models rather than reflecting contemporary local practices of prostitution.

WHY PROSTITUTE YOUR DAUGHTER?

Upon first consideration, motherhood itself seems like a severe disadvantage to a prostitute's lifestyle. Prostitutes, to an even greater degree than other female workers, are unable to work for some time due to pregnancy and childbirth. Childbirth was also a serious health risk in antiquity, and parenthood would have been a significant economic burden for women on the margins of society. Since prostitutes are frequently associated in ancient texts with contraceptives, abortifacients, and infant exposure, we might wonder why there are any stories about prostitutes and their daughters at all.[8] Since plentiful if unreliable information about abortion and contraception was readily available to prostitutes, and infant exposure was also socially tolerated, why would ancient prostitutes ever have taken the economic and physical risks of becoming mothers?

The answer lies in two distinct sources of concern for the freelance prostitute. In Greek and Roman societies, children were valued for their

ability to provide not only emotional gratification but also potential economic security. Children were expected to support and protect their elders when they were no longer able to fend for themselves.[9] Prostitutes, particularly given their lack of a larger family structure, must have desired protection and support in their old age as much as anyone else in antiquity.

This anxiety about the need for geriatric care would have been particularly cogent for prostitutes given their short career spans. Several texts tell us of the rapidly declining pay scales for middle-aged and elderly prostitutes in the ancient world.[10] Older prostitutes are generally characterized as ugly, cheap streetwalkers who were forced by necessity to perform more degrading sexual acts for less money. (There are exceptional women like Philinna or Charito, who supposedly still invoked fierce desire from her lovers at the age of sixty.)[11] Epicrates describes the reversal of fortune over time of the famous *hetaira* Laïs:

> When she was a chick and young, and made wild by the big bucks, you would have seen Pharnabazos sooner than her. But now since she has run the long course in years, and the structure of her body is relaxing, it's easier to see her than spit. She goes flying around, dashing everywhere: she takes a stater or three obols. (Epicrates, *Anti-Laïs* fr. 3.11–21)

Since marriage was rarely an option, and other women's work—like weaving—relatively unprofitable, the main retirement option for older prostitutes was to become a madam and live off a share of the earnings of younger, more attractive women. The easiest way to find such apprentices was to bear and raise them, although we also see examples from both literary and historical sources of madams buying young female children or adopting exposed infants. As a consequence, the ancient discourse concerning mother–daughter relationships among prostitutes is complicated by issues of economic necessity. While the mothers may wish success and happiness for their daughters, they also seek to ensure their own financial security and comfort.

FICTIONAL REPRESENTATIONS

In plays, poetry, and comic dialogue, prostitute-mothers are generally portrayed as antagonists to the young male hero or lover figure; they view their daughters largely as sources of potential profit. I shall primarily focus here on several examples from the second-century CE Greco-Roman au-

thor Lucian's *Dialogues of the Courtesans*, as these are both representative of the genre and feature extended conversations between madam-mothers and prostitute-daughters. The mothers echo the hostile, witch-like *lenae* (madams) and pseudo-maternal figures that we see elsewhere in Greek and Roman poetry, while the daughters are typically represented as the naïve victims of their mothers' greed and nagging.[12]

A representative example of maternal encouragement toward prostitution is Lucian's dialogue between the mother Crobyle and her daughter Corinna, who has just come back from her first night of work as a prostitute. Crobyle explains in detail the dire economic necessity that led to the prostitution of her daughter:

> CROBYLE: We've no other way of earning a living, you know, daughter. Do you realize how badly we've lived these last two years since your blessed father died? When he was alive, we had everything, with no problem. He worked metal and had a great name in Piraeus. . . . When he died, first of all I sold his fire-tongs and his anvil and his hammer for two *minae*, and we managed to live off of that for seven months. Then I earned our daily bread with difficulty, sometimes by weaving, sometimes by spinning the two kinds of thread, for woof and warp. I was feeding you, daughter, waiting for you to fulfill my expectations. . . . I reckoned that when you were the age you are now, you'd be able to look after me, and easily get yourself clothed well, grow rich, and have purple robes and maids.
>
> CORINNA: What do you mean, mother, how?
>
> CROBYLE: By spending your time with young men, drinking with them, and sleeping with them for money.
>
> (LUCIAN, *DIALOGUES OF THE COURTESANS* 6.1;
> TRANS. ADAPTED FROM SIDWELL [2005])

Crobyle is not a lazy or naturally immoral woman; she attempted to make a living through spinning and weaving, the more virtuous if less profitable types of work readily available to women.[13] However, Crobyle is also a widow who apparently lacks any natal family to assist her or her daughter. Corinna is her one profitable resource. Crobyle was not a prostitute herself, but she seems to find little immoral about the profession, presumably partially due to the genre of the comic dialogue itself. Corinna, meanwhile, is just postpubescent and quite naïve; much of the dialogue focuses on Crobyle's instructions to her on the proper behavior of an elite *hetaira*.

Despite the unorthodox nature of this family unit, Lucian emphasizes

the commonplace and humorous dynamic in their relationship. Crobyle holds up the example of her friend's daughter in an attempt to further encourage Corinna, noting, "Daphnis used to wear rags before her girl became old enough" (6.2). Crobyle is particularly focused not just on the necessities of life, like food, but on the potential to buy luxury items and feminine accessories with her daughter's earnings. This desire forms part of a long tradition of male condemnation of female greed and shallowness, but it also suggests a consciousness of class in this case. For ancient women, social and economic status was at least partially denoted by dress (as well as number of slaves); Crobyle wishes to leave rags behind for "purple robes and maids." Crobyle's final attempt to persuade her daughter into a life of prostitution assumes that her daughter feels a filial obligation to support her economically:

> Don't you want everyone pointing you out with their fingers very shortly and saying, "Do you see how very rich Crobyle's daughter Corinna is and how completely blissful she's made her mother?" What do you say? Will you do it? I know you will. (Lucian, *Dialogues of the Courtesans* 6.4; trans. adapted from Sidwell [2005])

There are two useful questions to be asked about this particular scenario of Lucian's. First, we may question its realism. Would Lucian's audience have considered plausible the possibility of a respectable smith's widow and daughter falling into prostitution? Ann Hanson's research on papyri from Hellenistic and Roman Egypt suggests that even wealthy widows and mothers of sons in antiquity were highly concerned with financial security after the death of their husbands.[14] Economic hardship for a mother of daughters without male kin to support her must have been both relatively common and dire. While prostitution was not the inevitable fate of young women in such a situation, it seems a reasonable possibility.

Why, then, would Lucian's audience have found this dialogue especially humorous, if it realistically depicted the stark economic choices available to nonelite widows and their daughters? The humor here lies not primarily in a Bakhtinian reversal of expectations but in the more conventional stereotyping and mockery of inferiors, as suggested by Aristotle.[15] Lucian's audience is presumably neither elite courtesans nor impoverished widows, but rather elite males of the leisure class. Such listeners must have laughed at the idea of an older woman nagging her daughter to prostitute herself in contrast with the more conventional scenario of mothers urging

their daughters to marry well. Both women conform to narrow misogynistic gender stereotypes in this dialogue; Lucian makes no attempt to evoke complex personalities or deep characterizations in his representation of either Crobyle or Corinna.

Kate Gilhuly also notes that this particular dialogue focuses on the gratification of male sexual desires as much as on female economic needs. Crobyle attempts to mold the Galataen Corinna into the perfect object for the male gaze, counseling her on how to eat, drink, and smile appropriately in order to attract lovers. At the same time, the mother herself interacts primarily with other women, their neighbors and friends, in similar straits.[16] The male–female relationship here is usually temporary and transactional, despite Corinna's wish to see her lover Eucritos again. In contrast, the female–female relationships are depicted as long-lasting and require both emotional and financial ties between mother and daughter.

Another typical scenario, featured in Lucian's dialogue between Musarion and her mother (7), involves the mother-madam criticizing her prostitute-daughter for taking a poor but handsome client. Musarion's lover Chaereas has been taking money from her rather than providing her with funds. When Musarion protests to her mother that her lover has promised to marry her as soon as his father dies, the mother responds:

> So if we need shoes, Musarion, and the shoemaker asks for the two drachmas, we're going to say to him, "We don't have the cash, but you can have a few of our hopes." And we'll say the same to the bread-man too. And if someone comes for the rent, we'll say, "Can you wait until Laches dies? I'll pay you straight after the wedding." (Lucian, *Dialogues of the Courtesans* 7.4; trans. Sidwell [2005])

In both Greek and Roman fiction, the madam-mother is generally an acerbic realist, willing to face the harsh facts and coach her daughter to abandon idealistic love for ready cash. She does perhaps love her daughter, but she also wants prototypically feminine comforts like clothes and jewelry, again feeding into male stereotypes of female interests and desires. These mothers may have real financial difficulties and worries about bread and rent money, but they are also fundamentally shallow in their longing for fashionable accessories. This dialogue also illustrates the madam-mother's concern with the ephemeral nature of a courtesan's career: "Do you think you're always going to be eighteen?" asks Musarion's mother. The daughter's career as a prostitute is only a temporary solution to the economic is-

sues faced by a household of women. In the best scenario, the daughter either finds a long-term relationship to support her or repeats the process with the next generation.

Sometimes, we are given the perspective of a young prostitute-mother. In one scene in the *Dialogues*, the *hetaira* Myrtion discusses her pregnancy with her lover Pamphilus, whom she fears is about to desert her for a legitimate bride:

> This is the only profit I've had of your passion, that you've made my stomach this size and I'll have to look after a child soon—a very difficult thing for a courtesan. I say "look after" because I'm not going to expose it, especially if it's male. I'm going to call him Pamphilus, and have him as a consolation for our love. And one day he'll throw it in your face that you were unfaithful to his poor mother. (Lucian, *Dialogues of the Courtesans* 2.1; trans. Sidwell [2005])

Myrtion places a high value on having a child, especially a son, who can offer the protection and eventual permanent support which girls like Corinna and Musarion cannot. She also views parenthood as an active choice, although the conception was presumably accidental and her plan involves significant career sacrifices.

Lacking a husband, Myrtion was able to choose her own fate as a mother. In conventional ancient families it was the father who had this power, not the mother. Greek and Roman fathers had the legal right to either raise or expose any child they wished. Mothers in conventional families normally lacked such power, although some might have the choice to expose a child in the case of divorce, if the father was uninterested in raising it.[17] Given the ready availability of exposure, all the children raised by a prostitute can be perceived as wanted children. While this dialogue, in contrast to the others, is one between a man and a woman, Myrtion does not appear to consider the father's power over this child at all. She remains outside the boundaries of the normal cross-gender familial relationships; as a courtesan, this control over children gives her both more power and more vulnerability.

Lucian's literary stereotypes of madam-mothers and prostitute-daughters appear to draw from common archetypes, as such characters are also found in Greek and Roman plays and poetry.[18] In the Roman playwright Terence's comedy *The Fair Andrian*, based on a play by the Greek playwright Menander, Chrysis, the Andrian prostitute in question, turns from weaving to prostitution in order to support her young sister.[19] In the *Eu-*

nuchus, the courtesan Thaïs is also the daughter of a madam and the foster sister of a virtuous maiden wrongly sold as a prostitute; Thaïs mentions
that her mother "taught [the girl] everything, and brought her up, just as
though she had been her own daughter."[20] The older sisters of the comedies
seem to be compassionate and protective of their virtuous maiden "sisters,"
and the original Greek plots revolve around the transition of the younger
girl from the status of prostitute to that of respectable wife.

This plot type stands in contrast to Lucian's dialogues and the depictions in poetry, however, where the prostitute-daughters remain courtesans, supporting their mothers in a female-run household. One possible
reason for this disparity is that the older sister is still fully capable of earning a living through her own sex work, unlike the older mothers of the dialogues. She plays the role of the attractive, crafty courtesan who uses her
wiles to ensure the best future for both herself and her female kin, generally
by tricking the hapless males of the comedy. The primacy of the female–
female relationship is maintained in these plays, but the strongly misogynistic aspect seen in Lucian's later mother-daughter dialogues is absent.

In contrast, later Roman and Greek elegiac poetry focused on trying to
drive a wedge between prostitute-daughters and their greedy, selfish mothers. As Sara Myers notes, the maternal figures generally serve as antagonists to the male poet-narrators or characters.[21] The Roman satirist Juvenal
complained that mothers taught their daughters how to be adulteresses or
even prostitutes: "For her own profit [*utile*] the shameful old woman brings
up her dear daughter for shame."[22] The Greek first-century CE poet Nicarchus warns his lover Philumena "not to listen to your mother" but to "try
and behave with propriety" and raise any child born while he is away.[23] The
Hellenistic poet Marcus Argentarius describes a scenario in which his intended seduction of the young woman Alcippe turned into a *ménage a trois*
with her mother, a different sort of remuneration for the older woman involved.[24] In these cases, the mothers are unconcerned either for their daughters' virtue or for their daughters' successful relationships with their lovers;
they want only profit or personal pleasure.

In other genres, the idea that a courtesan's household might frequently
consist of herself and her mother or other female kin seems to have been
readily accepted. In Xenophon's fourth-century BCE *Memorabilia*, for instance, the philosopher Socrates visits the *hetaira* Theodote, later the mistress of Alcibiades, and gives her advice on how to attract lovers. While
the dialogue is principally interesting in its comparison of Socrates himself to a courtesan, it includes the minor detail that Theodote supports her
mother with her work: "At this point Socrates noticed that she was sump-

tuously dressed, and that her mother at her side was wearing fine clothes and jewelry."[25] Whether or not this conversation is purely imaginary, Xenophon seems to expect his audience to find the presence of a mother who is economically supported by her courtesan daughter to be unremarkable. At the same time, the mother here does not have any obvious authority over Theodote; Theodote herself conducts the conversation with Socrates and is clearly the mistress of her own household.

SON OF A PROSTITUTE

Whereas the mothers of prostitute-daughters use their daughters only as temporary sources of dishonorable income, the prostitute-mothers of sons were sometimes able to achieve permanent comfort and upward social mobility through their offspring. On the literary side, there is the already discussed case of Musarion. A hypothetical law case imagined by the Roman first-century CE rhetorician Seneca the Elder debates the issue of whether a man can name as his heir his grandson by a disinherited son and a prostitute.[26] The prostitute-mother is depicted in the speech for the defense as a virtuous and loving woman, nursing her dying lover with "sad face and eyes cast down."[27] Here the woman's wifely devotion redeems her unorthodox status and offers an opportunity for her son. The opposing side criticizes the prostitute for her fertility, which is said to be inappropriate and uncharacteristic for prostitutes, who were supposedly experts with regard to contraceptives and abortifacients.[28] In this case, then, prostitute-like behavior—licentiousness and childlessness—is seen as incompatible with virtuous motherhood. However, this prostitute's ironic reward for her virtue is the loss of her child, as he is adopted into the aristocratic family and taken away from her; she achieves a better life for her child but not for herself.

Fourth-century BCE Athenian orators frequently cast aspersions on the sexual histories of their political rivals' mothers as a means of denigrating the men's social status. Demosthenes claims that his enemy Aeschines' mother Glaucothea was originally a common whore named Empusa.[29] Isaeus accuses the madam and prostitute Alce of scheming to establish her son as a legitimate Athenian citizen and the heir of her elite lover.[30] Most such slanders probably had little basis in fact, although they betray how little even the male neighbors of these men necessarily knew about the names and social background of the women in a household.[31] Women could of-

ten be accused of prostitution simply because there was no public record to prove otherwise.

Athenaeus offers an entire list of famous Greeks who were supposedly the sons of prostitutes, defending these lowly social origins on the grounds that "when such women change to a life of sobriety they are better than the women who pride themselves on their respectability."[32] In some versions of Roman legend, Romulus and Remus's foster mother was not a female wolf but a part-time prostitute named Acca Larentia or Lupa.[33] For men, these stories demonstrate that having a prostitute as a mother was shameful but did not necessarily doom the man himself to a lowly or dishonorable social status. Prostitute-mothers who were appropriately virtuous and self-sacrificing could produce elite sons, although they themselves do not seem to have benefited directly from their offspring's success.

LEGAL EXAMPLES OF MADAM-MOTHERS

Historical sources such as legal cases offer glimpses at more complex and mutually supportive relationships between prostitutes or former prostitutes and their "working girl" daughters. Nevertheless, these texts themselves are also highly charged and tend to present negative and somewhat stereotypical views of such ties.[34] As the authors and advocates were generally trying either to belittle or to whitewash the reliability and virtue of a female witness or defendant, they had little incentive to tell purely objective accounts. These trial cases are not designed solely for entertainment, unlike the comic dialogues, but they do still present, at best, a male-authored representation of historical female testimony and experience.

By focusing specifically on references to mother–daughter relationships rather than on the questions of the defendants' moral and social status, however, even these vituperative, misogynistic speeches provide useful insight into relationships among women. In the following examples I shall be focusing not on the guilt or innocence of the figures in each lawsuit but on what these cases can tell us about maternal attitudes toward the prostitution of their daughters.

The most famous and detailed relationship, as well as one of our only cases of a three-generation sequence, is that of the fourth-century BCE courtesan Neaira, her madam and maternal figure, Nicarete, and Neaira's daughter Phano. Our main source for the lives of these women is the prosecution speech of Apollodorus against Neaira; his agenda was to prove

both that Neaira was herself a notorious prostitute and that Phano was her daughter and not the legitimate citizen-daughter of Neaira's consort Stephanus by an Athenian citizen-wife.[35] As such, the facts of the case are arguable; Debra Hamel suggests that Phano may not have been Neaira's biological daughter at all.[36] In this case, however, I focus on the particular dynamics of the relationships between these mother–daughter pairs, rather than the underlying legal issues, and thus find Apollodorus's claims useful for that purpose.

Nicarete, a well-known madam and married freedwoman from Elis, apparently had a practice of adopting exposed attractive girl babies from the dung heap and "rearing and training them skillfully" to be courtesans.

> She used to address them as daughters, so that she might exact the largest fee from those who wished to have dealings with them, on the ground that they were freeborn girls; but after she had reaped her profit from the youth of each of them, one by one, she then sold the whole lot of them together, seven in all. (Apollodorus, *Against Neaira* 19)

While there was no biological tie between Nicarete and her prostitutes, she and possibly her husband Hippias functioned *in loco parentis* to these girls. Notably, the girls are publicly treated as daughters, but Apollodorus implies that, in private, Nicarete considered them to be slaves. He also alleges that Nicarete prostituted Neaira before she reached puberty and then, after making a large profit upon her, sold her as an exclusive concubine for two clients.[37] Such a scenario denotes the harshest possible representation of a relationship between a madam-mother figure and a prostitute-daughter. The madam uses the girl for prostitution at the earliest possible age and then sells her off, ending any pretense of a familial relationship.

Apollodorus claims that in the course of her own later career as a *hetaira*, Neaira herself had three children, the boys Proxenus and Ariston and a daughter, Phano, all of unknown parentage. Phano's parentage and citizenship status are at the crux of the trial, as she was later presented as the Athenian citizen-child of Neaira's lover and possible husband, Stephanus. Regardless of the veracity of the prosecution's argument about Phano's lack of citizenship, Neaira's interest in protecting and benefiting the girl is clear from the speech. Neaira and Stephanus first marry Phano off to an Athenian citizen, Phrastor, with a substantial dowry of thirty *minae*, the same as Neaira's own original purchase price.[38]

Apollodorus accuses Phano of having been brought up "in dissolute

ways, longing for her mother's way of life"; her marriage ultimately ended in divorce.[39] However, when Phano's ex-husband Phrastor fell ill, both Phano and her mother, Neaira, went to nurse him. As a result of their good care, the mother and daughter persuaded him to acknowledge Phano's own son as his legitimate heir.[40] This act of cooperative nursing suggests a continued relationship of familial support between Neaira and Phano, even after Phano had reached adulthood and marriage. Phano also seems to be living in the household of Neaira and Stephanus after her divorce. Since Apollodorus has no reason to portray Neaira or Phano sympathetically, the story of their care of Phrastor is likely to be accurate. Stephanus and Neaira subsequently remarried Phano to another Athenian, the king-archon for that year, again trying to improve her status and buy a good marriage by means of a substantial dowry and other monetary assistance for her husband.[41]

While Phano may have had some premarital sexual experience, Neaira worked hard to promote a respectable lifestyle for her daughter. She twice provided a dowry and arranged or tricked naïve Athenian men into marriage. Although the text of the speech is clearly hostile, it nevertheless gives substantial insights into the bonds of both responsibility and presumed affection between this alleged courtesan-mother and her daughter. We do not know the emotional nature of the relationship between Nicarete and Neaira, although Nicarete's regular sales of her "daughters" suggest that the tie was more economic than affectionate. However, rather than trying to profit from her own child, Neaira spent substantial sums to try to ensure a life free from prostitution for Phano.

When we read in between the lines of Apollodorus's exaggerated denunciation, we are given a brief glimpse of a devoted, hardworking prostitute trying to achieve prosperity and social respectability for her child. This glimpse also casts doubt on the romantic notion that Greek courtesans' lives were somehow superior to those of the sheltered, segregated Athenian wives. Neaira is very willing to sacrifice her daughter's independence and enjoyment of public life in return for the ordinary existence and long-term security of marriage.

In another example, the orator Isaeus's third speech concerns a lawsuit in which the husband of an Athenian woman named Phyle claims that she is her deceased father's heiress (*epikleros*) and thus has claim to his property. Isaeus's speech counters this claim by arguing that Phyle is merely the illegitimate daughter of her father, Phyrros, and a *hetaira*.[42] As in the case of *Against Neaira*, much of the argument revolves around the question of the

mother's social status and behavior. Isaeus claims that the mother was sere-naded by strangers and attended banquets with her "husband" in the company of men, but he can offer much less proof of her courtesan status than Apollodorus does for Neaira.[43] In any case, this supposed courtesan appears to have maintained a close relationship with her daughter, since the mother-prostitute is identified as a source of knowledge for her son-in-law during the lawsuit twenty years after her partner's death.[44]

Regardless of her mother's status, the daughter Phyle appears to be legitimately married to a respectable Athenian citizen, Xenocles, again suggesting that her mother or kin viewed marriage as highly preferable to a life of prostitution for her daughter. Isaeus alleges that Xenocles knowingly "took as his wife the daughter of a mistress," which, if true, establishes that the social distinctions between wife and *hetaira* in fourth-century Athens were more nebulous than cases like *Against Neaira* might suggest. While the respectability of mothers like Neaira and the unnamed courtesan here may have remained in question, these women were still able to marry off their daughters and thereby establish more conventional means of economic support for them. Their sons-in-law might also have been able to take care of the retired courtesans in their old age, providing a personal level of security as well as protection for their children and grandchildren.

In contrast, a late antique papyrus from Hermoupolis in Egypt paints a much grimmer picture of the typical historical mother–daughter relationship involving prostitution. According to the details of the fourth-/fifth-century CE case, an impoverished woman named Theodora sold her anonymous daughter to a pimp as a public prostitute, so that she might have economic support from the daughter's income.[45] The girl was subsequently killed in the line of work by one of her clients, the senator Diodemus. Theodora then sued Diodemus for financial support because of the resultant loss of her daughter's earnings, "a small consolation for her daughter's life," and was awarded 10 percent of the senator's property by the prefect.

The prefect describes the daughter as "a poor creature, who when she was alive was laid out for those who wanted her, like a dead body. The poverty of her lot was so insistent that she sold her body and brought dishonor upon her name and reputation and took on a prostitute's life with its many hardships." This is almost certainly a more common scenario for prostitute families than the extravagant lifestyle of Neaira and her family. The unnamed daughter was sold to gain basic sustenance for her mother and died as a result of the genuine dangers of her profession. Theodora presumably did not bear her child for the purpose of prostitution, but she was ready to make use of her for the economic benefit of the family. Indeed, given that

the prefect considered 10 percent of an elite senator's property to be fair recompense, it appears that Theodora may have profited quite substantially from the sale of her daughter.

When compared and examined as a whole, these different glimpses of life in mother–daughter prostitute households offer a startling alternative to the conventional father-dominated narratives of the ancient family. We cannot discount the misogyny and stereotypes present in these tales; even the law cases draw on general elite male assumptions about the greed of the female prostitute. Yet these stories also describe lifelong and mutually supportive relationships between mother and daughter. Just as the evidence about elite Roman matrons suggests that they maintained important relationships with their mothers well into adulthood, these lower class women also had their daughters as a primary tie.[46] For most prostitutes, daughters, if they existed, formed their only permanent familial bond, as relationships with lovers (and sons) were almost inevitably transient.

We can also see a striking contrast in attitudes toward the career of prostitution between historical and purely literary figures. The historical Athenian courtesan Neaira strove to prevent her daughter from following in her profession by repeatedly arranging respectable marriages for her. The purely fictional Crobyle, on the other hand, once a respectable smith's wife, goaded her daughter Corinna into prostitution without any apparent moral qualms. Lucian's dialogues and Greek New Comedy glamorized prostitution as a luxurious lifestyle, perhaps in order to reduce any unease among their male audience either about the fate of widows and female orphans or about wealthy men's treatment of ordinary prostitutes. The actions of Greek and Egyptian women in the legal cases, however, suggest that most women, even if economically desperate, did not view prostitution as a good option for their daughters. The fate of the daughter of Theodora—and mention should be made of Apollodorus's description of Neaira's gang rape (33)—offers a far harsher perspective on the reality of ancient sex work than any of the pretty dresses described by Lucian's Crobyle.

Both literary and legal texts describe women moving either from conventional family life to prostitution or vice versa; the plays and dialogues suggest more of a downward movement, whereas the legal texts chronicle the attempt of supposed prostitute-mothers to find respectable husbands for their daughters. These transitions between different social layers also suggest that there may have been more fluidity between the states of matron, madam, and prostitute than legal codes or prescriptive texts would imply, despite Apollodorus's famous doctrinaire statement:

We have courtesans [*hetairai*] for pleasure, and concubines [*pallakai*] for the daily service of our bodies, [and] wives [*gunaikēs*] for the production of legitimate offspring and to have a reliable guardian of our household property. (Apollodorus, *Against Neaira* 122)[47]

Courtesans in this schematic are explicitly not mothers, or at least not mothers of legitimate offspring, and yet this trial is an attempt to prove that Neaira herself is indeed the mother of Phano. For Apollodorus, the legal status of the mother–child relationship is key, rather than the emotional bond between the pair; what matters is not how Neaira and Phano feel about each other but whether Phano has the legal status of a citizen-daughter—the daughter of an Athenian father. Mothers are once again elided from the picture, even while putatively forming the object and focus of the trial.

It would be dangerous to read too much into this limited collection of legal cases and comic dialogues, especially in light of differences in genre and date. Nevertheless, given the paucity of other sources on ancient mother–daughter relationships, the discourse about such bonds in these texts suggests both the importance of the mother–daughter tie and the suspicion and denigration with which male authors treated it. The relationships between women depicted in these texts, whether literary or historical, are ones of mentorship and love as well as economic dependence.[48] The fictional stereotypical mothers of comedy and dialogue use their daughters for their own gain, but they also betray a genuine, plausible anxiety about the economic options available to women without male kin. In contrast, the successful historical courtesans seek to avoid their own fate by arranging traditional marriages for their daughters. While a modern audience may be startled by the idea of encouraging a daughter to become a prostitute, the goal of enabling a better life for one's children remains a constant in the history of motherhood.

NOTES

1. The major scholarship to date focuses almost exclusively on historical evidence about elite families; see Dixon (1988), 210–232; Hallett (1984), 259–262; Demand (1994), 28–35; Phillips (1978), 69–79.

2. See, for instance, Lucian, *Dialogues of the Courtesans* 2, 3, 6, 7; Juvenal 6.239–240; Plautus, *Cistellaria* 1–120, *Asinaria* 504–544, *Miles Gloriosus* 690f.; Terence, *Heauton Timorumenos* 233–234.

3. Euripides, *Iphigenia at Aulis* 1436–1456; Foley (2002), 124.

4. Foley (1994), 123–130.

5. Phillips (1978).

6. Dixon (1988), 210–232; Hallett (1984), 259–262.

7. The question of whether terminology for prostitutes in legal texts accurately described social and economic divisions between different types of sex workers is highly debated. Miner (2003) and Davidson (1997) discuss this issue extensively with regard to the Greek world. There has been no detailed analysis so far regarding the applicability of different Roman terms; the best current sources are Adams (1983) and Flemming (1999).

8. Demand (1994), 30; Hamel (2005), 48; Riddle (1992); see Hippocrates, *Fleshes* 19.

9. Golden (1990), 92–93; Rawson (2003), 220–225.

10. E.g., Aristophanes, *Ecclesiazusae* 1105–1110; Anacreon 346; *Greek Anthology* 5.204, 5.271, 5.273; 6.18–20, 6.48, 6.283.

11. Cokayne (2003), 136–140; Philodemus, *Greek Anthology* 5.13, 5.258, 5.282.

12. For Lucian specifically see Gilhuly (2007), 78; for representations of *lenae* in Roman poetry see Myers (1996), 2–3.

13. Two epigrams from the *Palatine Anthology* suggest that the transition from weaving to prostitution was not uncommon: *Palatine Anthology* 6.48, 6.285 ("Away, starving work of wretched women, that has the power to waste away the bloom of youth"). On the other hand, loomweights have been found in the alleged brothel of the Athenian Agora, and several classical Greek vases depict *hetairai* weaving, suggesting that prostitutes may also have multitasked as weavers during quiet times of the day: Davidson (1997), 86–87.

14. Hanson (2005), 86–87.

15. Aristotle, *Poetics* 1449a.

16. Gilhuly (2007), 78.

17. In the surviving law code of the ancient Cretan city of Gortyn (the language is Peloponnesian Doric), a divorced mother whose husband rejected her child in the presence of three adult witnesses was given the right to either expose or raise the baby: Demand (1994), 11, 187; Brunt (1971), 153.

18. Fantham (1975), 45.

19. Terence, *Andrian* 75–78.

20. Terence, *Eunuchus* 145f.

21. Myers (1996), 1.

22. Juvenal 6.239–240.

23. Nicarchus, *Palatine Anthology* 5.40.

24. Marcus Argentarius, *Palatine Anthology* 5.127.

25. Xenophon, *Memorabilia* 3.11.

26. Seneca, *Controversiae* 2.4.

27. Seneca, *Controversiae* 2.4.

28. Seneca, *Controversiae* 2.4.5.

29. Demosthenes, *On the Crown* 129.

30. Isaeus 6.18–24; Glazebrook (2005), 173.

31. Glazebrook (2005), 182.

32. Athenaeus, *Deipnosophistae* 13.

33. Livy 1.4. See also Prudence Jones's and Patricia Salzman-Mitchell's essays in this volume.

34. Glazebrook (2005), 181–182.

35. Apollodorus, *Against Neaira* 17; Hamel (2005), 80.

36. Hamel (2005), 88; Allison Glazebrook argues that all details should be considered with extreme skepticism, given the slanderous nature of Athenian oratory: Glazebrook (2005), 62. See also Patterson (1998), 205.

37. Apollodorus, *Against Neaira* 22.

38. Apollodorus, *Against Neaira* 50.

39. Apollodorus, *Against Neaira* 50.

40. Apollodorus, *Against Neaira* 55.

41. Apollodorus, *Against Neaira* 72.

42. Isaeus 3.6; Glazebrook (2005), 173–174.

43. Isaeus 3.13.

44. Isaeus 3.31.

45. Berlin papyrus 1024.6–8, exc. G. As translated in Lefkowitz and Fant (2005), no. 155.

46. Phillips (1978), 69–79.

47. For commentary on the specific use of these terms, see Davidson (1997), 73; Miner (2003), 19–35.

48. Phillips (1978), 78; Dixon (1988), 220–222.

WORKS CITED

Adams, James Noel. (1983). "Words for 'Prostitute' in Latin." *Rheinisches Museum* 126: 321–358.

Brunt, P. A. (1971). *Italian Manpower.* London: Oxford University Press.

Cokayne, Karen. (2003). *Experiencing Old Age in Ancient Rome.* London: Routledge.

Davidson, James. (1997). *Courtesans and Fishcakes.* New York: St. Martin's Press.

Demand, Nancy. (1994). *Birth, Death, and Motherhood in Classical Greece.* Baltimore: Johns Hopkins University Press.

Dixon, Suzanne. (1988). *The Roman Mother.* London: Croom Helm.

Fantham, Elaine. (1975). "Sex, Status, and Survival in Hellenistic Athens: A Study of Women in New Comedy." *Phoenix* 29.1:44–74.

Flemming, Rebecca. (1999). "*Quae corpore quaestum facit*: The Sexual Economy of Female Prostitution in the Roman Empire." *Journal of Roman Studies* 89:38–61.

Foley, Helene. (1994). *The Homeric Hymn to Demeter: Translation, Commentary, and Interpretive Essays.* Princeton: Princeton University Press.

———. (2002). *Female Acts in Greek Tragedy.* Princeton: Princeton University Press.

Gilhuly, Kate. (2007). "Bronze for Gold: Subjectivity in Lucian's Dialogues of the Courtesans." *American Journal of Philology* 128.1:59–94.

Glazebrook, Allison. (2005). "The Making of a Prostitute: Apollodoros' Portrait of Neaira." *Arethusa* 38:161–187.

Golden, Mark. (1990). *Children and Childhood in Ancient Athens*. Baltimore: Johns Hopkins University Press.

Hallett, Judith. (1984). *Fathers and Daughters in Roman Society: Women and the Elite Family*. Princeton: Princeton University Press.

Hamel, Debra. (2005). *Trying Neaira: The True Story of a Courtesan's Scandalous Life in Ancient Greece*. New Haven: Yale University Press.

Hanson, Ann Ellis. (2005). "The Widow Babatha and the Poor Orphan Boy." In R. Katzoff and D. Schapps, eds., *Law in the Documents of the Judean Desert*, 85–103. Leiden: Brill.

Lefkowitz, Mary, and Maureen Fant. (2005). *Women's Life in Greece and Rome*. 3rd ed. Baltimore: Johns Hopkins University Press.

Miner, Jess. (2003). "Courtesan, Concubine, Whore: Apollodorus' Deliberate Use of Terms for Prostitutes." *American Journal of Philology* 124.1:19–37.

Myers, K. Sara. (1996). "The Poet and the Procuress: The Lena in Latin Love Elegy." *Journal of Roman Studies* 86:1–21.

Patterson, Cynthia B. (1998). *The Family in Greek History*. Cambridge, MA: Harvard University Press.

Phillips, Jane. (1978). "Roman Mothers and the Lives of Their Adult Daughters." *Helios* 6.1:69–79.

Rawson, Beryl. (2003). *Children and Childhood in Roman Italy*. Oxford: Oxford University Press.

Riddle, John M. (1992). *Contraceptives and Abortion from the Ancient World to the Renaissance*. Cambridge, MA: Harvard University Press.

Sidwell, Keith, trans. (2005). *Lucian: Chattering Courtesans and Other Sardonic Sketches*. London: Penguin.

!

SEVEN

Tenderness or Taboo

IMAGES OF BREAST-FEEDING MOTHERS
IN GREEK AND LATIN LITERATURE

Patricia Salzman-Mitchell

Two taboos are involved in the representation of the nursing image: nudity and milk; two images of women: sexual and maternal.

BONFANTE (1997), 188

The topic of nursing in Greek and Roman culture has received some well-deserved attention from scholars in recent years. In particular, medical texts provide us with guidance and opinions surrounding the benefits and vicissitudes of nursing infants. But while medical and philosophical writers tend to view breast-feeding of children by their own mothers in a positive light, literary testimonies provide a more complex outlook. This essay will look at some examples in Greek and Roman literature of mortal mothers breast-feeding their own children and will draw connections and give general interpretations of them. The scope of this paper includes the works of Homer through the Augustan period.[1] Wet-nursing will not be a central part of the argument, as it has already been amply discussed.[2] I will instead concentrate on literary depictions of mortal mothers, though maternal goddesses will be mentioned at times as a point of contrast.[3]

Larissa Bonfante has observed that images of nursing mothers in art and literature tend to be followed by tragedy, and thus what should be a tender moment, which expresses women's vulnerability, acts as a dramatic contrast that stresses the misfortune that ensues.[4] I will go even further in this line of thought and propose that while usually emphasizing the unique bond forged between mother and nursling, at the same time these images are surrounded by the male fear of otherness; male authors express discom-

fort regarding a practice that seems unknown, even taboo, with a hue of incest, close to the animal side of nature rather than to the civilized world,
and present women as mysterious, polluting, dangerous, and different. The
calamities that follow the examples we will discuss might thus be interpreted as punishment for an act that is sometimes viewed as forbidden or
taboo. These literary images are thus complex, falling as they do between
the purely motherly and the sexual.

The feeding of infants with their mother's breast milk is deemed
by many—past and present—as a natural practice; humans are mammals, and therefore it is in their makeup to feed their young in this manner. Yet social perception complicates this simple tenet, and both anthropologists and psychoanalysts have remarked on the problems and taboos
involved in it. It is also an act from which men are explicitly excluded,
which gives rise to suspicion on their part. The most obvious taboo, as the
above quote from Bonfante states, is nudity. Breast-feeding, whether performed in public or not, involves some exposure of the breasts and thus
of an intimate part of the female body. But beyond this basic concept is
the idea that there is something sexual in lactation and that the boundaries between the motherly and the erotic might be blurred. Cindy Stears
observes that the breast-feeding experience is complicated by the conflict
between the sexualized breast—the primary interpretation of breasts, at
least in modern American society—and the nurturing side of the breast.[5]
In *Boundaries of Touch*, Jean Halley mentions that some modern theorists
of child-rearing oppose nursing beyond twelve months due to unease about
unnecessary touch between mother and child. The author states that "anxiety about incest is at the core of this concern."[6] Arlene Eisenberg and others, for example, worry that "breastfeeding will cross the line from good
maternal to sexual behavior."[7] Some psychologists and anthropologists
even see breast-feeding as the first form of human intercourse, as a penetra-
tion (that even includes the exchange of fluids) between one body and another. Though they see it as a kind of erotic experience, they avoid straightforward condemnation and consider it as a natural part of the human
experience.[8]

While proponents of lactation as the "most natural" form of infant
feeding have tried to free breast-feeding of these taboo nuances and define
it as purely motherly, traces of these sexual overtones are still latent in cultural products and literary representations.

SOME MEDICAL AND ARCHAEOLOGICAL EVIDENCE

Before moving to the literary evidence, let us cast a general look at the material and medical evidence on breast-feeding in order to gain a broader understanding of views of lactation in the ancient world.

In the material culture of Greece, as Bonfante has shown, the motif of the nursing mother is rather absent and does not really appear until the Hellenistic period, in contrast to Italy, where it is relatively abundant.[9] This observation is particularly striking in light of the fact that intimate scenes of family life are numerous on Greek vases and *stelai*.[10] Although in classical Greece breast-feeding seems to have been recommended, it is evident that bottle feeding was also practiced.[11] In contrast to ancient Greece, images of breast-feeding are pervasive in Italian art, particularly in Etruria, Southern Italy, and Sicily.[12] This evidence shows not only a widespread practice, but also a celebration of it in material objects.[13] Yet in Rome itself scenes of actual nursing are scarce and, as expected, images of mothers focus on the presentation of the family group.[14]

The earliest mentions of lactation in the medical writers appear in the Hippocratic corpus, which provides aphorisms "On Dentition" and offers observations on the intake of milk. It also comments on sucklings.[15] Aristotle referred to methods of infant feeding, and in the *Historia animalium* 8 he addresses the properties of different types of milk, indicating also that breast-feeding took place on the first day of life. Plato comments on the rearing of children in the ideal city and proposes that children should be kept all together and mothers be brought to nurse them when their breasts are full, though no mother would know her own child (*Republic* 5.460c).[16] Soranus in his treatise on *Gynecology* (1.19.24–25) gives extensive recommendations on how to choose a wet nurse and on nutrition for nursing women.[17] Interestingly, he thought that mother's milk was not good for forty days after delivery and that the infant ought to be fed by a wet nurse.[18] He believed that the most suitable woman should nurse the infant, not necessarily the mother, unlike what the Roman philosophers thought, as we will see. Galen also wrote a chapter on infant feeding, and his *De sanitate tuenda* gives advice to nursing women on how to preserve the quality of their milk, thus implying a positive encouragement of the practice. He, unlike Soranus, did not believe that mother's milk was bad immediately after childbirth.

NURSING IN GREEK LITERATURE

In contrast to the lack of archaeological evidence on nursing mothers in classical Greece, literature does furnish some remarkable examples. In this section I will discuss some of the most famous passages in Greek literature that deal with breast-feeding and explore how behind the tender images presented, sexual overtones are also at play.

The earliest mentions of the act of breast-feeding in Greek poetry appear in Homer. In the *Hymn to Hermes* the infant god stresses his innocence by explaining that he is still a tender baby who only wants to sleep and nurse: "I care for sleep and my mother's milk" (267). Nursing is thus set in the context of the innocence and sweetness of infancy, which, of course, in the case of the trickster god, sounds rather fake. And in fact Margo Kitts argues that gods do not drink mother's milk and that Hermes is indeed lying here.[19] Yet this text presents a goddess nursing her child, and thus it is a different case than what we will see in literary sources showing human mothers and their children. As we will observe in Roman examples as well, goddesses convey an idealized view of nursing unlike what we see among humans, and it is my contention that this is the case because deities are free of taboo (they marry their siblings, as Zeus and Hera do, for example), but mortals are not.

In the *Odyssey* there is a passing reference to Penelope as a young bride with an infant at her breast (*Od.* 11.447–449). We do know that Euryclea was Odysseus's nurse, who also breast-fed him, as the hero mentions: "Why do you wish to destroy me? You did suckle me yourself at your breast" (*Od.* 19.482–483). A more outstanding example is, however, found in the *Iliad*, where Hecuba makes a last desperate plea to Hector begging him to withdraw from battle. She exposes her breast to him:

μήτηρ δ' αὖθ' ἑτέρωθεν ὀδύρετο δάκρυ χέουσα
κόλπον ἀνιεμένη, ἑτέρηφι δὲ μαζὸν ἀνέσχε:
καί μιν δάκρυ χέουσ' ἔπεα πτερόεντα προσηύδα:
Ἕκτορ τέκνον ἐμὸν τάδε τ' αἴδεο καί μ' ἐλέησον
αὐτήν, εἴ ποτέ τοι λαθικηδέα μαζὸν ἐπέσχον:
τῶν μνῆσαι φίλε τέκνον
(*IL.* 22.79–84)

And his mother wailed now, standing beside Priam,
weeping freely, loosing her robes with one hand
and holding out her bare breast with the other,

her words pouring forth in a flight of grief and tears:
"Hector, my child! Look—have some respect for *this*!
Pity your mother too, if I ever gave you the breast
to soothe your troubles, remember it now, dear boy."[20]

This arresting gesture that reveals an intimate part of the female body is surprising in such a male-oriented war poem as the *Iliad*. Hecuba believes that the sight of her bare breast will have some power over Hector, as she intends it as a symbol of the special bond between mother and infant. Hecuba in particular mentions the calming effect of her breast on her son, the sense of comfort and protection it once gave him. And for her plea to appear credible, this gesture would have to be more powerful and persuasive than simple words.[21]

Yet there is more than the recollection of tenderness between mother and son here. During the lactation phase nursing mothers begin to perceive their breasts as a means of nurturing, as food, as a unique bond between them and their nurslings. Before and after this stage, in both the ancient and the modern worlds, the breasts tend to be sexualized, as elements of female beauty and femininity rather than motherhood.[22] One may wonder, however, whether these sexual connotations of the breast and the physical contact between a mortal mother and her son (interestingly, all the examples that I was able to find present mothers and sons, not daughters) are entirely erased in the act of nursing, and if still present even in a veiled way, there might be an odd allusion to incest in these scenes. It is perhaps this awkwardness, among other reasons, that made the use of wet nurses acceptable.

It is thus striking in the *Iliad* episode that after so many years, during which Hecuba's breasts have acquired a different significance, she brings that meaning of the breast as nourishing out again—presumably her son has not seen his mother's breasts since he was a baby. Even more poignant is that Hecuba begs him to look and thus encourages his scopophilic interest. This episode brings up the many contradictions and complexities involved in the act of nursing. Do we see tenderness or taboo here? The recollection of the intimate moment tries to appeal to the mother–infant early love, yet exposing one's breasts to a grown son, long after the lactation period has finished, conveys ambiguous, and possibly sexual, overtones. Even more disturbing is that Hecuba is usually seen as an aged woman, wife of "old Priam"; generally nudity in old women was an object of ridicule and contempt in Greek culture. The unusualness of the scene thus stems from the contradicting readings of Hecuba's breasts. She exposes them as a nurs-

ing mother, which she is not anymore, but Hector may be reading them in a different way; more importantly here, a modern reader views the scene with a sense of unease, the result of our own hang-ups about the sexual connotations of breast-feeding. We do not know where to look or what to do with the scene. Since, as Douglas Gerber has shown, naked breasts are loaded with eroticism in the Greek world, it is possible that ancient audiences also saw the scene as touching on the incest fantasy existing between son and mother.[23] We do not have a direct response to his parents' pleas from Hector, but the *Iliad* tells us that they are unsuccessful: "They could not shake the fixed resolve of Hector" (*Il.* 22.91).[24]

The image reveals some interesting aspects of the conceptualization of nursing in this early period of Greek literature, the first being that queens such as Hecuba would be expected to nurse their children themselves and not necessarily give them to a wet nurse. Second, we see that Hecuba is proud of having breast-fed her child and understands that it forged a strong emotional bond between her and Hector. Thus we learn that in the Homeric world, at least in the literary representation, upper-class women were honored for nursing their infant children, that breast-feeding was believed to nurture the child both physically and emotionally, and that it allowed a particularly meaningful connection between mother and nursling. This, of course, may simply be Hecuba's female perspective, but the male "author(s)" of the *Iliad* and the male world of this poem are certainly behind it. Yet at the same time, we notice the contradictions represented in the dual significance of the naked breast. As Nicole Loraux argues, one cannot make a strict distinction between a motherly way of exposing one's breast and a sexual way, which is especially valid in the context of the Trojan cycle, where we encounter Helen baring her breast to Menelaus in a seductive way as an appeal for mercy. For Loraux a separation of "la mère de la femme désirable" is artificial and not convincing. Thus both images are always superposed.[25]

For all its positive connotations, the outcome of the scene is a sorrowful one. Hector does not heed his mother's pleas, perhaps showing that the power of the breast and the recollection of the shared experience between mother and child are not as significant to him as to Hecuba, or, perhaps, they have the opposite effect. Hecuba's gesture attempts to bring about a very close physical union between mother and grown son. This action might actually generate fear and rejection on Hector's part, and he reacts by distancing himself from her even more. Hector moves on to fight Achilles and eventually dies at his hands. Hecuba's baring of her breast and her reminiscence of her having breast-fed her son are not only powerless and

fail in their purpose, but they are even made more dramatic due to the anticipation of the tragedy to come, the loss of her son at war and the final destruction of Troy. Henceforth, as we will see in other allusions to breast-feeding in Greek literature, the act of lactation, while implying a special affection between mother and child, at the same time conveys ominous connotations or a sorrowful fate. And perhaps these negative outcomes can be read almost as a punishment for a strong, physical closeness that verges toward the taboo, at least from the male perspective of the Homeric world.

A somewhat twisted recollection of this scene from the *Iliad* is presented in Aeschylus's *Libation Bearers* 896–898, where Clytemnestra tries to prevent the attack of her own son Orestes by, possibly, revealing her breast:[26]

ἐπίσχες, ὦ παῖ, τόνδε δ' αἴδεσαι, τέκνον,
μαστόν, πρὸς ᾧ σὺ πολλὰ δὴ βρίζων ἅμα
οὔλοισιν ἐξήμελξας εὐτραφὲς γάλα.

Stop[,] my son, honor this, child, the breast at which often while dozing you quaffed the nourishing milk with your gums.[27]

In this scene Orestes is about to avenge the death of his father Agamemnon at the hands of his mother by killing her. Just as in Homer, Clytemnestra shows that literary queens nursed their own children and that they viewed this experience as a positive and significant part of motherhood, or at least this is how Clytemnestra wants to use it to her own benefit.[28] In this episode she mentions not only the nourishment Orestes received through her, but also the soothing effect of nursing that would comfort and put the baby to sleep.[29] Both Hecuba and Clytemnestra try to force their sons to obey by reminding them of their nursing experience and, not surprisingly (as grown sons are unlikely to remember as mothers do), they both fail.

Likewise, in the same tragedy Clytemnestra dreams that she gives birth to a snake and gives the snake the breast. We already see here a much more perverted version of the Homeric scene. Orestes as nursing child is thus viewed as a poisonous serpent who will eventually attack his mother. In this we perceive a connection with Hera, who also gave her breast to Heracles, according to some accounts (*Il.* 5.392–394).[30] It is said that the hero bit her while nursing, and thus the Milky Way was formed. In the *Eumenides*, when the ghosts show the sleeping Furies the wounds on her heart (*Eum.* 103), it is implied that Orestes actually stabbed his mother in the breast.

Clytemnestra wants to recall the special bond involved in the act of

nursing: the tender image of an infant dozing off at the breast while drinking his mother's milk in her arms—to which one may add the loving gaze of the nursing mother upon the sweet baby. Yet this intimate image is perverted by the outcome of the scene and the matricide to be committed. Just as in Hecuba's case, this recollection has little power to alter the grown son's intentions. But this exposure of the female breast must also be seen as a theatrical dramatization. Stears observes that in the act of lactation "the body is in some ways a public good and thus open for public comment. . . . To the extent that breastfeeding occurs in the presence of others and/or symbolizes good mothering, it is also a visual performance of mothering with the maternal body at center stage."[31]

The image of baby Orestes sucking his mother's breast seems to have at least some effect on her adult son since Orestes hesitates about what to do next. The scene is disquieting: when it is presented as occurring between two adults, the bared breast and the recollection intimate sexual overtones, especially considering that illicit and inappropriate sexuality are traits of Clytemnestra, and the physical closeness between mother and son implied here may convey a hint of incest to the hero exposed to his mother's naked body. After Clytemnestra's baring of her breast and her allusion to the breast-feeding experience, Orestes is uncertain about whether to proceed ("Pylades, what shall I do? Shall I spare my mother's life out of respect?" *Libation Bearers* 900); he is finally persuaded to move forward by his friend and kills his mother after a long diatribe with her.

Orestes' reaction is the opposite of his mother's wishes: he kills her not necessarily because he has not been moved by this intimate image, but because he has experienced, and perhaps he needs to suppress, the incestuous fantasies that the breast may provoke. The revenge for his father's death is also merged with the rejection and need to repress the image (and possible desire) of his mother's semi-naked body. Loraux observes that *Libation Bearers* 827–832 assimilates Orestes to Perseus: "Keep up Perseus's spirit in your heart." Here, therefore, Clytemnestra is analogous to Medusa, who, as Sigmund Freud has proposed, is the image of dangerous, devouring, and destructive female sexuality that at the same time can provoke desire.[32] As Loraux mentions, in all these examples of sons exposed to a mother's breast, there is a refusal to look on the part of the males. Hector only has eyes for his rival Achilles, the children of Oedipus, as we shall see, disregard their mother's pleas and focus on fighting each other, and Orestes is like Perseus, averting his gaze from his mother/Medusa.[33]

The Homeric passage and Aeschylus's scene share a curious pattern of adult sons being exposed to their mother's breasts. While the notion of

mother and infant is a common and acceptable one, the picture presented here is odd and dramatic, intending to have a profound impact on the situation at hand. Both women make reference to the earlier intimacy only in the direst of circumstances, as a last recourse, when they feel their children or their own lives are in peril. Kitts states that "in Homer, infants who drink milk cling to their mothers and not yet to the hearth where socialized humans eat bread," and thus the image calls forth a "precultural stigma of childhood."[34] One can thus understand that this allusion to a more primal and less civilized stage in their lives may provoke rejection in two grown-up warriors who presume to have control of themselves and their countries and would not appreciate being drawn into a more primal, natural, and precivilized image. Just as in the Homeric scene, Clytemnestra's exposed breast—that which nourishes life—actually foreshadows murder, death, and a tragic outcome. It is an uncanny moment that shows female intimacy anticipating horror.[35] And this negative outcome may be the product of an image that is transgressive and taboo.

One final example worthy of mention is found in Euripides' *Phoenician Women* 1570, when Antigone narrates the death of her mother Jocasta after she tried to persuade her sons Eteocles and Polynices to stop fighting: "All saw her weep and heard her moan, as she rushed forth to carry to her sons her last appeal, a mother's breast."[36] While breast-feeding is not explicitly mentioned in this passage, Jocasta's gesture clearly resonates with Hecuba's and Clytemnestra's before. Yet these verses are particularly meaningful coming from a figure that itself embodies incest. The breast that Jocasta is now exposing to Eteocles and Polynices is the same one she presumably offered her son and husband Oedipus in a sexual act and possibly to him as a newborn in lactation, thus confusing and juxtaposing the sexual and the motherly even more clearly than the previous examples.[37] Here as well, the outcome of a mother's exposed breast in allusion to previous breast-feeding ends up in tragedy, the deaths of two brothers at each other's hands.

A somewhat different allusion to breast-feeding is found in Lysias' first speech, *On the Murder of Eratosthenes*. While the previous texts presume to give an account of breast-feeding from a female perspective, this speech is crafted with a male focalization. Here the defendant, Euphiletus, describes the situation in his household before he murdered his wife's lover, Eratosthenes. In his defense he tries to present himself as an overall good husband and good man, and thus he paints a very harmonious picture of his family life. He describes his relationship with his wife, whom he considered "the most excellent of wives; . . . a clever, frugal housekeeper [who] kept everything in the nicest order" (Lysias 1.7), as follows:

ἐπειδὴ δὲ τὸ παιδίον ἐγένετο ἡμῖν, ἡ μήτηρ αὐτὸ ἐθήλαζεν:
ἵνα δὲ μή, ὁπότε λοῦσθαι δέοι, κινδυνεύῃ κατὰ τῆς κλίμακος
καταβαίνουσα, ἐγὼ μὲν ἄνω διῃτώμην, αἱ δὲ γυναῖκες κάτω. καὶ
οὕτως ἤδη συνειθισμένον ἦν, ὥστε πολλάκις ἡ γυνὴ ἀπῄει κάτω
καθευδήσουσα ὡς τὸ παιδίον, ἵνα τὸν τιτθὸν αὐτῷ διδῷ καὶ μὴ βοᾷ.
(Lysias 1.9–10)

When the child was born to us, its mother suckled it; and in order that,
each time that it had to be washed, she might avoid the risk of descending by the stairs, I used to live above, and the women below. By this time
it had become such an habitual thing that my wife would often leave me
and go down to sleep with the child, so as to be able to give it the breast
and stop its crying.[38]

In Euphiletus's recollection, his (unnamed) wife not only gives the boy
the breast, but she also bathes him and even sleeps next to him, two circumstances of close physical contact and touch, while Euphiletus is distant, in a separate part of the house. Later he mentions that when the baby
was fussing, he told his wife to "go and give the child her breast, to stop its
howling" (Lysias 1.12). Here Euphiletus is defending himself against the ac-
cusation of murder and tries to give to the court a peaceful view of the situation in his household. He strives to appear as a tolerant, involved, and
understanding husband. Within this image of familial harmony, he explains how his wife nursed their son. This speech thus provides testimony
that upper-class women breast-fed their children in Athens and that possibly they were expected to. Even if other families used wet nurses, breast-
feeding is here presented as a virtue—it is what a good wife and mother
would do—and thus it is so shocking for the defendant to later learn that
his wife was not as pure as she seemed, that she was corrupted by another
man. Perhaps if they had used a wet nurse, we would have a more detached
mother here, and Euphiletus could have suspected her future deceit, but
she seems so virtuous and dedicated that her husband—he wants us to believe—could have never foreseen her treason. Yet again, as in previous examples, we see a pattern of ominous connotations behind the tender and
intimate domestic scene presented. In all these cases, the death to come
casts the nurturing scene in a negative light. Even more clearly in this case,
nursing is said to belong to the world of women—mysterious, unsettling,
and unknown to men.

In the speech the cries of the child were at some point even used to
hide the affair with Eratosthenes. Euphiletus feels alien to the child-rearing

experience, and he is even physically separated from it, living in the male quarters while his wife "sleeps" with the child. But again, one wonders if that closeness of the mother to the baby through the physical contact of breast-feeding may bring up incestuous thoughts in both Euphiletus and the audience, and thus the image brought to mind may actually provoke fear and revulsion in the jury. This observation is made even more compelling by the juxtaposition of the breast used in nursing and the breast, as a symbol of female sexuality, used in illicit sex, which seem to happen in parallel in this household. Euphiletus's wife is at the same time a motherly figure and a sexual object. The pureness of the nursing scene is thus tainted by the view of her naked body in her sexual affair with Eratosthenes, as Euphiletus finds him naked "in the act."

NURSING IN ROMAN LITERATURE

In the philosophical and moral texts of Rome, breast-feeding of children by their own mothers is recommended and is generally seen in a positive light, as it is said to forge strong bonds between mother and child and strengthen the character of the infant.[39] Plutarch, Tacitus, and Aulus Gellius point in this direction.[40]

Plutarch recalls that Cato's wife, Licinia, breast-fed her own son (*Life of Cato the Elder* 20.3). In several parts of the *Moralia* he states that the nursing of infants by their mothers was preferable to the use of wet nurses, and Tacitus also refers to breast-feeding as a good virtue of the past and criticizes the excessive use of wet nurses (*Dialogus de oratoribus* 28.4 and 29.1). Yet, as Keith Bradley observes, the example of Licinia and others suggests that breast-feeding may have been unusual rather than the norm.[41]

Aulus Gellius appears to share Plutarch's views in 12.1, where he refers to ideas of the sophist Favorinus. Plutarch objected to wet-nursing because he thought it prevented emotional bonding between mother and child. Favorinus even added that wet-nursing had a corrupting influence on children because the nurse's milk transmitted moral character.[42] But again the theory does not necessarily imply a widespread practice of maternal breast-feeding, and Soranus's extensive recommendations on how to select a wet nurse clearly show that wet-nursing was common in Rome, at least in the upper classes.[43] Yet there is a general sense that breast-feeding implies a stronger bond between mother and nursling and a more important emotional commitment.

Looking at the vocabulary used for the act of breast-feeding in Latin

can be quite revealing of Roman conceptions regarding nursing. The words *mamma* and *uber* (breast), for example, appear abundantly in Pliny.[44] They are found frequently in scientific texts like his *Natural History* and refer to issues of the breast in medical uses, in regards to animals and humans, and on its affections. Lucretius, in another didactic, quasi-scientific poem, also mentions breast-feeding. In *De rerum natura* (5.883–885), he gives testimony that even at three years of age, boys are often still nursing from their mother's breasts: *principio circum tribus actis impiger annis / floret equus, puer haut quaquam; nam saepe etiam nunc / ubera mammarum in somnis lactantia quaeret* ("At first a horse flourishes lively at around three years of age, unlike the boy, who even then often still seeks the milky nipples of the breast in his sleep"). Later he compares the earth to a mother's breasts filling with milk after childbirth (*De rerum natura* 5.812–815).[45]

In the first quote Lucretius, in the context of describing centaurs, is pointing at the difference between a horse's fast development and the fact that a boy is still almost a baby in the same amount of time. This passage gives evidence that the period of nursing in Rome could be a rather prolonged one. Just as we saw in Greek texts, the boy seeks the comfort of the breast to help him sleep, an interesting remark in reference to a three-year-old. Yet again, the image of nursing conveys a sense of comfort, physical closeness, and peacefulness. The second quote fits into a general use of milk in pastoral and natural contexts in Roman literature that point to a sense of abundance and richness of earth and its gifts. In general then, the idea of the nursing mother can bring forth a positive impression, as seen in the previous authors.

Specific mentions of lactation in Latin literature are, however, quite rare, and certainly less visible than in Greek literature. We do see a few allusions in comedy, though there are no direct scenes that present nursing or mothers recalling their nursing experience as we saw in Greek literature.[46] It is indeed intriguing that direct references to mothers nursing their own children are not found in a genre that presents the everyday life of the Romans in the Republic.

In the mythological and poetic texts of the Augustan period the act of breast-feeding among humans is even less frequent. Yet, for all the positive references to nursing in moral and philosophical texts, a more ominous view of nursing moments can be detected in literary texts. The beginnings of Roman civilization themselves are marked by an unusual act of nursing. In *Ab urbe condita* 1.4.6, Livy tells the story of how the twins Romulus and Remus were nursed by the *lupa*:

tenet fama cum fluitantem alveum, quo expositi erant pueri, tenuis in
sicco aqua destituisset, lupam sitientem ex montibus qui circa sunt ad
puerilem vagitum cursum flexisse; eam submissas infantibus adeo mitem
praebuisse mammas ut lingua lambentem pueros magister regii pecoris
invenerit—Faustulo fuisse nomen ferunt—ab eo ad stabula Larentiae
uxori educandos datos.

The story goes that when the floating cradle, where the boys were exposed, had been placed on dry land after the water retreated, a thirsty
she-wolf from the neighboring hills, turned her steps towards the crying babies, offered them her teats to suck and was so gentle to them that
the king's flock-master found her licking the boys with her tongue. They
say that his name was Faustulus. He took the infants to his hut and gave
them to his wife, Larentia, to rear.

The scene of the she-wolf nursing the twins is even today a powerful
symbol of Roman identity. There is a sense of tenderness in the image of
the animal offering her teats to the babies and lovingly caressing them with
her tongue.[47] But it is ironic that there is no real mother figure in the story
of the founding of Rome, a culture where the centrality of the *matrona*
was paramount. Instead, in this myth the mother figure is split in three,
since the boys are separated from their birth mother Rea Silvia, nursed by
the she-wolf, and then found by Faustulus and given by him to his wife,
Larentia, to raise as her own. Let us remember as well, that, as Livy 1.4.7
tells us, the image may be simply a deformation of Acca Larentia herself,
who was a "*lupa*," what the early Latins called a prostitute, who actually
nursed Romulus and Remus: *sunt qui Larentiam vulgato corpore lupam inter
pastores vocatam putent; inde locum fabulae ac miraculo datum* ("Some think
that Larentia, due to the unchaste use of her body, was called 'She-wolf'
amongst the shepherds, and that this was the origin of the story and the
miracle"). We thus recognize a sexualization of the nursing scene, through
the introduction of Acca Larentia as a woman who sells her sexual favors.[48]
In any case, this central image of the she-wolf in Roman culture may
well convey what the Romans thought about breast-feeding. We will see
that in Latin texts nursing seems to belong to the animal world, to evoke
nature rather than culture.[49] When it is placed in the context of nature it
does connote abundance, peace, and harmony; and images of milk are often involved in pastoral scenes. The image of the *lupa* and the twins, however, is somewhat uncanny. First we perceive an awkward mingling be-

FIGURE 7.1. *She-wolf nursing Romulus and Remus, bronze. Musei Capitolini, Rome. Photo: Vanni/Art Resource, NY, ART321670.*

tween the animal and the human worlds, and the reader and viewer of so many representations of this scene feels that something is out of place. The scene produces neither the sense of harmony found in nursing scenes between animals, nor the tenderness and intimacy of human allusions to breast-feeding as we have discussed. In the famous statue in the Capitoline museum, for example, the sitting babies raise their heads to the hanging teats while the she-wolf looks in a different direction (fig. 7.1).[50] There is no real physical contact beyond sucking between nurse and nursling and no exchange of loving gazes.

Other representations of the scene do, however, appear to show the she-wolf in a more involved stance. Some images show her turning her head backward and looking at the babies, and one interesting piece even represents her licking the twins (figs. 7.2 and 7.3). Yet, through the displaced sexually loaded body of Acca Larentia, the scene acquires erotic overtones; and if we follow Dale Glabach's language (see note 8), if she was actually the substitute mother nursing the twins, the act may be seen as a first erotic intercourse. Second, the outcome of the twins' lives also involves the mur-

der and fratricide located right at the center of Rome's foundation, with the death of Remus at his brother's hands, an image that even foreshadows the future civil wars of Roman history.

Quite remarkably, we find no descriptions of mothers breast-feeding their children in Vergil, though he does refer to animals as a source of milk

FIGURE 7.2. *She-wolf nursing Romulus and Remus, Romano-Campanian* didrachma *(or* stater*), Republican. Museo Civico Archeologico, Bologna. Photo: A. De Gregorio, © DeA Picture Library/Art Resource, NY, ART403983.*

FIGURE 7.3. *She-wolf nursing Romulus and Remus, limestone relief, second century BCE. Musée Romain, Avenches, Switzerland. Photo: A. De Gregorio, © DeA Picture Library/ Art Resource, NY, ART402812.*

and nourishment. The only reference—and it is odd—is to Metabus nursing his daughter with mare's milk (*Aeneid* 11.557). However, the idea of animal's milk is abundant in the *Georgics* and *Bucolics*, and it appears in a context of the peacefulness of nature and the countryside. For example, in *Georgics* 3.308, he refers to the milk of goats: *hinc largi copia lactis; / quam magis exhausto spumaverit ubere mulctra, / laeta magis pressis manabunt flumina mammis* ("From them comes a large supply of milk, the more the milking-pail has foamed from the drained udder, the more richly will the stream flow as the teats are pressed"). This passage alludes to the plentiful gifts of nature and is set within the tranquil context of farming, away from the corruption of civilization. The same idea can be appreciated in *Georgics* 2.519: *ubera vaccae / lactea dimittunt* ("the cows drop breasts full of milk"); and in *Eclogue* 7.3, when Vergil refers to Coridon's sheep (*distentas lacte capellas*). This harmonious symbolism of nature providing nourishment is conveyed in the figure of Tellus with full breasts on the Ara Pacis (illustrated in fig. 9.1 of this volume); though not explicitly doing so in this image, she is presumed to breast-feed the baby boys she holds. Yet, as we know, this idealized and poetic symbol of Earth and nature is a component of the Augustan political propaganda program and hints at the abundance, peace, and prosperity offered by the emperor.

In *Metamorphoses* 6, Ovid provides another example of a deity nursing her children, when Latona tries to quench her thirst in a pool, and the Lysian peasants prevent her from doing so. She carries her nursing children, Diana and Apollo: *Inque suo portasse sinu, duo numina, natos* (338). . . . *Uberaque ebiberant avidi lactantia nati* (342) ("In her arms she carried two babes. . . . They had drunk avidly from her full breasts"). Latona, as we know, is seen as a mother goddess who gives birth, provides, and nourishes; in this context, the act of nursing seems acceptable and appropriate. The tragedy that follows (the transformation of the peasants into frogs) falls upon the arrogant mortals and not on the nursing deity.

We can contrast this example with a most remarkable episode in book 9. When we are dealing with an actual mortal mother breast-feeding her child, the picture is very different:

> Venerat huc Dryope fatorum nescia, quoque
> indignere magis, nymphis latura coronas;
> inque sinu puerum, qui nondum impleverat annum,
> dulce ferebat onus tepidique ope lactis alebat.
> (*MET.* 9.336–339)

Dryope had come here unknowing her fate, and what would make you more indignant, she was going to bring garlands for the nymphs; she was carrying her son at her breast, who was not yet one year old, a sweet burden, and he was sucking her warm milk.

The scene is quite unique in Roman poetry in portraying the nursing moment. Dryope is here presented not only as a good mother, but also as a devotee of the nymphs who thus observes and respects her religious duties. In a very Ovidian way, the scene shows the sweetness and intimacy between mother and child. Words like *dulce* and *tepidi* emphasize the tenderness of the scene and the idea of the mother as kind nourisher. Yet, as is common in *Metamorphoses*, pleasant scenes are used to draw contrasts to tragic events to come. Soon Ovid describes how Dryope accidentally picked a flower which used to be a nymph. The flower began to bleed and then Dryope gradually began to harden into a tree, including her full breasts:

At puer Amphissos (namque hoc avus Eurytus illi
addiderat nomen) materna rigescere sentit
ubera, nec sequitur ducentem lacteus umor.
(*MET.* 9.356–358)

But the child Amphissos (for his grandfather Eurytus had given him this name) feels his mother's breasts harden, and the flow of milk stops as he sucks.

Dryope is being turned into a tree as punishment for killing the nymph Lotis, who had fled from Priapus. This woman is being dehumanized and becomes part of the natural world. She hardens and loses the tenderness and softness emphasized in the passage before. The focus on the transformation of the breast is thought-provoking. We as readers here experience a reification of the female body. She has lost autonomy and independence, like other virgins turned into trees in the poem, such as Daphne. Yet the motherly breast with flowing milk now becomes part of the landscape, which, in Ovid, often recalls rape and violence against women for the reader and viewer. In this transformation she loses the fluid and the softness of her breasts, and the contrast makes the metamorphosis even more dramatic. We find again in this episode that nursing, while presented as a tender moment, is involved in a scene that will end up in tragedy and a sort of death, or at least the death of Dryope's humanity and motherly qualities.

Just as in Homer and Greek tragedy then, we observe that allusions to

breast-feeding in mythological and narrative texts are presented in a dark context; they seem to foreshadow and contrast with the horrors to come. Interesting as well, is the fact that the nursling here is a son (*puerum*), as in the passages of Greek literature we have discussed. Perhaps the explicitness and vividness of the scene also conveys an uncomfortable feeling in the (male) reader, and the physical closeness between mother and son may be somewhat disturbing, to the point that it is inevitably followed by tragedy and separation of mother and child.[51]

From the examples we have discussed we notice that there is a generally positive view of breast-feeding one's own children in medical, philosophical, and moral texts. Likewise, when we deal with examples of nursing deities, the act also seems appropriate and acceptable. In Latin literature, nursing and milk in the animal world fit into the pastoral idea of the abundance and peacefulness of nature in contrast with the corrupt civilized world. Yet this favorable view of mother's milk as nourishment—both of the body and the soul—is cast in a darker light in literary texts that deal with specific examples of breast-feeding mothers. In both Greek literature and the few examples found in Latin texts, we see that the tenderness of the breast-feeding experience tends to foreshadow tragedy and carries with it a sense of doom. This misfortune can be seen as a result of the taboo aspect of the practice, given the extremely close physical connection between mothers and sons. Male authors and ancient readers must have comprehended nursing with a sense of discomfort, otherness, and shame that hints at incest—a reading far removed from the depicted female experience.

NOTES

I would like to thank Prudence Jones, Jean Alvares, and Lauren Petersen for suggestions helpful to this essay.

1. Newbold (2000) provides an excellent survey of milk and breasts in Nonnus's *Dionysiaca* (fifth century CE), a text that I will not address in this essay.

2. For good studies of wet-nursing at Rome see Bradley (1986); Dixon (1988), 120–129; Joshel (1986); and also Fildes (1986), 17–36.

3. According to Kitts (1994), the evidence shows that no god "drink[s] milk in infancy," but the gods are nursed with ambrosia, which gives them immortality; thus to have taken their mother's breasts is a sign of mortality (142–143).

4. Bonfante (1997), 174–177.

5. See Stears (1999), 308ff., for a very insightful discussion. As Gerber (1978) and others have shown, breasts were also a locus of eroticism in ancient Greece.

6. Halley (2008), 100.

7. Halley (2008), 100, with her quote from Eisenberg et al. (1994). This issue is also approached by Stears (1999) and Dettwyler (1995).

8. Glabach (2001); and see Freud's recognition of breast-feeding as an early sexual experience, and his belief that the mother was the baby's "first seducer" (Freud [1995], 188).

9. There are some striking examples of adults being breast-fed, in particular the famous Pompeian fresco of Pero suckling her father to save him from starvation (House of Lucretius Fronto, V.4.a). See also Galen's recommendations on the use of breast milk, preferably directly from the breast, to aid elderly people (7.701). On breast milk as nurture for adults see Corbeill (2004), 100ff., who also connects breast-feeding with funerary practices.

10. Bonfante (1997), 174ff.

11. Feeding bottles have been found in children's graves. See esp. Bartsocas (1978); Wickes (1953), 155; and images in Fildes (1986), 18, 24, and 36.

12. See Bonfante (1997). "Etruscan art, in fact, is characterized by the appearance of breasts in unexpected contexts" (179).

13. See examples in Bonfante (1997), 178–181.

14. Bonfante (1997), 183. For specific examples in Roman art, see Bonfante (1997), 184. Bonfante also remarks on a general aversion to large breasts in Greek literature. See also the evidence in Lucretius, *De rerum natura* 4.1168 and Terence, *Eunuchus* 2.3. According to Bonfante (1997), 185: "It was also a sign of civilization for a lady to be freed from this embarrassingly physical necessity, all too reminiscent of our lowly animal nature"; and "In Greek and Roman formal art only Barbarians and wild creatures, such as female centaurs, nurse their young."

15. For a full discussion of lactation in ancient writers, see Wickes (1953); and Fildes (1986), 17–36.

16. See references in Fildes (1986), 18–21.

17. Soranus, as other earlier texts, recommends withholding colostrum and not breast-feeding for the few days postpartum (*Gynecology* 11.17).

18. But see how Galen himself acknowledges that not everyone agrees with this view—Damastes, for example (*Gynecology* 11.18).

19. Kitts (1994), 143.

20. Translations of the *Iliad* are taken from Fagles (1998).

21. O'Neill (1998), 229, gives a good intertextual account of this passage in relation to the Aeschylean moment we will analyze later.

22. This is seen, for example, in the fact that many nursing mothers feel free to bare their breasts in public to breast-feed, while they would be ashamed to do so if they were not tending to their infants. Stears (1999) provides an interesting survey of women's perceptions of their bodies and their appropriate use while nursing in public and comments, "In doing breastfeeding in front of others, women negotiate the definitions of their nursing behaviors as sexual or nurturing" (310). On the eroticism of breasts in Greek literature see Gerber (1978), and Newbold (2000), 17, on the erotic appeal of breasts in Nonnus's *Dionysiaca*.

23. Let us recall here, for example, Oedipus gazing upon his mother's naked body.

24. This is not the first instance where Hector is involved in the act of nursing. In *Iliad* 24.58, the bard tells us that "Hector is mortal. He sucked a woman's breast," which according to Kitts is "just one expression of a primal dimension of mortal being that categorically separates Hector, other humans and other mammals from the lofty gods" (143).

25. Loraux (1986), 100.

26. Not all authors believe that she actually revealed a breast, since actors were male. See discussion in DeForest (1993), 129. For other instances of actors exposing breasts, see possibly Aristophanes, *Wasps* 1374, *Lysistrata* 83, and *Thesmophoriazousae* 638ff. DeForest does, however, believe that since "the Athenians had the technology to permit a male actor to reveal an artificial breast, we may presume that Aeschylus composed the scene with the intention that Clytemnestra's breast be revealed on the stage. Otherwise, he would have composed the scene differently" (129).

27. Translation taken from DeForest (1993), 129.

28. Various authors question the sincerity of Clytemnestra's feelings. See DeForest (1993), 130; Goldhill (1992), 37–45; Winnington-Ingram (1983), 106–108; and Kitto (1961), 84. On the other hand, Garvie (1970), 79–91, *ad loc.*, does not doubt her feelings. On the connections of this scene with Homer's, see in particular O'Neill (1998) and Whallon (1958).

29. Rousseau (1963) thinks that Orestes was never nursed by his mother. For a discussion of whether Clytemnestra actually breast-fed Orestes, see Whallon (1958), 84.

30. As DeForest (1993), 130, notes, the image of Clytemnestra also conveys connections with Mother Earth, Demeter, and Hera: "In her splendid robes, pointing to her bared breast, Clytemnestra would have looked like the images of the Earth goddess, who, in statues throughout the Aegean, points to her naked breast—indeed, this is a universal image for her as the great κουροτρόφος." On representations of kourotrophic deities, see Price (1978).

31. Stears (1999), 308–309.

32. Loraux (1986), 90ff.

33. Loraux (1986), 101.

34. Kitts (1994), 144. Interestingly, Kitts ([1994], 145) also remarks that other milk-drinking and cheese-eating creatures like shepherds or maenads are seen as "childlike, barbaric or exotic" and thus precultural and pre-agricultural. This notion is evident in the confrontation of the civilized Odysseus and the savage Cyclops.

35. The ominous connotation given to the image of the nursing mother in Greece is also reflected in art. As Bonfante mentions, another remarkable example is the image of Eriphyle nursing her child after she had sent her husband, Amphiaraos, to Thebes, bribed by the necklace of Harmonia. This image also evokes the matricide that will later take place. One can compare it to the figure of Andromache nursing Astyanax in Polygnotus's mural painting of the *Iliupersis*, referred to by Pausanias in 10.25.5 (Bonfante [1997], 175). In the *Iliad*, it is the nurse who appears to be breast-feeding Hector's

son (*Iliad* 6.470ff.). Here, as Bonfante (1997), 175, states, "the horror to come is underscored by the private, moving scene of the mother nursing the child, an image of vulnerability not normally shown, and therefore special."

36. Translation by Coleridge in Oates and O'Neill (1938).

37. On this scene see Loraux (1986), 101.

38. Translations of Lysias 1 are taken from Lamb (1930).

39. See Dixon (1988), 122–123.

40. See also Dixon (1988), 3.

41. Bradley (1986), 201. Note how in a generalizing phrase Cicero mentions a nurse rather than a mother: "We almost seem to have drunk in deception with our nurse's milk" (Cicero, *Tusculanae Disputationes* 3.2). Tacitus's comments on nursing by mothers among Germanic tribes implies that this practice was not the norm among the Romans of his time (Tacitus, *Germania* 20.1). On this notion, see Dixon (1988), 120.

42. Aulus Gellius 12.1.17–32; Soranus, *Gynecology* 2.19; Macrobius, *Saturnalia* 5.11.15–18.

43. Epigraphic evidence shows that possible reasons for wet-nursing were that the mother was dead or unable to nurse, or when infants exposed at birth were then reclaimed as slaves. Slave owners may have had one *nutrix* in their family in charge of nursing all the slave infants so that the mothers could go back to work, or breed more slaves (the contraceptive effects of lactation were known to the Romans: Plutarch, *De liberis educandis* 5). See Bradley (1986), 207 and 212. Bradley suggests that the use of wet nurses had to do with the avoidance of emotional commitment on the part of the parents in regard to a child that may not survive, as infant death was very common in Rome (218ff.).

44. A search of the words *mamma*, *uber*, and *lacto* ("to breast-feed") reveals that the overwhelming majority of *loci* are found in Pliny the Elder.

45. On further medical uses of breast milk see Laskaris (2008).

46. In the prologue of Plautus's *Menaecmi*, for example, it is said that the twins were so identical that not even their "breast-mother" (i.e., their wet nurse) or their birth mother could distinguish them (18–21), stressing that the "breast-mother" has a profound knowledge of her nursling. Further, in *Truculentus*, Phronesium pretends to have just had a child and orders the slaves to nurse a baby she has procured to make the *miles* believe it is hers (*puero isti date mammam*, *Truc.* 449). The use of a wet nurse is implied in this scene. Terence also presents a case of wet-nursing when in *Adelphoi* 975, Syrus mentions that his wife Phrygia was the first to suckle Deamea's grandson that day (*Et quidem tuo nepoti, huius filio, / hodie primam mammam dedit haec*).

47. A similar combination of human and beast in the act of nursing is seen in a puzzling image of Pasiphae nursing the Minotaur. In addition, there is the case of Telephus suckled by a deer as an important ancestor of the Romans. See Corbeill (2004), 105.

48. Acca Larentia was also a goddess of earth and fertility of Etruscan origin connected with the worship of the Lares. A later sculpture by Jacopo Della Quercia (1371–1438) portrays her with nude breasts and holding an infant in her arms, thus pointing

to her nursing capabilities and nature. Corbeill (2004) states that breast milk has life-giving powers, and in connection with funerary rites, monuments, and myths it serves to nurture the deceased into a new life (104–105).

49. See Kitts (1994) here as well.

50. It is worth recalling that in this statue the babes are from the Renaissance, and a new theory holds that the wolf herself is of medieval manufacture; see Mazzoni (2010), esp. chap 1.

51. Although the scope of this essay does not go beyond the time of Augustus, there is the remarkable testimony of the Christian martyr Perpetua, one of our only first-person accounts of a breast-feeding mother, in *Acts of the Christian Martyrs* (Roman Carthage, 203 CE). As in previous examples, the nursing moment is also followed by a tragic outcome: "A few days later, we were lodged in prison. . . . I was tortured with worry for my baby there. . . . I nursed my baby, who was faint from hunger. . . . Then I got permission for my baby to stay with me in prison. At once I recovered my health. My prison had suddenly become a palace. . . . One day while we were eating breakfast we were suddenly hurried off for a hearing. . . . 'Are you a Christian,' said Hilarianus. And I said 'Yes, I am.' Then Hilarianus passed sentence on all of us: we were condemned to the beasts, and we returned to prison in high spirits. But my baby had got used to being nursed at the breast and to staying with me in prison. So I sent the deacon Pomponius straightaway to my father to ask for my baby back. But father refused to give him over. But as God willed; and, the baby had no further desire for the breast, nor did I suffer any inflammation; and so I was relieved of any anxiety for my child and of any discomfort in my breasts." Translation taken from Lefkowitz and Fant (2005), no. 445.

WORKS CITED

Bartsocas, C. S. (1978). "Ancient Greek Feeding Bottles." *Transactions and Studies of the College of Physicians of Philadelphia* 45.6:297–298.

Bonfante, Larissa. (1997). "Nursing Mothers in Classical Art." In Ann Olga Koloski-Ostrow and Claire L. Lyons, eds., *Naked Truths: Women, Sexuality, and Gender in Classical Art and Archaeology*, 174–196. London: Routledge.

Bradley, Keith. (1986). "Wet-Nursing at Rome: A Study in Social Relations." In Beryl Rawson, ed., *The Family in Ancient Rome: New Perspectives*, 201–229. Ithaca: Cornell University Press.

Corbeill, Anthony. (2004). *Nature Embodied: Gesture in Ancient Rome*. Princeton: Princeton University Press.

DeForest, Mary. (1993). "Clytemnestra's Breast and the Evil Eye." In Mary DeForest, ed., *Woman's Power, Man's Game*, 129–148. Wauconda: Bolchazy-Carducci.

Dettwyler, Katherine. (1995). "Beauty and the Breast: The Cultural Context of Breast-feeding in the United States." In Patricia Stewart-Macadam and Katherine Dettwyler, eds., *Breastfeeding: Biocultural Perspectives*, 167–216. New York: Aldine.

Dixon, Suzanne. (1988). *The Roman Mother*. London: Routledge.

Eisenberg, Arlene, Heidi Murkoff, and Sandee Hathaway. (1994). *What to Expect the Toddler Years*. New York: Workman.

Fagles, Robert, trans. (1998). *Homer: The Iliad*. New York: Penguin.

Fildes, Valerie A. (1986). *Breasts, Bottles, and Babies: A History of Infant Feeding*. Edinburgh: Edinburgh University Press.

Freud, Sigmund. (1995). *The Complete Works (The Standard Edition)*, vol. 23. London: Hogarth Press.

Garvie, A. F. (1970). "The Opening of the *Choephori*." *Bulletin of the Institute of Classical Studies of the University of London* 17:79–91.

Gerber, Douglas E. (1978). "The Female Breast in Greek Erotic Literature." [Issue title: *Women in the Ancient World*.] *Arethusa* 11.1/2:203–212.

Glabach, Dale. (2001). "Naturally Sexual Breast-Feeding: An Evolutionary Prescription for Emotional Health." *Journal of Prenatal and Perinatal Psychology and Health* 16.2:151–166.

Goldhill, Simon. (1992). *Aeschylus: The Oresteia*. Cambridge: Cambridge University Press.

Halley, Jean. (2008). *Boundaries of Touch: Parenting and Adult–Child Intimacy*. Urbana: University of Illinois Press.

Joshel, Sandra R. (1986). "Nursing the Master's Child: Slavery and the Roman Child-Nurse." *Signs* 12:3–22.

Kitto, H. D. (1961). *Greek Tragedy*. London: Routledge.

Kitts, Margo. (1994). "Two Expressions for Human Mortality in the Epics of Homer." *History of Religions* 34.2:132–151.

Lamb, W. R. M., trans. (1930). *Lysias*. Cambridge, MA: Harvard University Press.

Laskaris, Julie. (2008). "Nursing Mothers in Greek and Roman Medicine." *American Journal of Archaeology* 112.3:459–464.

Lefkowitz, Mary R., and Maureen B. Fant. (2005). *Women's Life in Greece and Rome: A Sourcebook in Translation*. 3rd ed. Baltimore: Johns Hopkins University Press.

Loraux, Nicole. (1986). "Matrem nudam: Quelques versions grecques." *L'Écrit du Temps* 11:90–102.

Mazzoni, Cristina. (2010). *She-Wolf: The Story of a Roman Icon*. Cambridge: Cambridge University Press.

Newbold, R. F. (2000). "Breasts and Milk in Nonnus' *Dionysiaca*." *Classical World* 94.1:11–23.

Oates, Whitney J., and Eugene O'Neill, Jr. (1938). *Euripides: The Complete Greek Drama*, vol. 2: *The Phoenissae*. Trans. E. P. Coleridge. New York: Random House.

O'Neill, K. (1998). "Aeschylus, Homer, and the Serpent at the Breast." *Phoenix* 52.3/4:216–229.

Price, Theodora H. (1978). *Kourotrophos: Cults and Representations of the Greek Nursing Deities*. Leiden: Brill.

Rousseau, G. S. (1963). "Dream and Vision in Aeschylus' *Oresteia*." *Arion* 2:101–126.

Stears, Cindy. (1999). "Breastfeeding and the Good Maternal Body." *Gender and Society* 13.3:308–325.

Whallon, W. (1958). "The Serpent at the Breast." *Transactions of the American Philological Association* 89:271–275.

Wickes, Ian G. (1953). "A History of Infant Feeding, Part I. Primitive Peoples: Ancient Works: Renaissance Writers." *Archives of Disease in Childhood* 28:151–158.

Winnington-Ingram, Reginald P. (1983). *Studies in Aeschylus' Oresteia*. Cambridge: Cambridge University Press.

EIGHT

Mater Patriae

CLEOPATRA AND ROMAN IDEAS

OF MOTHERHOOD

Prudence Jones

Cleopatra VII was the mother of four children. Caesarion (Ptolemy XV Philopator Philometor Caesar, 47–30 BCE) was, Cleopatra claimed, the son of Julius Caesar. Mark Antony fathered her three youngest children, twins Alexander Helios (40– ca. 29–25 BCE) and Cleopatra Selene II (40 BCE–6 CE), and son Ptolemy Philadelphos (36–29 BCE). For Cleopatra, the role of mother also constituted an integral part of her political program in Egypt. In sources from the Roman world, however, we find a surprising lack of attention paid to Cleopatra the mother. This essay will examine some possible reasons for this apparent neglect of an important aspect of Cleopatra's identity. On one hand, Cleopatra's status as a female head of state must have seemed incongruous and even dangerous to the Romans (recall Dido, the failed queen of Carthage). On the other hand, the ways in which she communicates her status as a mother would have been all too familiar to a Roman audience and, thus, would have had the potential to create a public relations disaster if seen against Octavian's attempts to demonize the woman upon whom he had to focus his attacks, lest his conflict with Mark Antony be perceived as civil war.

Before proceeding, we must first consider public portrayals of motherhood in pre-Ptolemaic and Ptolemaic Egypt and look at the ways in which Cleopatra used these images of motherhood to present herself to her Egyptian subjects. This topic, along with motherhood as it appears in the public sphere during the Roman monarchy and Republic, will form the backdrop for looking at the ways in which Octavian erases motherhood from the identity of the Cleopatra he presents to the Romans.

In Egypt, motherhood was essential to the mythology of the female pharaoh. As the earthly incarnation of Isis, the female pharaoh represents

FIGURE 8.1. *Wall relief of Khonsu, Hathor, and Sobek (*left to right*). Kom Ombo Temple, Egypt. Photo: Rémih.*

the mother of Horus, the divine counterpart of the male pharaoh. As tends to be the case in hereditary monarchies, women, and specifically mothers, play a far greater role in politics than do their counterparts in forms of government not based on familial succession.[1]

Motherhood also had a prominent place in both the religious traditions of Egypt and the government established by the Ptolemies, and so it was natural—and probably inevitable—that Cleopatra should include motherhood as a part of her public image. Two goddesses who were important in Egyptian religion, particularly where the pharaohs were concerned, were Hathor and Isis, both of whom were seen as mother figures. Hathor was associated with the female pharaoh and Horus, as mentioned, with the male pharaoh. Hathor's name, which means "house of Horus," associates her specifically with the lineage of the pharaoh.[2] Her iconography includes a headdress that consists of horns (she could be represented as a cow) surrounding a sun-disc, a symbol that becomes part of the representation of Isis, and which Cleopatra adopts as well (figs. 8.1, 8.2, and 8.3). This iconography not only connects Cleopatra with Isis and Hathor, but specifically links her to the motherly aspect of these goddesses. Throughout the Mediterranean world and even further east, the cow was a powerful

FIGURE 8.2. *Isis and Horus, bronze.* © *Trustees of the British Museum.*

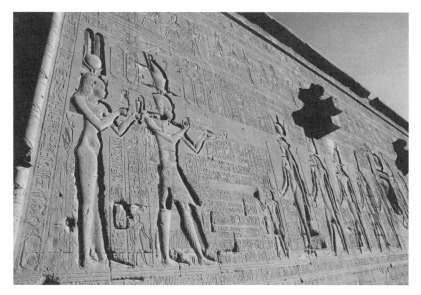

FIGURE 8.3. *Cleopatra (left) and Caesarion. Dendera. Photo: Prudence Jones.*

symbol of motherhood. As Catherine Clément and Julia Kristeva note, "Like the goddess Hathor in Egypt, the sacred cow in India is the envelope of the universe, since it is within the sewn skin of a cow that the first man was born. . . . The cow is thus maternal and enveloping."[3] In this way, the crown of horns surrounding the sun-disc connects Cleopatra with the generative force in the universe.

Isis, as she appears in the Ptolemaic period, combines attributes of several other goddesses, including Hathor, but without the ferocity sometimes associated with mother goddesses: rather, Isis was a tender and compassionate deity,[4] whereas Hathor was at times paired with Sekhmet, a "lioness goddess who personified brute power."[5] Like Hathor, however, Isis included motherhood as one of her primary associations, and she had a significant role in guaranteeing the perpetuation of the royal family, as the mother of Horus. In statuettes that show Isis nursing Horus, the goddess may have Hathor's headdress of horns and sun-disc (see fig. 8.2), or she may have a crown in the shape of the hieroglyphic symbol for "throne."[6]

We also see prominent women in the Macedonian and Ptolemaic monarchies, which were, along with the pharaohs, models for the Ptolemaic dynasty in Egypt.[7] In Macedonia, Olympias, the mother of Alexander the Great, had a significant role in public life. Indeed, during Alexander's reign, Macedonian royal women enjoyed greater prominence and

influence than they ever had previously. Two factors played a role in this increased public visibility for the women of Alexander's family. Alexander did
not marry until near the end of his life, and so, for much of his reign, his
mother, Olympias, along with his sister Cleopatra, were his official family.
In addition, with Alexander away from Macedonia expanding his empire
from 334 BCE on, the only members of the royal family in the capital at
Pella were women.[8] Ptolemy I, who ruled Egypt after the death of Alexander the Great, imposed his own family as the new dynasty, but also assimilated them to the Egyptian pharaohs. By the second generation of the Ptolemies, we see that dynasty adopting the custom of brother–sister marriage.[9]
Ptolemy I married his half-sister Berenike I. Their children, Arsinoë II and
Ptolemy II, married and were worshiped in their lifetime as *theoi adelphoi,* "sibling gods," and each took the epithet Philadelphos, "sibling-lover"
(fig. 8.4).

Cleopatra inherits this tradition and uses images of motherhood successfully to consolidate her power. Her role as a mother, and specifically
as the mother of Julius Caesar's son Caesarion, was essential in legitimiz-
ing her rule. After engineering the deaths of her brothers and successive co-
rulers, Cleopatra had to rely on her son Caesarion to be the Horus to her
Isis, as women of the Ptolemies did not generally rule without a male partner. Upon his birth, Cleopatra issued coins showing her as Isis nursing an
infant (fig. 8.5).[10] The reliefs on the Temple of Hathor at Dendera also as-

FIGURE 8.4. *Gold* octodrachm *of
Ptolemy II and Arsinoë II.* © *Trustees of
the British Museum.*

FIGURE 8.5. *Bronze coin: Cleopatra VII
with infant Caesarion.* © *Trustees of the
British Museum.*

sociate Cleopatra and Caesarion with the Egyptian gods, as the pair appears making offerings to the gods and is shown with pharaonic iconography (see fig. 8.3). By identifying Caesarion with Horus, Cleopatra claims divinity for him and presents him as the boy who could bring new prosperity to Egypt as heir to the Egyptian empire (and perhaps to the Roman empire as well).[11]

Near the end of her reign, in her relationship with Mark Antony, Cleopatra again identifies herself with Isis. Cassius Dio tells us that Cleopatra and Antony posed for portraits as Isis and Osiris (*Roman History* 50.5). In their famous meeting at Tarsus in 41 BCE, Cleopatra may have evoked Isis, although Plutarch refers to her as representing Aphrodite. The goddesses have a number of similar qualities, however, and the two were consciously identified with each other in the Hellenistic period, particularly in the East.[12] In Plutarch's description of Cleopatra's arrival at Tarsus, we can see aspects of Isis, even though Plutarch mentions only Aphrodite:

> Πολλὰ δὲ καὶ παρ' αὐτοῦ καὶ παρὰ τῶν φίλων δεχομένη γράμματα
> καλούντων, οὕτως κατεφρόνησε καὶ κατεγέλασε τοῦ ἀνδρός, ὥστε
> πλεῖν ἀνὰ τὸν Κύδνον ποταμὸν ἐν πορθμείῳ χρυσοπρύμνῳ, τῶν
> μὲν ἱστίων ἁλουργῶν ἐκπεπετασμένων, τῆς δ' εἰρεσίας ἀργυραῖς
> κώπαις ἀναφερομένης πρὸς αὐλὸν ἅμα σύριγξι καὶ κιθάραις
> συνηρμοσμένον. αὐτὴ δὲ κατέκειτο μὲν ὑπὸ σκιάδι χρυσοπάστῳ,
> κεκοσμημένη γραφικῶς ὥσπερ Ἀφροδίτη, παῖδες δὲ τοῖς γραφικοῖς
> Ἔρωσιν εἰκασμένοι παρ' ἑκάτερον ἑστῶτες ἐρρίπιζον. (Plutarch, *Life
> of Antony* 26.1–3)

> She had received many letters from Antony and his friends summoning her, but she disdained and mocked the man by sailing up the River Cydnus in a ship with a golden stern, with purple sails fluttering, with rowers pulling with silver oars as flutes played accompanied by pipes and lyres. Cleopatra reclined beneath a canopy embroidered with gold, decked out to resemble a painting of Aphrodite, and boys, made to look like the Erotes we see in art, stood on either side and fanned her.[13]

An arrival by water is certainly fitting for Aphrodite, given her birth from sea foam, but it is appropriate for Isis as well. Isis was a patron goddess of seafarers; the festival known as the *Navigium Isidis* involved a procession leading to the seashore, and one of its messages was the spread of Isis's cult beyond Egypt. In the East, especially in Tarsus, Isis was worshiped under the cult name Isis Pelagia, or Isis of the Sea.[14] Apuleius describes the festival:

Ibi deum simulacris rite dispositis navem faberrime factam picturis miris Aegyptiorum. . . . Huius felicis alvei nitens carbasus litteras [votum] <auro> intextas progerebat: eae litterae votum instaurabant de novi commeatus prospera navigatione. Iam malus insurgit pinus rutunda, splendore sublimis, insigni carchesio conspicua, et puppis intorta chenisco, bracteis aureis vestita fulgebat omnisque prorsus carina citro limpido perpolita florebat. . . . donec muneribus largis et devotionibus faustis completa navis, absoluta strophiis ancoralibus, peculiari serenoque flatu pelago redderetur. (Apuleius, *Metamorphoses* 11.16)

There the gods' statues were duly set in place, and the chief priest named and consecrated to the goddess a ship which had been built with splendid craftsmanship, and which was adorned on all its timbers with wonderful Egyptian pictures. . . . The bright sail of this blessed craft carried upon it woven letters in gold, bearing those same petitions for trouble-free sailing on its first journeys. The mast was of rounded pine, gloriously tall and easily recognized with its striking masthead. The stern was curved in the shape of a goose, and gleamed with its covering of gold leaf. . . . Eventually the ship, filled with generous gifts and propitious offerings, was loosed from its anchor-ropes and launched on the sea before a friendly, specially appointed breeze.[15]

Note in particular the detail of the gold-covered stern in both descriptions. Although Plutarch emphasizes the Hellenizing aspects of Cleopatra's spectacle, the associations with Isis would not have been lost on Plutarch, himself the author of *On Isis and Osiris*, or on his audience of Greek speakers living in the Roman empire.

Cleopatra's children also emphasize her connection with Isis. The names of the twins she had with Antony, Alexander Helios (the sun) and Cleopatra Selene (the moon), evoke the earliest identity of Horus, the son of Isis; the earliest Egyptian concept of Horus was as a sky god whose two eyes represented the sun and the moon. The *Donations of Alexandria*, an explicitly dynastic ceremony, also featured Cleopatra identifying herself with Isis. Plutarch reports, "On this occasion she wore the sacred garment of Isis and bore the title the New Isis" (*Life of Antony* 54.9). In a possible echo of their meeting at Tarsus, Antony dressed as Dionysus. The ceremony—in which Cleopatra's children (Caesarion as well as her children with Antony) received titles and lands to rule (some of which were yet to be conquered)—illustrates the close identification of family and politics in Ptolemaic Egypt.

Cleopatra's identification with Isis, a goddess known for her connection to motherhood and nurturing, thus sets the stage for the central role her children play in political life in Alexandria. While this mixing of motherhood and politics might seem specific to Egypt, it probably was not a concept foreign to the Romans. They saw in their own history a number of mothers who were pivotal figures in Rome's development.

In Rome, as in Egypt, motherhood occupied a prominent, if sometimes problematic, place in the society's understanding of its own origins. Rome's foundation story and early legends are full of tales that hinge on motherhood. In Rome's foundation story, motherhood is a dangerous and, therefore, powerful force. Romulus and Remus were born to a woman whom others attempted to prevent from being a mother and who was an unwilling mother herself after being raped by the god Mars. The first of the twins' substitute mothers, a she-wolf, was another unlikely nurturer, as wolves were seen as antithetical to civilization.[16] The twins' second foster mother was a shepherd's wife. In the ancient world, the occupation of shepherd likewise carried with it connotations of wildness. It is possible, in fact, that the wolf and the shepherd's wife were one and the same. Livy tells us (*Ab urbe condita* 1.4) that some considered "wolf" a euphemism for "prostitute" (yet another un-ideal mother figure).[17]

There are two other tales in which motherhood plays a central role in establishing Rome: the Sabine women and the rape of Lucretia. The Sabine women, another group of unwilling mothers, overcame their circumstances and, through the bonds forged by motherhood, brought the Romans and the Sabines together.[18] Just as the Sabine women participated in the birth of the Roman state, another violated woman accomplished the transition from monarchy to Republic. Lucretia, raped by the king's son, commits suicide and, in doing so, motivates the birth of the Roman Republic. In this way, motherhood becomes an important symbol in the Roman conception of the culture's origins.

Thus, in stories of origins from both Egyptian and Roman traditions, motherhood marks transitions: it is the irrepressible force that produces Horus, even under seemingly impossible conditions (the preceding death of his father, Osiris); it produces and ensures the survival of Romulus and Remus, despite the best efforts of those in power; it secures Rome's viability as a state; and it is perhaps even a metaphor for the origin of the Republic.

During the Republic, there was a direct connection between Egypt and Roman ideas about motherhood. The cult of Isis was present in Rome from the early first century BCE, so Romans would have gained a familiarity with the Egyptian iconography associated with motherhood (i.e., that of

Isis).[19] It is important to note this point of contact because Roman familiarity with Isis indicates that the significance of Cleopatra associating herself with this goddess would not have been lost on a Roman audience.

Roman mothers had an important, if indirect, role in public life. The ideal of the Roman *matrona* called for a woman who was strong, virtuous, self-sacrificing, and devoted to the education and political advancement of her family. Children conferred posterity on their parents, and mothers were responsible for the earliest education of children in the household.[20] Thus the Romans recognized mothers as shaping great leaders. The best example is Cornelia, the mother of the Gracchi. Plutarch gives Cornelia a great deal of credit for the deeds of her sons (*Life of Tiberius* 1). He writes of them: "These she brought up with such care, that though they were without dispute in natural endowments and dispositions the first among the Romans of their time, yet they seemed to owe their virtues even more to their education than to their birth."[21] Cornelia became, for the Romans of the late Republic, the epitome of what a Roman mother should be, and her story reinforced the idea that mothers were essential to Rome's greatness.

Octavian, always a canny manipulator of symbolism, inherited these images of Roman motherhood and had to be careful of evoking them in his portrayal of Cleopatra, whom he had declared an enemy of Rome. The first step he took in removing from Cleopatra associations of motherhood was a reversal of gender roles: Cleopatra was masculinized and Antony feminized. In creating this propaganda, Octavian drew on certain preexisting prejudices; Antony's affinity for the Greek East, and specifically the wild and intemperate god Dionysus, was well known and proved to be a handy contrast to Octavian's ideal of rustic Italian simplicity.[22] The East was, for the Romans, associated not only with excessive wealth and luxury, but also with a lack of mental and physical toughness. Eastern peoples were regarded as effeminate as compared to Romans.[23] Antony also was feminized based on his relationship with Cleopatra. She was seen as the dominant partner, and Antony as helpless under her spell and captivated by the enervating luxuries of the East. Furthermore, Antony was fond of boasting his descent from Hercules; Octavian countered that if Antony was Hercules, he was Hercules enslaved to Queen Omphale.[24]

Cleopatra, for her part, was portrayed as having designs on ruling at Rome. Depicting her as the dominant partner in her relationship with Antony not only was useful in emphasizing the reversal of gender roles, but it also made it clear that Cleopatra was the primary aggressor against Rome. Plutarch reflects this characterization (as well as the feminization of Antony) when he notes qualities Cleopatra had in common with Fulvia, An-

tony's former wife and the mother of two of his children, Marcus Antonius Antyllus (47–30 BCE) and Iullus Antonius (45–2 BCE):

ἀπαλλαγεὶς γὰρ ἐκείνου τοῦ βίου γάμῳ προσέσχε, Φουλβίαν
ἀγαγόμενος τὴν Κλωδίῳ τῷ δημαγωγῷ συνοικήσασαν, οὐ ταλασίαν
οὐδ' οἰκουρίαν φρονοῦν γύναιον οὐδ' ἀνδρὸς ἰδιώτου κρατεῖν
ἀξιοῦν, ἀλλ' ἄρχοντος ἄρχειν καὶ στρατηγοῦντος στρατηγεῖν
βουλόμενον, ὥστε Κλεοπάτραν διδασκάλια Φουλβίᾳ τῆς Ἀντωνίου
γυναικοκρασίας ὀφείλειν, πάνυ χειροήθη καὶ πεπαιδαγωγημένον
ἀπ' ἀρχῆς ἀκροᾶσθαι γυναικῶν παραλαβοῦσαν αὐτόν. (Plutarch, *Life
of Antony* 10.5–6)

His bride was Fulvia, the former wife of Clodius the demagogue. She had no use for women's work like spinning or housekeeping and was not interested in presiding over a husband who was not in the public eye: rather, she wanted to rule a ruler and command a general. As a result, Cleopatra should have paid Fulvia tuition for schooling Antony to obey a woman, so docile and trained to obey a woman's commands was he when she took him on.

The areas in which Fulvia (and by implication Cleopatra) shows deficiency—spinning and housekeeping—are the emblematic tasks of the proper Roman matron (Lucretia's spinning won her the contest of womanly virtue). The language of ruling and commanding that characterizes Fulvia's preferred activities is from the masculine sphere. We sense no maternal leanings here; she is the antithesis of Roman motherhood, despite her two children, who are conveniently omitted from this description.

It is not just Octavian's manipulation of Cleopatra's image that veils her status as a mother. His actions effectively erase her children from public memory. In particular, his treatment of Cleopatra's children minimizes the maternal aspect of her public persona. He had Caesarion put to death, but not publicly. He also dealt with Cleopatra's other children, who were shown clemency, in relative privacy, partly, no doubt, to avoid the risk of arousing public sympathy:

βουλευομένου δὲ Καίσαρος, Ἄρειον εἰπεῖν λέγουσιν
    οὐκ ἀγαθὸν πολυκαισαρίη.
Τοῦτον μὲν οὖν ὕστερον ἀπέκτεινε μετὰ τὴν Κλεοπάτρας
τελευτήν. (Plutarch, *Life of Antony* 81.5–82.2)

As Octavian was considering what to do with Caesarion, Areius is said to have paraphrased:

It is not good to have too many Caesars.[25]

Octavian had Caesarion killed later, after Cleopatra's death.

τοὺς δὲ λοιποὺς Ὀκταουΐα παραλαβοῦσα μετὰ τῶν ἐξ ἑαυτῆς ἔθρεψε. καὶ Κλεοπάτραν μὲν τὴν ἐκ Κλεοπάτρας Ἰόβᾳ τῷ χαριεστάτῳ βασιλέων συνῴκισεν. (Plutarch, *Life of Antony* 87.2)

The remaining children Octavia took in and raised with her own children. And she arranged that Cleopatra, daughter of Cleopatra, be married to Juba, the most accomplished of kings.

Plutarch treats the fate of her children as incidental information: he presents the details in a matter-of-fact style, and the information is not part of Cleopatra's dramatic death scene. It is mentioned in two different places in the narrative, the first before and the second after Cleopatra's death, which is clearly the centerpiece. By dealing with her children privately, Octavian avoids, as much as possible, the sympathy the orphaned children might evoke for their mother.

Octavian also avoided connotations of motherhood in his shaping of the way Cleopatra was remembered. He seems to have had Caesarion's image removed from the statue of Cleopatra that resided in the Temple of Venus Genetrix, a temple that calls attention to Venus's role as progenitor of the Julian family.[26] Complete removal of a rival certainly provided one motive for Octavian, but eliminating the child from a mother-and-child sculpture in a temple devoted to the motherly aspect of Venus effectively abrogates Cleopatra's role as a mother and transforms Cleopatra from a woman central to the perpetuation of one of Rome's leading families to that of a captive. In its new significance, Cleopatra's statue becomes spoils of war and perhaps resembles personifications of conquered provinces, the iconography of which does not feature children.[27] When non-Roman children are represented in Roman art, they tend to appear in military contexts, either in battleground scenes or scenes of triumph.[28] According to Jeannine Uzzi, these types of images "underscore the dominance of Rome by equating conquered non-Romans with children. The inclusion of children also increases the pathos of such scenes."[29] Such an image in this instance, however, would run the risk of reminding viewers that the enemy was a woman and a mother. In addition, by removing Caesarion, Octavian effectively ed-

its his family tree. If Caesarion was, as Cleopatra claimed, the son of Caesar, the boy not only could be seen as a potential rival for Octavian, but also created a familial bond between Octavian and Cleopatra, perhaps a circumstance Octavian did not want memorialized in the temple dedicated to his family origins.

We can see some of Octavian's agenda reflected in Augustan poetry. In his famous "Cleopatra Ode" (1.37), Horace first shows the queen beset by ill-fated megalomania and drunk on wine and delusions of grandeur:

> . . . quidlibet inpotens
> sperare fortunaque dulci
> ebria. sed minuit furorem
>
> vix una sospes navis ab ignibus
> mentemque lymphatam Mareotico
> redegit in veros timores
> Caesar . . .
> (HORACE, *ODES* 1.37.10–16)

> She was mad
> to hope for anything at all and
> drunk on good fortune. But scarcely one ship
>
> safe from the fires cooled her fury,
> and Caesar snatched her mind,
> crazed with Mareotic wine, back to
> true fears . . .

Her lack of control and rationality stand in stark contrast to the reality check Octavian delivers by means of military force. Here, Cleopatra's qualities are clearly Eastern and feminine, while Octavian's are Roman and masculine.

In the next stanza, however, Cleopatra's gender begins to shift:

> . . . quae generosius
> perire quaerens nec muliebriter
> expavit ensem nec latentis
> classe cita reparavit oras,
> (HORACE, *ODES* 1.37.21–24)

The queen,
seeking to die more nobly, did not, womanish,
shrink from the sword, nor did she retreat
in her swift fleet to hidden shores.

Now Cleopatra's actions are explicitly not those expected of a woman, and
she displays bravery in battle. In the ode's final stanza, she turns defeat into
her own triumph, as she gains the control she so emphatically lacked earlier in the poem:

deliberata morte ferocior:
saevis Liburnis scilicet invidens
privata deduci superbo
non humilis mulier triumpho.
(HORACE, *ODES* 1.37.29–32)

More defiant in a deliberate death,
begrudging the cruel Liburnian ships
to be led, a queen no longer,
but never humbled, in a showy triumph.

Written in the immediate aftermath of the Battle of Actium, Horace's poem
elevates Cleopatra to the status of an enemy worthy of Octavian.

Propertius and Vergil also describe Cleopatra's death, but in terms that
make her the female victim:

fugisti tamen in timidi vaga flumina Nili:
    accepere tuae Romula vincla manus.
bracchia spectasti sacris admorsa colubris,
    et trahere occultum membra soporis iter.
"Non hoc, Roma, fui tanto tibi cive verenda!"
    dixit et assiduo lingua sepulta mero.
(PROPERTIUS, *ELEGIES* 3.11.51–56)

And yet you fled to the meandering streams of the cowardly Nile,
your hands accepted Romulus's chains.
I saw your arms bitten by sacred snakes,
and the hidden course of sleep overtake your limbs.
"You need not have feared me, Rome, when you had such a citizen
protecting you!" She spoke, though strong wine had overwhelmed her
    tongue.

illam inter caedes pallentem morte futura
fecerat ignipotens undis et Iapyge ferri,
contra autem magno maerentem corpore Nilum
pandentemque sinus et tota veste vocantem
caeruleum in gremium latebrosaque flumina victos.
(VERGIL, *AENEID* 8.709–713)

The lord of fire had fashioned her, pale with approaching death,
amid the slaughter, impelled by the waves and the Northwest wind.
Opposite, the mourning Nile with open arms
receives the conquered into his folds,
into his blue embrace and sheltering streams.

Despite the increased pathos in these two descriptions, neither poet
portrays Cleopatra as a mother. Indeed, elsewhere in 3.11, Propertius refers
to her as the "whore-queen" (3.11.39). The sympathy Vergil evokes comes
not from Cleopatra's status as a mother, but from her link to Dido, another victim of Rome's march toward world power. Not only do biographical details unite Cleopatra and Dido (both were Eastern, female rulers in
northern Africa), but Vergil underscores the link through intratextual reference. The phrase *pallentem morte futura* (8.709) recalls *pallida morte futura*
(4.644), Vergil's description of Dido on her funeral pyre. In addition to having words, sounds, and sense in common, the phrases occupy the same met-
rical position, thus creating a link between Cleopatra's death and Dido's.[30]

As we have seen above, in Egypt Cleopatra was able to present herself
as a head of state in such a way that the concepts of power and motherhood
(and womanhood in general) reinforce one another. In the Roman conception of Cleopatra, which was shaped by Octavian's negative propaganda,
however, feminine qualities were not a source of strength; rather, they appeared to add to the unease a Roman audience would feel about an Eastern ruler or to arouse sympathy for a fallen enemy. This sympathy seems to
have been dispensed in measured doses, and depicting her orphaned children might have made her too tragic a figure.

Octavian does seem to have taken a lesson from Cleopatra, however,
as Diana Kleiner points out in her recent book, *Cleopatra and Rome*. After the defeat of Antony and Cleopatra, Octavian's own dynastic aspirations become clear. His family becomes the "first family" of Rome and his
repeated attempts to secure a successor leave little doubt as to his goal. His
wife, Livia, took a more prominent role in public life than had been cus-
tomary for Roman women, who in the Republic tended to support their
husbands' political ambitions from behind the scenes. Livia's image, how-

FIGURE 8.6. *Head of Livia.* © *Trustees of the British Museum.*

FIGURE 8.7. *Statue of a Ptolemaic queen: Cleopatra. Metropolitan Museum of Art, New York, Gift of Joseph W. Drexel 1889.2.660.* © *Metropolitan Museum of Art/Art Resource, NY, ART358164.*

ever, began to appear on coins, reliefs, and statues.[31] Despite Augustus's sometimes controversial family life (in particular the scandal involving his daughter Julia), he creates for public consumption an idealized first family, of which Livia is the *materfamilias*.

As Augustus dealt with the issue of succession, Livia took on a key role as the mother of his successor. She continued to have a prominent position during the reign of Tiberius as the mother of the emperor. Several ancient sources record the Roman Senate's desire to commemorate that role with the title *Mater Patriae* ("Mother of the Fatherland"), but report that Tiberius vetoed the honor (Tacitus, *Annals* 1.14.1; Suetonius, *Tiberius* 50.2–3; Cassius Dio, *Roman History* 57.12.4). This notion of Livia as the mother of her country clearly evokes the role Cleopatra emphasized through her association with Isis. Kleiner even sees a visual detail borrowed from Cleopatra's portraiture: Livia's *nodus* hairstyle approximates the triple *uraeus* that often adorns Cleopatra's forehead (figs. 8.6 and 8.7).[32] On the *Ara Pacis*,

Livia's portrait resembles that of Tellus, a resemblance that also casts Livia as a mother figure.[33]

The contrasts between the way Cleopatra presents her image to her subjects in Egypt and the way Octavian portrays her to the Romans point to a conscious effort on Octavian's part to decrease Cleopatra's impact as a mother when she is presented to audiences in the Roman empire. The political significance of motherhood in both Egypt and Rome makes it a powerful symbol through which the origins and continuity of a community can be understood. Thus, those who hold political power, whether they are male or female, must be mindful of the messages images of motherhood send. Because motherhood in its political context evokes images of creation and nurturing common to both Roman and Egyptian traditions, Octavian risked humanizing and assimilating his enemy Cleopatra if he portrayed her as a mother. Already aware that his conflict with Antony might be viewed as civil war (he was careful to declare war only on Cleopatra), in his characterization of Cleopatra Octavian stresses the foreign and threatening aspects of her persona, while directing attention to his own family as a model for the Roman citizenry.

NOTES

1. Pomeroy (1990), 8.

2. Frankfort and Kramer (1978), 171.

3. Clément and Kristeva (2001), 28.

4. Carney (2000), 85.

5. Lesko (1999), 117.

6. Silverman and Brovarski (1997), 71. For a large collection of representations of Isis nursing Horus, see Tran Tam Tinh (1997).

7. Alexander the Great was the last king of the Macedonian monarchy. Alexander extended his empire into Egypt and India. After his death in 323 BCE, several of his generals ruled portions of his empire. Ptolemy I continued the tradition of hereditary monarchy in Egypt, on the model of the Macedonian monarchy as well as the Egyptian pharaohs.

8. Pomeroy (1990), 9.

9. According to Pomeroy (1990), 16, Ptolemaic brother–sister marriage may have been based on a misunderstanding of pharaonic tradition.

10. Carradice (1995), 96.

11. Kleiner (2005), 88.

12. Dunand (2007), 258. Both Isis and Aphrodite were goddesses associated with fertility and reproduction. Both also were associated with the sea (see below).

13. Except where noted, translations are from Jones (2006).

14. Hughes-Hallett (1990), 85.

15. Translated by Walsh (1999), 228–229.

16. *Sic omnem illum populum luporum animos inexplebiles sanguinis atque imperii divitiarumque avidos ac ieiunos habere* ("so the whole people has the souls of wolves, who cannot be sated with blood and are always hungry and greedy for power and wealth," Pompeius Trogus, *Historiae Philippicae* book 38, fr. 152, line 98 [ed. Seel (1956)]). The wolf as symbol of the warrior has Indo-European roots (Speidel [2002], 256).

17. Although see Anise Strong's essay in this volume. For the *lupa* and its connections with prostitution see Patricia Salzman-Mitchell in this volume as well.

18. The Sabine women, kidnapped to provide the fledgling community of Rome with women, become devoted wives after giving birth to their captors' children (Livy 1.9).

19. Heyob (1975), 15.

20. Dixon (1992), 116, 120.

21. διαγενομένους οὕτως φιλοτίμως ἐξέθρεψεν, ὥστε πάντων εὐφυεστάτους Ῥωμαίων ὁμολογουμένως γεγονότας, πεπαιδεῦσθαι δοκεῖν βέλτιον ἢ πεφυκέναι πρὸς ἀρετήν.

22. See Plutarch, *Life of Antony* 9.8, 24.4 and Pelling (1988) *ad* 24.4; Zanker (1990), 240; Russell (1998), 121–137; Southern (2008), 158, 163; and Krostenko (2001), 294, on Antony's association with the East and extravagance. On Augustus projecting an image of rustic simplicity, see Zanker (1990), 240.

23. Williams (1999), 177.

24. Plutarch likens Antony to Hercules enslaved to Omphale in his *Comparison of Demetrius and Antony* 3.3. A visual representation of the myth that dates to ca. 30 BCE may be an attempt to ridicule Antony. See Zanker (1990), 59.

25. The line Areius paraphrases is Homer, *Iliad* 2.204.

26. Kleiner (2005), 153.

27. Smith (1988), 59, 70–71.

28. Uzzi (2005), 120.

29. Uzzi (2005), 121. Also see Zanker (2000), 168.

30. Jones (2008), 113.

31. Kleiner (2005), 255–256.

32. Kleiner (2005), 155. On the triple *uraeus* as characteristic of Cleopatra, see Ashton (2001), 155.

33. Kleiner (2005), 259–260.

WORKS CITED

Ashton, Sally-Ann. (2001). "Identifying the Egyptian-Style Ptolemaic Queens." In Susan Walker and Peter Higgs, eds., *Cleopatra of Egypt: From History to Myth*, 148–155. Princeton: Princeton University Press.

Carney, Elizabeth. (2000). *Women and Monarchy in Macedonia.* Norman: University of Oklahoma Press.

Carradice, Ian. (1995). *Greek Coins.* London: British Museum Press.

Clément, Catherine, and Julia Kristeva. (2001). *The Feminine and the Sacred.* New York: Columbia University Press.

Dixon, Suzanne. (1992). *The Roman Family.* Baltimore: Johns Hopkins University Press.

Dunand, Françoise. (2007). "Isis." In Daniel Ogden, ed., *A Companion to Greek Religion* (Blackwell Companions to the Ancient World), 258–262. Hoboken, NJ: Wiley-Blackwell.

Frankfort, Henri, and Samuel Noah Kramer. (1978). *Kingship and the Gods: A Study of Ancient Near Eastern Religion as the Integration of Society and Nature.* Chicago: University of Chicago Press.

Heyob, Sharon Kelly. (1975). *The Cult of Isis in the Graeco-Roman World.* Leiden: Brill.

Hughes-Hallett, Lucy. (1990). *Cleopatra: Histories, Dreams, and Distortions.* New York: Harper Perennial.

Jones, Prudence. (2006). *Cleopatra: A Sourcebook.* Norman: University of Oklahoma Press.

———. (2008). "Teaching Reception via Dido and Cleopatra." *New England Classical Journal* 35.2:111–121.

Kleiner, Diana E. E. (2005). *Cleopatra and Rome.* Cambridge, MA: Harvard University Press.

Krostenko, Brian. (2001). *Cicero, Catullus, and the Language of Social Performance.* Chicago: University of Chicago Press.

Lesko, Barbara. (1999). *Great Goddesses of Egypt.* Norman: University of Oklahoma Press.

Pelling, C. B. R., ed. (1988). *Plutarch: Life of Antony.* New York: Cambridge University Press.

Pomeroy, Sarah. (1990). *Women in Hellenistic Egypt: From Alexander to Cleopatra.* Detroit: Wayne State University Press.

Russell, B. F. (1998). "The Emasculation of Antony: The Construction of Gender in Plutarch's *Life of Antony.*" *Helios* 25:121–137.

Seel, Otto, ed. (1956). *Pompei Trogi fragmenta.* Leipzig: Teubner.

Silverman, David P., and Edward Brovarski. (1997). *Searching for Ancient Egypt: Art, Architecture, and Artifacts from the University of Pennsylvania Museum of Archaeology and Anthropology.* Ithaca: Cornell University Press.

Smith, R. R. R. (1988). "*Simulacra gentium*: The *Ethne* from the Sebasteion at Aphrodisias." *Journal of Roman Studies* 78:50–77.

Southern, Patricia. (2008). *Antony and Cleopatra.* Stroud: Tempus.

Speidel, Michael. (2002). "Berserks: A History of Indo-European 'Mad Warriors.'" *Journal of World History* 13.2:253–290.

Tran Tam Tinh, V. (1997). *Isis lactans: Corpus des monuments gréco-romains d'Isis allai-*

tant Harpocrate. Études préliminaires aux religions orientales dans l'empire romain 37. Leiden: Brill.

Uzzi, Jeannine. (2005). *Children in the Visual Arts of Imperial Rome*. Cambridge: Cambridge University Press.

Walsh, P. G., trans. (1999). *Apuleius: The Golden Ass*. Oxford: Oxford University Press.

Williams, Craig Arthur. (1999). *Roman Homosexuality: Ideologies of Masculinity in Classical Antiquity*. New York: Oxford University Press.

Zanker, Paul. (1990). *The Power of Images in the Age of Augustus*. Ann Arbor: University of Michigan Press.

———. (2000). "Die Frauen und Kinder der Barbaren auf der Markussäule." In John Scheid and Valérie Huet, eds., *La colonne Aurélienne: Autour de la colonne Aurélienne*, 163–174. Turnhout: Brepols.

NINE

Mater Amoris

MOTHERS AND LOVERS IN AUGUSTAN ROME

Genevieve Liveley

In 2005 Ayelet Waldman's controversial *New York Times* essay on motherhood in the twenty-first century provoked fierce debate among women on both sides of the Atlantic—fueling arguments in and out of the media about hot moms, MILFs ("mothers I'd like to fuck"), the yummy mummy (the British incarnation of the MILF), and the character of (post)modern motherhood. In her article "Modern Love: Truly, Madly, Guiltily" and in subsequent interviews, Waldman openly confessed to being a "bad" mother for loving her husband more than her four children, for loving but not "being in love" with her new baby. The essay begins like this:

> I have been in many mothers' groups—Mommy and Me, Gymboree, Second-Time Moms—and each time, within three minutes, the conversation invariably comes around to the topic of how often mommy feels compelled to put out. Everyone wants to be reassured that no one else is having sex either. These are women who, for the most part, are comfortable with their bodies, consider themselves sexual beings. These are women who love their husbands or partners. Still, almost none of them are having any sex.[1]

The reason for this lack of sex, Waldman argues, is that

> the wife's passion has been refocused. Instead of concentrating her ardor on her husband, she concentrates it on her babies. Where once her husband was the center of her passionate universe, there is now a new sun in whose orbit she revolves. Libido, as she once knew it, is gone, and in its place is all-consuming maternal desire.[2]

From this paradigm of twenty-first-century motherhood a binary opposition between the good and bad mother emerges. Indeed, Waldman herself confesses:

> If a good mother is one who loves her child more than anyone else in the world, I am not a good mother. I am in fact a bad mother. I love my husband more than I love my children.[3]

Waldman maps the model of modern motherhood as a quasi-romantic relationship in which maternal love for a child comes to eclipse erotic desire for a partner, and in which the role of mother subsumes and replaces that of lover. Yet this model of "modern love," of motherhood good and bad, is not the modern phenomenon that Waldman and her critics suppose. In particular, we can extrapolate similar models of good and bad mothering from the literature and art of Augustan Rome, which shows motherhood in the first century BCE as an early site of contestation between an idealized and sentimental model of maternity and the eroticized paradigm that has become central to twenty-first-century debates on mothering and motherhood.

Throughout antiquity, the relationship between mother and child was regarded as taking precedence over that between husband and wife. Aristotle (in the *Nicomachean Ethics* 8.12) saw the relationship between husband and wife as secondary in both status and emotional intensity to that between parent and child. Most Stoic philosophers similarly privileged parental over marital relationships; according to Beryl Rawson:

> Mothers' love for their children is one of the qualities which Musonius Rufus (frag. 3) argued was developed by philosophy. . . . A woman trained in philosophy is best situated to protect the interests of husband and children; she loves . . . her children more than life itself. These were ideals continually set in front of wives and daughters.[4]

We can map a similar attitude toward motherhood across the extant literature and art of classical Greece and Rome.[5] Yet in Augustan representations of motherhood (particularly those with a political and ideological brief to promote larger families among the social elite), we may trace particular tensions and paradoxes between mother and lover, maternal and erotic love, which specifically parallel those highlighted by Waldman. Here we see clear evidence of mothers behaving as lovers, as in Ovid's *Ars amatoria*, where he reassures mothers—Augustan MILFs, perhaps—that they can still be both sexually active and attractive (*Ars amatoria* 3.81–88), reminding

them that Venus herself enjoyed sex with the youthful Adonis after she had given birth to her son Aeneas: *ut Veneri, quem luget adhuc, donetur Adonis: / unde habet Aenean Harmoniamque suos?* (*Ars amatoria* 3.85f).[6] In this light, he also advises women who have already borne children, and who bear the stretch marks to prove it, about the best positions to take up during sex: *tu quoque, cui rugis uterum Lucina notavit, ut celer aversis utere Parthus equis* (*Ars amatoria* 3.785f). Clearly, motherhood and sex are not mutually exclusive in this text or context, and sex for mothers can apparently be enjoyed for the purposes of recreation no less than for procreation.

However, alongside "sexy mothers" in Augustan representations of motherhood we also see representations of "bad" mothers, who fall short of the maternal ideal through the improper privileging of erotic or sexual relationships over their maternal responsibilities: Ovid's Corinna, who aborts her unborn child (*Amores* 2.13, 2.14); Ovid's Helen, who abandons her young daughter Hermione when she sails to Troy with Paris (*Heroides* 8); and Dido—who is emphatically not Ascanius's mother, nor Aeneas's wife, and so seems prevented from assuming the role of good mother in Vergil's Augustan narrative *a priori*.[7] We also encounter artistic representations of "good" mothers, who seem to exemplify but at the same time to complicate the maternal ideal: images of Venus Genetrix highlight Venus's status as nurturing mother, protective parent, and founder-mother of the Julian line; a panel of the Ara Pacis shows the Terra Mater, the "mother goddess of Augustan art" holding two infants and advertising the privileged status of Augustan motherhood (fig. 9.1).[8] Yet even in these ostensibly propagandist portraits, mothers and lovers are confused: the Terra Mater, whose garment is shown slipping seductively from one shoulder, is also identifiable as Venus, whose status and reputation as goddess of erotic love—as "*mater Amoris,*" mother of Love (Ovid, *Amores* 3.15.1), and "*tenerorum mater Amorum,*" mother of tender Love (Ovid, *Ars amatoria* 1.30)—destabilizes attempts to configure both the Terra Mater and Venus Genetrix as respectable images of "good" Augustan motherhood.

This essay will use both textual and visual *exempla* to extrapolate on such models of good and bad mothering in Augustan Rome, and so to examine motherhood as a site of contestation between the tensions and paradoxes of mother and lover, maternal and erotic love. It will show that the idealized and sentimental model of motherhood in the art and literature of Augustan Rome offers an eroticized paradigm that continues to influence twenty-first-century debates on good parenting.

Mothers mattered to Augustus—for many reasons.[9] The grandson of Caesar's sister, he was adopted as Caesar's heir and given his name as a

FIGURE 9.1. *Tellus panel, Ara Pacis, 13–9 BCE. Rome. Photo: Richard Huxtable (by kind permission of the Sovraintendenza Comunale Beni Culturali di Roma).*

direct consequence of this maternal connection; his own sister Octavia (who also raised Antony's children by Fulvia and Cleopatra), mother of Marcellus, gave Augustus his first adopted heir; and after Marcellus's early death, his only child, Julia, as mother of Gaius and Lucius, gave him two adopted sons. His wife, Livia, although subsequently unable to provide Augustus with children of their own, was mother of two sons by her former marriage, Tiberius and Drusus, and it was she who ultimately provided Augustus with an adopted heir and imperial successor.[10] His daughter, Julia, was the most "successful" mother of the first family, bearing five children—including those two all-important boys, for which she was honored by Augustus in having her portrait as the "first mother of Rome" (alongside that of her two sons) depicted on Rome's official coinage.[11] However, Julia was less of a success as a wife, and she was banished by Augustus in 2 BCE for her adulterous erotic activities.[12] This complicated image of motherhood—and some of these mothers themselves—can be seen reflected and represented in the art and literature of the Augustan age, in which a complex and contradictory model of the good and bad Augustan mother emerges.

As we saw in the previous essay, such representations and reflections of mothers and motherhood appear problematized *ab initio* in Augustan Rome by the maternal legacy of Cleopatra, queen of Egypt, living goddess, mistress of both Julius Caesar and Mark Antony, and mother of Caesarion—Caesar's son, "biological heir," and therefore potential rival to the adopted heir Octavian.[13] In this light, Cleopatra was a dangerously "hot mom." And, as Diana Kleiner observes, the associations of Cleopatra with Venus Genetrix, *magna mater* of the Julian clan, would have been particularly threatening to Augustus:[14]

> Caesarion was not just some foreign pharaoh but a real presence in Rome. He had stayed in Caesar's villa with his mother and was proudly featured by his father in a gilded statue of Cleopatra with Caesarion on her shoulder. Even more worrisome was that the statuary group was audaciously paired with that of the Julian family's patron deity Venus in her temple in Caesar's forum in Rome.

The image of a mother carrying her son upon her shoulders is certainly potent and, in this context, also highly suggestive, echoing as it does the iconic image of Aeneas leaving Troy to found Rome carrying his father upon his shoulders and leading his young son, Iulus (eponymous ancestor of the Julian clan), by the hand—the statue group with which Augustus would later particularly associate himself, both in coinage and in his own forum.[15]

However, re-imagined and re-presented in literary form in the guise of Dido in Vergil's *Aeneid*, Cleopatra's role as mother—and above all, as frustrated would-be founder-mother of Rome's greatest dynasty—is subtly defused. For Dido, queen of Carthage, favorite of Juno, mistress of Aeneas, is represented unequivocally as a "bad" mother, who confuses her unspeakable passion (*infandum . . . amorem*) for Aeneas with her maternal affection for his motherless son, Ascanius. Indeed, early in book 4 of the *Aeneid*, the love-struck Dido infamously holds Ascanius upon her lap as a sort of child-substitute for his father (*gremio Ascanium genitoris imagine capta / detinet, infandum si fallere possit amorem* [4.84–85], "captivated by the image of his father, she holds Ascanius on her lap as if she might cheat her unspeakable love"). The childless Dido's unspeakable (erotic) love, her *infandum amorem*, for Aeneas here fuses both figuratively and linguistically with her motherly love for the *infant* Ascanius. But Dido is emphatically *not* Ascanius's mother or stepmother, and neither is she Aeneas's wife. For, as Susan Treggiari has pointed out, "*Matrimonium* means an institution for making mothers (*matres*)" and a "good" mother in this Augustan context means precisely a *married* mother.[16]

This neat, albeit somewhat reductive, model of "good" motherhood, ostensibly reconciling and smoothing over tensions between the roles of wife and mother, would have been as ideologically charged in Augustan Rome as it is in—and out—of mothers' groups today. Yet in the context of Augustan concerns—and legislation—regarding morality and sexual behavior, Dido's relationship with both the child and his father (described by Ovid in *Tristia* 2.536 as "*non legitimo foedere iunctus amor*") is deemed illegitimate and thus dangerous. Indeed, by the end of book 4, Dido's maternal instincts and motherly love for the child will have become corrupted and confused by her passion for the father. She imagines herself as Agave, as Medea, as Procne, tearing apart Aeneas's body, serving up Ascanius on toast to his father:

non potui abreptum divellere corpus et undis
spargere? non socios, non ipsum absumere ferro
Ascanium patriisque epulandum ponere mensis?
(*AENEID* 4.600–602)

Could I not have grabbed his body, torn it apart and scattered it on the waves? Couldn't I have put his friends to the sword and Ascanius, and set him on his father's table to be eaten?

Significantly, in each of these fantasies of revenge against her lover, Dido identifies herself as a "murderous" mother. Indeed, she identifies with the

most notoriously "bad" mothers from the classical mythological and literary tradition—each of whom kills her own child (and in Medea's case, children) as a result of improperly privileging another relationship over her maternal responsibilities. Agave privileges her cultic (and perhaps quasi-erotic) devotion to Bacchus over her maternal affection for Pentheus; Medea privileges her erotic passion for Jason over her maternal love for her (and his) children; and it is Procne's love for her sister Philomela no less than her passionate hatred for her husband, Tereus, that drives her to butcher her infant son, Itys.

In Ovid's *Heroides*, Dido similarly confuses the roles of mother and lover, and again identifies herself as a murderous "bad" mother.[17] Initially, positioning herself as a "good" mother, she seems to show appropriately maternal concern for the well-being and safety of young Ascanius as he is about to set sail on stormy seas. But it immediately becomes clear that she is couching her desire for her lover to stay with her a little longer in this maternalistic expression of love and concern for his child:

> Da breve saevitiae spatium pelagique tuaeque;
>> grande morae pretium tuta futura via est.
> nec mihi tu curae; puero parcatur Iulo.
>> te satis est titulum mortis habere meae.
> quid puer Ascanius, quid di meruere Penates?
> (*HEROIDES* 7.73–77)

> Allow a little time for the savagery of the sea, and your own;
> a safe voyage will be a rich reward for your delay.
> And though you care little for me, spare the boy Iulus.
> It will be enough for you to take the credit for *my* death.
> What has the boy Ascanius, what have your Penates done to
>> deserve this?

However, we soon see Dido engaging in a Medean fantasy of revenge against Aeneas, threatening the death of his unborn child if he leaves her:

> Forsitan et gravidam Didon, scelerate, relinquas
>> parsque tui lateat corpore clausa meo.
> accedet fatis matris miserabilis infans
>> et nondum nato funeris auctor eris.
> cumque parente sua frater morietur Iuli.
> (*HEROIDES* 7.133–137)

And perhaps it is a pregnant Dido, wicked one, whom you abandon,
and a part of you lies concealed within my body.
The poor baby will share the fate of its mother,
you will be the murderer of your unborn child,
and with his mother the brother of Iulus will die.

As in Vergil, Dido's maternal instincts regarding the protection of her child
have here become corrupted and confused by her passion for the father. The
fantasy of pregnancy as a surrogate for union with the child's father has become a fantasy of revenge against him. Her dark threats to kill her unborn
child, moreover, hold echoes of abortion, particularly as evinced in Ovid's
writing on this theme in the *Amores* (2.13 and 2.14). Having castigated
Corinna for almost killing herself along with her unborn child, Ovid controversially speculates on what might have happened if Venus had dared to
abort her unborn son, Aeneas, thereby robbing the world of its future Caesars (*si Venus Aenean gravida temerasset in alvo, / Caesaribus tellus orba futura fuit* [*Amores* 2.14.17–18]). Aligned with an elegiac *puella* in this way—
the literary antithesis of a maternal *matrona*—Dido, then, is certainly not
a "good" mother, not least of all because she lacks a legitimate husband to
validate her status as *mater*.

Indeed, Ovid's provocative "what if" speculation concerning Venus as
magna mater of the Julian clan and her putative abortion of Aeneas is also
suggestive here. For the "first lady" among the pantheon of Augustan bad
mothers is surely Vergil's Venus, whose son Aeneas complains of her cru-
elty and neglect, and who (when she does offer him some form of maternal
support) reminds us of both her son's "illegitimacy" and her own adultery
in seducing her husband, Vulcan, into forging Aeneas's (somewhat unnecessary) new armor. In the first book of the *Aeneid*, this *mater* (1.314) is described as possessing the look of a virgin (*virginis os habitumque gerens et
virginis arma* [1.315]); she impatiently and somewhat unsympathetically in-
terrupts her son's account of his woes (*nec plura querentem / passa Venus me-
dio sic interfata dolore est* [1.385f.]), telling him in so many words to "get on
with it" (*perge modo et, qua te ducit via, derige gressum* [1.401]). And it is
only when she turns to leave him, that she reveals her true identity as Aeneas's mother:

dixit, et avertens rosea cervice refulsit,
ambrosiaeque comae divinum vertice odorem
spiravere, pedes vestis defluxit ad imos,
et vera incessu patuit dea. ille ubi matrem

agnovit, tali fugientem est voce secutus:
"quid natum totiens, crudelis tu quoque, falsis
ludis imaginibus? cur dextrae iungere dextram
non datur, ac veras audire et reddere voces?"
talibus incusat, gressumque ad moenia tendit.
(*AENEID* 1.402–410)

She spoke, and as she turned away, her rosy neck gleamed, while from
her head her heavenly hair breathed a divine fragrance; her robes slipped
down to her feet and in her step she was revealed as a true goddess. Then
he recognized her as his mother [*matrem*], and as she fled he followed
her with these words: "Why are you too cruel, why do you play [*ludis*]
with your son [*natum*] with false appearances? Why am I not allowed to
take your hand in mine or to hear and to speak honest words?" So he re-
proaches her and turns his feet towards the citadel.

In this epic encounter between mother and son, there is an odd blend
of the maternal and the erotic: this mother looks and behaves just like a virgin—the epitome of the yummy mummy;[18] she half-listens to her child's
complaints but is principally concerned not with his prattle but with the
larger affairs of grown-ups (that is, of the gods); she reveals her true identity to her son—in one possible translation of *pedes vestis defluxit ad imos*—
by taking off her clothes to reveal (what must surely be) her naked body;
she "plays" with her child (*ludis*)—but cruelly, without affection; and she
refuses him the maternal intimacy of contact or conversation. This sexy
mother is clearly both neglectful of and unavailable to her child. In this description, she is physically detached from her child, refusing even to take
his hand in hers (in Vergil's ambiguously erotic terms, refusing to "give"
[*datur*] or to "join" [*iungere*] anything of herself to her son).
     The antithesis of the mother for whom all-consuming maternal desire
replaces sex, Venus appears to reserve her body entirely for erotic pursuits
and to deny her child any physical expression of maternal love. We might
hesitate to label Venus a "bad" mother, but on the basis of this encounter
with her son, she could hardly be identified as a "good" mother. What is
more, as Ellen Oliensis has observed, Aeneas's complaint that his mother is
"cruel too" or "cruel like others" (*crudelis tu quoque* [1.407]) carries threatening undertones of motherhood turned bad:[19]

The phrase derives from *Eclogue* 8 (47–48): "savage Love taught the
mother to stain her hands with her children's blood; you too are cruel,

mother" (*crudelis tu quoque, mater*). The cruel mother of the eclogue may be Medea, the child-killing mother, or Venus, the mother of "savage Love." But the very fact that the referent is unclear draws the two mothers together.[20]

Vergil's Venus, mother of Aeneas, mother of "savage Love," and founder-mother of the Julian line, presents a complicated image of motherhood. And in particular, her status as a divinity of erotic love seems to destabilize and undermine her status as a loving mother in Vergil's epic.

Turning from Augustan epic to elegy, we find that this tension between eroticism and motherhood is similarly exploited (as we might expect) in Ovid's writing, where Venus appears once again as the embodiment of the mother of Love, or *mater Amoris*. In the *Fasti* (4.1–6), Ovid addresses her as "nurturing mother of the twin Loves," and in his love poetry Ovid plays heavily upon his own quasi-filial relationship with Venus, emphasizing both the goddess's associations with love and sex, and her assumed role as patron/matron of love poets. In both the *Amores* and *Ars amatoria*, Venus features prominently, addressed in the *Amores* as "*tenerorum mater Amorum*," or "mother of tender Love" (3.15.1). Controversially, he even prays to her for inspiration for his poem on the arts of love, addressing her again as the "*mater Amoris*," or "mother of Love" (1.30), playfully combining her two familiar Augustan roles as divine mother and heavenly lover.

Other Augustan representations of Venus at this time, however, accented her maternal role above all others, highlighting Venus's status as nurturing mother and protective parent in the divine form of Venus Genetrix, and downplaying her more traditional role as the goddess of Love. In the development of his public image, Augustus played heavily upon his associations with Venus, emphasizing his family connection through Venus's identification as Genetrix, or founder-mother, of the Roman people in general and of the Julian line in particular. Moreover, Augustus's active and official encouragement of motherhood was initiated by his restoration of the statue to Cornelia, "*mater Gracchorum*," and by the official promotion of Venus Genetrix as never before.

Indeed, Venus had not traditionally been associated with motherhood or maternity; Varro (*Res rustica* 1.1.6) and Macrobius (*Saturnalia* 1.12.12) describe her as a rustic goddess of horticulture and gardens. Her worship and association with motherhood in Augustan Rome emerges directly from her "adoption" by the imperial family. Suzanne Dixon (discussing Suetonius, *Julius* 6) reminds us further of the prominent role played by Venus as *magna mater* of the Julian clan in both Julian and Augustan ideology:

In his funeral oration on his paternal aunt Julia, Julius Caesar praised her ancestry as deriving from kings on the maternal side and the goddess Venus in the paternal line [. . .] On the eve of Pharsalus, Caesar vowed a temple to Venus Victrix (Appian *BC* 2.68). Yet the temple actually erected in the Forum Iulium was to Venus Genetrix, the founder of the Julian house. [. . .] Augustus' temple to Mars Ultor in the Forum Augustum dedicated in 2 BC . . . included a statue of Venus (Ovid, *Tristia* 2.295f). [. . .] The *Aeneid* reinforced the image of Venus as Genetrix, the "Ancestress," the forceful mother pushing her son to his divine destiny and inextricably associating the fortunes of Rome and the Julian house.[21]

The relative "novelty" of Augustus's familial relationship with Venus perhaps goes some way toward explaining its repeated emphasis in the poetry of the period: Vergil draws an explicit line of descent from Venus, through Aeneas, to Julius and Augustus Caesar (*Aeneid* 6.756–807); Horace (*Odes* 4.15.31f.) similarly refers to the genealogical relationship between Venus, Aeneas, and Augustus, and in his *Carmen Saeculare* (50) he associates Venus with Augustus; Propertius (3.4.19f. and 4.1.46f.) repeats this association, which is further echoed in Ovid.

Indeed, Ovid's representation of Augustus as the direct descendant of Venus is a particular area of provocation and play in numerous poems. In his *Fasti* Ovid draws attention to this intimate connection between Augustus and Venus, explicitly inviting the emperor to see the fourth month and the fourth book of the *Fasti*, dedicated to Venus, as the most personally significant part of the calendar and the poem (4.19f.). However, Venus is addressed in the opening line of book 4 not as the *alma mater*, or "nurturing mother," of Augustus or even the Roman people, but as the "mother of the twin Loves" (*alma . . . geminorum mater Amorum*), as Ovid signals that he has in mind not only Venus Genetrix, but also the erotic Venus, "*tenerorum mater Amorum*" and goddess of love and sex. He claims that April, the fourth month, belongs to her (4.13f.), but traditionally the fourth month did *not* belong to Venus. According to the Roman calendars used by Ovid to form the foundation of his *Fasti*, April was neither named after nor especially associated with Venus, so he is required to offer a detailed aetiological and etymological explanation for this assertion; he suggests that April did indeed take its name from Venus—although not from the Latin but rather from the Greek form of her name, Aphrodite, a word which is itself etymologically derived from the Greek word for "sea spray" (4.61f.).[22] He then makes a further tenuous connection between Venus and the month of

April, incorporating the more traditional Roman etymological derivation of *Aprilis* from the Latin *aperire* (to spring open) in his claim that

> nec Veneri tempus, quam ver, erat aptius ullum
> (vere nitent terrae, vere remissus ager;
> nunc herbae rupta tellure cacumina tollunt,
> nunc tumido gemmas cortice palmes agit).
> (4.125–128)

No time was more fitting to Venus than spring:
In spring the earth gleams, in spring the soil is loose;
Now the plants lift pointed shoots pushed up through the soil,
Now the blossom drives the bud through the swelling bark.

In a related celebration of the goddess's associations with reproduction, he also offers an elaborate—and overstated—description of Venus as sovereign of the world:

> illa quidem totum dignissima temperat orbem,
> illa tenet nullo regna minora deo,
> iuraque dat caelo, terrae, natalibus undis,
> perque suos initus continet omne genus.
> (4.91–94)

Indeed, she deservedly rules the whole world;
She owns a kingdom greater than any god,
She gives laws to heaven and earth and her birthplace, the sea,
And through her every species keeps going.

This exaggerated account of Venus's power might seem to offer an enthusiastic tribute to the goddess and to her descendent Augustus (who might more legitimately be said to rule the whole world, own a kingdom greater than any god, and give laws to all). But the implicit source of Venus's universal power and authority in this eulogy is sex.[23] Thus, Ovid reminds his audience that the mother of Aeneas and Augustus is not only Venus Genetrix but also Mater Amoris.[24]

Similarly complicating the maternal ideal of Venus Genetrix as nurturing mother, protective parent, and founder-mother of the Julian line is a relief on the east panel of the Ara Pacis that shows a female figure (presumably) nursing two infants and advertising the privileged status of motherhood in Augustan Rome (see fig. 9.1).

A matronly deity in classicizing drapery sits in dignified posture on her rocky seat. She holds in her arms two babies who reach for her breast, while her lap is filled with fruit and her hair adorned with a wreath of grain and poppies. . . . The woman's physical presence, her posture and garments are evidently intended to invoke many different associations in the viewer. But whether we wish to call this mother goddess Venus, because of the motif of the garment slipping off the shoulder, Ceres, on account of the veil and stalks of grain, or the earth goddess Tellus, because of the landscape and rocky seat, it is immediately obvious that she is a divinity whose domain is growth and fertility.[25]

The wide domain of this goddess is, like that of Ovid's Venus, fertility, reproduction, and motherhood, and although Paul Zanker designates this figure variously as Tellus, Italia, Ceres, and Pax Augusta as well as Venus, he ultimately decides that she is the "mother goddess of Augustan art, whatever we call her."[26] The identification of this maternal deity has challenged generations of archaeologists, art historians, and classicists, but Karl Galinsky has argued persuasively that although the polysemy of this iconographic relief draws variously upon Mother Earth, Ceres, and Pax, it is Venus—as Venus Genetrix, Victrix, and Caesaris—who is unequivocally depicted here.[27] Indeed, even those who argue for an alternate identification of this "mother goddess" allow that the evocation of Venus in the representation is significant. So, Barbette Spaeth argues for a reading of the "mother goddess" panel that strongly points to the identification of the goddess as Ceres, but she allows that, given the unambiguous iconographic connections of this deity with Venus, there is strong evidence to suggest a dual reference here, concluding that "the Ara Pacis figure may be meant to combine features of both Demeter/Ceres and Aphrodite/Venus."[28]

But if the mother goddess whose garment is shown slipping seductively from one shoulder *is* identified as Venus, her status and reputation as goddess of erotic love—as "*mater Amoris*" (*Amores* 3.15.1) and "*tenerorum mater Amorum*" (*Ars amatoria* 1.30)—destabilize her configuration here as an unambiguously respectable image of Augustan motherhood. Indeed, if we look closely at the relief (reminiscent of Ovid's description of Venus as "nurturing mother of the twin Loves"[29]), we can see that one of the two infants on her lap seems to be reaching for her breast and is tugging at her dress, pulling her gown down from her shoulder in the process. A breast exposed by and for a hungry babe is unequivocally positive, a nurturing gesture of maternity. Indeed, this innocent gesture—of a child tugging at the garment of a parent, a motif not seen in Roman art before the Ara Pacis—

is mirrored in the scenes of the imperial family depicted on the south frieze of the Ara Pacis and is later transferred as a motif to Augustan funerary reliefs depicting parents and children.[30]

When this figure is viewed as Venus—even as Venus Genetrix—the erotic implications of "one of the twin Loves" reaching up to expose the goddess of Love's breast are unavoidable. And if we follow Elaine Fantham's suggestion that Ovid's reference in the *Fasti* to Venus as "nurturing mother of the twin Loves" specifically alludes to *Amor* (Affection) and *Cupido* (Desire), then the duality of Venus's representation here can also be read as explicitly figuring a relationship between (maternal) affection and (erotic) desire.[31] From this perspective, we can see the Ara Pacis Venus as yummy mummy, as MILF—confusing the distinctions between maternal and erotic love, fusing the roles of mother and lover.[32]

This tantalizing possibility is further complicated by the suggestion that the "mother goddess" figure on the Ara Pacis looks a lot like Livia, the wife of Augustus and mother of his adopted sons and imperial heirs, the yummy mummy whose marriage to the *princeps* was effected with remarkable haste just three days after she gave birth to her second son, Drusus.[33] The veiled Ara Pacis "Venus" certainly shares not only facial features but also dress, attitude, and expression with the veiled figure (designated S-31) depicted in the procession on the south frieze, and identified through portrait comparison as Livia.[34] What is more, the altar was dedicated on January 30, 9 BCE, Livia's forty-ninth birthday, suggesting that the Ara Pacis was intended to confer some particular honor to her—whether or not we identify the maternal figure here explicitly as Livia herself. Indeed, such identification fits neatly within the design schema and narrative of the Ara Pacis. According to Kleiner, "Nothing was more important to Augustus in the last two decades of the first century BCE than the creation of a dynasty and Livia was at the core of that particular enterprise."[35] Thus, she argues, the preponderance of women—and more particularly, *mothers*—on the Ara Pacis helps to configure a narrative thread that leads us as we walk in procession alongside these mothers and their children toward the future of Rome:

> The narrative that was spun established a lineage for these women and for the sons whom they provided their husbands, male heirs who ensured the continuity of dynasty and Rome. As the procession moves from east to west and along the north and south sides of the altar, it passes from the maternal world to the paternity of men.[36]

It would, of course, be Livia who ultimately provided Augustus with his adopted heir and imperial successor. However, at the time of the commissioning and dedication of the Ara Pacis, the mother whose face would, perhaps, have better fitted the Venus figure in the monument's east panel—and indeed the narrative schema of the altar as a whole—was not Livia but Julia. By 9 BCE, Julia had provided Augustus with two male biological heirs, celebrating (albeit at one remove) his own paternity and thus, it must then have seemed, ensuring the continuity of his dynasty.[37] If the already polysemantic character of the Ara Pacis's *magna mater* includes partial identification with Livia, then it seems not only possible but probable that we are also invited to see Julia represented here, the two babies recalling her own sons, Gaius and Lucius Caesar—in the same grouping of mother and two sons celebrated by Augustus on contemporary coinage.[38] Given the comprehensive destruction of Julia's sculptural portraits later ordered by Augustus in the aftermath of her very public disgrace, it is difficult to make a case that the Venus figure on the Ara Pacis looks particularly like Julia. However, if we take as a model the portraits of the imperial family depicted in the processional frieze that runs along the Ara Pacis, it is clear that the east panel's *magna mater* looks a lot like both Livia *and* Julia. Indeed, Kleiner suggests that here, as in all visual representations of Augustus and his extended family, "all members were depicted as interchangeable. Although not related by blood, Livia, Octavia, and Julia were clones of one another."[39] It would seem that the polysemous identity of the maternal figure on the Ara Pacis calls upon plural, overlapping portraits of mortal no less than immortal mothers, and that Julia is almost certainly one of these.

The back-shadow cast upon Julia's reputation by subsequent public scandal and charges of serial adultery (including punishment under her father's own laws on marriage and morality) has obscured the qualification of this notorious "hot mom" to be taken seriously as a mother; because Julia turned out to be a "bad" wife her status as a "good" mother has been undermined. But the Ara Pacis, with its celebration of mothering, reminds us that Augustan motherhood was ever a site of contestation revealing the tensions and paradoxes inherent in being a mother and a lover.

Augustus's Julian and Papian-Poppaean laws on marriage and adultery introduced measures on one hand to promote legitimate childbearing and motherhood and on the other to criminalize adultery, treating the two together through restrictive legislation and taxation. Ironically, however, one of the effects of this approach toward the legislation of private behaviors

seems to have been the explicit association in Augustan literature and art of illicit sexual *mores* with *matres*—albeit through determined official efforts to draw a clear line between legitimate and illegitimate sexual relations and the reproduction of children and heirs, between recreational and procreational sex.[40] Thus, we see in the literature and art of this period both the idealization and the eroticization of motherhood. We see the fusion and occasional confusion of mother and lover in the many figures of the Augustan *mater amoris*—*magna mater* and founder-mother of the modern MILF and yummy mummy.

NOTES

Thanks to all the sexy mothers I know, and especial thanks to those who have helped to parent this paper: Lisa Hau, Sarah Kennedy, Lauren Petersen, and Pat Salzman-Mitchell.

1. Waldman (2005).

2. Waldman (2005). For an alternate view of modern, or "millennial," motherhood, see Warner (2005), who argues that having a baby refocuses rather than replaces libido and that mothering can be an erotic experience (127–128).

3. Waldman (2005).

4. Rawson (2003), 237.

5. As examined in Dixon (1988), (1991); Foucault (1984); Rawson (2003), (1991); Rouselle (1988); Wiedemann (1989) (although Wiedemann, significantly, has no entry for "mother" or "motherhood" in his index). On the representation of parental vs. marital relationships, Dixon (1988) notices "the tendency . . . in literature from the late Republic on to idealise and sentimentalise conjugal *and* parental relations" (73; emphasis mine).

6. Although a goddess may be allowed the sort of sexual license that would certainly not be permitted a mortal woman.

7. She is also, of course, assimilated to Cleopatra, whose own self-representation as mother and mistress resonates here. See Prudence Jones's essay in this volume.

8. Zanker (1988), 175.

9. In her study of "Women in the Time of Augustus" (2005), Treggiari draws attention to "the prominent position given in [Horace, *Odes* 3.14] to Augustus' closest women associates, and the selection of mothers and the young to represent the population of Rome on this occasion. . . . The imperial family itself is represented by two senior women, both mothers" (131).

10. See Treggiari (2005), 140.

11. See Kleiner (2005), 200–202.

12. Suetonius, *Life of Augustus* 65; Velleius Paterculus, *History of Rome* 2.100.2–

5; Dio Cassius 55.10.12–16; Seneca, *De beneficiis* 6.32.1–2. See also Fantham (2006), 138–146.

13. See Kleiner (2005), 199.

14. See Kleiner (2005), 199.

15. See Zanker (1988), 193–215. See also Prudence Jones's discussion of this statue in this volume.

16. Treggiari (2005), 133.

17. Provocatively, Ovid's Dido also refers to herself as Venus's daughter-in-law (*Heroides* 7.31) and describes Venus, Aeneas's mother, as mother of Loves (*quia mater Amorum / nuda Cytheriacis edita fertur aquis* [*Heroides* 7.59ff.]).

18. According to Oliensis (1997), 305: "Like Creusa [Ascanius's mother], Dido blends the features of mother and bride."

19. Oliensis (1997), 306.

20. *saevus Amor docuit natorum sanguine matrem / commaculare manus; crudelis tu quoque, mater* (*Eclogue* 8.47ff.).

21. Dixon (1988), 74. Indeed, it was during the *ludi Veneris Genetricis*, hosted by Augustus, that the soul of Julius was believed to have achieved *his* divine destiny in his apotheosis (Pliny, *Natural History* 2.93–94); see Johnson (1996), 130.

22. According to Pliny (*Natural History* 35.91), the Temple of Divus Julius dedicated by Augustus in 29 BCE housed a painting of the birth of Venus, where she is emerging from the sea as in Hesiod's account of the birth of Aphrodite, reinforcing this association between the Julian/Augustan Venus and her erotic Greek counterpart. Ovid may or may not have been aware of the false etymology here.

23. Compare *Ars amatoria* 2.480.

24. For a detailed discussion of Ovid's controversial and provocative representation of *Venus Amatoris*, see Johnson (1996), 131–133.

25. Zanker (1988), 173–174, refers to "the many-sided and eclectic iconography of the figure."

26. Zanker (1988), 175. On the contested identity of the "mother goddess" figure depicted on the Ara Pacis, see Strong (1937); Booth (1966); Kleiner (1978); Zanker (1988); de Grummond (1990); Galinsky (1992); Spaeth (1994).

27. See Galinsky (1996), 148–149: "Venus relates best to the dynastic dimension illustrated also by Augustus and his family, and by the presence of Aeneas, Venus's son and the Julian ancestor, on the east side." For the identification of the two side figures that flank the central deity in this panel as representing the celestial and marine aspects of Venus, see Booth (1966); Galinsky (1966), (1969), (1992); Thornton (1983); Spaeth (1994).

28. Spaeth (1994), 77.

29. *Fasti* 4.1–6. Fantham (1998) suggests that "the two Loves are probably a reference to *Amor* (Affection) and *Cupido* (Desire), not the Platonic *Eros* and *Anteros*. Given the representation of Venus with two cupids on a coin of one of Julius Caesar's kinsmen in 94 or 90 BC, and O.'s preoccupation with the Julian Venus . . . , we should not exclude reference to a contemporary cult image familiar to O.'s readers but now lost." Fan-

tham bases her view on the work of Antonie Wlosok (1975) and argues persuasively that Ovid's insistence upon the "duality" of the twin loves here "is specific, distinct from the usual collective of *Erotes* as in Catullus 3.1 (*lugete, o Veneres Cupidinesque*)" (89–90).

30. See Galinsky (1996), 150–151.

31. *Fasti* 4.1–6. Fantham (1998), 89–90 (and see note 29 above).

32. This image also reminds the viewer of the *physicality* of both mothering and sex, and the ways in which both a baby and a lover demand physical intimacy with a woman's body. See also Patricia Salzman-Mitchell's essay in this volume.

33. On the identification of the babies in the east panel see Pollini (1987), 21–28; Rose (1990), 467. See also Zanker (1988). Kleiner (1992) and de Grummond (1990) suggest that the children may be identified as Livia's own children Tiberius and Drusus. Spaeth objects to this identification on the grounds that Livia's "children" were already adults at the time the Ara Pacis was erected (89, n. 207).

34. On the identification of Venus as Livia see Bonnano (1976), 28; Pollini (1987), 100; Kleiner (1992), 98; (2005), 223; and Spaeth (1994), 88.

35. Kleiner (2005), 223.

36. Kleiner (2005), 224.

37. I am grateful to the anonymous reader for the University of Texas Press for making this point to me.

38. See Kleiner (2005), 200–202.

39. Kleiner (2005), 212.

40. On the links between the Ara Pacis and Augustan social policy, see Kleiner (1978), 772–776.

WORKS CITED

Bonnano, Anthony. (1976). *Roman Relief Portraiture to Septimius Severus*. Oxford: Oxford University Press.

Booth, A. (1966). "Venus on the Ara Pacis." *Latomus* 25:873–879.

De Grummond, Nancy. (1990). "The Goddess Peace on the Ara Pacis." *American Journal of Archaeology* 94:663–677.

Dixon, Suzanne. (1988). *The Roman Mother*. London: Routledge.

———. (1991). "The Sentimental Ideal of the Roman Family." In Beryl Rawson, ed., *Marriage, Divorce, and Children in Ancient Rome*, 99–113. Oxford: Oxford University Press.

Fantham, Elaine. (1998). *Ovid: Fasti Book IV*. Cambridge: Cambridge University Press.

———. (2006). *Julia Augusti: The Emperor's Daughter*. London: Routledge.

Foucault, Michel. (1984). *L'histoire de la sexualité*, vol. 3: *Le souci de soi*. Paris: Gallimard.

Galinsky, Karl. (1966). "Venus in a Relief of the Ara Pacis Augustae." *American Journal of Archaeology* 70:223–243.

————. (1969). *Aeneas, Sicily, and Rome.* Princeton: Princeton University Press.

————. (1992). "Venus, Polysemy, and the Ara Pacis Augustae." *American Journal of Archaeology* 96:457–475.

————. (1996). *Augustan Culture.* Princeton: Princeton University Press.

Johnson, Patricia. (1996). "Constructions of Venus in Ovid's *Metamorphoses* V." *Arethusa* 29:125–149.

Kleiner, Diana. (1978). "The Great Friezes of the Ara Pacis Augustae." *Mélanges de l'École français de Rome, Antiquité*: 753–785.

————. (1992). *Roman Sculpture.* New Haven: Yale University Press.

————. (2005). "Semblance and Storytelling in Augustan Rome." In Karl Galinsky, ed., *The Cambridge Companion to the Age of Augustus,* 197–233. Cambridge: Cambridge University Press.

Oliensis, Ellen. (1997). "Sons and Lovers: Sexuality and Gender in Virgil's Poetry." In Charles Martindale, ed., *The Cambridge Companion to Virgil,* 294–311. Cambridge: Cambridge University Press.

Pollini, John. (1987). *The Portraiture of Gaius and Lucius Caesar.* New York: Fordham University Press.

Rawson, Beryl, ed. (1991). *Marriage, Divorce, and Children in Ancient Rome.* Oxford: Oxford University Press.

————. (2003). *Children and Childhood in Roman Italy.* Oxford: Oxford University Press.

Rose, C. Brian. (1990). "Princes and Barbarians on the Ara Pacis." *American Journal of Archaeology* 94:453–467.

Rouselle, Aline. (1988). *Porneia: On Desire and the Body in Antiquity.* Oxford: Oxford University Press.

Spaeth, Barbette. (1994). "The Goddess Ceres on the Ara Pacis Augustae and the Carthage Relief." *American Journal of Archaeology* 98:65–100.

Strong, Eugénie. (1937). "Terra Mater or Italia?" *Journal of Roman Studies* 27:114–126.

Thornton, M. (1983). "Augustan Genealogy and the Ara Pacis." *Latomus* 42:619–628.

Treggiari, Susan. (2005). "Women in the Time of Augustus." In Karl Galinsky, ed., *The Cambridge Companion to the Age of Augustus,* 130–147. Cambridge: Cambridge University Press.

Waldman, Ayelet. (2005). "Truly, Madly, Guiltily." *New York Times,* March 27, I11.

Warner, Judith. (2005). *Perfect Madness: Motherhood in the Age of Anxiety.* New York: Riverhead.

Wiedemann, Thomas. (1989). *Adults and Children in the Roman Empire.* London: Routledge.

Wlosok, Antonie. (1975). "Amor and Cupid." *Harvard Studies in Classical Philology* 79:165–179.

Zanker, Paul. (1988). *The Power of Images in the Age of Augustus.* Ann Arbor: University of Michigan Press.

[TEN]

Per hunc utero quem linquis nostro

MOTHERS IN FLAVIAN EPIC

Antony Augoustakis

In the three epic poems of the Flavian period (Valerius Flaccus's *Argonautica*, Statius's *Thebaid*, and Silius Italicus's *Punica*),[1] the dichotomy between such concepts as Roman and non-Roman (barbarian), Greek and non-Greek, same and other is negotiated from the perspective of an idealized cosmopolitanism, a transformation concomitant with the expansion of the borders of the empire. Whereas in Vergil and Ovid the epic narrative is steered toward the foundation of a center in Rome, in the heart of Italy, the Flavian poets are rather preoccupied with the confrontation of other, marginal sites outside the Italian peninsula (Colchis, Thebes, Carthage, and Saguntum, respectively).

In this study, I shall address the role of some "*other*," non-Roman mothers in Flavian epic poetry and explore the transformed manifestations of motherhood through the representation of otherness. As we shall see, mothers are given a prominent role in these narratives, either as destructive powers, possessed by bacchic frenzy, who undermine the predominant male ideological code, or as a constructive apparatus, who affirm and abet the achievements of the male protagonists toward the manufacture of an imperial ideology. The manipulation of women's actions in these poems highlights the fluctuating mobility of both gender and cultural hierarchies and speaks to the construction of Romanness from an often idealized and utopian perspective.

SILIUS ITALICUS'S *PUNICA*

Let us first look at the city of Saguntum in the *Punica*, with whose siege Silius opens his monumental historical epic on the Second Punic War,

from the beginning of the hostilities to the victorious battle at Zama and Hannibal's annihilating defeat (218–202 BCE).[2] In the poem, Saguntum is the first city attacked by the Carthaginian general. This Spanish city is a Greco-Roman colony that, as the poet explains from the very beginning, should not—and indeed could not—be exclusively called Roman. Its inhabitants descend from Greek colonists, from Zacynthus (an island in the Ionian Sea) and Hercules' homonymous friend, who dies onsite in Spain, as the poet informs us (*Pun.* 1.274–290); the Zacynthians then subsequently merged with immigrants from the Italian city of Ardea (*Pun.* 1.291–295). It is through this amalgamation, then, that the Saguntines came into existence.

What makes this poem especially intriguing in this discussion of motherhood and identity in Flavian epic is the spin that Silius gives to one particular episode, otherwise well documented in the historical record: through her instrument—the Fury Tisiphone—Juno inspires a frenzy in the Saguntine mothers and pushes them to commit mass suicide after killing many of their male kinsmen (*Pun.* 2.526–680). In this way Juno—the fervent supporter of her protégé, Hannibal, throughout the poem—puts an end to the prolonged siege of Saguntum and facilitates the victorious outcome for Carthage.

Before this massacre of epic proportions, the reader is presented with a remarkable scene, where the Saguntines—confronted with death—burn the heirlooms that once accompanied their ancestors from faraway Zacynthus in Greece and Ardea in Italy, and thus destroy any evidence of their present, past, and future:

> certatim structus surrectae molis ad astra
> in media stetit urbe rogus; portantque trahuntque
> longae pacis opes quaesitaque praemia dextris,
> Callaico vestes distinctas matribus auro
> armaque Dulichia proavis portata Zacyntho
> et prisca advectos Rutulorum ex urbe penates.
> huc, quicquid superest captis, clipeosque simulque
> infaustos iaciunt enses et condita bello
> effodiunt penitus terrae gaudentque superbi
> victoris praedam flammis donare supremis.
> (*PUN.* 2.599–608)

A pyre, zealously built, stood in the middle of the city, whose height rose to the stars; they drag and carry the wealth of a long peace and the prizes

won by valor, that is the clothes embroidered by the mothers with Gallician gold, the Dulichian weapons brought by their ancestors from Zacynthus, and the household gods carried across the sea from the ancient city of the Rutulians. Here the conquered people throw whatever is left to them, and their shields too and their cursed swords. And from the bowels of the earth, they dig up what they had hidden during the war and they rejoice in giving to the last fire the booty of the arrogant victor.[3]

Silius particularly focuses on the act of burning, that is, on the destruction of both works of peace, such as the clothing produced by women, and of weapons, carried by men in war. In addition, the poet underscores the conflagration of Saguntine identity, namely the burning of the images of the homeland gods, tokens that once defined the arrival of the newcomers and the establishment of the new city in Spain. The burning at the instigation of the Erinys constitutes the annulment of the Saguntines' recognition of their identity as either "Ardeans" or "Zacynthians."[4] They become a hybrid nation now, just before death. The Dionysiac frenzy will result in a Stoic, Roman, death which nevertheless wipes out the Saguntines' ties with their Roman and subsequently Greek *patriae*.

In their stirring of the earth's bowels, the Saguntine mothers reverse the act of founding a city, as we know it from the story of the foundation of Carthage, for instance: in *Punica* 2.410–411, Silius informs us that Dido and her companions dig up the earth and discover the head of a horse, a symbol of the city's future invincibility in war (*ostentant caput effossa tellure repertum / bellatoris equi atque omen clamore salutant*, "having dug up the earth, they display the found head of a fighting horse and they greet the omen with a shout"). At the same time, however, the mothers' act constitutes a jarring, public reversal of the ritual of burial; this is a funeral pyre without subsequent burial, without hope for the future rest of souls that is normally ensured by the return of the dead to Mother Earth. This pyre then can itself be read as the Saguntines' tomb, since there will be no actual burial after their suicide and the burning of the city. This is a "tomb," however, in which Roman identity is incinerated. In hybrid Saguntum, this becomes not a story of founding, but rather one of utter destruction. The eradication of anything that reminds the citizens of their origins is only one step away from what occurs next. This obliteration of their entire material inheritance progresses to the utter devastation of family ties. The public and the private merge into one and the same.

For instance, the death of a pair of twin brothers, Eurymedon and Ly-

cormas, adds to the confusion created by the bacchic madness and contributes further to the annihilation of memory and identity:

> vos etiam primo gemini cecidistis in aevo,
> Eurymedon fratrem et fratrem mentite Lycorma,
> cuncta pares, dulcisque labor sua nomina natis
> reddere et in vultu genetrici stare suorum.
> iam fixus iugulo culpa te solverat ensis,
> Eurymedon, inter miserae lamenta senectae,
> dumque malis turbata parens deceptaque visis
> "quo ruis? huc ferrum" clamat "converte, Lycorma,"
> ecce simul iugulum perfoderat ense Lycormas.
> sed magno "quinam, Eurymedon, furor iste?" sonabat
> cum planctu geminaeque notis decepta figurae
> funera mutato revocabat nomine mater,
> donec transacto tremebunda per ubera ferro
> tunc etiam ambiguos cecidit super inscia natos.
> (*PUN.* 2.636–649)

Also you, twin brothers, fell in your prime, Eurymedon and Lycormas, each an exact likeness of the other, alike in every point. It was a sweet toil for your mother to recognize her sons by name and to decide who is who, by looking at each son's face. Now the sword that had pierced your neck, had already freed you from the blame, Eurymedon, amidst the lament of your poor old mother; and while the parent, disturbed by the sorrow and deceived by whom she thought she had seen, exclaims: "Where do you rush? Turn your blade here, Lycormas,"—behold! Lycormas had already stabbed his throat with the sword. But she cried with a big groan: "What kind of fury is this, Eurymedon?," and deceived by the likeness of the twins, the mother kept calling back the dead by their wrong names, until, with a sword driven through her quivering breasts, she fell over her sons, whom even then she could not distinguish.

The mother is unable to identify her sons properly and thus annuls the ancestral Roman custom of *conclamatio*, the calling of the dead person's name three times, for it is futile in this case. Although the poet addresses such deeds of apparent bravery as *infelix gloria* ("pitiable glory," 2.613) and *laudanda monstra* ("praiseworthy monstrosities," 2.650), the result of the mass suicide remains dubious: the outcome is "scorned by the unfair gods" (*iniustis neglecta deis*, 2.657). As Alison Keith rightly points out, "Silius both

praises the Saguntines for their fidelity . . . and abhors the carnage with its overtones of civil discord."[5]

What we witness here is the Saguntines' effort to delete their identity by burning, and killing, reminders of their city's former self. Destructive motherhood operates on the level of the relationship between colony and *metropolis*; Saguntum expunges her association with the Roman state, since Rome herself, the mother *polis* for Saguntum and a staunch ally before the siege, is conspicuously absent from Saguntum's ordeal. As a result of internal conflict and disagreement among the chief Roman officers at the time, Saguntum is effectively abandoned by Rome. A reflection of this civil conflict can be seen in the instances of destructive motherhood examined above, mothers killing their offspring in a bacchic frenzy.

Here in the second book of the seventeen-book poem, the *cosmos* of the *Punica* is threatened by the same chaotic powers that pervade the nefarious world of Statius's epic landscape, as we shall see next. The women's centralized, public, and yet marginal status acutely interrogates what true Romanness betokens. While it is found lacking in the center, old-fashioned Romanness may be situated in the margins. Rome cannot rise to the circumstance by protecting Saguntum and by dealing with Hannibal effectively; therefore, as a consequence of the lack of Roman *virtus* in the center of the empire, Saguntum emerges as the city that teaches Rome a lesson in *pietas* and *virtus* through the mass suicide.

And yet at the end of the Saguntine episode the poet undercuts any such easy conclusion. Is the Spanish city really setting an example of a city in the periphery that is conspicuous for its Romanness? The chief Saguntine mother-heroine in this scene, Tiburna, and her Saguntine companions are in truth silent; their voice is not their own but instead on loan from the fury, Tisiphone. Therefore, just as Saguntum itself becomes a monument of *fides* for future generations, so too does the act of her people to obliterate any traces of what is tantamount to their former identity: they are no longer Greeks or Romans, they have become Saguntines, and such an act sharply emphasizes the ineffective control that Rome exercises on its subjects at the time. What the poet stresses at the end of the second book is the fact that the Romans ought to search for the signification of *Romanitas* and abandon their inertia; the need for a new spin in the Roman center conspicuously emerges as an important issue in the first ten books of the poem, culminating in the disastrous battle at Cannae, where the Roman army is annihilated. There is need for a new, effective general to undertake the long war. Only after Scipio is sanctioned as the sole capable conqueror of Hannibal does Rome rise to the height of her glory.

Saguntum's silenced existence will speak volumes in the remainder of the *Punica* as the city becomes exemplary for her hybridity and unique nature as an *urbs* in the periphery that strives for her own identity, away from the big centers of either Rome or Carthage. Emphasis on the bacchant (m)others-murderers reflects on what we could call Silius's "poetics of defeat." It is from this chaotic and civil war–like narrative that Rome is going to emerge as an idealized entity, destined to lead the world's future. The "foreign" mothers of Saguntum, a city from the periphery, are now teaching true Romanness to the Romans in the center of the empire.[6]

STATIUS'S *THEBAID*

Although Rome emerges victorious from her struggle with Hannibal at the end of the *Punica*, Statius—an epicist contemporary to Silius—opts for a different route, by means of a mythological epic on the Theban *oikos* of Oedipus's offspring. In the *Thebaid*, Statius recounts the civil war between the two sons of Oedipus for the throne of Thebes: Eteocles, the incumbent king, who refuses to alternate with his brother, and Polynices, the exile, who finds refuge and alliance in the court of the Argive king, Adrastus. The struggle for power comes to a horrendous conclusion, as the two siblings kill each other on the battlefield.

It is intriguing, however, that Statius delays the battle between the two brothers until the eleventh book, paying attention in the meantime to the periphery rather than the center of the action. A long digression occupies the central books of the poem (from the end of book 4 through the end of book 6), during which Hypsipyle, former queen of Lemnos, narrates—for the Argive army's "entertainment"—another epic story, namely, the murder of the Lemnian husbands by their wives and the subsequent stop of the Argonauts at the nefarious island.[7]

In Hypsipyle's narrative, the poet exploits the Lemnian woman's otherness as a foreigner. For instance, the adjective *Lemnias* is extensively used to point to Hypsipyle's odd status as a nurse in the Nemean palace, an exile from her former *patria*, Lemnos (*Theb.* 4.775, 5.29, 5.500, 5.588). First and foremost, then, the Lemnian queen is presented to the reader as a dislodged mother with misplaced affections: after the Lemnian massacre, when as a result of a punishment from Venus, the Lemnian women kill the entire male population on the island, Hypsipyle is proclaimed the queen of the disturbed matriarchal society, even though she helped her father, Thoas, escape unscathed; when the truth about this rescue is uncovered, she is sep-

arated from her children and by extension her country, though she is still identified as *Lemnias* and *mater* throughout the narrative. Hypsipyle's task in Nemea is to tend to Opheltes, the baby son of King Lycurgus, and to lull him into sleep, to nurse him as a mother does, and to protect him against the dangers hidden in the Nemean landscape. Her forgetfulness, however, turns Hypsipyle into a "lost" (m)other, who chooses an unreliable proxy, *tellus*, for the completion of a task that should have been her own, and thus perpetuates the horror of death and destruction that haunts her past:

> at puer in gremio vernae telluris et alto
> gramine nunc faciles sternit procursibus herbas
> in vultum nitens, caram modo lactis egeno
> nutricem plangore ciens iterumque renidens
> et teneris meditans verba inluctantia labris.
> (*THEB.* 4.786–790)

> But the boy in the bosom of the vernal earth, the lush herbage, now butts and levels the soft grasses with his forward plunges, now calling for his dear nurse, crying thirsty of milk; and again he smiles and endeavors for words that struggle with his tender lips.[8]

Because Hypsipyle leaves Opheltes alone and untended, a huge serpent is subsequently able to kill him. The heroine fails in her role as a nurse because when she meets the army of Argives, she hastens to quench their thirst by leading them to a stream nearby, abandoning the baby in the process.

Hypsipyle's ambivalent status of foreigner and exile gives her the freedom to recount her toils and weave a story that lulls the Argives into a metaphorical sleep, during which they forget the purpose of their expedition. Hypsipyle's narrative, however, is transformed into a story of civil conflict, foreshadowing the upcoming war against Thebes: the Lemnian women kill their husbands and Hypsipyle saves her father, but when she is discovered, she is sent into exile and forced to abandon the children she begot from Jason.

To be sure, Hypsipyle paradoxically became an alien to her native environment by transgressing the already transgressive rules set by the other Lemnian women. The poet creates a version of Hypsipyle that defies any norm or categorization. At the outset of the digression in book 4, Statius associates Hypsipyle, as she tends the baby Opheltes, with a foreign goddess, the mother of the gods, who gives orders to the Curetes for the nursing of Jove:

> . . . qualis Berecyntia mater,
> dum parvum circa iubet exultare Tonantem
> Curetas trepidos; illi certantia plaudunt
> orgia, sed magnis resonat vagitibus Ide.
> (*THEB.* 4.782–785)

> . . . like Cybele, while she bids the trembling Curetes dance around the
> infant Thunderer; they sound their mystic cymbals in competition, yet
> still the baby's mighty wails resound around Ide.

Just as he did for Thrace, Lemnos, and Thebes, so Statius also casts a mae-
nadic shadow over the Nemean landscape from the outset, this time as the
place of the baby's death, an event to be remembered by a festival not coinci-
dentally called *trieteris* (4.729), a noun appropriate for the cult of Bacchus.

Most importantly, the didactic story narrated by Hypsipyle translates
into the unsuccessful, wickedly vicious world of the poem. Hypsipyle remains an exile, and the Argives' first stop in Nemea becomes just a first test
of and taste for the war at Thebes that will result in the permanent alienation of the two peoples, the Thebans and the Argives, leading to the perpetuation of an endless war, now and in the future, with the attack of the
Epigonoi, the next generation of Peloponnesian warriors that will attack
Thebes. Indeed, the female narrator's own identity is blurred, as Hypsipyle
hastened to save her father, while at the same time she seemingly erased
any ties with her own family: even on Lemnos, Hypsipyle had been in reality an "exile," a female who does not comply with the behavior of the rest
of the female population but who is, rather, marginalized when she is portrayed saving her father from the slaughter.

Hypsipyle's fixation with the narrative of civil war crimes alienates her
from her own gender, as she is presented at odds with womanhood itself.
Consider, for instance, how she highlights the description of the burning of
her father's weapons and garments:

> ipsa quoque arcanis tecti in penetralibus alto
> molior igne pyram, sceptrum super armaque patris
> inicio et notas regum velamina vestes,
> ac prope maesta rogum confusis crinibus asto
> ense cruentato, fraudemque et inania busta
> plango metu, si forte premant, cassumque parenti
> omen et hac dubios leti precor ire timores.
> (*THEB.* 5.313–319)

I too in the secret recesses of my house build a high-flaming pyre and cast on it my father's scepter and weapons and his well-known garments, the dress of kings. In sadness with disordered hair and bloody sword I stand nearby and fearfully lament the fraud, the empty mound, hoping to cover up. And I pray that the omen bring no harm to my father and that doubting fears of his death be so discharged.

In this scene, Statius fuses two important intertexts: from Vergil, in particular Dido's preparation of her own funeral pyre in *Aeneid* 4;[9] and from Lucan, specifically Cornelia's preparation of a pyre-cenotaph for Pompey, in *De bello civili* 9, even though the Roman general had already been burned and buried in Egypt.[10] Like Cornelia, Hypsipyle performs an empty ritual, and just like Dido, the Lemnian woman brings about her own downfall, by means of a fraud.[11] At the same time, however, as Joanne Brown has observed, Hypsipyle's false lamentation for Thoas calls into question her reliability as a narrator.[12] How are we then to believe Hypsipyle's lamentation for Opheltes as a sincere expression of motherhood? In the perverted world of the *Thebaid*, no narrative is impervious to the *nefas* that looms large over the Argive, Theban, and Nemean landscapes. Ultimately, Hypsipyle cannot escape the foreboded doom. She brings about Opheltes' death, unintentionally, just like the Lemnian mothers who were possessed by Tisiphone and Venus when they were committing their crimes.

Moreover, Hypsipyle's careless mothering of the baby can be traced back to her unwilling impregnation by Jason. After the story of the Lemnian massacre and the saving of her father, Thoas, Hypsipyle narrates at length the stay of the Argonauts on the infamous island. The Argonauts' influence on the women seems favorable in the beginning, as the advent of the male warriors coincides with the reinstitution of gender hierarchies on the island, boundaries that had been previously transgressed through the slaughter of the male population. The female figures, once out of their *sexus*, are now reconstructed: *rediit sexus* ("our sex returned to our hearts," *Theb.* 5.397). The threat of matriarchy is safely closeted for the time being. And yet even when the "natural order" is restored, Hypsipyle fashions herself as a dislocated person. Although previously a virgin,[13] when the slaughter began, she now loses her innocence to Jason and is impregnated by him:

> cineres furiasque meorum
> testor ut externas non sponte aut crimine taedas
> attigerim (scit cura deum), etsi blandus Iason
> virginibus dare vincla nouis . . .

iam nova progenies partusque in vota soluti,
et non speratis clamatur Lemnos alumnis.
nec non ipsa tamen, thalami monimenta coacti,
enitor geminos, duroque sub hospite mater
nomen avi renovo;
(*THEB.* 5.454–457, 461–465)

By the ashes and the avenging ghosts of my own kin, I swear—the
gods care and know—that by no will of mine and guiltless I became a
stranger's wife, though Jason used his charm to ensnare young virgins
. . . Now comes new progeny and births to answer prayer. Lemnos is loud
with unhoped-for children. I too with the rest bring forth twins, memori-
als of a forced bed though they be, and made a mother by my rough guest
I revive their grandfather's name.

Words such as *alumnus*, applied to Hypsipyle's offspring, remind us of
similar use in the case of Opheltes, who is at this very moment in the dangerous lap of *tellus* (*Theb.* 4.786–787). Hypsipyle describes her reluctance to
enter into a relationship with Jason, based on her knowledge of subsequent
events.[14] The Argonauts soon leave, while she is forced into exile. Repetition of the past proves dangerous; the naming of Jason's child after Thoas
is a stark reminder of Hypsipyle's hidden truth about her father. Substitution betokens an aborted renewal and a fresh start doomed to failure. And
indeed, a new beginning for the island, a renovation of gender hierarchies,
has failed anew.

Hypsipyle's actual infatuation with Jason is evident in her reunion
with her sons, Thoas and Euneos (*Theb.* 6.343). Her first reaction is cold,
but when she recognizes them as the true offspring of Jason, she completely
changes her attitude toward them:

illa velut rupes inmoto saxea visu
haeret et expertis non audet credere divis.
ut vero et vultus et signa Argoa relictis
ensibus atque umeris amborum intextus Iason,
cesserunt luctus, turbataque munere tanto
corruit, atque alio maduerunt lumina fletu.
(*THEB.* 5.723–728)

She like a stony rock, with a gaze unmoved, does not react nor does she
dare to believe the gods she knows well. But when she recognized their
faces and the signs of Argo on the swords left behind and Jason's name

interwoven on their shoulders, her grief departed and collapsed disturbed by such great gift; her eyes became wet by other tears.

Finally, Hypsipyle's transformation from an impassionate and compassionate narrator into a stone is memorialized also in the ekphrasis on Opheltes' tomb, where the nurse now becomes the object of the narrative itself:

> stat saxea moles,
> templum ingens cineri, rerumque effictus in illa
> ordo docet casus: fessis hic flumina
> monstrat Hypsipyle Danais, hic reptat flebilis infans,
> hic iacet.
> (*THEB.* 6.242–246)

There stands a mass of stone, a great temple for the ashes, and therein a sculptured series tells the story: here is Hypsipyle showing the stream to the weary Danai, here crawls the poor baby, here he lies dead.

Hypsipyle is transformed from mobile to static, from narrator to the object of the narrative, from woman to marble, from animate to inanimate. This portrayal of Hypsipyle in stone highlights the affinity of the Lemnian woman with Niobe, a Theban heroine who is metamorphosed into stone—a rock—after the loss of her offspring.[15] Even though Hypsipyle casts herself as someone who can easily dupe the rest of the Lemnian women by pretending to burn and bury her father in book 6, the poet fixes the heroine on a real tomb, of her nursling Opheltes. Statius transfers the heroine's former mobility to the eternal flow of the *flumina*, as if Hypsipyle had merged into the landscape of Nemea forever.

Through the anaphora of *hic*, we are left only with some pointers of Hypsipyle's former presence in the poem; meaning is generated through silence, a mute stillness that nevertheless speaks volumes. The transformation of Hypsipyle into stone completes the process: the queen of Lemnos from her conspicuous position as the narrator now becomes part of the story, failed motherhood memorialized in verse and in marble.

VALERIUS'S *ARGONAUTICA*

I would like to conclude by addressing the importance of polarities such as center and periphery for the culture and society of Domitianic

Rome, by way of Valerius Flaccus's Roman *Argonautica*.[16] Valerius's version of Hypsipyle's saga is quite different from Statius's rather ominous narrative in *Thebaid* 4–6. Hypsipyle's piety in saving her father is stressed, as well as her willingness to bear offspring to Jason, as opposed to Statius's strong language of Hypsipyle being forced to yield and marry the best of the Argonauts, which we saw above.

> praecipueque ducis casus mirata requirit
> Hypsipyle, quae fata trahant, quae regis agat vis
> aut unde Haemoniae molem ratis: unius haeret
> adloquio et blandos paulatim colligit ignes,
> iam non dura toris Veneri nec iniqua reversae
> et deus ipse moras spatiumque indulget amori.
> (ARG. 2.351–356)

> And most of all, Hypsipyle in awe inquires about the leader's fortunes, which fates draw him, the power of which king drives him forth, or when comes the mass of the Haemonian ship: she clings upon his words and slowly she gathers in the sweet flames, no longer opposing the beds of Venus and well disposed toward the return of the goddess; even the god himself likes the delay and allows space for the love affair.[17]

Through an aversion to repeating the Aeneas–Dido encounter from *Aeneid* 4, Valerius fashions Hypsipyle as a willing and conscious participant in the Argonautic saga; she is part of the story, a story in which she happily acts as a helper of Jason's progress toward his *telos*. As Debra Hershkowitz has noted, "Hypsipyle [does] not seem to harbour any guilt over losing her long-protected virginity to Jason."[18]

By a striking contrast to what Statius chooses to do—memorializing Hypsipyle in an ekphrasis that tells Opheltes' story—Valerius presents Hypsipyle as the creator of an artifact instead, a cloak for Jason described in an ekphrasis telling her own story:

> . . . chlamydem textosque labores
> illic servati genitoris conscia sacra
> pressit acu currusque pios: stant saeva paventum
> agmina dantque locum; viridi circum horrida tela
> silva tremit; mediis refugit pater anxius umbris . . .
> tunc ensem notumque ferens insigne Thoantis
> "accipe," ait "bellis mediae ut pulvere pugnae

sit comes, Aetnaei genitor quae flammea gessit
dona dei, nunc digna tuis adiungier armis.
i, memor, i, terrae quae vos amplexa quieto
prima sinu, refer et domitis a Colchidos oris
vela, per hunc utero quem linquis Iasona nostro."
(*ARG.* 2.409–413, 418–424)

. . . a tunic with a woven handiwork. There she has embroidered with a
needle the ceremony, witness of her father's rescue, and the pious char-
iot: the savage group of the Lemnians stand in fear and allow her to pass;
all around in green thread, the horrified forest trembles; in the middle of
the shades the father seeks refuge, in agony . . . Then bringing the sword,
with the well-known emblem of Thoas: "Take this," she said, "that it may
be your companion in war and in the dust where the battle is the thick-
est, the fiery gifts of the god of Aetna which my father bore, now worthy
to be worn together with your weapons. Go now, go, and remember the
land, which first embraced you in her quiet bosom! And from the shores
of Colchis, once you conquer them, bring back your sails here, in the
name of this Jason, whom you leave in our womb."

The queen's "generosity" in letting the epic hero pursue the *telos* of his
trip could be considered unique, inasmuch as it is an anti-Didoesque moment in the narrative. "Hypsipyle is the Sense to Dido's Sensibility, and,
in contrast to Dido's increasingly barbaric character, she is presented as a
Romanized daughter and wife," as Hershkowitz correctly observes.[19] In
contrast to Statius's account, Hypsipyle's gifts here are seen to be the very
items that she commits to the fire in the *Thebaid*: the clothes of her father
(*chlamydem, Arg.* 2.409 ~ *notas regum velamina vestes, Theb.* 5.315) and his
weapons (*ensem, Arg.* 2.418 ~ *armaque patris, Theb.* 5.314). In Valerius's reconstruction of the story, Hypsipyle gives expression to her act of *pietas*
by embroidering the saving of Thoas on the cloak. In this creation of the
chlamys, Hypsipyle finds recourse to the power of ekphrasis, rather than
becoming part of it herself. Instead, what she heavily underscores in her
farewell speech is the *pignus amoris*, her offspring, which will be an in-
delible mark on Jason's future as a father of a little Jason.[20] Whereas Statius's Hypsipyle calls upon the ashes and the Furies (*cineres furiasque meo-
rum testor, Theb.* 5.454–455), Valerius's heroine holds a much more powerful
"tool," *per hunc utero quem linquis Iasona nostro*, whereby she directs us
with an outlook toward the future, not with a foot stuck in the abomina-
ble past.

Placing the *Argonautica* in the middle of the Vespasianic regime, since the poem was probably finished around or before 79 CE,[21] it is tempting to read this scene in the light of the hopes placed on the new *gens* that rules Rome, namely Vespasian and his two sons, the positive rebirth of the city and the empire after the decadence of the Julio-Claudians. In Valerius's utopia of a Roman Jason civilizing the barbarians, the public facet of motherhood is encouragingly abetting the forces of imperialism, thus reviving those good ol' Roman values. And yet, the problematization of motherhood in Flavian epic poetry, as we saw in Silius and certainly Statius, in the later years of the Flavian rule goes beyond the confines of a poetically recreated mythological and historical past and is inextricably intertwined with the anxieties of a male regime that has no prominent wives or mothers to display, a sharp contrast to the Julio-Claudian house. Vespasian does not remarry after the death of Domitilla, having secured succession; Domitian and Domitia Longina lose their baby son early on, the only *spes regni*, while Domitian himself does not attempt adoption until late in his reign, and then quite unsuccessfully.[22]

In surviving Flavian art, motherhood seems completely elided, an unimportant theme when compared, for instance, to the Augustan imagery of fertility and abounding motherhood in the Ara Pacis.[23] Instead we find symbols of virginity, of Minerva especially, the protectress of the emperor (punishing Arachne in the frieze of the Forum Transitorium), or of Roma in Amazonian dress, or other personified virtues. Cancelleria Relief B portrays Vespasian's *adventus* to the city in 70 CE, with Domitian on his side. On the left side of the fragmented relief, the viewer's gaze is directed toward the personification of Roma, in Amazonian costume, accompanied by one of the Vestals. In relief A, Domitian is the central figure, in either a *profectio*, setting out for war in the frontiers of the empire, or an *adventus*, a victorious return from his war against the Chatti (fig. 10.1). The last of the Flavians is accompanied by Minerva and Mars on the left and an Amazonian figure (possibly Roma) on the right who appears to be urging him on. Whereas literature problematizes the relationship between virginity, *pudicitia*, and the dangers of motherhood, art elides the latter, refocusing the lens solely on the former.

In their epic poems, the Flavian poets construct an idealized discourse on gender and ethnicity that aims at destabilizing stereotypical boundaries. In such reconstructions, Roman sameness and non-Roman otherness seem-

FIGURE 10.1. Profectio *of Domitian, frieze from the Cancelleria Reliefs, ca. 93–95 CE. Museo Gregoriano Profano, Vatican Museums, Vatican State. Photo: Scala/Art Resource, NY, ART80416.*

ingly converge, while simultaneously these same boundaries are reshaped from the male perspective of the epic diction. Epic narrative traditionally celebrates the κλέα ἀνδρῶν ("glories of men"), and thus the Flavian epicists expectedly hasten to satisfy the generic expectations for a marginal, abject female voice. I believe the conclusion can be drawn that the construction of Roman identity ultimately rests upon the absorption of elements from outside that bear the marks both of the radically different—the monstrous—and of Rome's truest self, that is, its idealized virtues and merits. The Flavian epicists then subvert by deconstructing or espouse by helping build a utopia, where boundaries are reset or destabilized according to the authorial vision of the empire's future or lack thereof.

Through this quick overview of the Flavian epic landscape, I hope to trigger further interest in a period fascinating in its own right from our modern perspective—a big empire that reaches its peak, with a growing anxiety concerning its future, and a profound questioning of the Vergilian aphorism *sine fine.* Upon this multifaceted tableau, the poets embroider several female figures as both compelling and captivating women, and unexpected and yet predictable (m)others.

NOTES

This article draws on material presented in greater detail in Augoustakis (2010), with some additions.

1. On similar preoccupations in Statius's unfinished *Achilleid*, see Augoustakis (forthcoming).

2. On the episode of Saguntum's siege in Silius, see for example, von Albrecht (1964), 25–28, 55–62, 181–183; Vessey (1974); Küppers (1986); McGuire (1997), 207–219; Ripoll (1998), 406–411; and Bernstein (2008), 179–187.

3. The Latin text of the *Punica* comes from Delz's Teubner edition (1987); translations are taken from Duff's Loeb edition (1934), with modifications.

4. *Pace* Bernstein (2008), 182, who sees an indirect assertion of the dominance of Rutulian identity in the mass suicide.

5. See Keith (2000), 92; cf. also: "His [the poet's] attribution of praise and blame in the episode also demonstrates an unfaltering commitment to the 'natural' hierarchy of gender in the structure of Roman epic warfare, for the glorious achievement of the Saguntines is inspired by Hercules, who sends Loyalty to fortify the citizens out of concern for the city he founded . . . , while their unheroic mutual slaughter is provoked by Tisiphone" (92–93).

6. Cf. Spentzou (2008): "Late first-century A.D. Rome was a thriving and bewildering empire with 'Others' that form a disturbing, festering but also challenging and liberating part of its hegemony. As forms of social and political order are opened to revision in Silius's Rome, there are opportunities for new identifications, such as Silius's Hannibal" (144).

7. The Hypsipyle episode has received a lot of critical attention in the past few years; see, for instance, Dominik (1994), 54–63; Ganiban (2007), 71–95; and McNelis (2007), 88–93. For its relationship with Valerius Flaccus's version of the slaughter in Lemnos in *Arg.* 2.77–427 (and Apollonius's *Arg.* 1.601–909), see Vessey (1985); Aricò (1991); and Gibson (2004).

8. The Latin text of the *Thebaid* comes from Hill's Brill edition (1996); translations are taken from Shackleton Bailey's Loeb edition (2003), with modifications.

9. On Hypsipyle as Dido, see Ganiban (2007), 86–88.

10. On Cornelia's cenotaph of Pompey in Lucan's *De bello civili* 9, see Augoustakis (2011).

11. Nugent (1996) explores the role of the absent father Thoas in Hypsipyle's narrative and links it to that ever-present, poetic father figure in Statius's poetry, Vergil: "She would have no narrative without him; but she would have no narrative with him" (71).

12. Brown (1994), 122–123.

13. Consider also Hypsipyle's representation of her fearful maidenhood, when she refers to her betrothed Gyas, one of the slaughtered Lemnian sons: *fortemque, timebam / quem desponsa, Gyan vidi lapsare cruentae / vulnere Myrmidones* ("and strong

Gyas, whom I was fearing as his fiancée, I saw fall by the stroke of bloody Myrmidone";
Theb. 5.223–224).

14. *Contra* Dominik (1997), who claims that Hypsipyle's refusal to submit to
erotic, baser passions inspired by Venus demonstrates "the nobility of her character and
shows that she is morally superior to the other Lemnian women" (46).

15. The Nemeans accompany the burial of Opheltes with a dirge, a *carmen* reported to have been sung by. Niobe in the Phrygian manner at the funeral of her children (*Theb.* 6.124–125). On Niobe in Ovid's *Metamorphoses* 6 (a mere coincidence?) and
Statius, see Rosati (2005), 159–160.

16. On Valerius's Hypsipyle, see Hershkowitz (1998), 136–146; Schenk (1999),
341–387; and most recently Clare (2004).

17. The Latin text of the *Argonautica* comes from Liberman's most recent Budé
edition (2003); translations are mine.

18. Hershkowitz (1998), 140; cf. also her discussion of the ekphrasis on the cloak,
where she interprets the myth of Ganymede as "symbolizing both Hypsipyle's 'rape' of
young (virgin) Jason (and, likewise, Jason's 'rape' of the young virgin Hypsipyle) and
Jason's forced departure from Lemnos on Jovian business" (142–143, n. 143).

19. Hershkowitz (1998), 146. Also cf. Apollonius Rhodius's description of Jason's
cloak before he meets Hypsipyle, a work of Athena there (*Argonautica* 1.721–768).

20. Cf. Deidamia's similar address and use of the deictic prayer in Statius's *Achilleid* 1.952–954, coupled with the emphasis on the possibilities of Achilles becoming a
father via a foreign woman also: *attamen hunc, quem maesta mihi solacia linquis, / hunc
saltem sub corde tene et concede precanti / hoc solum, pariat ne quid tibi barbara coniunx*
("But this boy, whom you leave with me as a sad comfort, this boy at least hold in your
heart and grant this to me begging you, this thing only, let no barbarian wife bear a
child for you").

21. On the chronology, see most recently Stover (2008).

22. See Newlands (2006), 203.

23. See Margaret Woodhull's essay, which follows.

WORKS CITED

Aricò, Giuseppe. (1991). "La vicenda di Lemno in Stazio e Valerio Flacco." In Matthias
Korn and Hans Jurgen Tschiedel, eds., *Ratis omnia vincet: Untersuchungen zu den
Argonautica des Valerius Flaccus*, 197–210. Hildesheim: Olms.
Augoustakis, Antony. (2010). *Motherhood and the Other: Fashioning Female Power in
Flavian Epic.* Oxford: Oxford University Press.
———. (2011). "*Sine funeris ullo ardet honore rogus*: Burning Pyres in Lucan and Silius
Italicus' *Punica*." In Paolo Asso, ed., *Brill Companion to Lucan*, 185–198. Leiden:
Brill.

————. (Forthcoming). "Raping Achilles and the Poetics of Manhood: Re(de)fining Europe and Asia in Statius' *Achilleid.*" *Classical World*.

Bernstein, Neil. (2008). *In the Image of the Ancestors: Narratives of Kinship in Flavian Epic.* Toronto: University of Toronto Press.

Brown, Joanne. (1994). "Into the Woods: Narrative Studies in the *Thebaid* of Statius with Special Reference to Books IV–VI." Ph.D. diss., Cambridge University.

Clare, Ray. (2004). "Tradition and Originality: Allusion in Valerius Flaccus' Lemnian Episode." In Monica Gale, ed., *Latin Epic and Didactic Poetry: Genre, Tradition, and Individuality*, 125–147. Swansea: Classical Press of Wales.

Delz, Josef, ed. (1987). *Silius Italicus Punica.* Stuttgart: Teubner.

Dominik, William. (1994). *The Mythic Voice of Statius: Power and Politics in the Thebaid.* Leiden: Brill.

————. (1997). "*Ratio et dei*: Psychology and the Supernatural in the Lemnian Episode." In Carl Deroux, ed., *Studies in Latin Literature and Roman History*, 8:29–50. Brussels: Latomus.

Duff, James, trans. (1934). *Silius Italicus.* Loeb Classical Library. Cambridge, MA: Harvard University Press.

Ganiban, Randall. (2007). *Statius and Virgil: The Thebaid and the Reinterpretation of the Aeneid.* Cambridge: Cambridge University Press.

Gibson, Bruce. (2004). "The Repetitions of Hypsipyle." In Monica Gale, ed., *Latin Epic and Didactic Poetry: Genre, Tradition, and Individuality*, 149–180. Swansea: Classical Press of Wales.

Hershkowitz, Debra. (1998). *Valerius Flaccus' Argonautica: Abbreviated Voyages in Silver Latin Epic.* Oxford: Clarendon Press.

Hill, Donald, ed. (1996). *P. Papini Stati Thebaidos libri XII.* 2nd ed. Leiden: Brill.

Keith, Alison. (2000). *Engendering Rome: Women in Latin Epic.* Cambridge: Cambridge University Press.

Küppers, Jochem. (1986). *Tantarum causas irarum: Untersuchungen zur einleitenden Bücherdyade der Punica des Silius Italicus.* Berlin: de Gruyter.

Liberman, Gauthier, ed. (2003). *Valerius Flaccus: Argonautiques,* 1: *Chants I–IV.* Paris: Les Belles Lettres.

McGuire, Donald. (1997). *Acts of Silence: Civil War, Tyranny, and Suicide in the Flavian Epics.* Hildesheim: Olms-Weidmann.

McNelis, Charles. (2007). *Statius' Thebaid and the Poetics of Civil War.* Cambridge: Cambridge University Press.

Newlands, Carole. (2006). "Mothers in Statius's Poetry: Sorrows and Surrogates." *Helios* 33:203–226.

Nugent, Georgia. (1996). "Statius' Hypsipyle: Following in the Footsteps of the *Aeneid.*" *Scholia* 5:46–71.

Ripoll, François. (1998). *La morale héroïque dans les épopées latines d'époque flavienne: Tradition et innovation.* Louvain: Peeters.

Rosati, Gianpiero. (2005). "Il 'dolce delitto' di Lemno: Lucrezio e l'amore-guerra nel-

l'Ipsipile di Stazio." In Renato Raffaelli, ed., *Vicende di Ipsipile: Da Erodoto a Metastasio*, 141–167. Urbino: Quattroventi.

Schenk, Peter. (1999). *Studien zur poetischen Kunst des Valerius Flaccus: Beobachtungen zur Ausgestaltung des Kriegsthemas in den Argonautica*. Munich: Beck.

Shackleton Bailey, David Roy, trans. (2003). *Statius*. Loeb Classical Library. Cambridge, MA: Harvard University Press.

Spentzou, Efrossini. (2008). "Eluding *Romanitas*: Heroes and Antiheroes in Silius Italicus's Roman History." In Sinclair Bell and Inge Lyse Hansen, eds., *Role Models in the Roman World: Identity and Assimilation*, 133–145. Ann Arbor: University of Michigan Press.

Stover, Tim. (2008). "The Date of Valerius Flaccus' *Argonautica*." *Papers of the Langford Latin Seminar* 13:211–229.

Vessey, David. (1974). "Silius Italicus on the Fall of Saguntum." *Classical Philology* 69:28–36.

———. (1985). "Some Aspects of Valerius Flaccus, *Argonautica* II, 77–305." *Classical Journal* 80:326–339.

Von Albrecht, Michael. (1964). *Silius Italicus: Freiheit und Gebundenheit römischer Epik*. Amsterdam: Schippers.

ELEVEN

Imperial Mothers and Monuments in Rome

Margaret L. Woodhull

When Augustus's nephew, Marcellus, his favored heir, died unexpectedly in 23 BCE, he left unfinished a building project begun with his mother, Octavia Minor, the emperor's sister.[1] Octavia completed the project, a renovation of an older Republican portico, the Porticus Metelli, at the southern end of the Campus Martius.[2] In it, she recorded the traces of her maternal grief in the form of two memorial libraries for Marcellus, which she added to the older plan (Ovid, *Ars amatoria* 1.69).[3] The refurbished monument, the Porticus Octaviae, marks the first major architectural project by a woman in Rome's history (fig. 11.1). It initiates a long tradition of imperial mothers as patrons and honorands of architecture in the capital city. Scholars study these monuments individually, but none considers them collectively as a measure of the dynastic strategy that defined the imperial woman by her role as mother producing successive generations of Rome's heirs.

This essay examines five of the monuments built in imperial Rome by or for imperial women from the Julio-Claudian through the Antonine eras: the Augustan porticoes by Octavia and by Livia; the second-century temple for the Deified Matidia; the lost monument thought to have been Sabina's consecration altar; and the Antonine temple of *diva* Faustina (fig. 11.2). When studied together, these monuments allow us to highlight the use of maternal motifs and concepts and trace shifts in how they were deployed to address the changing realities of dynastic inheritance. The picture that emerges from considering these buildings within the framework of imperial motherhood modifies a prevailing scholarly view that sees the power of the imperial mother waning in the second century of empire—instead arguing for her continued potency as a stabilizing presence in succession politics.[4]

FIGURE 11.1. *Porticus Octaviae, southwest façade, main propylon. Campus Martius, Rome. Photo: Fototeca Unione, American Academy in Rome, nr. 5656.*

In general, the diminished archaeological, literary, and historical evidence for the early second-century imperial women is held to indicate their political demotion and its resulting diminution of their representations as central figures in dynastic inheritance. In response to this model, recent scholarship has begun to focus on the ascendant image of the emperor as a father figure during this time.[5] Yet when we consider the architectural evidence for imperial motherhood during these first two centuries, we find a different picture: in contrast to the monuments built by their Julio-Claudian predecessors, the buildings for second-century imperial women aggrandize them as mothers in ways Livia and Octavia never enjoyed.

MOTHERS, SONS, AND MONUMENTS
IN EARLY IMPERIAL ROME

Architectural patronage in Rome radically changed in the transition from Republic to empire. A practice dominated by elite men, the building of monuments traditionally offered Republican military heroes and politicians the opportunity for permanent self-aggrandizement in the fabric

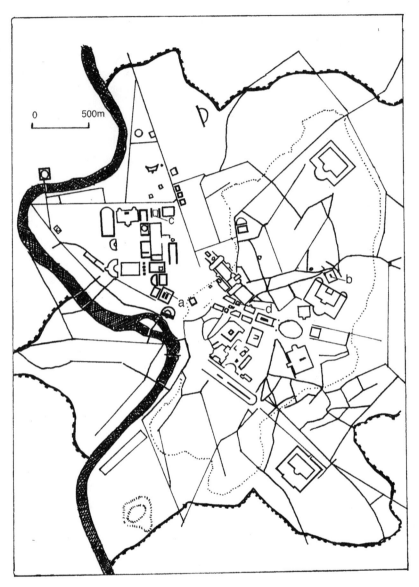

FIGURE II.2. *Plan of Rome: (a) Porticus Octaviae, (b) Porticus Liviae, (c) Temple of Matidia and basilicas of Matidia and Marciana, (d) Temple of Faustina I and Antoninus Pius.. Drawing by M. Woodhull.*

of the city. Republican women, by contrast, rarely contributed to civic embellishment.

The shift to dynasty in the early decades of Augustus's rule changed the profile of the typical architectural benefactor in two discernible ways. Increasingly, monumental patronage fell to the hands of one family, the Julio-Claudians, a reflection of their principal role in emerging dynastic politics. At the same time, Julio-Claudian women involved themselves in Augustus's programmatic rebuilding of Rome. As Augustus and his family concentrated building in their own hands, a cohesive plan for urban renewal and regeneration evolved, and a new, visually unified Rome emerged. Imperial Rome revealed its new political order through beautiful public buildings and temples, revamped amenities, and refurbished monuments of the Republic.[6]

It was early in this transition that Octavia and her son rebuilt the portico that bore her name. For an elite Republican society habituated to traditional gender roles, Octavia's involvement in the masculine world of city-building surely challenged Roman sensibilities. Augustus seems to have been sensitive to the political tensions such perceived transgressions might incite, for he fostered new social roles that translated the private activities of feminine domesticity into publicly acceptable practices. An evolving public image of the imperial woman was effectively framed with the values of women's traditional place in the home, specifically as mothers.[7] Civic space for the imperial family was domesticated; Rome was its family, and motherhood became a public and political role for its women. For female members of the new first family, this shift naturalized the transition from elite woman in the private sphere to public figure with political power as producer of heirs. The buildings associated with them reflected this role.

The portico of Octavia is especially instructive here, for it emphasized motherhood in various ways. Begun in the first half of the 20s BCE, it joined a host of other buildings in the Campus Martius either undergoing renovation or being built anew by members of the imperial family (see fig. 11.2:a). Together these monuments initiated a change in the character of the Campus Martius from one whose monuments signaled Republican politics and militarism to one identified with family and dynasty. The plan and design of Octavia's portico probably differed very little from the Republican building it supplanted. However, its celebration of mothers, symbolized in its new patron and the artwork it housed, stood in stark contrast to its predecessor, a portico erected by the military hero Q. Caecilius Metellus from his extensive victory spoils.

The monument's traditional four-sided, double colonnade design en-

closed two preexisting Republican temples dedicated to Juno Regina and Jupiter Stator, the two memorial libraries for Marcellus noted above, a cu- ria, and, like other public porticoes, an extensive collection of sculpture and paintings displayed about the grounds.[8] Grand art collections were a regular feature of the Republican portico, but in the Augustan era these were increasingly cultivated to focus attention not just on the identity of the benefactor, but on the cultural values associated with his or her spe- cific social and familial role. Often dedicatory inscriptions, architectural designs, and cultic associations within the complex played off of one an- other to cultivate specific meanings for a viewer. For visitors to Octavia's portico, decoration and artworks occasioned instances of maternal expres- sion. Through the interplay of these forms, one message was quite distinct: The Roman mother was the link between an old and new Rome. Various artworks attest as much.[9]

Perhaps the most famous statue in the portico was the image of a seated Cornelia, mother of the second-century statesmen of populist causes, Ti- berius and Gaius Gracchus (Pliny, *Natural History* 34.31).[10] Although the statue itself is not preserved, its base emerged in excavations in 1878.[11] Its in- scription identifies Cornelia by her family filiation, with emphasis on her role as mother: CORNELIA AFRICANI F. GRACCHORUM.[12] Recent studies of the base argue for an Augustan date for the inscription and sug- gest that the statue of Cornelia replaced a bronze image of a seated goddess. If correct, then the substitution of Cornelia's image reinforces the idea that the Augustan renovation of the complex was especially motivated to em- phasize a particular ideal of Roman motherhood concerned with a mother's cultivation of her citizen sons.[13] In the 20s when the colonnade was begun, Marcellus was quickly becoming a favorite of his uncle; he was married to the emperor's daughter, Julia, and had begun his march up the *cursus ho- norum*, proving himself in his military affairs. As his mother, Octavia evi- denced the maternal oversight that fostered Marcellus's rise.

For Romans, Octavia appeared a natural successor to the earlier Cor- nelia, whose sons' political achievements were often attributed to their mother's grooming. The image of Cornelia in Octavia's portico pointed up for visitors the parallels between the two women; it collapsed the dis- tance between mothers of Rome's noble past and those of its present. For both women, good mothering had been a fact of life. Moreover, numer- ous other details of their biographies would have further linked them to one another. Both were widowed young and remained unmarried (*univi- rae*), and both were publicly honored with statues for acknowledged rec- titude. Indeed, Octavia's role as a chaste Roman mother had recently cap-

tured the public's attention. As her marriage to Mark Antony unraveled, Octavian seized the opportunity to champion her maternal image over her identity as the scorned wife of his co-triumvir. Despite the public humiliation of abandonment for a foreign queen, Octavia pressed on as a devoted Roman mother, raising Antony's children by other marriages alongside her own (Plutarch, *Life of Antony* 54). In 35 BCE, the senate recognized Octavia's virtue with the grant of tribunician sacrosanctity and public statues.[14] Widowed by Antony's death in 31 BCE, she remained alone for nearly two decades. For a Roman audience, Cornelia and Octavia were so well paired that it is tempting to see in the portico's art collection a portrait of Octavia alongside her Republican counterpart,[15] constituting the virtues of motherhood in Augustus's renewed Republic.

Other mothers were also represented by artworks in the portico.[16] Several statues showing Venus (Pliny, *Natural History* 36.35) surely alluded to Venus Genetrix, the maternal founder of the Julian line. At least one representation of the goddess appeared in each of the temples in the complex, and another version elsewhere in the precinct, by Phidias, was arguably the model for Cornelia's statue, perhaps a pendant to it (Pliny, *Natural History* 36.35).[17] Related to these, a statue of Venus's son, Cupid, holding a thunderbolt alluded to the divine mother–son duo, forecasting their descendants, Octavia and Marcellus (Pliny, *Natural History* 36.28).

These miniature family couplings in the context of the commission reinforced the emerging value of motherhood in the production of a dynastic heir. Framing this rich imagery were decorative details in the architectural elements (small reptiles and foliage), which located the portico's display within an Augustan program concerned with fecundity and life-nurturing values, such as viewers saw in the nearby Ara Pacis Augustae.[18] The early appearance of these symbolic devices suggests that Octavia's portico offered an experimental site for building a visual discourse on motherhood for the evolving Augustan line.

Marcellus's death diminished Octavia's importance,[19] and for the remaining years of her life, we find little evidence for her activities within the family, testimony to the close connection between her image as a mother of an heir and her elevation in public life. Her own death, however, occasioned unprecedented honors for a woman, with special rites held for her in Rome's main Forum (Cassius Dio 54.35). With Octavia's passing, however, a formidable image of the imperial mother arose in her sister-in-law, the empress Livia.

When Livia herself died in 29 CE, nearly five decades later, she left a record of public works that would exceed all other imperial women of the

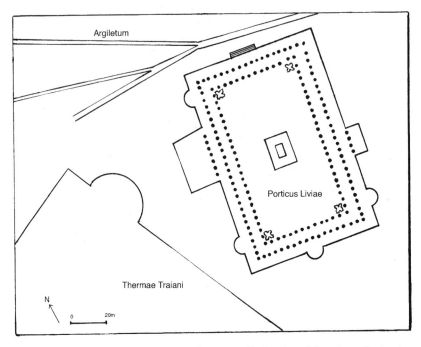

FIGURE 11.3. *Porticus Liviae. Drawing by M. Woodhull, adapted from Pannella (1987).*

first two centuries of empire and rival many of Rome's imperial men. Most of the monuments attributed to Livia were closely connected with the concerns of women (the temples of Fortuna Muliebris, Bona Dea, Pudicitia Plebeia, and Patricia, for example);[20] yet it was the grand portico named for the empress and its shrine to the goddess Concordia on the Esquiline hill that best expressed the politics of motherhood for the imperial woman.[21] Despite their childless marriage (or perhaps in response to it), Augustan propaganda had for some time propounded an image of Livia as mother of Rome's future leaders, but this facet of her character had not been so carefully honed, especially while Octavia still lived. In 9 BCE, however, the death of Livia's son, Drusus, occasioned portrait statues of the empress, specially honoring her as a grieving mother.[22] Shortly after this event, Livia and her remaining son, Tiberius, built the Porticus Liviae (figs. 11.2:b, 11.3).

Dedicated on January 16, 7 BCE, Livia's portico rose from the slopes of the Esquiline, a gleaming marble building overlooking central Rome from its perch within the congested Subura. Although the monument is now lost, its history and reception are known from assorted literary references, and its general plan, preserved in fragments of the well-known Severan marble

map (Ovid, *Fasti* 6.639–642; Cassius Dio 54.23, 55.8; Pliny, *Epistulae* 1.5.9; and *Forma Urbis Romae* fr. nos. 10, 11). Together these sources flesh out the image of an enclosed colonnade close in style to Octavia's and similarly embellished.[23] Ovid noted that famous paintings were displayed about the colonnade (*Ars amatoria* 1.71–72), and Pliny made special note of its lush gardens (*Natural History* 14.11). For visitors to the area, the monument's wide, open plan surely contrasted to good effect with the tightly knit apartment buildings and narrow streets of the neighborhood. The small rectangular design at the center of the portico is thought to be the *aedes Concordia* ascribed to Livia by Ovid in his *Fasti* (6.637–640),[24] wherein he notes its dedication by the empress alone some six months after the portico's dedication by the mother and son team. The date of the shrine's dedication, on June 11, was the holiday Roman mothers celebrated the goddess Mater Matuta—in essence, Rome's equivalent of Mother's Day.

Much of the scholarship on the portico complex focuses on the meaning and symbolism of the *aedes Concordia* and its dedication to the goddess at the expense of the portico that surrounded it. The story of the complex that emerges emphasizes the way Concordia symbolized Livia's uxorial duties. For Romans, Concordia was the guardian of marital health and family life as well as political stability in the state. When Livia dedicated her shrine to Concordia, her actions sent a clear message to Rome's citizenry that the well-being of the royal couple's marriage and its family rested on the rectitude of the wife; marital harmony between emperor and empress, in turn, created political stability.[25]

What gets underplayed in this traditional reading of the monument is the portico itself and the fact that it was dedicated by the empress with her son, Tiberius, in her role as mother.[26] In most studies, Livia-as-wife supersedes Livia-as-mother. Such oversights by modern eyes are understandable, for in the absence of any visible evidence for the monument it is difficult to remember that before visitors to the complex encountered the shrine, they first found themselves confronted by a beautiful new portico. Indeed, its magnificence caused Strabo to extol it as one of Augustan Rome's architectural jewels (Strabo 5.236). Its benefactors were no doubt well advertised in an inscription across its façade (likely similar to one the patroness Eumachia inscribed across the portico she built on her own and her son's behalf in the forum in Pompeii).[27] If so, then visitors to the Porticus Liviae walking up the Argiletum, the main road to the portico, would *first* encounter the empress symbolized as mother of a potential successor to Augustus, and only *secondarily*, after entering the portico, would they discover Concordia's shrine, with its allusions to Livia's role as the emperor's wife.

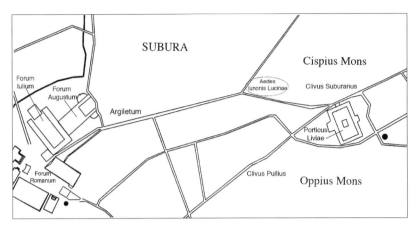

FIGURE II.4. *Area plan, Porticus Liviae and temple for Juno Lucina. Drawing by M. Woodhull.*

Motherhood, then, was visually the first order of symbolism for Livia's portico. Cast up front, it signaled to viewers that the political goodwill emanating from the *princeps* toward Tiberius was largely owed to his mother. Although Tiberius was shown favor by the emperor, it was far from clear, even after Drusus's death, that he would succeed him. Augustus did not adopt Tiberius until 4 CE, and thus Livia's joint benefaction with Tiberius is best comprehended as a pragmatic gesture of a mother furthering her son's political trajectory.[28]

This attempt to separate out maternal from uxorial symbolism is admittedly somewhat artificial. To the Roman mind, these roles went hand-in-hand for an elite woman, a reality borne out by the fact that Livia's Concordia shrine celebrating her marriage was dedicated on Rome's Mother's Day. Nevertheless, the confrontation with the external portico and its representation of Livia as an active mother who had produced a potential successor necessitates a reading of the monument in which motherhood dominates the building's symbolic narrative.

An argument for emphasis on the maternal can be pressed further if we consider the site's topography, an observation that has not garnered much if any attention. Augustus inherited the lands on the Esquiline from the unsavory Vedius Pollio (Cassius Dio 54.23.5);[29] yet why it was Livia, not the emperor, who built up the parcel is unclear until we consider the proximity of the late Vedius's holdings to the shrine of Juno Lucina, the goddess sacred to mothers seeking favor in childbirth, which was just a short walk across the Argiletum (fig. 11.4).[30] According to Ovid, Juno Lucina's cult had

originated here with Rome's Sabine foremothers (*Fasti* 3.167–258). From Ovid's description, the celebration of the goddess's cult was enormously popular. Macrobius even connects it with renewal rituals of the Vestal Virgins (*Saturnalia* 1.12.6). Moreover, other Roman holidays tied to women's cult life clustered around both Juno's and Concordia's dedication dates.[31] A monument built here by Rome's premier mother, then, was ideal. Enriched by Livia's portico, this traditionally squalid region of the city found itself heavily identified with the symbols of mothering and animated by its celebration.

The porticoes built by Octavia and Livia established a new mode of architectural benefaction, engaging time-honored symbolic capital—Roman social tradition, maternal divinities, visual allusion—to manifest their motherhood in the public buildings they erected. Although speculative, it is further possible that typologically the quadriportico favored by them overlapped semantically with values tied to mothering. In general, Romans preferred the four-sided design for its ability to create an enclosed respite from the hustle and bustle of the city outside. Vitruvius noted that this plan offered protection and a healthful environment for the city's inhabitants (*De architectura* 5.9.5–9).[32] His emphasis on physical well-being is provocative. From the classical through the early modern era, the types of architectural monuments employed by women patrons most often share a concern for the health or well-being of the community for which they are built.[33] We might understand this "protective" design, coming from the hands of a female patron, to represent a nurturing characteristic of the mother of Rome's first family that is extended to its citizenry.

Pliny makes clear that Livia's portico with its trailing vines was a respite, a break from the brick and stone city, suffused with nature. The description conjures an image not unlike the "Tellus" panel on the Ara Pacis with its overtones of feminine fecundity and the health of the natural world. Such allusions might have foreshadowed Livia's later association in coinage with the legend *Salus Augusta*.[34] Pliny's soothing portrait of the portico further suggests the orderly vistas favored by Romans and a tranquility rarely found in the city. These porticoes would have thus served a regenerative and beneficial need, a gift with life-affirming assets. A portico had, too, the unique characteristic of being neither fully public nor fully private, an apt metaphor for the emerging public image of the imperial mother, figured so frequently in nurturing terms, but in a manner that ushered those domestic symbols into the public spaces of the city as the family of the emperor became the family of state.[35]

Perhaps stronger evidence that Romans sometimes conceived porti-

coes in feminine terms comes less from an apparent ideological program demanded by the patron and expressed in imagery than from subversive poetic responses found in literature. Propertius and Ovid notoriously reconceived a variety of Augustan monuments in sexualized terms never intended by the *princeps* in his benefactions.[36] Ovid pointedly locates sexual intrigue in Livia's and Octavia's porticoes in a way that strongly contrasts with their established symbols of motherhood (*Ars amatoria* 1.71–72; 3.391). As scholars have noted, the rhetorical power of such literary imagery grows from the contrast between a popular notion of finding illicit sex with disreputable women in these spaces and the *exemplum* of the Roman mother evinced throughout.[37] To be sure, Romans were not so literal in their architectural designs as to allow easy claims to biological and cultural metaphors, but buildings where metaphor focused meaning did exist—such as the Pantheon—and, thus, may offer ways for understanding how building types and patronage intersected for women patrons.

Livia's and Octavia's patronage was remarkably experimental. Before Augustus's rise, structures like these rested exclusively in the hands of men. They typically celebrated masculine virtues of military triumph, political leadership, and economic power. Until the principate, elite mothers rarely appeared on the public stage; far fewer merited monumental honors.[38] New Rome, however, told a story of new political order and indicated this in many novel features of its physical spaces, not the least of which were buildings erected by women. As incipient steps, then, the experimental patronage the early Julio-Claudian women engaged in demanded the veil of tradition. The mother–son benefactions were in line with traditional activities of an elite Republican mother expected to further her son's political ambitions through her own family ties and social relations.[39] Although the marble manifestations of Octavia and Livia were a far cry from these older intangible and often covert expressions of maternal patronage, the institution of the Republican mother provided imperial women a conventional path into public life, and monumental patronage endowed it with tangible forms.[40]

The characteristic experimentation of this generative era with its imperial mothers functioning as active agents in the development of their public roles declined as the Julio-Claudian line died out and successive dynasties arose. By the early second century, a run of barren empresses had come to define the era of the adoptive emperors. Imperial women no longer took an active role in building Rome, but instead received monumental honors posthumously.[41] Motherhood, nevertheless, remained a dominant concept in the monuments built for them.

MOTHERHOOD, MONUMENTS, AND
IMPERIAL WOMEN OF THE ADOPTIVE ERA

In contrast to the abundant historical, literary, and visual record
for Rome's first imperial women, comparable evidence for their second-
century counterparts is paltry. Mary Boatwright correlates this impover-
ishment with the fact that the Hadrianic and Trajanic women failed to produce male heirs. For this reason, then, they were far less potent in political
life than Julio-Claudian women. As Boatwright puts it, "the biological role
of women in the transfer of power was obsolete."[42] Motherhood, it would
seem, was in danger of losing its political clout for imperial women. Yet if
in life these Hadrianic and Trajanic women (namely Trajan's wife, Plotina;
his niece, Matidia; his sister and the mother to Matidia, Marciana; and
great-niece, Sabina) merited little attention, then it is all the more striking
that in death they bore tremendous symbolic power, often receiving monumental honors rarely enjoyed by their predecessors. Moreover, it is rather
ironic that despite the failure of biological reproduction to produce a male
heir, it was often the reproductive body and symbolic mothers who were
commemorated in these monuments. Two Hadrianic structures in particular—the Temple of Deified Matidia (fig. 11.2:c), with its accompanying basilicas for Matidia and her mother, Marciana, and the so-called Sabina Altar—mark the first of a series of known architectural monuments solely
honoring imperial women as *divae*.[43]

Evidence for the Matidian monument is scanty at best. A fragment
of the Severan map preserves a corner of the building's plan (*Forma Urbis
Romae* fr. no. 36b). A *fistula* inscribed *Templo Matidiae* (*Corpus Inscriptionum Latinarum* [*CIL*] 15.7248) and fragments of cipollino columns distrib-
uted around the area of Piazza Capranica are its principal archaeological remains. References to it in the Regionary Catalogues place the monument
in Region IX and next to a basilica of Neptune commonly associated by
scholars with the Stoa of Poseidon in the Saepta.[44] From these bits, scholars surmise that the complex rose between the forecourt of Hadrian's refurbished Pantheon to its west and his renovated Saepta to its south. After
Hadrian's death and deification in 138, Antoninus Pius erected a temple to
the new *divus*, the Hadrianeum, directly to the east of the temple, and thus
the Matidian monument formed the central element in a Hadrianic commemorative complex in the mid Campus Martius. Surprisingly, the diam-
eter of the columns for Matidia's temple (1.7 m) places their height somewhere between 13.7 and 17 m, thereby exceeding the façade elevation of the
Pantheon.[45] Thus, its height dominated hierarchically its Hadrianic neigh-

FIGURE 11.5. *Hadrianic medallion showing Templum Matidiae, ca. 120–121 CE. Photo: Fototeca Unione, American Academy in Rome, nr. 6490F.*

bor in this complex, a striking fact for a monument devoted to a woman for whom other evidence is so meager, and testimony to the deep symbolism Hadrian's mother-in-law held for the emperor.

A rare Hadrianic medallion (ca. 120–121 CE) hints at the overall design of the complex (fig. 11.5).[46] Here, a prostyle temple houses an unidentifiable cult statue (perhaps Matidia?) and is flanked symmetrically by smaller shrines in which two other cult statues stand. Extending from this central grouping at either side are two wings of double-colonnaded porticoes typically identified as the two basilicas for Matidia and Marciana.[47] Here they form a forecourt for the temple, one that perhaps visually complemented a similar configuration for the Pantheon to the west. Scholars associate portions of recently discovered green granite columns with these porticoed basilicas.[48] Judging from Hadrian's use of such varied stones, Matidia and Marciana's monuments shared his predilection for coloristic effects found in the stonework of the adjacent Pantheon, a unifying feature of the complex here.[49]

The erection of the Temple of Deified Matidia and its basilicas was occasioned by its honorand's death and consecration ca. 119–121 CE.[50] It numbered among a group of projects in the central Campus Martius commissioned by Hadrian, but stood out among these as an entirely new construction (see fig. 11.2).[51] Most of Hadrian's building projects in this area were renovations to earlier Augustan buildings, initiated with an eye to creating a symbolic link between himself and Rome's first dynast.[52] The new complex by contrast was unfettered by historical associations and occasioned the opportunity for the emperor to highlight important figures of his own dynastic family. Hadrian's choice to deify his mother-in-law and honor

her mother alongside her with a new temple and basilicas is puzzling at first glance, for a more logical recipient might have been Trajan's wife, Plotina, held to have favored Hadrian (Historia Augusta, *Life of Hadrian* 2.10) and credited with orchestrating his marriage to Matidia's daughter, Sabina, and ultimately, his accession. Plotina's death and consecration (ca. 121/2 CE) shortly after Matidia's certainly would have put her in the running as the new temple's honoree. Hadrian, however, honored Plotina as Trajan's wife, by adding her name to the temple he built for the late deified emperor.

What, then, motivated Hadrian to build one of the largest temples to date in the Campus Martius to a seemingly retiring member of his family?[53] The answer is best understood in the context of accession politics, for Matidia's body, unlike Plotina's, had produced, in Sabina, a child—albeit a daughter—through whom Hadrian secured imperial ancestry, traced to Trajan through three generations of mothers and daughters beginning with his wife. Although Hadrian and Trajan shared a common ancestor (M. Ulpius Traianus),[54] the relation was somewhat distant. Through Sabina's mother, Hadrian bolstered his weak connection to the late emperor, with the added benefit of displacing any contest of his own somewhat shady adoption. The deification of women in the imperial family other than the empress had few precedents, and the apotheosis of a non-emperor had been discredited as a practice by Vespasian.[55] Hadrian's return to the practice for his mother-in-law and her mother, then, indicates how critical their production of a child (Matidia in Marciana's case and Sabina in Matidia's) through whom Hadrian secured accession truly was. Motherhood—or more precisely, a reproductive figurehead—then, motivated the benefaction. Its acknowledgment in such monumental scale and the innovative form of the *diva* temple draw attention to the perceived fragility of the dynastic model because of its extreme dependency on sustaining some concept of motherhood for its stability.[56]

If producing a child who directly connected Hadrian to Trajan merited built honors for Matidia and Marciana, then it is ironic that the "fictive fertility" of their progeny, Sabina, who produced no heir, was later celebrated in this same region.[57] The so-called Altar of Sabina, now lost, was likely erected by Hadrian for the empress's consecration and included a collection of marble panels reused on the late-antique Arco di Portogallo.[58] One panel is especially interesting for its unique conceptualization of Sabina (fig. 11.6). In the panel, Sabina rises heavenward on the back of Aeternitas in the first known monumental depiction of an empress's apotheosis (ca. 136–138 CE). A personification of the Campus Martius, the senate, and a seated Hadrian watch from below.

FIGURE 11.6. *Apotheosis of Sabina, relief, 136–138 CE. Musei Capitolini, Rome. Photo: Alinari/Art Resource, NY, ART187909.*

Although evidence for the altar is slim, recent studies situating the apotheosis within Sabina's portraiture emphasize an ideological fictionalizing of the empress's fertility. Sabina's idealized youthfulness belied her forty-eight years to foster the image of an empress ever-ripe for childbearing. The veil she raises hints at an equally fictive harmonious marriage to Hadrian

with its allusion to matronly scenes of Pudicitia and Hera.[59] Penelope Davies develops the discussion of this iconography and proposes that before the late-antique reworking of the panel, a strong play of sunlight raked across the empress, to powerful effect, casting her in a celestial glow as she ascended to the heavens; Hadrian below sat rather diminished by comparison.[60] In Davies's analysis, the visual composition places Sabina physically, but more significantly, symbolically, above Hadrian, elevated by her fictive fertility. While it is impossible to know the original design of the monument, multiple allusions situate Sabina's altar within the context of imperial mothers' monumental honors. For example, the visual hierarchy of the figures in the apotheosis panel recalls the provocative architectural hierarchy of Matidia's monument, while the iconography of apotheosis relates the new empress *diva* Sabina to her predecessor, *diva* Plotina. By contrast, however, Sabina's monument honors the imperial mother not for real (and active) childbearing but as an abstract virtue of the political role. The empress's fecundity is made iconic, and its relationship to reality is suppressed. Indeed, Sabina's celestial setting reinforces the timelessness and idealization of such a virtue as an inherent and natural characteristic.

Two major observations emerge from this look at the Hadrianic commemorations. First, as in the Julio-Claudian monuments before them, these were experimental and unprecedented. The Matidian temple honored a *diva* in Rome's cityscape for the first time, and its scale drew attention to its significance. Similarly, Sabina's apotheosis image from her altar marks the first time an empress's image appeared in public in this manner. In both cases the honorees were passive recipients, honored posthumously. For modern historians, the shift here from first-century imperial women as active patrons to the second-century commemoration of mothers is palpable. Yet for ancient visitors to the Campus Martius, this shift probably seemed less dissonant, for as commemorations, they fit squarely into the funereal character the Campus Martius developed in the imperial era. Moreover, the move back to this model of honoring a mother satisfied traditional sensibilities concerning women's behavior in society. Still, so few women enjoyed commemoration here that those who merited it were notable. The new Matidian works must have recalled other monuments by and for Roman mothers, like Octavia's portico to the south, featuring commemorative libraries dedicated to Marcellus. Although Octavia's building may have attested to a different sort of imperial woman, the more educated visitor, familiar perhaps with Octavia's history, might recall that both she and Matidia had received the rare honor of a formal public eulogy.[61]

Matidia's complex must have also evoked ties to an earlier monu-

ment honoring Julius Caesar's beloved daughter, Julia, whose tumulus rose nearby.[62] Julia's death in 54 BCE in childbirth left Caesar, her husband Pompey, and the people of Rome bereft, and resulted in their insistence—despite senatorial misgivings—that her body be interred in the Campus Martius.[63] Like Octavia's memorial libraries, it symbolized the liabilities of motherhood. Other circumstances link the three monuments. Like Matidia and Octavia, Julia was eulogized in the Forum; like Matidia's temple, Julia's funeral monument marked a watershed for women in monumental Rome, for no woman before Julia had received honorary burial in the Campus Martius. Filippo Coarelli places the tumulus just north of the Hadrianeum, and, if Boatwright's orientation of the Matidian buildings to the north is correct, then Matidia's temple and her cult statue inside faced symbolically toward her Republican predecessor, and the tombs of Augustus and Hadrian.[64]

THE TEMPLE OF *DIVA* FAUSTINA: THE IMPERIAL MOTHER REVIVED

The symbolic hierarchy expressed by the Hadrianic monuments was further advanced some four years later when the death and deification of their successor, Faustina the Elder, wife of Antoninus Pius, occasioned the senate's vow of a temple to honor the newest *diva*. Erected in 141 CE, the temple is one of Rome's best preserved, and like its Hadrianic predecessors, it marks an unprecedented use of architecture to celebrate an imperial mother; in this case, it was the first time a woman was represented in a building in Rome's most politically charged arena, its ancient Forum (figs. 11.2:d, 11.7).[65] Coin images show an iron gate across the lower, axial steps where an altar stood just inside it on the staircase. The temple proper housed an over life-sized cult statue of the empress.[66] Rising from its nearly sixteen-foot-tall (4.6 m) podium, Faustina's temple looms above other monuments in the Forum and along the Via Sacra.[67] From this beacon, Faustina the Elder looked out across the ancient center and dominated the space for nearly two decades until the death and deification of her husband, Antoninus Pius, called for the addition of his name next to hers.[68]

It is generally agreed that the temple was intended to honor both the empress and the emperor posthumously, but because Faustina predeceased her husband by twenty years, it is likely that the empress's earlier death provided the impetus for building the monument. The dedicatory inscription, which fills the lower architrave of the monument's façade, DIVAE

FIGURE 11.7. *Temple of Faustina I and Antoninus Pius. Rome. Photo: Scala/ Art Resource, NY, ART117171.*

FIGURE 11.8. *Detail of architrave, Temple of Faustina I and Antoninus Pius. Drawing by M. Woodhull, adapted from Cassatella (1993), 370, fig. 25.*

FAVSTINAE EX S C (*CIL* 6.1005), was inscribed in the wake of her consecration, ca. 141. Only after the emperor's death in 161 would the dedicatory inscription for him, DIVO ANTONINO ET ([*CIL* 6.1005], fig. 11.8), have been added on the logic that it was unusual—dangerous even—for an emperor to assume divinity before his actual death (hence, the carved relief of griffins and candelabra still flanking the emperor's inscription probably continued across the front until 161). We, then, forget that symbolically Faustina alone held oversight of the Forum for twenty years, and thus

we rarely consider what merits justified Faustina's honors and the effect her presence here had on ancient viewers. How, then, might a visitor to the Forum have understood the empress's monument?

In some ways, the temple's reception enjoyed two conceptual phases over time. After Antoninus's death, the monument honored the royal couple together, but made clear the emperor's dominance: visually the inscription that bears his name runs across the frieze above hers and the lettering for his name is larger and more easily read. In this later phase, the monument surely brought to mind the Hadrianic temple for Plotina and Trajan. In the monument's initial phase, however, the empress's reproductive virtues appear to have justified the monument's erection. During the two decades it honored Faustina, it shared similarities with Hadrian's temple for *diva* Matidia. Like Matidia, Faustina produced not a male heir but instead a daughter through whom her husband's adopted successor, Marcus Aurelius (chosen along with Lucius Verus prior to the emperor's death), might advance more securely. Matidia's temple thus offered a strong precedent, and because it was the only other *diva* temple in Rome at the time, viewers no doubt understood the similarities between the two monuments and knew that motherhood had merited both women this unusual honor.

Although neither the extant monument nor our archaeological and literary sources suggest any programmatic displays of motherhood in the form of statues or mother–son benefactions such as we find in the Augustan monuments above (however, this does not preclude their presence originally), there is considerable circumstantial evidence that indicates that Faustina's commemoration here owed a debt to her public identity as the mother both of the Antonine line and the Roman people. A rich body of Antonine coinage and art fleshes out this picture.[69] In particular, posthumous numismatic portraits show a bust of *diva* Faustina on the obverse of coins where Juno or Ceres appear on the reverse. The association between the empress and Juno intimated a congruence between the two figures. Here *diva* Faustina is compared to the wife of the principal god of the Roman state, Jupiter, a deity to whom emperors were often equated. But Juno was also, as we saw, associated with childbirth and a potent fertility goddess who, for Romans, closely harmonized with the Earth Mother.[70] Similarly, Faustina's posthumous association with the fertility goddess Ceres is attested in an image from Ostia.[71] The establishment of alimentary distributions to the *puellae Faustininae* to commemorate the empress highlighted Faustina's identity in life as a nurturer and maternal figurehead.[72] Finally, the location of the temple honoring her directly across the Via Sa-

cra from the Atrium and Temple of Vesta was surely calculated to project Faustina as Rome's contemporary maternal guardian juxtaposed with its symbolic ancient ones (see fig. 11.2).

Initially, then, the temple had to be understood to honor *diva* Faustina alone, and the facet of her character that most merited consecration seems to have been her centrality to the line. For twenty years, Faustina stood vigilant over the oldest part of the Roman Forum celebrating the new *diva* as a maternal figure. Later, in its second phase, as the Temple of the Divine Faustina and Antoninus Pius, the monument built on this symbolism by celebrating a marital union and parental oversight that made for stability in the family that was Rome, a theme foreshadowed just up the road from the temple in Livia's portico a century and a half earlier, and reiterated in much Antonine art and culture.[73]

A few observations worth further exploration emerge from this analysis of the Hadrianic and Antonine material. Hadrian's benefactions for Matidia, Marciana, and Sabina and their emphasis on mothers and fertility call for modification of the scholarly paradigm of the impotent imperial woman of the early second century. This model assumes an imperial woman's diminished personal and economic agency in her lived experience as the standard for assessing her decreased power. Yet the architectural commemoration of these women in the Campus Martius challenges this notion, attesting instead to their powerful and enduring symbolic capital as mothers, even if only as a potentiality.[74] The dependency of the dynastic model on the concept and role of the mother places imperial women at the heart of Rome's political stability. This core function was perhaps acknowledged metaphorically by the centrality of Matidia's monument within the Hadrianic complex in the Campus Martius, and by Faustina's temple in the Roman Forum. Indeed, if as is often the case, representation of maternal attributes of an imperial woman (be they a reproductive body or a nurturing aspect) intensifies during moments of dynastic turnover, then motherhood in built form offered an enduring and sustaining rhetoric at such times.

Imperial women's monuments of the first two centuries of Rome's empire tell the story of Julio-Claudian empresses as agents of change crafting a public image for their new roles within an emerging political order that depended on the mother for its endurance. Their engendering of Rome's built spaces correlates with and was a function of their active production of male heirs. It corresponds, too, to a generative era in Rome's political history when the casting of a new rule permitted experimentation for women. Building patronage represented the most experimental expres-

sion of imperial women's novel activities, for it left permanent evidence of them in the city. Experimentation, however, demanded the cloak of tradition, and for the Julio-Claudian women their active engagement as patrons of monumental Rome was moderated by evoking the traditional Republican mother. Their buildings thus incorporate familial relationships, commemorate their personal losses, and honor them with a biographical specificity lacking in the later monuments.

Conversely, the archaeological and textual evidence for their second-century successors leaves us relatively nothing of the personal lives of Trajanic, Hadrianic, and Antonine women, a lacuna that is commonly held to signal the loss of the imperial mother's status, as they failed to provide male issue. When the architectural evidence for these women is evaluated, however, this picture brightens. Using an analytic matrix defined by scale and space, we note that the second-century monuments for the imperial women are by far grander and more centrally staged in the civic space than those of the Julio-Claudians. Although actual, feminine agency endowed by virtue of real motherhood declined from the first to the second century, it was replaced by a greater symbolic power that was manifested in the unprecedented aggrandizement that second-century imperial women received in architectural honors.

Architecture provided the dynastic ideology of motherhood an enduring presence that transcended the uncertainties of the reproductive body and stabilized its political force. Embedded in the city, buildings anchored the concept of the imperial mother with a repetitive force that demanded attention. It was an apt mode, for it constituted an especially thick sense of motherhood as blocks of stone formed new buildings and brought new life to an old city. One of the most stable symbols of the intact family, the mother, coupled with these durable forms to create an enduring image of the eternal city and its undying political order. Imperial women's architectural monuments were erected continually from that first structure built by Octavia through to late antiquity, creating a network of maternal references that strengthened the fabric of dynasty as much as it did the fabric of the city. In this network, motherhood intersected with architecture to open a complex discursive space for the imperial woman.

NOTES

Many thanks to the editors of this volume for their careful reading and editing and to Mary T. Boatwright for sharing her work on monumental Antonine Rome in advance of its publication.

1. On Marcellus: Plutarch, *Life of Marcellus* 30; Vergil, *Aeneid* 6.860–886; and Propertius 3.18; *Consolatio ad Liviam* 441–444; Wood (2000), 29–35, 58, 64, 102.

2. On the Metellan colonnade: Boyd (1953); Lauter (1980–1981); and Rodríguez-Almeida (1981) on a Severan reconstruction.

3. Viscogliosi (1999), 141–145; Richardson (1992), 317–318; Woodhull (2003).

4. Boatwright (1991).

5. Kampen (2009), esp. chap. 2.

6. Favro (1996), 24–78.

7. Severy (2003), Milnor (2005), and Kampen (2009) reflect the wealth of recent scholarship on family discourses in imperial culture.

8. Cassius Dio 55.8; Josephus, *De bello Judaico* 7.5.4; Pliny, *Natural History* 36.28; *Forma Urbis Romae* fr. nos. 31, 31aa, 31bb, 31cc, 31u, 31v, 31z.

9. Woodhull (1999), 71ff., and (2003) elaborates many of the ideas sketched here.

10. Coarelli (1978); Kajava (1989); Fantham et al. (1994), 265–266.

11. Pellegrini (1861) and (1868); Lanciani (1878).

12. Coarelli (1978), 13–28; Kajava (1989), 119–132; *Inscriptiones Latinae Liberae Rei Publicae* 336.

13. Hemelrijk (2005), 312–313; Ruck (2004). I am grateful to the anonymous reader for these references.

14. Scardigli (1982); Flory (1993), 292–294; Hemelrijk (2005).

15. Lewis (1988).

16. Woodhull (1999), 116–129.

17. Coarelli (1978), 21.

18. Lanciani (1897), 467; Viscogliosi (1999), 159; Woodhull (1999), for analysis of the scholarship and evidence.

19. Cf. Bartman (1999), 80.

20. Barrett (2002), 199–205, for an overview of these benefactions with notes and bibliography; also Welch (2004), 68–73; on Livia and temple for *divus* Augustus, Torelli (1993).

21. Panella (1993), 127–129; Woodhull (1999).

22. Flory (1993), 299ff.

23. Panella (1987) on excavations of the site.

24. Flory (1984); Coarelli (1995), 215; cf. Platner and Ashby (1929), 138; and Richardson (1978), 269.

25. Flory (1984), 314–317; on politicized Concordia, Levick (1978).

26. Cassius Dio 55.8.1.

27. *Corpus Inscriptionum Latinarum* (*CIL*) 10.810; Richardson (1978) demonstrates that Eumachia's building followed the plan and concept of Livia's monument.

28. Generally, see Corbier (1995); Barrett (2002), 146–173, for influence on Tiberius's career.

29. Grimal (1943), 145; Flory (1984), 325–328.

30. Richardson (1992), 214–215; Gianelli (1996); Woodhull (1999), 93–102.

31. Flory (1984).

32. Favro (1996), 174–175.

33. Valone (2001).

34. Bartman (1999), 112–115.

35. Cf. Milnor (2005) and Severy (2003).

36. On Propertius, Welch (2004); on Ovid, Edwards (1996), 23–24.

37. Edwards (1996), 25.

38. The few familiar instances—such as Cornelia's statue in the Campus Martius—are sculptural and sufficiently unusual as to have been noteworthy.

39. Dixon (1983) and (1988), 175.

40. Cf. Buckley (1999).

41. Boatwright (1991), whose study considers primarily the Trajanic and Hadrianic women.

42. Boatwright (1991), 536.

43. The role of *divae* and their monuments in imperial cult is beyond the scope of this essay, but deserves fuller attention.

44. Valentini and Zucchetti (1940–1953), 1:125, 153, 176, 184–185, as cited in Boatwright (1987), 59, n. 74.

45. Boatwright (1987), 44–45 and 60.

46. Dressel (1906).

47. Boatwright (1987), 61, explains that the use of the term *basilica* in this period comports well with descriptions of similar second-century complexes with porticoes.

48. Richardson (1992), 53; granite columns, see also Lissi Caronna (1973), 403; and Boatwright (1987), 61.

49. Boatwright (1987), 61. There is much to explore within this visual and symbolic juxtaposition.

50. Temporini (1978), 186–259.

51. De Caprariis (1996); Richardson (1992), 246. Here I draw extensively on Boatwright's (1987) reading of the monument and its date, ca. 119, cf. 58ff., nn. 73–75, 80; an altar is attested (*CIL* 6.31893b.10) and probably stood in the complex.

52. Temporini (1978), 45; Boatwright (1987), 72–73.

53. Temporini (1978), 259, also notes that both Matidia and Marciana had eastern cities named for them.

54. Boatwright (1991), 517.

55. Oliver (1949), 39.

56. Oliver (1949), 37–38, further elaborates Marciana's role here.

57. Davies (2000), 102–119, coined the phrase in her analysis of the often-fictionalized fertility of the empresses depicted in monuments.

58. Kleiner (1992), 253–254; cf. Boatwright (1987), 229, 231–234.

59. Davies (2000), 113–114.

60. Davies (2000), 116.

61. Octavia's eulogy (Cassius Dio 54.35); for Matidia's eulogy: *CIL* 14.3579 = Smallwood (1966), 114.

62. On the tumulus Iuliae, see de Caprariis (1996), 233; and Richardson (1992), s.v. *tumulus Iuliae.*

63. Livy, *Letter* 106; Plutarch, *Life of Pompey* 53 and *Life of Caesar* 23; Cassius Dio 39.64; Suetonius, *Julius Caesar* 84.

64. Coarelli (1999), 291; Boatwright (1987), 60.

65. Historia Augusta, *Life of Antoninus Pius* 6.7; *CIL* 6.1005; Cassatella (1993), 46–47; Boatwright (2011). I thank Prof. Boatwright for generously sharing her essay before its publication.

66. *Roman Imperial Coinage* 3.162 no. 1115 = *Coins of the Roman Empire in the British Museum* 4.242, no. 1507, pl. 36.3.

67. Boatwright (2011), n. 32.

68. Cassatella (1993), 46.

69. Fittschen (1996). Cf. Kleiner and Matheson (1996), cat. nos. 34, 35, 37, 38, 39 with bibliography; Kleiner (1992), 242, 278–280.

70. Kleiner and Matheson (1996), 77; Davies (2000), 114.

71. Kleiner and Matheson (1996), 77 and n. 2. Cf. Davies (2000), 116, who argues that Faustina's dominance of the central vertical line of the apotheosis panel on the base of the Antonine funerary column emphasizes her, albeit fictive, fertility in securing dynastic succession.

72. Boatwright (2011), citing Walentowski (1998), 79.

73. Boatwright (2011).

74. Cf. Boatwright (1991), 535 and n. 86.

WORKS CITED

Barrett, Anthony. (2002). *Livia: First Lady of Imperial Rome.* New Haven: Yale University Press.

Bartman, Elizabeth. (1999). *Portraits of Livia: Imaging the Imperial Woman in Augustan Rome.* New York: Cambridge University Press.

Boatwright, Mary T. (1987). *Hadrian and the City of Rome.* Princeton: Princeton University Press.

———. (1991). "The Imperial Women of the Early Second Century A.C." *American Journal of Philology* 112.4:513–540.

———. (2011). "Antonine Rome: Security in the Homeland." In Björn C. Ewald and Carlos F. Noreña, eds., *The Emperor and Rome: Space, Representation, and Ritual* (Yale Classical Studies), 169–197. New York: Cambridge University Press.

Boyd, M. J. (1953). "The Porticoes of Metellus and Octavia." *Papers of the British School at Rome* 21:152–159.

Buckley, Cheryl. (1999). "Made in Patriarchy: Theories of Women and Design: A Reworking." In Joan Rothschild, ed., *Design and Feminism: Re-Visioning Spaces, Places, and Everyday Things,* 109–118. New Brunswick: Rutgers University Press.

Cassatella, Alessandro. (1993). "Antoninus, Divus et Faustina, Diva, Aedes, Templum."

In Marguerite Steinby, ed., *Lexicon Topographicum Urbis Romae*, 1:46–47. Rome: Edizioni Quasar.

Coarelli, Filippo. (1978). "La statue de Cornélie, mère des Gracques et la crise politique à Rome au temps de Saturninus." In Hubert Zehnacker, ed., *Le dernier siècle de la République romaine et l'époque augustéenne*, 13–28. Strassbourg: A.E.C.R.

———. (1995). *Roma*. 2nd ed., rev. Rome: Guida Laterza.

———. (1999). "Sepulcrum: Iulia (Tumulus)." In Marguerite Steinby, ed., *Lexicon Topographicum Urbis Romae*, 4:291. Rome: Edizioni Quasar.

Corbier, Mireille. (1995). "Male Power and Legitimacy through Women: The *domus Augusta* under the Julio-Claudians." In Richard Hawley and Barbara Levick, eds., *Women in Antiquity: New Assessments*, 178–193. London: Routledge.

Davies, Penelope J. E. (2000). *Death and the Emperor: Roman Imperial Funerary Monuments from Augustus to Marcus Aurelius*. Cambridge: Cambridge University Press.

De Caprariis, Francesca. (1996). "Matidia, Templum." In Marguerite Steinby, ed., *Lexicon Topographicum Urbis Romae*, 3:233. Rome: Edizioni Quasar.

Dixon, Suzanne. (1983). "A Family Business: Women's Role in Patronage and Politics at Rome, 80–44 B.C." *Classica et Mediaevalia* 34:91–112.

———. (1988). *The Roman Mother*. Norman: University of Oklahoma Press.

Dressel, H. (1906). "Der Matidiatempel auf einem Medaillon des Hadrianus." In *Corolla Numismatica in Honour of Barclay Head*, 16–28. London: Oxford University Press.

Edwards, Catharine. (1996). *Writing Rome: Textual Approaches to the City*. Cambridge: Cambridge University Press.

Fantham, Elaine H., et al. (1994). *Women in the Classical World*. New York: Oxford University Press.

Favro, Diane. (1996). *The Urban Image of Augustan Rome*. Cambridge: Cambridge University Press.

Fittschen, Klaus. (1996). "Courtly Portraits of Women in the Era of the Adoptive Emperors (A.D. 98–180) and Their Reception in Roman Society." In Diana Kleiner and Susan Matheson, eds., *I, Claudia: Women in Ancient Rome*, 42–52: Austin: University of Texas Press.

Flory, Marleen B. (1984). "*Sic exempla parantur*: Livia's Shrine to Concordia and the Porticus Liviae." *Historia* 33:309–330.

———. (1993). "Livia and the History of Public Honorific Statuary for Women in Rome." *Transactions of the American Philological Association* 123:287–292.

Giannelli, Giuseppe. (1996). "Iuno Lucina, Aedes." In Marguerite Steinby, ed., *Lexicon Topographicum Urbis Romae*, 3:122–123. Rome: Edizioni Quasar.

Grimal, Pierre. (1943). *Les jardins romains à la fin de la République et aux deux premiers siècles de l'Empire: Essai sur le naturalisme romain*. Paris: Éditions de Boccard.

Hawley, Richard, and Barbara Levick, eds. (1995). *Women in Antiquity: New Assessments*. London: Routledge.

Hemelrijk, Emily. (2005). "Octavian and the Introduction of Public Statues for

Women in Rome." *Athenaeum: Studi Periodici di Letteratura e Storia dell'Antichità* 93:309–317.

Kajava, Mika. (1989). "Cornelia Africani F. Gracchorum." *Arctos* 23:119–132.

Kampen, Natalie B. (2009). *Family Fictions in Roman Art.* New York: Cambridge University Press.

Kleiner, Diana E. E. (1992). *Roman Sculpture.* New Haven: Yale University Press.

Kleiner, Diana E. E., and Susan B. Matheson, eds. (1996). *I, Claudia: Women in Ancient Rome.* Austin: University of Texas Press.

Lanciani, Rodolfo. (1878). "Scavi nel portico d'Ottavia." *Bullettino dell'Istituto di Corrispondenza Archeologica*, 209.

———. (1897). *The Ruins and Excavations of Ancient Rome: A Companion Book for Students and Travelers.* Boston: Houghton, Mifflin, and Company.

Lauter, Hans. (1980–1981). "Porticus Metelli–Porticus Octaviae: Die baulichen Reste." *Bullettino della Commissione Archeologica Comunale di Roma* 87:37–46.

Levick, Barbara. (1978). "Concordia at Rome." In R. A. G. Carson and Colin M. Kraay, eds., *Scripta Nummaria Romana. Essays Presented to Humphrey Sutherland*, 217–233. London: Spink and Son.

Lewis, R. G. (1988). "Some Mothers . . ." *Athenaeum* 66:198–200.

Lissi Caronna, Elisa. (1973). "Roma: Rinvenimenti in Piazza Capranica, 78." *Notizie degli Scavi di Antichità*, ser. 8, 26:398–403.

Milnor, Kristina. (2005). *Gender, Domesticity, and the Age of Augustus: Inventing Private Life.* Oxford: Oxford University Press.

Oliver, James. (1949). "The Divi of the Hadrianic Period." *Harvard Theological Review* 42:35–40.

Panella, Clementina. (1987). "L'organizzazione degli spazi sulle pendici settentrionali del colle Oppio tra Augusto e i Severi." *L'Urbs: Espace urbain et histoire (Ier siècle av. J.-C.–IIe siècle ap. J.-C.). Collection de l'École française de Rome* 98:611–651.

———. (1993). "Porticus Liviae." In Marguerite Steinby, ed., *Lexicon Topographicum Urbis Romae*, 4:127–129. Rome: Edizioni Quasar.

Pellegrini, Angelo. (1861). "Scavi del Portico di Ottavia." *Bullettino dell'Istituto di Corrispondenza Archeologica*, 241–245.

———. (1868). "I Tempii di Giove e di Giunone nei Portici di Metello e di Ottavia." *Annali dell'Istituto di Corrispondenza Archeologica*, 108–132.

Platner, Samuel Ball, and Thomas Ashby. (1929). *A Topographical Dictionary of Ancient Rome.* London: Oxford University Press.

Richardson, Lawrence, Jr. (1978). "Concordia and Concordia Augusta: Rome and Pompeii." *La Parola del Passato* 33:260–272.

———. (1992). *A New Topographical Dictionary of Ancient Rome.* Baltimore: Johns Hopkins University Press.

Rodríguez-Almeida, Emilio. (1981). *Forma Urbis Marmorea: Aggiornamento generale.* 2 vols. Rome: Edizioni Quasar.

Ruck, Brigitte. (2004). "Das Denkmal der Cornelia in Rom." *Mitteilungen des Deutschen Archäologischen Instituts, Römische Abteilung* 111:477–494.

Scardigli, Barbara. (1982). "La sacrosantitas tribunicia di Ottavia e Livia." *Annali della Facoltà di Lettere e Filosofia dell'Università di Siena* 3:61–64.

Severy, Beth. (2003). *Augustus and Family at the Beginning of Empire.* New York: Routledge.

Smallwood, E. Mary. (1966). *Documents Illustrating the Principates of Nerva, Trajan, and Hadrian.* Cambridge: Cambridge University Press.

Steinby, E. Marguerite, ed. (1993–2000). *Lexicon Topographicum Urbis Romae.* 6 vols. Rome: Edizioni Quasar.

Temporini, Hildegard. (1978). *Die Frauen am Hofe Trajans.* Berlin: de Gruyter.

Torelli, Mario. (1993). "Augustus, Divus, Templum (Novum); Aedes." In Marguerite Steinby, ed., *Lexicon Topographicum Urbis Romae,* 1:145–146. Rome: Edizioni Quasar.

Valentini, Roberto, and Giuseppe Zucchetti. (1940–1953). *Codice topografico della città di Roma.* 4 vols. Rome: Istituto Storico Italico.

Valone, Carolyn. (2001). "Matrons and Motives: Why Women Built in Early Modern Rome." In Sheryl Reiss and David Wilkins, eds., *Beyond Isabella: Secular Women Patrons of Art in Renaissance Italy,* 319–336. Kirksville, MO: Truman State University Press.

Viscogliosi, Alessandro. (1999). "Porticus Octaviae." In Marguerite Steinby, ed., *Lexicon Topographicum Urbis Roma,* 4:141–145. Rome: Edizioni Quasar.

Walentowski, Sabine. (1998). *Kommentar zur Vita Antoninus Pius der Historia Augusta.* Bonn: Habelt.

Welch, Tara. (2004). "Masculinity and Monuments in Propertius 4.9." *American Journal of Philology* 125:61–90.

Wood, Susan E. (2000). *Imperial Women: A Study in Public Images, 40 B.C.–A.D. 68.* Leiden: Brill.

Woodhull, Margaret L. (1999). "Building Power: Women as Architectural Patrons during the Early Roman Empire." Ph.D. diss., University of Texas at Austin.

———. (2003). "Engendering Space: Octavia's Portico in Rome." *Aurora: Journal of the History of Art* 4:13–33.

Notes on Contributors

ANTONY AUGOUSTAKIS is associate professor of classics at the University of Illinois, Urbana-Champaign. He is the author of *Motherhood and the Other: Fashioning Female Power in Flavian Epic* (Oxford University Press, 2010), *Brill's Companion to Silius Italicus* (Brill, 2010), *Plautus' Mercator* (Bryn Mawr Latin Commentary, 2009), *Silvae and the Poetics of Intimacy* (with Carole Newlands, Johns Hopkins University Press, 2007), *Statius's Thebaid 8* (forthcoming), and *The Blackwell Companion to Terence* (forthcoming), as well as numerous articles on Greek and Latin literature.

YURIE HONG is assistant professor of classics at Gustavus Adolphus College. She earned her B.A. in classics at UCLA and her Ph.D. at the University of Washington. Her research and teaching interests include sex and gender in antiquity, ancient medicine, feminist pedagogy, and classics and feminism in popular culture. She is currently working on a book about representations of pregnancy and childbirth in Archaic and Classical Greek literature.

PRUDENCE JONES is associate professor of classics at Montclair State University. She is the author of two books on Cleopatra VII: *Cleopatra (Life and Times)* (Haus, 2006) and *Cleopatra: A Sourcebook* (University of Oklahoma Press, 2006); and of *Reading Rivers in Latin Literature and Culture* (Lexington Books, 2006). She has also written various articles on Latin literature and the reception of Cleopatra.

MIREILLE M. LEE is assistant professor of art history and classical studies at Vanderbilt University. She is a specialist in the social functions of ancient Greek dress and has published widely in journals and edited volumes. She has been the recipient of fellowships from the Center for Hellenic Studies and the American Council of Learned Societies. Her book-length study of the body and dress in early Greece is in preparation.

GENEVIEVE LIVELEY is senior lecturer in classics at the University of Bristol. Her principal research interests are Augustan literature, critical theory, and the classical tradition. She is co-editor and contributor to *Latin Elegy and Narratology: Fragments of Story* (Ohio State University Press, 2008), and is the author of *Ovid's Metamorphoses: A Reader's Guide* (Continuum, 2011) and *Ovid: Love Songs* (Duckworth, 2005).

Her other publications include articles and essays on the classical tradition, cyborgs, and chaos theory.

LAUREN HACKWORTH PETERSEN is associate professor of art history at the University of Delaware. She is the author of *The Freedman in Roman Art and Art History* (Cambridge University Press, 2006) and has published in the *Art Bulletin* and *Arethusa*, among others. She is the recipient of awards from the Getty Foundation, the American Academy in Rome, the National Endowment for the Humanities, and the American Council of Learned Societies.

PATRICIA SALZMAN-MITCHELL is associate professor of classics at Montclair State University. She is the author of *A Web of Fantasies: Gaze, Image, and Gender in Ovid's Metamorphoses* (Ohio State University Press, 2005) and contributor to and co-editor of *Latin Elegy and Narratology: Fragments of Story* (Ohio State University Press, 2008). She has published several articles on Ovid, Latin literature, and the classical tradition in art and film.

ANISE K. STRONG is assistant professor of history at Western Michigan University. A Roman social historian specializing in the study of Roman women and their sexuality, she has published articles on incest in the ancient world and on deviant sexuality in HBO's *Rome* series. She is currently completing a book on the representation of Roman prostitutes in ancient literature and art.

ANGELA TARASKIEWICZ is lecturer in foreign languages and literatures at Valparaiso University, and a Ph.D. candidate in the Committee on Social Thought at the University of Chicago. Her dissertation research examines ritual and narrative intertextuality in Euripidean tragedy.

ANGELIKI TZANETOU is associate professor of classics at the University of Illinois, Urbana-Champaign. Her research interests include Greek drama, Greek political theory, gender, and religion. She is the author of *City of Suppliants: Tragedy and the Athenian Empire* (University of Texas Press, forthcoming 2012); and co-editor with Maryline Parca of *Finding Persephone: Women's Rituals in the Ancient Mediterranean* (Indiana University Press, 2007). She has also published articles on ritual and gender in drama and on tragedy and politics.

MARGARET L. WOODHULL is the director of the Graduate Interdisciplinary Studies program at the University of Colorado Denver. She has been the recipient of a Fulbright Fellowship, a Woodrow Wilson Foundation Grant in Women's Studies, and the Archaeological Institute of America's Woodruff Traveling Fellowship, among others. Her research focuses on women and building patronage in classical antiquity. Currently she is working on a book-length study entitled *Women Building Rome: Gender and the Built Environment in Early Imperial Rome*.

Index

Page numbers in italics refer to images.

LaVergne, TN USA
15 November 2010
204986LV00003B/154/P